*Everyman, I will go with thee,*
*and be thy guide*

## THE EVERYMAN
## LIBRARY

*The Everyman Library was founded by J. M. Dent
in 1906. He chose the name Everyman because he wanted
to make available the best books ever written in every
field to the greatest number of people at the cheapest possible
price. He began with Boswell's 'Life of Johnson';
his one thousandth title was Aristotle's 'Metaphysics',
by which time sales exceeded forty million.*

*Today Everyman paperbacks remain true to
J. M. Dent's aims and high standards, with a wide range
of titles at affordable prices in editions which address
the needs of today's readers. Each new text is reset to give
a clear, elegant page and to incorporate the latest thinking
and scholarship. Each book carries the pilgrim logo,
the character in 'Everyman', a medieval morality play,
a proud link between Everyman
past and present.*

William Shakespeare

# AS YOU LIKE IT

*Edited by*
JOHN F. ANDREWS
*Foreword by*
MICHAEL KAHN

EVERYMAN
J. M. DENT · LONDON
CHARLES E. TUTTLE
VERMONT

First published in Everyman by J. M. Dent 1997
Published by permission of GuildAmerica Books, an imprint
of Doubleday Book and Music Clubs, Inc.

J. M. Dent
Orion Publishing Group
Orion House
5 Upper St Martin's Lane, London WC2H 9EA
and
Charles E. Tuttle Co.
28 South Main Street, Rutland, Vermont
05701, USA

Photoset by Deltatype Ltd, Birkenhead, Merseyside
Printed in Great Britain by
The Guernsey Press Co. Ltd, Guernsey, C.I.

British Library Cataloguing-in-Publication Data
is available upon request

ISBN 0 460 87627 9

# CONTENTS

# NOTE ON THE AUTHOR AND EDITOR

WILLIAM SHAKESPEARE is held to have been born on St George's day, 23 April 1564. The eldest son of a prosperous glove-maker in Stratford-upon-Avon, he was probably educated at the town's grammar school.

Tradition holds that between 1585 and 1592, Shakespeare first became a schoolteacher and then set off for London. By 1595 he was a leading member of the Lord Chamberlain's Men, helping to direct their business affairs, as well as being a playwright and actor. In 1598 he became a part-owner of the company, which was the most distinguished of its age. However, he maintained his contacts with Stratford, and his family appears to have remained there.

From about 1610 he seems to have grown increasingly involved in the town's affairs, suggesting a withdrawal from London. He died on 23 April 1616, aged 52, and was buried at Holy Trinity two days later.

JOHN F. ANDREWS has recently completed a 19-volume edition, *The Guild Shakespeare*, for the Doubleday Book and Music Clubs. He is also the editor of a 3-volume reference set, *William Shakespeare: His World, His Work, His Influence*, and the former editor (1974–85) of the journal *Shakespeare Quarterly*. From 1974 to 1984 he was director of Academic Programs at the Folger Shakespeare Library in Washington and Chairman of the Folger Institute. He now heads the Shakespeare Guild, which bestows the annual Sir John Gielgud Award for Excellence in the Dramatic Arts.

# CHRONOLOGY OF SHAKESPEARE'S LIFE

---

| Year[1] | Age | Life |
|---|---|---|
| 1564 | | Shakespeare baptized 26 April at Stratford-upon-Avon |
| 1582 | 18 | Marries Anne Hathaway |
| 1583 | 19 | Daughter, Susanna, born |
| 1585 | 21 | Twin son and daughter, Hamnet and Judith, born |
| 1590–1 | 26 | *The Two Gentlemen of Verona* & *The Taming of the Shrew* |
| 1591 | 27 | *2 & 3 Henry VI* |
| 1592 | 28 | *Titus Andronicus* & *1 Henry VI* |
| 1592–3 | | *Richard III* |
| 1593 | 29 | *Venus and Adonis* published |

[1] It is rarely possible to be certain about the dates at which plays of this period were written. For Shakespeare's plays, this chronology follows the dates preferred by Stanley Wells and Gary Taylor, the editors of The Oxford Shakespeare. Publication dates are given for poetry and books.

# CHRONOLOGY OF HIS TIMES

| Year | Literary Context | Historical Events |
|---|---|---|
| 1565–7 | Golding, Ovid's *Metamorphoses*, tr. | Elizabeth I reigning |
| 1574 | *A Mirror for Magistrates* (3rd ed.) | |
| 1576 | London's first playhouse built | |
| 1578 | John Lyly, *Euphues* | |
| 1579 | North, Plutarch's *Lives*, tr. Spenser, *Shepheardes Calender* | |
| 1587 | Marlowe, *I Tamburlaine* | Mary Queen of Scots executed |
| 1588 | Holinshed's *Chronicles* (2nd ed.) | Defeat of Spanish Armada |
| 1589 | Kyd, *Spanish Tragedy* Marlowe, *Jew of Malta* | Civil war in France |
| 1590 | Spenser, *Faerie Queene*, Bks I–III | |
| 1591 | Sidney, *Astrophel and Stella* | Proclamation against Jesuits |
| 1592 | Marlowe, *Dr Faustus* & *Edward II* | Scottish witchcraft trials Plague closes theatres from June |
| 1593 | Marlowe killed | |

| Year | Age | Life |
|------|-----|------|
| 1594 | 30 | *The Comedy of Errors. The Rape of Lucrece* published |
| 1594–5 | | *Love's Labour's Lost* |
| 1595 | 31 | *A Midsummer Night's Dream, Romeo and Juliet,* & *Richard II.* An established member of Lord Chamberlain's Men |
| 1596 | 32 | *King John.* Hamnet dies |
| 1596–7 | | *The Merchant of Venice* & *1 Henry IV* |
| 1597 | 33 | Buys New Place in Stratford The Lord Chamberlain's Men's lease to play at the Theatre expires; until 1599 they play mainly at the Curtain |
| 1597–8 | | *The Merry Wives of Windsor* & *2 Henry IV* |
| 1598 | 34 | *Much Ado About Nothing* |
| 1598–9 | | *Henry V* |
| 1599 | 35 | *Julius Caesar.* One of syndicate responsible for building the Globe in Southwark, where the Lord Chamberlain's Men now play |
| 1599–1600 | | *As You Like It* |
| 1600–1 | | *Hamlet* |
| 1601 | 37 | *Twelfth Night.* His father is buried in Stratford |
| 1602 | 38 | *Troilus and Cressida.* Invests £320 in land near Stratford[2] |
| 1603 | 39 | *Measure for Measure.* The Lord Chamberlain's Men become the King's Men. They play at court more than all the other companies combined |
| 1603–4 | | *Othello* |
| c.1604 | 40 | Shakespeare sues Philip Rogers of Stratford for debt |
| 1604–5 | | *All's Well That Ends Well* |
| 1605 | 41 | *Timon of Athens.* Invests £440 in Stratford tithes |
| 1605–6 | | *King Lear* |

[2] A schoolmaster would earn around £20 a year at this time.

| Year | Literary Context | Historical Events |
|---|---|---|
| 1594 | Nashe, *Unfortunate Traveller* | Theatres reopen in summer |
| 1594–6 | | Extreme food shortages |
| 1595 | Sidney, *An Apologie for Poetry* | Riots in London |
| 1596 | | Calais captured by Spanish Cadiz expedition |
| 1597 | Bacon, *Essays* | |
| 1598 | Marlowe and Chapman, *Hero and Leander* Jonson, *Every Man in his Humour* | Rebellion in Ireland |
| 1599 | Children's companies begin playing Thomas Dekker's *Shoemaker's Holiday* | Essex fails in Ireland |
| 1601 | 'War of the Theatres' Jonson, *Poetaster* | Essex rebels and is executed |
| 1602 | | Tyrone defeated in Ireland |
| 1603 | Florio, Montaigne's *Essays*, tr. | Elizabeth I dies, James I accedes Raleigh found guilty of treason |
| 1604 | Marston, *The Malcontent* | Peace with Spain |
| 1605 | Bacon, *Advancement of Learning* | Gunpowder plot |

| Year | Age | Life |
|------|-----|------|
| 1606 | 42 | *Macbeth* & *Antony and Cleopatra* |
| 1607 | 43 | *Pericles*. Susanna marries the physician John Hall in Stratford |
| 1608 | 44 | *Coriolanus*. The King's Men lease Blackfriars, an indoor theatre. His only grandchild is born. His mother dies |
| 1609 | 45 | *The Winter's Tale*. 'Sonnets' and 'A Lover's Complaint' published |
| 1610 | 46 | *Cymbeline* |
| 1611 | 47 | *The Tempest* |
| 1613 | 49 | *Henry VIII*. Buys house in London for £140 |
| 1613–14 | | *The Two Noble Kinsmen* |
| 1616 | 52 | Judith marries Thomas Quiney, a vintner, in Stratford. On 23 April Shakespeare dies; is buried two days later |
| 1623 | | Publication of the First Folio. His widow dies in August |

| Year | Literary Context | Historical Events |
|------|------------------|-------------------|
| 1606 | Jonson, *Volpone* | |
| 1607 | Tourneur, *The Revenger's Tragedy*, published | Virginia colonized<br>Enclosure riots |
| 1609 | | Oath of allegiance<br>Truce in Netherlands |
| 1610 | Jonson, *Alchemist* | |
| 1611 | Authorized Version of the Bible<br>Donne, *Anatomy of the World* | |
| 1612 | Webster, *White Devil* | Prince Henry dies |
| 1613 | Webster, *Duchess of Malfi* | Princess Elizabeth marries |
| 1614 | Jonson, *Bartholomew Fair* | |
| 1616 | Folio edition of Jonson's plays | |

Biographical note, chronology and plot summary compiled by John Lee, University of Bristol, 1996.

# FOREWORD TO *As You Like It*

*As You Like It* is one of Shakespeare's most sweetly deceptive plays. Its effortless comedy and accessible romantic appeal often cause it to be regarded and produced as the playwright's concession to popular taste. But remove this preconception, and an examination of the text reveals Shakespeare brilliantly using this popular form to explore the themes that inform all his major work: life, honour, the nature and regenerative power of love, illusion and reality, the breakdown of the natural order and its restoration, and, indeed, the very Nature of Man.

The play begins in a world informed by usurpation and loss; a world where children are fatherless and brothers are at war; a world where the only goal is power and where the only punishable crime is to be good and 'enchantingly beloved'. Orlando, nobly born but deprived of his inheritance and education, and Rosalind, educated but female and powerless, are, as a result of the innate goodness of their natures, forced to flee and take refuge in the Forest of Arden.

But contrary to the pastoral convention, this Arden is not an idyllic fantasy. It is a very real place where the 'Icy Fang and churlish Chiding of the Winter's Wind' chill the bones and remind its inhabitants of the precarious frailty of man and suggest the hard lesson that 'Sweet are the Uses of Adversity'. Described most often by its new inhabitants as a 'desert', it becomes a testing ground for previously accepted values as the social codes and set roles of a dangerous and superficial world are examined and transformed.

Rosalind changes her banishment into liberty by assuming male disguise. With the freedom to approach Orlando as an equal, she provides his education and discovers her power. Proposing to cure Orlando of love, she submits him to self-analysis. Intending to test his ardor, she witnesses his anguish. But in the process she does not spare herself. The young woman who early in the play considered the act of falling in love a sport, now uncovers and rejects all the superficial and socially acceptable feminine responses to the emotion and finds that love is so deep it cannot be sounded − but like man himself it must be stripped of all false notions to allow it to mature and endure.

As Touchstone learns the essential nature of honour and behaviour, as Jaques moves from an easy cynicism to understanding, as Oliver accepts the depth of brotherhood, as the banished Duke discovers his true power in the acceptance of himself as a fallible man, the communal values emerging from shared hardship are absorbed by all.

And as the characters emerge from their winter of discontent and trial into the spring of renewal and reconciliation, these newly acquired values are restored to the temporal world and we see that Shakespeare might well have entitled this wise and moving comedy, 'As It Really Is'.

*Michael Kahn*

MICHAEL KAHN is Artistic Director of The Shakespeare Theatre in Washington, D.C., and Chairman of New York's Juilliard School Acting Department. He was previously Artistic Director of the American Shakespeare Festival in Stratford, Connecticut, and New York's The Acting Company. His wide-ranging directorial credits include a Broadway production of *Showboat*, Handel's opera *Julius Caesar*, and an award-winning *Measure for Measure* in Central Park for the New York Shakespeare Festival.

# EDITOR'S INTRODUCTION TO
## *As You Like It*

---

*As You Like It* is often referred to as a 'festive' comedy, and there can be no doubt that it is among the happiest of Shakespeare's theatrical accomplishments.

The date usually assigned to the script is 1599, when the dramatist was entering his thirty-sixth year. It displays the gifts of an artist in the prime of his creative life, and it shows him experimenting with a genre in which he had already demonstrated unprecedented mastery. It introduces two character types, the court jester and the melancholic malcontent, who would proceed to more serious roles in Shakespeare's major tragedies. It focuses on how men and women think and feel. And it delves into what different personalities do to attain the things they most desire.

When you're fortunate enough to experience a capable performance of this sprightly revel, you realize that it engages your imagination with uncommon directness. Like *Twelfth Night*, it places you in a position to ponder 'what you will'. In the process it encourages you to puzzle over the problematic relationships between the 'real' world it reflects and the 'fictional' world it conjures into the magic circle, the 'Wooden O' (*Henry V*, Prologue.13), for which it was originally devised. When all's said and done, it leaves you meditating on the elusiveness of such concepts as Nature and Art, Fate and Freedom, and Wisdom and Folly.

*As You Like It* derives much of its plot, and a foretaste of its title, from a prose romance by Thomas Lodge. In his preface to *Rosalynde, or Euphues' Golden Legacy* (1590), the popular Elizabethan writer tells readers 'If you like it, so'. We know that at least one of Lodge's contemporaries did like what he encountered in those evocative pages, and he raided *Rosalynde* for many of the incidents in what some regard as his most skilfully crafted play. What we discern if we set Shakespeare's work and its forebear side by side, though, is that as usual his modifications were at least as significant as his borrowings.

In Lodge, for example, the conflict that opens the story is grimmer than the one we observe in Shakespeare's handling of a similar situation. In Lodge, the first-born who becomes Oliver in Shakespeare's comedy has subverted his father's will in order to cheat his youngest brother out of a bequest that was larger than Saladyne's own. In Lodge, rather than merely authorize the Duke's wrestler to use his full might against an Orlando who has rashly challenged him, as happens in *As You Like It*, Saladyne instigates the combat himself and then secretly bribes the gladiator to grant Rosader no mercy. In Lodge, the main event is preceded by preliminary bouts in which the wrestler kills rather than maims his opponents. And in Lodge, the youngest brother does more than silence his overconfident adversary with a stunning 'Fall' that resembles a 'Thunderbolt' (I.ii.214, 224); unlike Orlando, the Rosader of Lodge's *Rosalynde* keeps fighting until he slays a brute with none of the appeal we witness in our initial meeting (I.i.161–72) with Shakespeare's Charles the Wrastler.

What the playwright does here is soften the harsh edges of the tale he read in his source. But some of his other revisions are of another sort. His Oliver may appear just as mean-spirited as the oldest brother in Lodge's narrative, for example, but in fact the malice of *As You Like It*'s cruel sibling is prompted, not by greed or by an understandable sense of injured merit, but by an irrational 'humour', an envious obsession with his youngest sibling's innate goodness. At the same time, as compared to his counterpart in Lodge, the 'Last and Least' (*King Lear*, I.i.84) in Shakespeare's play has little basis for attributing all his woes to the first-born; no, Orlando's deprivations owe as much to an inflexible system of primogeniture as they do to Oliver's refusal to yield the pittance his youngest brother has been bequeathed by Sir Rowland de Boys. In any case, as discordant as they seem, the confrontations between the two brothers in *As You Like It* prove far less violent than the ones to be found either in Lodge or in the poem from which Lodge himself had drawn, a fourteenth-century *Tale of Gamelyn* in which the youngest brother becomes an outlaw, a 'Prodigal' and a 'Robin Hood' (I.i.40, 123) who finally reaps his revenge when the sibling who had oppressed him expires at the end of a hangman's rope.

What Shakespeare does to the Oliver and Orlando story is analogous to what he does with the relationship between the two dukes. He alters Lodge's narrative by making the noblemen brothers. To reinforce the parallel with Oliver, moreover, he portrays the usurping Frederick as a 'humorous' tyrant, arbitrary and menacing but not so reprobate that he must ultimately be put to the sword in battle, as in Lodge. Rather than attempting to 'motivate' either the reprehensible crimes or the remarkable conversions of the wicked Oliver and Frederick, however, Shakespeare simply represents them as phenomena of the kind of cosmos in which 'strange Events' (V.iv.135) will have their way. The net effect of these and other changes is to render *As You Like It* less realistic and more allegorical in spirit than Lodge's *Rosalynde*.[1]

Since much of what transpires in *As You Like It* would seem too implausible to accept if it occurred in an ordinary setting, Shakespeare induces us to suspend our disbelief by moving the action almost immediately from a familiar if constraining environment at court to a liberating, and at times exotic, forest where virtually anything becomes conceivable. Commentators sometimes speak of Arden as a benign, garden-like demesne with affinities to the Eden of biblical lore and the Golden Age of classical antiquity. This is how it is depicted in the play's first allusion to a 'Golden World' in which men 'fleet the Time carelessly' (I.i.125–26) without concern for the hypocrisy and 'Peril' (II.i.4) of Duke Frederick's court. But once everyone gets to the forest, even such cheerful figures as Old Adam perceive that it offers something quite distinct from the ease and plenty that had long been celebrated in myth and romanticized in pastoral poetry. To be sure, Arden has its literary lads and lasses, its Silviuses and

---

[1] For a more extended discussion of this topic, see the excerpt by Sylvan Barnet in the 'Critical Perspectives' section. For other comments on Shakespeare's treatment of the sources and traditions he echoed, see the selections by William Warburton, Walter Whiter, G. G. Gervinus, Frederick S. Boas, John W. Draper, Harold Jenkins, Helen Gardner, Harry Morris, Alan Taylor Bradford and Louis Adrian Montrose.

Phebes; but it also has its crude and inarticulate rustics, its Audreys and its Williams. This forest may provide a context for friendly shepherds, like the sensible, well-meaning Corin, but the playwright emphasizes that it also contains its share of unreasonable, stingy landowners, like the churlish overlord who has decided to sell his faithful tenant's sheepcote. And far from supplying limitless abundance and perpetual sunshine, the Arden we tour in *As You Like It* appears to be a cold and largely 'desert' expanse, uncultivated and almost completely uninhabited, where food and comfort are hard to come by. In short, Shakespeare's Forest of Arden is an uninviting locale with few of the advantages of civilization and more than the normal admixture of 'Winter and rough Weather' (II.v.8). The lot it fosters may be 'sweet' for Duke Senior and his band of loyal followers, but the blessings it affords are reserved for those rare philosophical characters who can 'translate the Stubbornness of Fortune' into a 'Stile' that enables them to surmount, and find profitable 'Uses' for, 'Adversity' (II.i.1–20).

For two of the court denizens this proves difficult. The dyspeptic Jaques complains that the banished Duke is abusing the forest, expropriating it from its 'native Burghers', the poor deer whose 'round Haunches' must be 'goar'd' to maintain a human 'City' in exile (II.i.23–28). In comparable fashion the unimpressionable Touchstone says 'now I am in Arden, the more Fool I: when I was at home, I was in a better place' (II.iv.16–17). Notwithstanding the poses with which he satirizes the sentiments of others, Touchstone eventually accommodates himself to the imperatives of his rural surroundings; at the end of the play he presses in 'amongst the rest of the Country Copulatives' (V.iv.57–58) for the wedding feast that promises 'to make all this Matter even' (V.iv.18). But the contemplative Jaques insists on marching to another 'Measure' (see V.iv.180–87, 201); in the final reckoning 'Monsieur Melancholy' (III.ii.313) knows that he is not destined to couple and then go 'Dancing' back to court, so he resolves to stay and converse with the 'Convertites' on 'the Skirts of this wild Wood' (V.iv.192–204)

For the remainder of its visitors, Arden turns out to be a restorative, if temporary, retreat. Here an Orlando who 'cannot speak' (I.ii.268) to his Rosalind at court finds 'Tongues in Trees' (II.i.16) and counsel from a disguised 'Ganimed' (I.iii.129) who prepares him for matrimony with warnings about the worst that may befall him if he persists in his pursuit of the woman he woos. Here an Oliver who is hell-bent on becoming another Cain discovers what it really means to be a brother's keeper. Here a Celia disposed to renounce any inheritance she receives from her father and return it to the cousin from whom it has been withheld is rewarded with wedlock to a gentleman who pledges to cherish her as his princess. And here a Rosalind who enters the forest bearing little more than her wit and resourcefulness emerges as the presiding genius over a sylvan realm that she alone sees steadily and as a whole. Her prize is a Hercules whose patient labours have certified him both as a worthy husband for herself and as a proper heir for her father, a benevolent patriarch who's just been reinstated as duke.

Rosalind may be the most sane and balanced of Shakespeare's heroines. She embodies the tenderness and sensitivity of humanity's 'weaker vessels' (see II.v.6). She loves ardently and cares profoundly: at a key moment in her pilgrimage she faints at the sight of her future spouse's blood. To her credit she recognizes and acknowledges her vulnerability, but for much of her sojourn in Arden she masks this consciousness with a sagacious 'Counterfeiting' (III.iv.172) that enables her to explore her deepest self while she guides her companions to a better understanding of their own natures.

*As You Like It* concludes with 'Music' and with an 'Epilogue' in which Shakespeare's surrogate 'Magician' solicits her audience to 'like as much of this Play as please you' (V.i.186, 208, 34, 220–21). Another mature comedy, *Twelfth Night*, draws to its close with a Clown telling us that 'Man's Estate' is a steady diet of 'the Wind and the Rain' (V.i.399–402). Feste's words sound a more sombre note than do Rosalind's; but like the sentences that round off *As You Like It*, they keep us aware that, whenever we need a respite from our travels and travails, we can look for solace in the company of a troupe who will 'strive to please' us 'every Day' (*Twelfth Night*, V.i.414).

# THE TEXT OF THE EVERYMAN SHAKESPEARE

## Background

### THE EARLY PRINTINGS OF SHAKESPEARE'S WORKS

Many of us enjoy our first encounter with Shakespeare when we're introduced to *Julius Caesar* or *Macbeth* at school. It may therefore surprise us that neither of these tragedies could ever have been read, let alone studied, by most of the playwright's contemporaries. They began as scripts for performance and, along with seventeen other titles that never saw print during Shakespeare's lifetime, they made their inaugural appearance as 'literary' works seven years after his death, in the 1623 collection we know today as the First Folio.

The Folio contained thirty-six titles in all. Of these, half had been issued previously in the small paperbacks we now refer to as quartos.* Like several of the plays first published in the Folio, the most trustworthy of the quarto printings appear to have been set either from Shakespeare's own manuscripts or from faithful copies of them. It's not impossible that the poet himself prepared some of these works for the press, and it's intriguing to imagine him reviewing proof-pages as the words he'd written for actors to speak and embody were being transposed into the type that readers would filter through their eyes, minds, and imaginations. But, alas, there's no indisputable evidence that Shakespeare had any direct involvement with the publication of these early editions of his plays.

What, then, about the scripts that achieved print for the first time in the Folio? Had the dramatist taken any steps to give the

---

* Quartos derived their name from the four-leaf units of which these small books were comprised: large sheets of paper that had been folded twice after printing to yield four leaves, or eight pages. Folios, volumes with twice the page-size of quartos, were put together from two-leaf units: sheets that had been folded once after printing to yield four pages.

permanency of book form to those texts before he died? We don't know. All we can say is that when a fatal illness seized him in 1616, Shakespeare was denied any opportunities he might otherwise have taken to ensure that his 'insubstantial Pageants' survived the mortal who was now slipping into the 'dark Backward and Abysm of Time'.

Fortunately, two of the playwright's colleagues felt an obligation, as they put it, 'to procure his Orphans Guardians'. Some time after his death John Heminge (or Heminges) and Henry Condell made arrangements to preserve Shakespeare's theatrical compositions in a manner that would keep them vibrant for posterity. They dedicated their endeavour to two noblemen who had helped see England's foremost acting company through some of its most trying vicissitudes. They solicited several poetic tributes for the volume, among them a now-famous eulogy by fellow writer Ben Jonson. They commissioned an engraved portrait of Shakespeare to adorn the frontispiece. And they did their utmost to display the author's dramatic works in a style that would both dignify them and make them accessible to 'the great Variety of Readers'.

As they readied Shakespeare's plays for the compositors who would set them into stately Folio columns, Heminge and Condell (or editors and scribes designated to carry out their wishes) revised and augmented many of the entrances, exits, and other stage directions in Shakespeare's manuscripts. They divided most of the works into acts, and many into both acts and scenes.* For a number of plays they appended 'Names of the Actors', or casts of characters. Meanwhile they made every effort to guarantee that the Folio printers had reliable copy-texts for each of the titles: authoritative manuscripts for the plays that had not been published previously, and good quarto printings (annotated in some instances to insert staging details, mark script changes, and add supplementary material) for the ones that had been issued prior to the Folio. For several titles they supplied texts that were

---

* The early quartos, reflecting the unbroken sequence that probably typified Elizabethan and Jacobean performances of the plays, had been printed without the structural demarcations usual in Renaissance editions of classical drama.

substantively different from, if not always demonstrably superior to, the quarto versions that preceded them.

Like even the most accurate of printings that preceded it, the Folio collection was flawed by minor blemishes. But it more than fulfilled the purpose of its generous-minded compilers: 'to keep the memory of so worthy a Friend and Fellow alive as was our Shakespeare'. In the process it provided a publishing model that remains instructive today.

## MODERN EDITIONS OF THE PLAYS AND POEMS

When we compare the First Folio and its predecessors with the usual modern edition of Shakespeare's works, we're more apt to be impressed by the differences than by the similarities. Today's texts of Renaissance drama are normally produced in conformity with twentieth-century standards of punctuation and usage; as a consequence they look more neat, clean, and, to our eyes, 'right' than do the original printings. Thanks to an editorial tradition that extends back to the early eighteenth century, if not before, most of the rough spots in the early printings of Shakespeare have long been smoothed away. Textual scholars have ferreted out redundancies and eradicated inconsistencies. They've mended what they've perceived to be errors and oversights in the playscripts, and they've systematically attended to what they've construed as misreadings by the copyists and compositors who transmitted these playscripts to posterity. They've added '[Within]' brackets and other theatrical notations. They've revised stage directions they've judged incomplete or inadequate in the initial printings. They've regularized disparities in the speech headings. They've gone back to the playwright's sources and reinstated the 'proper' forms for many of the character and place names which a presumably hasty or inattentive author got 'wrong' as he conferred identities on his dramatis personae and stage locales. They've replaced obsolete words like *bankrout* with their modern heirs (in this case *bankrupt*). And in a multitude of other ways they've accommodated Shakespeare to the tastes, interests, and expectations of latter-day readers.

The results, on the whole, have been splendid. But interpreting the artistic designs of a complex writer is always problematical, and the task is especially challenging when that writer happens to have been a poet who felt unconstrained by many of the 'rules' that more conventional dramatists respected. The undertaking becomes further complicated when new rules, and new criteria of linguistic and social correctness, are imposed by subsequent generations of artists and critics.

To some degree in his own era, but even more in the neoclassical period (1660–1800) that came in its wake, Shakespeare's most ardent admirers thought it necessary to apologise for what Ben Jonson hinted at in his allusion to the 'small Latin, and less Greek' of an untutored prodigy. To be sure, the 'sweet Swan of Avon' sustained his popularity; in fact his reputation rose so steadily that by the end of the eighteenth century he'd eclipsed Jonson and his other peers and become the object of near-universal Bardolatry. But in the theatre most of his plays were being adapted in ways that were deemed advisable to tame their supposed wildness and bring them into conformity with the decorum of a society that took pride in its refinement. As one might expect, some of the attitudes that induced theatre proprietors to metamorphose an unpolished poet from the provinces into something closer to an urbane man of letters also influenced Shakespeare's editors. Persuaded that the dramatist's works were marred by crudities that needed expunging, they applied their ministrations to the canon with painstaking diligence.

Twentieth-century editors have moved away from many of the presuppositions that guided a succession of earlier improvers. But a glance at the textual apparatus accompanying virtually any modern publication of the plays and poems will show that emendations and editorial procedures deriving from such forebears as the sets published by Nicholas Rowe (1709), Alexander Pope (1723–25, 1728), Lewis Theobald (1733, 1740, 1757), Thomas Hanmer (1743–45, 1770–71), Samuel Johnson (1765), Edward Capell (1768), George Steevens (1773), and Edmond Malone (1790) retain a strong hold on today's renderings of the playwright's works. The consequence is a 'Shakespeare' who offers the tidiness we've come to expect in our libraries of treasured authors, but not necessarily the playwright a 1599 reader of the Second Quarto of *Romeo and Juliet* would still be able to recognize as a contemporary.

### OLD LIGHT ON THE TOPIC

Over the last two decades we've learned from art curators that paintings by Old Masters such as Michelangelo and Rembrandt look a lot brighter when centuries of grime are removed from their surfaces – when hues that had become dulled with soot and other extraneous matter are allowed to radiate again with something approximating their pristine luminosity. We've learned from conductors like Sir Neville Marriner and Christopher Hogwood that there are aesthetic rewards to be gained from a return to the scorings and instruments with which Renaissance and Baroque musical compositions were first presented. We've learned from twentieth-century experiments in the performance of Shakespeare's plays that an open, multi-level stage, analogous to that on which the scripts were originally enacted, does more justice to their dramaturgical techniques than does a proscenium auditorium devised for works that came later in the development of Western theatre. We've learned from archaeological excavations in London's Bankside area that the foundations of playhouses such as the Rose and the Globe look rather different from what many historians had expected. And we're now learning from a close scrutiny of Shakespeare's texts that they too look different, and function differently, when we accept them for what they are and resist the impulse to 'normalize' features that strike us initially as quirky, unkempt, or unsophisticated.

## The Aims that Guide the Everyman Text

Like other modern editions of the dramatist's plays and poems, the Everyman Shakespeare owes an incalculable debt to the scholarship that has led to so many excellent renderings of the author's works. But in an attempt to draw fresh inspiration from the spirit that animated those remarkable achievements at the outset, the Everyman edition departs in a number of respects from the usual post-Folio approach to the presentation of Shakespeare's texts.

### RESTORING SOME OF THE NUANCES
### OF RENAISSANCE PUNCTUATION

In its punctuation, Everyman attempts to give equal emphasis to sound and sense. In places where Renaissance practice calls for heavier punctuation than we'd normally employ – to mark the caesural pause in the middle of a line of verse, for instance – Everyman sometimes retains commas that other modern editions omit. Meanwhile, in places where current practice usually calls for the inclusion of commas – after vocatives and interjections such as 'O' and 'alas', say, or before 'Madam' or 'Sir' in phrases such as 'Ay Madam' or 'Yes Sir' – Everyman follows the original printings and omits them.

Occasionally the absence of a comma has a significant bearing on what an expression means, or can mean. At one point in *Othello*, for example, Iago tells the Moor 'Marry patience' (IV.i.90). Inserting a comma after 'Marry', as most of today's editions do, limits Iago's utterance to one that says 'Come now, have patience.' Leaving the clause as it stands in the Folio, the way the Everyman text does, permits Iago's words to have the additional, agonizingly ironic sense 'Be wed to Patience'.

The early texts generally deploy exclamation points quite sparingly, and Everyman follows suit. Everyman also follows the early editions, more often than not, when they use question marks in places that seem unusual by current standards: at the conclusion of what we'd normally treat as exclamations, for example, or at the ends of interrogative clauses in sentences that we'd ordinarily denote as questions in their entirety.

The early texts make no orthographic distinction between simple plurals and either singular or plural possessives, and there are times when the context doesn't indicate whether a word spelled *Sisters*, say, should be renedered *Sisters*, *Sisters'*, or *Sister's* in today's usage. In such situations the Everyman edition prints the word in the form modern usage prescribes for plurals.

### REVIVING SOME OF THE FLEXIBILITY
### OF RENAISSANCE SPELLING

Spelling had not become standardized by Shakespeare's time, and that meant that many words could take a variety of forms. Like

James Joyce and some of the other innovative prose and verse stylists of our own century, Shakespeare revelled in the freedom a largely unanchored language provided, and with that in mind Everyman retains original spelling forms (or adaptations of those forms that preserve their key distinctions from modern spellings) whenever there is any reason to suspect that they might have a bearing on how a word was intended to be pronounced or on what it meant, or could have meant, in the playwright's day. When there is any likelihood that multiple forms of the same word could be significant, moreover, the Everyman text mirrors the diversity to be found in the original printings.

In many cases this practice affects the personalities of Shakespeare's characters. One of the heroine's most familiar questions in *Romeo and Juliet* is 'What's in a Name?' For two and a half centuries readers – and as a consequence actors, directors, theatre audiences, and commentators – have been led to believe that Juliet was addressing this query to a Romeo named 'Montague'. In fact 'Montague' *was* the name Shakespeare found in his principal source for the play. For reasons that will become apparent to anyone who examines the tragedy in detail, however, the playwright changed his protagonist's surname to 'Mountague', a word that plays on both 'mount' and 'ague' (fever).* Setting aside an editorial practice that began with Lewis Theobald in the middle of the eighteenth century, Everyman resurrects the name the dramatist himself gave Juliet's lover.

Readers of *The Merchant of Venice* in the Everyman set will be amused to learn that the character modern editions usually identify as 'Lancelot' is in reality 'Launcelet', a name that calls attention to the clown's lusty 'little lance'. Like Costard in *Love's Labour's Lost*, another stage bumpkin who was probably played by the actor Will Kemp, Launcelet is an upright 'Member of the Commonwealth'; we eventually learn that he's left a pliant wench 'with Child'.

Readers of *Hamlet* will find that 'Fortinbras' (as the name of the

---

* For anyone who doubts that Shakespeare's alteration of Romeo's family name was part of a conscious artistic plan, it may be worth noting that 'Capulet', like 'Capilet' in *Twelfth Night* and *All's Well That Ends Well*, means 'small horse'.

Prince's Norwegian opposite is rendered in the First Folio and in most modern editions) appears in the earlier, authoritative 1604 Second Quarto of the play as 'Fortinbrasse'. In the opening scene of that text a surname that meant 'strong in arms' in French is introduced to the accompaniment of puns on *brazen*, in the phrase 'brazon Cannon', and on *metal*, in the phrase 'unimprooued mettle'. In the same play readers of the Everyman text will encounter 'Ostricke', the ostrich-like courtier who invites the Prince of Denmark to participate in the fateful fencing match that draws *Hamlet* to a close. Only in its final entrance direction for the obsequious fop does the Second Quarto call this character 'Osrick', the name he bears in all the Folio text's references to him and in the usual modern edition of Shakespeare's most popular tragedy.

Readers of the Everyman *Macbeth* will discover that the fabled 'Weird Sisters' appear only as the 'weyward' or 'weyard' Sisters. Shakespeare and his contemporaries knew that in his *Chronicles of England, Scotland, and Ireland* Raphael Holinshed had used the term 'weird sisters' to describe the witches who accost Macbeth and Banquo on the heath; but presumably because he wished to play on *wayward*, the playwright changed their name to *weyward*. Like Samuel Johnson, who thought punning vulgar and lamented Shakespeare's proclivity to seduction by this 'fatal Cleopatra', Lewis Theobald saw no reason to retain the playwright's weyward spelling of the witches' name. He thus restored the 'correct' form from Holinshed, and editors ever since have generally done likewise.

In many instances Renaissance English had a single spelling for what we now define as two separate words. For example, *humane* combined the senses of 'human' and 'humane' in modern English. In the First Folio printing of *Macbeth* the protagonist's wife expresses a concern that her husband is 'too full o'th' Milke of humane kindnesse.' As she phrases it, *humane kindnesse* can mean several things, among them 'humankind-ness', 'human kindness', and 'humane kindness'. It is thus a reminder that to be true to his or her own 'kind' a human being must be 'kind' in the sense we now attach to 'humane'. To disregard this logic, as the protagonist and his wife will soon prove, is to disregard a principle as basic to the cosmos as the laws of gravity.

In a way that parallels *humane*, *bad* could mean either 'bad' or 'bade', *borne* either 'born' or 'borne', *ere* either 'ere' (before) or 'e'er' (ever), *least* either 'least' or 'lest', *lye* either 'lie' or 'lye', *nere* either 'ne'er' or 'near' (though the usual spellings for the latter were *neare* or *neere*), *powre* either 'pour' or 'power', *then* either 'than' or 'then', and *tide* either 'tide' or 'tied'.

There were a number of word-forms that functioned in Renaissance English as interchangeable doublets. *Travail* could mean 'travel', for example, and *travel* could mean 'travail'. By the same token, *deer* could mean *dear* and vice versa, *dew* could mean *due*, *hart* could mean *heart*, and (as we've already noted) *mettle* could mean *metal*.

A particularly interesting instance of the equivocal or double meanings some word-forms had in Shakespeare's time is *loose*, which can often become either 'loose' or 'lose' when we render it in modern English. In *The Comedy of Errors* when Antipholus of Syracuse compares himself to 'a Drop / Of Water that in the Ocean seeks another Drop' and then says he will 'loose' himself in quest of his long-lost twin, he means both (a) that he will release himself into a vast unknown, and (b) that he will lose his own identity, if necessary, to be reunited with the brother for whom he searches. On the other hand, in *Hamlet* when Polonius says he'll 'loose' his daughter to the Prince, he little suspects that by so doing he will also lose his daughter.

In some cases the playwright employs word-forms that can be translated into words we wouldn't think of as related today: *sowre*, for instance, which can mean 'sour', 'sower', or 'sore', depending on the context. In other cases he uses forms that do have modern counterparts, but not counterparts with the same potential for multiple connotation. For example, *onely* usually means 'only' in the modern sense; but occasionally Shakespeare gives it a figurative, adverbial twist that would require a nonce word such as 'one-ly' to replicate in current English.

In a few cases Shakespeare employs word-forms that have only seeming equivalents in modern usage. For example, *abhominable* (derived, however incorrectly, from *ab*, 'away from', and *homine*, 'man') which meant 'inhuman', 'nonhuman', or 'subhuman' to the poet and his contemporaries, is not the same word as our *abominable* (ill-omened, abhorrent). In his advice to the visiting players Hamlet complains about incompetent actors who imitate 'Humanity so abhominably' as to make the characters they depict seem unrecognizable as men. Modern readers who don't realize the distinction between Shakespeare's word and our own, and who see *abominable* on the page before them, don't register the full import of the Prince's satire.

Modern English treats as single words a number of word-forms that were normally spelled as two words in Shakespeare's time. What we render as *myself*, for example, and use primarily as a reflexive or intensifying pronoun, is almost invariably spelled *my self* in Shakespeare's works; so also with *her self*, *thy self*, *your self*, and *it self* (where *it* functions as *its* does today). Often there is no discernible difference between Shakespeare's usage and our own. At other times there is, however, as we are reminded when we come across a phrase such as 'our innocent self' in *Macbeth* and think how strained it would sound in modern parlance, or as we observe when we note how naturally the self is objectified in the balanced clauses of the Balcony Scene in *Romeo and Juliet*:

> Romeo, doffe thy name,
> And for thy name, which is no part of thee,
> Take all my selfe.

Yet another difference between Renaissance orthography and our own can be exemplified with words such as *today*, *tonight*, and *tomorrow*, which (unlike *yesterday*) were treated as two words in Shakespeare's time. In *Macbeth* when the Folio prints 'Duncan comes here to Night', the unattached *to* can function either as a preposition (with *Night* as its object, or in this case its destination) or as the first part of an infinitive (with *Night* operating figuratively as a verb). Consider the ambiguity a Renaissance reader would have detected in the original publication of one of the most celebrated soliloquies in all of Shakespeare:

> To morrow, and to morrow, and to morrow,
> Creeps in this petty pace from day to day,
> To the last Syllable of Recorded time:
> And all our yesterdayes, have lighted Fooles
> The way to dusty death.

Here, by implication, the route 'to morrow' is identical with 'the way to dusty death', a relationship we miss if we don't know that for Macbeth, and for the audiences who first heard these lines spoken, *to morrow* was not a single word but a potentially equivocal two-word phrase.

### RECAPTURING THE ABILITY TO HEAR WITH OUR EYES

When we fail to recall that Shakespeare's scripts were designed initially to provide words for people to hear in the theatre, we sometimes overlook a fact that is fundamental to the artistic structure of a work like *Macbeth*: that the messages a sequence of sounds convey through the ear are, if anything, even more significant than the messages a sequence of letters, punctuation marks, and white spaces on a printed page transmit through the eye. A telling illustration of this point, and of the potential for ambiguous or multiple implication in any Shakespearean script, may be found in the dethronement scene of *Richard II*. When Henry Bullingbrook asks the King if he is ready to resign his crown, Richard replies 'I, no no I; for I must nothing be.' Here the punctuation in the 1608 Fourth Quarto (the earliest text to print this richly complex passage) permits each *I* to signify either 'ay' or 'I' (*I* being the usual spelling for 'ay' in Shakespeare's time). Understanding *I* to mean 'I' permits additional play on *no*, which can be heard (at least in its first occurrence) as 'know'. Meanwhile the second and third soundings of *I*, if not the first, can also be heard as 'eye'. In the context in which this line occurs, that sense echoes a thematically pertinent passage from Matthew 18:9: 'if thine eye offend thee, pluck it out'.

But these are not all the implications *I* can have here. It can also represent the Roman numeral for '1', which will soon be reduced, as Richard notes, to 'nothing' (o), along with the speaker's title, his worldly possessions, his manhood, and eventually his life. In Shakespeare's time, to become 'nothing' was, *inter alia*, to be emasculated, to be made a 'weaker vessel' (1 Peter 3:7) with 'no thing'. As the Fool in *King Lear* reminds another monarch who has abdicated his throne, a man in want of an 'I' is impotent, 'an O without a Figure' (I.iv.207). In addition to its other dimensions, then, Richard's reply is a statement that can be formulated mathematically, and in symbols that anticipate the binary system behind today's computer technology: '1, o, o, 1, for 1 must o be.'

Modern editions usually render Richard's line 'Ay, no; no, ay; for I must nothing be'. Presenting the line in that fashion makes good sense of what Richard is saying. But as we've seen, it doesn't make total sense of it, and it doesn't call attention to Richard's paradoxes in the same way that hearing or seeing three undifferentiated *I*'s is likely to have done for Shakespeare's contemporaries. Their culture was more attuned than ours is to the oral and aural dimensions of language, and if we want to appreciate the special qualities of their dramatic art we need to train ourselves to 'hear' the word-forms we see on the page. We must learn to recognize that for many of what we tend to think of as fixed linkages between sound and meaning (the vowel 'I', say, and the word 'eye'), there were alternative linkages (such as the vowel 'I' and the words 'I' and 'Ay') that could be just as pertinent to what the playwright was communicating through the ears of his theatre patrons at a given moment. As the word *audience* itself may help us to remember, people in Shakespeare's time normally spoke of 'hearing' rather than 'seeing' a play.

In its text of *Richard II*, the Everyman edition reproduces the title character's line as it appears in the early printings of the tragedy. Ideally the orthographic oddity of the repeated *I*'s will encourage today's readers to ponder Richard's utterance, and the play it epitomizes, as a characteristically Shakespearean enigma.


## OTHER ASPECTS OF THE EVERYMAN TEXT

Now for a few words about other features of the Everyman text.

One of the first things readers will notice about this edition is its bountiful use of capitalized words. In this practice as in others, the Everyman exemplar is the First Folio, and especially the works in the Folio sections billed as 'Histories' and 'Tragedies'.* Everyman makes no attempt to adhere to the Folio printings with literal exactitude. In some instances the Folio capitalizes words that the Everyman text of the same passage lowercases; in other instances Everyman capitalizes words not uppercased in the Folio. The objective is merely to suggest something of the flavour, and what appears to have been the rationale, of Renaissance capitalization, in the hope that today's audiences will be made continually aware that the works they're contemplating derive from an earlier epoch.

Readers will also notice that instead of cluttering the text with stage directions such as '[Aside]' or '[To Rosse]', the Everyman text employs unobtrusive dashes to indicate shifts in mode of address. In an effort to keep the page relatively clear of words not supplied by the original printings, Everyman also exercises restraint in its addition of editor-generated stage directions. Where the dialogue makes it obvious that a significant action occurs, the Everyman text inserts a square-bracketed phrase such as '[Fleance escapes]'. Where what the dialogue implies is subject to differing interpretations, however, the Everyman text provides a facing-page note to discuss the most plausible inferences.

Like other modern editions, the Everyman text combines into 'shared' verse lines (lines divided among two or more speakers) many of the part-lines to be found in the early publications of the plays. One exception to the usual modern procedure is that Everyman indents some lines that are not components of shared verses. At times, for example, the opening line of a scene stops short of the metrical norm, a pentameter (five-foot) or hexameter (six-foot) line comprised predominantly of iambic units (unstressed syllables followed by stressed ones). In such cases Everyman uses indentation as a reminder that scenes can begin as well as end

---

* The quarto printings employ far fewer capital letters than does the Folio. Capitalization seems to have been regarded as a means of recognizing the status ascribed to certain words (*Noble*, for example, is almost always capitalized), titles (not only King, Queen, Duke, and Duchess, but Sir and Madam), genres (tragedies were regarded as more 'serious' than comedies in more than one sense), and forms of publication (quartos, being associated with ephemera such as 'plays', were not thought to be as 'grave' as the folios that bestowed immortality on 'works', writings that, in the words of Ben Jonson's eulogy to Shakespeare, were 'not of an age, but for all time').

in mid-line (an extension of the ancient convention that an epic commences *in media res*, 'in the midst of the action'). Everyman also uses indentation to reflect what appear to be pauses in the dialogue, either to allow other activity to transpire (as happens in *Macbeth*, II.iii.87, when a brief line 'What's the Business?' follows a Folio stage direction that reads, '*Bell rings. Enter Lady*') or to permit a character to hesitate for a moment of reflection (as happens a few seconds later in the same scene when Macduff responds to a demand to 'Speak, speak' with the reply 'O gentle Lady, / 'Tis not for you to hear what I can speak').

Readers of the Everyman edition will note that many word-forms are printed with apostrophes to indicate contractions (*to't* for 'to it', for example, or *o'th'* for 'of the') or syllabic elisions (*look'd* for 'looked', for instance, or *nev'r* or *ne'er* for 'never'). In many cases these departures from ordinary spelling occur in verse contexts that call for the deletion of syllables which if voiced would result in minor violations of the metrical norm. Thus in *Twelfth Night*, II.iv.107, *loved* is syncopated to *lov'd* in Viola's statement 'My Father had a Daughter lov'd a Man'. On the other hand, in *A Midsummer Night's Dream*, II.i.26, *loved* is treated as a full voiced two-syllable word in 'But she, perforce, withholds the loved Boy'. In situations such as these Everyman almost invariably retains the word-forms to be found in the early printings that have been adopted as control texts. At times this policy results in lines whose metre can be construed in different ways by different interpreters. In *A Midsummer Night's Dream*, III.ii.292, to cite one line for illustrative purposes, it could be argued that the first *Personage* should be syncopated to *Pers'nage* when Hermia says, 'And with her Personage, her tall Personage'. By the same token it could be maintained that words such as *even*, *Heaven* and *whether* should be syncopated in pronunciation when, as is usual, they occur in positions that would normally demand a sound with the metrical value of a single syllable. The frequency with which syllabic elisions crop up in the original editions of Shakespeare's works would seem to suggest that the playwright and his colleagues placed a premium on metrical regularity. At the same time, the frequent absence of syncopated or contracted word-forms in settings where the metre would lead us to expect them (*I am* is only rarely rendered as *I'm*, for example, though it continually appears in positions that invite compression to one syllable) could be viewed as evidence that Shakespeare was anything but rigid in such matters, and may even have consciously opted for the subtle variations that derive from occasional unstressed syllabic additions to an otherwise steady march of iambic feet. Given the metrical ambiguity of the early texts, it is difficult if not impossible to determine how 'smooth' the verse-speaking was intended to be in the theatres for which Shakespeare wrote his scripts. Rather than impose a fixed order that might be incompatible with the poet's own aesthetic principles, then, the Everyman text merely preserves the metrical inconsistencies to be observed in the Quarto and Folio printings of Shakespeare's plays and poems.

Everyman also retains many of the other anomalies in the early texts. In some instances this practice affects the way characters are depicted. In *A Midsummer Night's Dream*, for example, the ruler of Athens is usually identified in speech headings and stage directions as 'Theseus', but sometimes he is referred to by his title as 'Duke'. In the same play Oberon's merry sprite goes by two different names: 'Puck' and 'Robin Goodfellow'.

Readers of the Everyman edition will sometimes discover that characters they've known, or known about, for years don't appear in the original printings. When they open the pages of the Everyman *Macbeth*, for example, they'll learn that Shakespeare's audiences were unaware of any woman with the title 'Lady Macbeth'. In the only authoritative text we have of the Scottish tragedy, the protagonist's spouse goes by such names as 'Macbeth's Lady', 'Macbeth's Wife', or simply 'Lady', but at no time is she listed or mentioned as 'Lady Macbeth'. The same is true of the character usually designated 'Lady Capulet' in modern editions of *Romeo and Juliet*. 'Capulet's Wife' makes appearances as 'Mother', 'Old Lady', 'Lady', or simply 'Wife'; but she's never termed 'Lady Capulet', and her husband never treats her with the dignity such a title would connote.

Rather than 'correct' the grammar in Shakespeare's works to eliminate what modern usage would categorize as solecisms (as when Mercutio says 'my Wits faints' in *Romeo and Juliet*), the

Everyman text leaves it intact. Among other things, this principle applies to instances in which archaic forms preserve idioms that differ slightly from related modern expressions (as in the clause 'you are too blame', where 'too' frequently functions as an adverb and 'blame' is used, not as a verb, but as an adjective roughly equivalent to 'blameworthy').

Finally, and most importantly, the Everyman edition leaves unchanged any reading in the original text that is not manifestly erroneous. Unlike other modern renderings of Shakespeare's works, Everyman substitutes emendations only when obvious problems can be dealt with by obvious solutions.

## The Everyman Text of As You Like It

Our sole authority for the text of *As You Like it* is the version of the comedy that appeared in the 1623 First Folio. From all indications the Folio compositors set type either from an authorial transcript that had been lightly annotated (to provide act and scene divisions, for example, which are adapted in the Everyman edition from the Folio printing) or from a theatrical promptbook based upon a clean authorial copy. The F1 text presents no serious problems, and the alterations from it that appear in the later seventeenth-century folios are usually construed as emendations that were introduced without reference to an authoritative independent source.

In a few passages Everyman emends the First Folio text. For each item in the following list the first entry, in boldface type, is the reading adopted by Everyman (with a parenthetical reference to F2, F3, or F4 if the non-F1 reading derives from the 1632 Second Folio, the 1663–4 Third Folio, or the 1685 Fourth Folio), and the second entry, in regular type, is the reading to be found in the 1623 First Folio.

| | | |
|---|---|---|
| I.i. | 52 | **What,** What |
| | 115 | **she** (F3) hee |
| | 172 | **[OLIVER]** (F2) No speech heading in F1. |
| I.ii. | 86 | **mean'st** means't |
| | 88 | **[CELIA]** ROSALIND |
| | 269 | **overthrown:** overthrown |

| | | |
|---|---|---|
| I.iii. | 12 | **Working-day** working day |
| | 82 | **her** (F2) per |
| | 130 | **be** by |
| II.i. | 6 | **Fang** phange |
| | 49 | **much** (F2) must |
| II.iii. | 10 | **some** (F2) seem |
| | 16 | **[ORLANDO]** (F2) Line concludes Adam's speech in F1. |
| | 29 | **[ORLANDO]** (F2) *Ad.* |
| II.iv. | 44 | **their Wound** (F2) they would (Most editions adopt 'thy wound', the emendation proposed by Nicholas Rowe in 1709.) |
| | 70 | **you, Friend** (F2) your friend |
| II.v. | 46–47 | *No . . . Weather. &c.* |
| II.vii. | 38 | **Brain** (F2) braiue |
| | 64 | **Sin** (F2) fin |
| | 87 | **any Man.** any. man |
| | 182 | **Then** The |
| | 201 | **Master** masters |
| III.ii. | 29 | **good** (F2) pood |
| | 134 | **No** Noe |
| | 136 | **show** shoe |
| | 137 | **back,** back |
| | 165 | **withal** withall (so also in III.ii.331) |
| | 167 | **back,** back |
| | 241 | **Size.** (F3) size, |
| | 393 | **are** (F2) art |
| | 401 | **Revenue). Then** revenue) then |
| | 406 | **Point-** point |
| III.iii. | 97 | **[CLOWN]** (F2) *Ol.* (*Oliver*) |
| | 108 | *Exeunt. Exit.* (preceded by '*Exeunt Jaques, Touchstone, and Audrey.*' after III.iii.106) |
| III.iv. | 33 | **of a** of |
| III.v. | 37 | **have** (F2) hau |
| IV.i. | 1 | **me be** (F2) me |
| | 19 | **which** in which |
| | 20 | **Rumination** rumination, |
| | 108 | **Nun,** Nun; |
| | 112 | **Chroniclers** (F2) Chronoclers |
| | 210 | **it** (F2) in |
| IV.iii. | 106 | **Top** (F2) top, |

| V.i. | 11 | **Clown.** (F4) Clowne, |
| | 24 | **Wast** Was't |
| | 40 | **do, Sir** (F2) do sit |
| | 63 | **Do,** (F4) Do |
| | 64 | **merry,** (F4) merry |
| V.ii. | 53 | **Heart –** heart |
| | 63 | **are** (F2) arc |
| V.iii. | 19 | ***In Spring*** *In the spring* |
| | | ***Ring*** *rang* |
| | 34–36 | ***And ... Prime,*** In the Folio these verses come immediately after line 21. |
| V.iv. | 25 | ***Exeunt*** *Exit* |
| | 81 | **to** (F2) ro |
| | 129 | **adieu.** adieu |
| | 179 | **were** (F2) vvete |
| | 194 | **bequeath:** bequeath |
| | 206 | **trust** trust, |

In a number of passages that distinguish it from other modern editions, the Everyman text retains First Quarto readings, spelling forms, or punctuation styles. For each listing below, the first entry, in boldface type, is the reading to be found in Everyman; the second entry, in regular type, is the reading adopted by some if not most of today's editions.

| I.i. | 14 | **deerly** dearly (compare I.ii.3, 286, I.iii.33, 35, 37, 54, 70, II.vi.1, III.v.27, IV.i.54, 190, V.ii.79, V.iv.155) |
| | 29 | **a-part** apart (compare IV.iii.44) |
| | 45 | **I** Ay (compare I.ii.76, 163, 258, II.iv.16, IV.i.58, 126, 140, V.i.8, 25, 31, V.ii.32) |
| | 49 | **borne** born (compare I.iii.55, II.v.63, IV.i.228, IV.ii.16, V.i.24) |
| | 58 | **me Villain** me, villain |
| | 60 | **Boys,** Boys: |
| | 65 | **so, thou** so. Thou |
| | 66 | **patient,** patient; |
| | 77 | **Testament,** testament; |
| | 82 | **Will,** will. |
| | 86 | **Reward:** reward? |
| | 94 | **Charles** Charles, |
| | | **Wrastler** wrestler, |
| | 99 | **to morrow** tomorrow (compare I.i.127, 133, 169, II.i.29, V.ii.17, 48, 52, 55, 76, 82, 120, 122, 124, 126, V.iii.1, 2) |

106 **Brother** brother,
111 **Rosalind** Rosalind,
112 **Daughter** daughter,
113 **Daughter** daughter,
    **Cousin** cousin,
128 **Duke.** Duke?
131 **Brother** brother,
132 **Orlando** Orlando,
137 **loth** loath
140 **withall** withal (compare I.ii.29, II.vii.48, III.ii.165)
154 **Discretion,** discretion;
160 **Devise** device (F3; so also in I.i.177)
165 **anathomize** anatomize (F3; compare II.vii.56)
181 **long,** long;

I.ii.
    3 **Celia;** Celia,
    4 **yet were merrier:** yet I were merrier?
    9 **waight** weight (compare I.ii.267)
   31 **then** than (so also in I.ii.277, II.v.23, II.vii.138,
       III.ii.242, 407, 413, IV.i.210, V.iv.201, 209)
   34 **Houswife** hussif
   47 **No;** No?
   58 **hath** and hath
   88 ROSALIND CELIA
       **him** him;
   89 **enough;** enough.
       **him,** him;
   92 **wisely,** wisely
       **Wisemen** wise men
   96 **Beu** [Le] Beau
  102 **Boon-iour** Bon jour
  110 **decrees** decree
  111 **said, that** said! That
  113 **loosest** losest (compare II.vii.112)
  155 DUKE DUKE [FREDERICK] (so also throughout I.ii, I.iii,
       and II.ii)
  161 **Cousin:** Cousin? cousin?
  170 **hether** hither (so also in V.iv.121; compare I.iii.94)
  188 **Sir,** sir;
  201 **onely** only (so also in II.vii.34, 44, III.iv.13, V.iii.13,
       19, 25, 31, 37, V.iv.110)
  210 **Gallant,** gallant
  234 **else,** else:
  239 **Youth,** youth.
  241 **Coze** Coz (so also in I.ii.257, 266)

252 **deserv'd,** deserv'd.
253 **Love;** love, *or* love
256 **Fortune** fortune,
257 **more,** more
261 **Quintine** quintain
    **liveless** lifeless
262 **Fortunes,** fortunes;
269 **Orlando!** Orlando,
    **overthrown** overthrown!
271 **counsaile** counsel
273 **Love;** love,
276 **humorous,** humorous:
277 **, then** than (so also in II.v.23, III.ii.407, 413, IV.i.210,
    V.iv.201, 209; compare I.ii.31)
279 **Duke,** Duke
282 **taller** smaller
286 **Sisters:** sisters.
293 **well,** well.
299 **Rosaline** Rosalind (so also in I.iii.1, 94)

I.iii.
    5 **Curs,** curs;
    11 **Father:** father.
    12 **oh** O (compare II.iii.2, 3, 14, 56, II.iv.22, 33, II.vii.33,
        III.v.18)
    15 **Foolery,** foolery;
    18 **Coat,** coat;
    26 **you:** you!
        **try** cry
    27 **despight** despite (so also in II.v.49; compare V.ii.89)
    46 **Uncle.** uncle?
        **Cousin,** cousin.
    56 **Traitors,** traitors:
    61 **Likelihoods** likelihood (F2)
        **depends?** depends.
    67 **me,** me?
    68 **much,** much
    76 **Remorse,** remorse.
    81 **subtile** subtle
        **Smoothness;** smoothness,
    82 **per** her (F2)
    83 **Fool,** fool;
    86 **Lips,** lips:
    87 **Dombe,** doom
    91 **your self,** yourself;
    94 **whether** whither (so also in I.iii.105, 110, II.iii.29, 30;

compare I.ii.170)

| | |
|---|---|
| 99 | **me** me, |
| 113 | **far** far! |
| 117 | **you, so** you. So |
| | **along,** along |
| 120 | **man,** man? |
| 122 | **Bore-spear** boar-spear |
| 123 | **Lye** Lie |
| 135 | **Travail** travel (F3; so also in II.iv.75, IV.i.30) |
| 137 | **woe** woo (so also in II.iii.50, II.vii.10, III.ii.433, 454, IV.i.155; compare II.vii.148) |
| 139 | **Time,** time |
| 141 | **in we** we in |

**II.i.**

| | |
|---|---|
| 6 | **Seasons** seasons' |
| 13 | **ougly** ugly |
| 18 | **it, happy** it. Happy |
| | **Grace** grace, |
| 20 | **Stile** style (compare IV.iii.31–32) |
| 25 | **goar'd** gor'd |
| 30 | **antic** (anticke F1) antique |
| 33 | **Stag** stag, |
| 46 | **Stream;** stream: |
| 50 | **Friend** friends |
| 55 | **greazy** greasy |
| 59 | **of** of the (F2) |
| 63 | **dwelling place** dwelling-place |
| 66 | **place,** place. |
| 68 | **strait** straight (so also in III.v.136; compare V.ii.73) |

**II.ii.**

| | |
|---|---|
| 2 | **be,** be. |
| 4 | **her,** her. |
| 5 | **Ladies** ladies, |
| | **Chamber** chamber, |
| 10 | **Hisperia** Hisperia, |
| | **Gentlewoman** gentlewoman, |
| 14 | **sinowy** sinewy |
| 15 | **believes** believes, |
| | **gone** gone, |
| 17 | **Brother,** brother; |
| | **hither,** hither. |
| 18 | **me,** me; |

**II.iii.**

| | |
|---|---|
| 2 | **Master,** master? |
| 4 | **Rowland;** Rowland! |
| 11 | **Enemies,** enemies? |
| 15 | **it?** it! |
| 18 | **lives** lives. |

|       | 19 | Brother, brother – |
|-------|----|--------------------|
|       | 21 | Father, father – |
|       | 35 | can, can. (F3) |
|       | 40 | foster foster- |
|       | 46 | you, you; |
|       |    | Servant, servant. |
|       | 51 | Debility, debility; |
|       | 53 | you, you; |
|       | 58 | Meed: meed! |
|       | 64 | yield, yield |
|       | 65 | Husbandry, husbandry. |
|       | 71 | seventy seventeen |
|       | 73 | seventy seventeen |
|       | 74 | Week, week; |

II.iv.

| 1 | merry weary |
|---|-------------|
|   | Spirits? spirits! |
| 8 | Petty-coat petticoat |
| 19 | so so, |
| 33 | hartily, heartily! (compare II.v.28, III.ii.263) |
| 38 | Wearing Wearying (F2) |
| 40 | Company, company |
| 43 | Shepherd, shepherd! (shepherd F1) |
| 48 | a night a-night |
|    | Smile, Smile; |
| 66 | Food, food; |
| 67 | Holla; Holla! |
| 74 | our selves, ourselves |
| 82 | wreaks reaks *or* recks |
| 84 | Besides Besides, |
|    | Coate cote |
| 85 | Sheep-coat sheepcote (so also in IV.iii.78) |
| 98 | me, me; |

II.v.

| 1 | Under [AMIENS] Under |
|---|----------------------|
|   | green wood greenwood |
| 12 | more, I can more. I can |
| 26 | Complement compliment |
| 33 | while, while; |
| 39 | *Altogether All together* (compare V.ii.120) |
| 51 | Thus JAQUES Thus [*Amy.* Thus F1] |
| 63 | first borne first-born (compare IV.i.228) |
| 65 | Banket banquet |

II.vi.

| 5 | thee: live thee? Live |
|---|------------------------|

II.vii.  0  *Enter . . . Lord[s]. Enter Duke Senior, [Amiens,] and Lord[s].*
         9  **Monsieur,** monsieur?
            **this** this,
        13  **a** ah
        37  **Courtier** courtier,
        42  **Fool,** fool!
        55  **Seem** Not to seem
        56  **anathomiz'd** anatomiz'd (F3; compare I.i.165)
        71  **Party:** party?
        73  **ebb.** ebb?
        83  **what then,** what then?
        87  **come** comes (F2)
        94  **first,** first.
        95  **Shew** show (compare III.ii.457, III.v.20, IV.i.217, V.ii.30, 87)
        96  **in-land** inland
       106  **you,** you;
       112  **Loose** Lose
       115  **sate** sat
       152  **Canon's** cannon's
       160  **wide,** wide
       162  **treble Pipes,** treble, pipes
       174  **Blow** [AMIENS] Blow
       181  **fayning** feigning
       196  **witness,** witness
       197  **limn'd,** limn'd
       198  **hither:** hither.
       199  **Father,** father.

III.i.   5  **is,** is;
          6  **Candle:** candle;
          9  **thine,** thine
         10  **seizure,** seizure

III.ii.   2  **thrice** thrice-
          4  **Name,** name
         16  **well:** well;
         19  **well:** well;
         21  **well:** well,
         57  **Courtiers** courtier's
         94  **Rosalinde** Rosalind (so also in III.ii.96, 98, 100, 108, 110, 112, 114, 116, 118)
        101  **so,** so
            **together;** together,
        102  **Sleeping** sleeping-

115  **sowrest** sourest
118  **Prick,** prick
119  **Verses,** verses:
125  **Medler** medlar
133  **this** this a
143  **Bows** boughs (so also in IV.iii.105)
151  **wide** wide-
     **enlarg'd,** enlarg'd.
153  **his** her
156  **Lucrecia's** Lucretia's (F4)
160  **pris'd** priz'd
167  **now,** now?
204  **Complection** complexion
210  **powre** pour (compare V.i.45)
253  **forth** such (forth such F2)
260  **the** thy
263  **Hart** heart (compare II.iv.33)
264  **Burthen,** burden;
266  **Woman, when** woman? When
273  **too,** too
292  **Cloath** cloth
296  **me, and** me? And
301  **change,** change
305  **Brook,** brook;
310  **you,** you.
356  **Shepherdess** shepherdess,
369  **Lectors** lectures (F3)
370  **Woman** woman,
376  **half Pence** halfpence
380  **Physic,** physic
385  **defying** deifying (F2)
389  **Love-shak'd,** love-shak'd:
393  **art** are (F2)
397  **blew** blue
407  **Accoustrements** accoutrements
420  **love,** love
427  **cur'd,** cur'd
435  **longing,** longing
446  **meerly** merely
453  **Coat** cote (compare II.iv.84–85)

III.iii.

7  **Poet** poet,
   **Ovid** Ovid,
8  **Gothes** Goths
9  **ill** ill-
19  **faining** feigning

28  **hard** hard-
39  **Gods,** gods`
40  **it,** it
56  **Horns;** horns?
57  **so poor** so. Poor
    **alone.** alone?
69  OLIVER [SIR] OLIVER (*Ol.* F1)
75  **Sir, you** Sir? You
76  **Company,** company.
77  **you, even** you. Even
82  **Desires,** desires;
88  **Wainscot,** wainscot;
91  **mind,** mind

III.iv.

3   **consider,** consider
35  **Tapster,** tapster:
44  **Man, he** man! he
46  **travers** traverse,
61  **remove,** remove;

III.v.

1   **not, Phebe, not, Phebe;** (F3)
5   **Neck,** neck
8   **Executioner,** executioner;
10  **Eye,** eye;
11  **pretty sure** pretty, sure
12  **Eyes that** eyes, that
17  **why** why?
20  **thee,** thee:
43  **Sale-work?** sale-work.
45  **it,** it.
50  **Rain,** rain?
63  **Shepherd,** shepherd;
75  **Olives,** olives
88  **Love** love,
98  **Gladness,** gladness
109 **him,** him;
134 **tanting** taunting (F4)
137 **Heart,** heart;

IV.i.

6   **abhominable** abominable
19  **by** my
42  **Lover?** lover!
47  **Love?** love!
52  **Heart hole** heart-whole (F4)
60  **Joincture** jointure (F2)
74  **holi-day** holiday

|        |     |                                                            |
|--------|-----|------------------------------------------------------------|
|        | 82  | **warn** warrant                                           |
|        | 83  | **Lovers,** lovers                                         |
|        | 103 | **Love Cause** love-cause                                  |
|        | 180 | **have,** have                                             |
|        | 192 | **Dinner,** dinner;                                        |
|        | 195 | **prove,** prove;                                          |
|        | 226 | **Venus,** Venus                                           |
|        | 228 | **borne** born (compare I.iii.55, IV.ii.16, V.i.24, V.iv.30) |
|        | 230 | **judge,** judge                                           |
| IV.ii. | 0   | *Lords, Foresters* Lords [as] Foresters                    |
|        | 1   | **Dear** deer (so also in IV.ii.5, 11)                     |
|        | 2   | LORD [1] LORD                                              |
|        | 8   | LORD [2] LORD                                              |
|        | 11  | **What** [2 LORD] What                                     |
|        | 14  | **the ... Burthen.** *The ... Burthen.* [treated as a stage-direction] |
| IV.iii.| 5   | **forth** forth –                                          |
|        | 11  | **Tenure** tenor                                           |
|        | 14  | **Swaggerer,** swaggerer:                                  |
|        |     | **all:** all!                                              |
|        | 18  | **hunt,** hunt;                                            |
|        | 34  | **giant rude** giant-rude                                  |
|        | 40  | **turn'd?** turn'd,                                        |
|        | 41  | **burn'd.** burn'd?                                        |
|        | 44  | **a part** apart (F2; compare I.i.29)                      |
|        | 74  | **Lover** lover, (F4)                                      |
|        | 77  | **Purlews** purlieus                                       |
|        | 78  | **Olive-trees.** olive trees?                              |
|        | 79  | **Bottom** bottom,                                         |
|        | 98  | **Handkercher** handkerchief                              |
|        | 102 | **befell:** befell!                                        |
|        | 109 | **guilded** gilded                                         |
|        | 113 | **was** was –                                              |
|        |     | **Cestos** Sestos (F2)                                     |
|        | 130 | **Nature** nature,                                         |
|        | 143 | **I'brief** (I brief F1) In brief (F2)                     |
|        | 156 | **Died** Dy'd                                              |
|        |     | **this** his (F2)                                          |
|        | 163 | **pray you** pray you,                                     |
|        |     | **Arm.** arm?                                              |
|        | 167 | **counterfeited,** counterfeited!                          |
|        | 168 | **counterfeited:** counterfeited.                          |
| V.i.   | 40  | **do sit** do, sir (F2)                                    |
|        | 34  | **Wiseman** wise man (F4)                                  |

172  **him** them
181  **shrew'd** shrewd
196  **Love,** love
198  **long,** long
201  **other, then** other than (compare II.v.23)
205  **Rights** rites
206  **end** end,
       ***Exit. Exeunt** [all but Rosalind]*.
216  **Play?** play!

# AS YOU LIKE IT

# NAMES OF THE ACTORS

DUKE SENIOR, banished to the Forest of Arden
DUKE FREDERICK, his Brother and usurper

ROSALIND, Daughter to Duke Senior
CELIA, Daughter to Duke Frederick

AMYENS [AMIENS]  } Lords attending on Duke Senior
JAQUES

LE BEU [LE BEAU] a Courtier attending upon Duke Frederick
CHARLES, Wrestler to Duke Frederick

OLIVER
JAQUES    } Sons of the late
ORLANDO     Sir Rowland de Boys

ADAM
DENNIS  } Servants to Oliver

TOUCHSTONE, a Clown
SIR OLIVER MAR-TEXT, a Vicar

CORIN
SILVIUS  } Shepherds

WILLIAM, a Country Fellow in love with Audrey

PHEBE, a Shepherdess beloved by Silvius
AUDREY, a Country Wench
HYMEN, God of Marriage

**LORDS**
**PAGES**
**FORESTERS**
**ATTENDANTS**

I.i.   The opening scene takes place in the 'Orchard' (line 43), of
       Oliver, the oldest son of Sir Rowland de Boys. Orlando is
       complaining to Adam (an old retainer) about the lot of a
       younger son with a negligible inheritance.

2      **by Will**  in my father's last will and testament.
       **but poor a**  a paltry.

3      **Crowns**  in England, coins worth five shillings each.
       **charg'd**  commanded.

4      **on his Blessing**  both (a) on his receiving his blessing from his
       dying father (a ritual that recalls Genesis 27), and (b) on the
       penalty of his losing that blessing if he fails to adhere to Sir
       Rowland's wishes.
       **breed**  bring up, educate.

5      **Jaques**  the 'second brother' (middle sibling) in the de Boys
       household. His only appearance in the action occurs after
       V.iv.158.

6      **goldenly**  with glittering praise. Compare lines 124–26.

7      **Profit**  benefit, progress in his studies (but with the implication
       that the learning and discipline he acquires will also equip him
       to profit socially and economically once he enters his chosen
       profession).
       **keeps**  (a) maintains, as opposed to (b) 'stays' (line 8) or
       constrains (like a prisoner). The 'School' to which Orlando
       refers is probably a university; compare *Hamlet*, I.ii.112–17.
       **rustically**  like a menial rural labourer, cut off from civilized
       society.

8      **stays**  detains, blocks my way.

9      **unkept**  unprovided for. Orlando's references to 'Keeping'
       allude to Genesis 4:9, where Cain asks, 'Am I my brother's
       keeper?'

11     **Stalling**  stabling, keeping in a stall. Another meaning of
       *Stalling*, 'impeding' or 'delaying', reinforces *stays* (line 8).

12     **fair**  healthy and handsome.

13     **taught their Manage**  trained to comport themselves and bear
       riders in an appropriate manner (with the proper paces).

14     **deerly hir'd**  engaged at great cost. Here the Folio spelling,
       *deerely*, may involve wordplay on (a) *deerly*, 'deerlike' (see the
       note to line 20), and (b) *dearly*, 'expensively' and 'lovingly'.

# ACT I

## Scene 1

*Enter Orlando and Adam.*

ORLANDO   As I remember, Adam, it was upon this
fashion bequeath'd me by Will, but poor a
thousand Crowns, and as thou sayst, charg'd my
Brother on his Blessing to breed me well: and
there begins my Sadness. My brother Jaques he          5
keeps at School, and Report speaks goldenly of
his Profit. For my part, he keeps me rustically
at home, or (to speak more properly) stays me
here at home unkept: for call you that Keeping
for a Gentleman of my Birth, that differs not         10
from the Stalling of an Ox? His Horses are bred
better, for besides that they are fair with
their Feeding, they are taught their Manage,
and to that end Riders deerly hir'd. But I (his
Brother) gain nothing under him but Growth, for       15
the which his Animals on his Dunghills are as
much bound to him as I. Besides this Nothing
that he so plentifully gives me, the Something
that Nature gave me his Countenance seems to

---

17   **bound**   both (a) beholden, indebted, and (b) connected (like a
     branch or graft on a tree).

19–20 **his . . . me**   his treatment appears contrived to deprive me of. In
     this passage *Countenance* plays on several possible meanings:
     (a) face (expression, here conveying aloofness, if not hostility),
     (b) appearance, demeanour, and (c) patronage, favour, or
     approval (here meant ironically).

20 **Hinds** both (a) farmhands, and (b) young female deer (compare *Romeo and Juliet*, I.i.68).

21 **bars me** bars me from, withholds from me.
**place of a Brother** both (a) a place at his own table as a social equal (see line 20), and (b) a position in the household that befits a sibling, as distinguished from a 'hind', a hired hand.

22–23 **mines . . . Education** both (a) exploits (like a mine owner who profits from the extraction of gold, coal, or other valued minerals), and (b) undermines (erodes) my inherited qualities as a man of gentle blood by the way he 'educates' me. Compare *Hamlet*, III.iv.145–46.

23 **grieves me** both (a) aggrieves me, gives me legitimate cause for grievance (complaint against unjust treatment), and (b) 'begins my Sadness' (line 5).

25–26 **this Servitude** his treating me as if I were no better than a servant. We soon learn that the old man to whom Orlando complains *is* a servant, but one who is demeaned in a way that would be 'Improper for a Slave' (*King Lear*, V.iii.221). Orlando's name is the Italian equivalent of *Rowland*, so he is justified in his sense that he is animated by the 'Spirit' of his 'Father'.

29 **Go a-part** stand aside, where you will not be seen.

30 **shake me up** abuse and upset me.

31 **what make you** what are you doing. Oliver's implication is that Orlando is 'here' when he should be elsewhere (see lines 5–9, 20–21); Oliver is suspicious of the 'Idleness' (line 36) of a loiterer who would 'be better employ'd' (line 37) in the barn or in the field than in a setting where his leisure permits him to plot insurrections against his 'Master' (line 28).

32 **make** create, do.

33 **mar** abuse, disfigure. 'Make and mar' was a proverbial pairing. Compare *Romeo and Juliet*, II.iii.121–30.

34 **Marry** truly (with wordplay on *mar*). *Marry* originated as 'Mary', an oath in the name of the virgin 'handmaid' (Luke 1:38) whom 'God made' (line 35) the earthly mother of his incarnate Son.

36 **Idleness** Orlando means (a) lack of cultivation or proper employment (like a plot of arable land that is not being put to agricultural use), as contrasted with (b) laziness or reckless abandon.

take from me: he lets me feed with his Hinds,                    20
bars me the place of a Brother, and as much as
in him lies, mines my Gentility with my
Education. This is it, Adam, that grieves me,
and the Spirit of my Father, which I think is
within me, begins to mutiny against this          25
Servitude. I will no longer endure it, though
yet I know no wise Remedy how to avoid it.

*Enter Oliver.*

ADAM   Yonder comes my Master, your Brother.
ORLANDO   Go a-part, Adam, and thou shalt hear how
   he will shake me up.                          30
OLIVER   Now Sir, what make you here?
ORLANDO   Nothing: I am not taught to make any thing.
OLIVER   What mar you then, Sir?
ORLANDO   Marry Sir, I am helping you to mar that
   which God made, a poor unworthy Brother of     35
   yours, with Idleness.
OLIVER   Marry Sir, be better employ'd, and be
   naught a while.
ORLANDO   Shall I keep your Hogs, and eat Husks
   with them? what prodigal Portion have I spent,  40
   that I should come to such Penury?

---

37–38 **be naught**   be nothing, go to the Devil, disappear. *Naught*
      echoes lines 17–20.

40    **prodigal Portion**   Orlando alludes to the story of the Prodigal
      Son in Luke 15:11–32, who 'wasted' his 'portion of the
      goods' due to him and 'would fain have filled his belly with
      the husks that the swine did eat'.

41    **Penury**   both (a) poverty and (b) pain, as a penalty (Latin
      *poena*) for 'riotous living' (Luke 15:13).

45     **I**   both (a) I [do], and (b) Ay (yes).
       **knows**   both (a) recognizes, and (b) understands, respects, and
       loves accordingly.

47–48 **so know me**   in the same way regard me – as your brother, a
       gentleman of the same 'Blood' (genetic makeup) that
       determines your 'Condition' (both disposition and rank).

48     **Courtesy of Nations**   universally accepted customs and norms,
       what Hector calls the 'moral Laws / of Nature and of
       Nations' in *Troilus and Cressida*, II.ii.183–84. Here Orlando
       refers to the 'Tradition' (line 50) of primogeniture, which
       provided for the first-born to inherit an estate in its entirety.

48–49 **allows . . . better**   acknowledges you as my social and
       property-owning superior.

49     **borne**   both (a) carried, and (b) born.

50     **Blood**   gentility (as the son of a gentleman). But *Blood* can also
       refer to the impulses and passions a son derives from his
       father; compare II.iii.36–37, V.iv.57–59.

53–54 **is nearer to his Reverence**   entitles you to (a) more of his
       favour, and (b) more of the standing he himself enjoyed.

54     **coming before me**   arrival prior to my birth.

55     **Boy**   then as now, a term of disrespect, in this case one that
       reduces Orlando to the status of a page or lowly servant.
       Compare *Romeo and Juliet*, III.i.69–70, *Coriolanus*,
       V.vi.99–109, and *Antony and Cleopatra*, V.ii.214–19.

57     **young**   both (a) immature, rash, and (b) inexperienced, inferior.
       Oliver has probably tried to strike Orlando, and Orlando now
       grasps him in a wrestling hold. Orlando is telling his older
       brother that the real boy 'in this' altercation is Oliver.

58     **me Villain**   both (a) me as a villain, and (b) me, you villain.

59     **Villain**   Orlando uses the term in its original sense: peasant or
       serf (from the French *villein*). Oliver has used it to mean
       rascal (line 58), and Orlando picks up on that sense in lines
       61–62. Here *thrice* means not only 'three times' but 'many
       times'; compare *très* in French.

65     **rail'd on**   insulted.

66–67 **for your Father's Remembrance**   (a) out of respect for your
       father's memory, and (b) bearing in mind your father's
       honour and declared 'Will' (lines 1–5, 70–71).

OLIVER    Know you where you are, Sir?

ORLANDO    O Sir, very well: here in your Orchard.

OLIVER    Know you before whom, Sir?

ORLANDO    I, better than him I am before knows me:    45
I know you are my eldest Brother, and in the
gentle Condition of Blood you should so know
me. The Courtesy of Nations allows you my
better, in that you are the first borne, but
the same Tradition takes not away my Blood,    50
were there twenty Brothers betwixt us. I have
as much of my Father in me as you, albeit I
confess your coming before me is nearer to his
Reverence.

OLIVER    What, Boy.    55

ORLANDO    Come, come, elder Brother, you are too
young in this.

OLIVER    Wilt thou lay Hands on me Villain?

ORLANDO    I am no Villain: I am the youngest Son
of Sir Rowland de Boys, he was my Father, and    60
he is thrice a Villain that says such a Father
begot Villains. Wert thou not my Brother, I
would not take this Hand from thy Throat till
the other had pull'd out thy Tongue for saying
so, thou hast rail'd on thy self.    65

ADAM    Sweet Masters, be patient, for your Father's
Remembrance, be at accord.

OLIVER    Let me go, I say.

ORLANDO    I will not till I please: you shall hear
me. My Father charg'd you in his Will to give    70
me good Education: you have train'd me like a

72–73 **obscuring . . . Qualities** literally, keeping me under a shadow, and trying to prevent me from even knowing about the attributes that would make my 'Condition' a 'gentle' one (line 47).

74 **grows strong** rises up in accordance with its native 'Growth' (lines 14–17).

75 **Exercises** physical and mental training, gentlemanly pursuits.

77 **poor Allottery** meagre allotment. Orlando is probably punning on *Lottery*; compare *The Merchant of Venice*, II.i.15–16.
**by Testament** in his will.

78 **buy my Fortunes** invest the talents I've been bequeathed (see Matthew 25:14–30) and thereby acquire such 'Fortunes' as my efforts will yield. See the notes to lines 7, 31, 40, 48.

80 **get you in** get out of my garden. Oliver's reference to begging (lines 79–80) is another allusion to the lot of the Prodigal Son; see Luke 25:14, 17–19.

82 **your Will** (a) what you so wilfully demand, as distinguished from (b) your portion from our father's will (see lines 91–92, which echo lines 1–4).

83 **offend** trouble, inconvenience, displease.

83–84 **becomes me** is in keeping with proper behaviour.

90–91 **grow upon me** both (a) grow large enough to challenge me in stature, and (b) encroach upon me, threaten me. *Grow* echoes lines 73–74.

91 **physic your Rankness** both (a) cure your disease (by lancing you as a physician does a festering boil), and (b) curb your growth (by pruning you as a gardener does an overgrown, or 'rank' tree). Oliver's plan to discipline his younger brother might be defended as responsible 'keeping' (see the note to line 9) if Orlando really needed to be controlled and if Oliver were really doing it for his charge's own good.

94 **Duke's Wrastler** a wrestler who enjoys the patronage (sponsorship and support) of the Duke. Most editions insert parenthetical commas around the phrase *the Duke's Wrastler*; here as elsewhere, Everyman follows the First Folio text and adds no punctuation. Compare lines 106, 111–13, I.ii.9–11, 131–32. II.ii.5, 10.

97 **importunes access to you** begs to see you. The literal meaning of *importunes* is 'seeks admission to a portal ["the Door", line 96]'.

Peasant, obscuring and hiding from me all
Gentleman-like Qualities. The Spirit of my
Father grows strong in me, and I will no longer
endure it: therefore allow me such Exercises 75
as may become a Gentleman, or give me the poor
Allottery my Father left me by Testament, with
that I will go buy my Fortunes.

OLIVER   And what wilt thou do? beg when that is
spent? Well Sir, get you in. I will not long 80
be troubled with you: you shall have some part
of your Will, I pray you leave me.

ORLANDO   I will no further offend you than becomes
me for my good.

OLIVER   – Get you with him, you old Dog. 85

ADAM   Is 'old Dog' my Reward: most true, I have
lost my Teeth in your Service. God be with my
old Master, he would not have spoke such a
Word.                              *Exeunt Orlando [and] Adam.*

OLIVER   – Is it even so, begin you to grow upon 90
me? I will physic your Rankness, and yet give
no thousand Crowns neither. – Holla, Dennis.

### *Enter Dennis.*

DENNIS   Calls your Worship?

OLIVER   Was not Charles the Duke's Wrastler here
to speak with me? 95

DENNIS   So please you, he is here at the Door,
and importunes access to you.

99    **a good way**   Oliver means 'a good way (route, means) to physic his brother's rankness'. Having been his 'brother's keeper' (see the note to line 9) in a sense that involves malign neglect, Oliver is now prepared to deal with Orlando in a way that resembles the paradigmatic older brother, Cain, even more forcibly.

      **to morrow**   tomorrow. But here as occasionally elsewhere, the Elizabethan orthography permits a two-word phrase to be construed in ways that go beyond the meaning of the modern single-word form. Compare lines 127, 133, 169.

101   **morrow**   morning.

107   **loving Lords**   lords who love, and remain loyal to, the old Duke.

109   **Revenues**   profits from the use of the lands. The situation at the 'new Court' (line 103) is a variation on that which obtains in the estate of Sir Rowland de Boys. The usurpation at court, where a 'younger Brother' has managed to 'grow upon' (line 90) his older sibling and supplant him and all that he has legally inherited, benefits an irresponsible landholder who 'mines' the 'Gentility' (line 22) of his blood relative and all of his followers. So eager is Oliver to avoid the fate of 'the old Duke' (line 105) that he tyrannizes Orlando and prevents him from claiming even the small monetary inheritance that is due him. The relationship between the daughters of the two dukes is an implicit rebuke to the perverted relationships between the two sets of brothers; though they are merely cousins (see lines 111–19), Rosalind and Celia are bound together as intimately as if they were sisters.

110   **good . . . wander**   welcome permission to take leave of their estates.

114–  **being . . . together**   inasmuch as they have been brought up like
15     siblings since they were infants. *Bred* echoes lines 3–4, 11–12.

116   **to stay behind her**   to remain behind if her cousin were to follow her father into exile. Charles refers to Celia, the daughter of the usurping Duke Frederick, and Rosalind, the daughter of the banished Duke Senior. *Stay* echoes lines 8–9.

121–  **the Forest of Arden**   Shakespeare combines the features of two
22     forests: (a) the Ardennes, on the river Meuse in what are now France, Luxembourg, and Belgium, and (b) the Arden, north of the river Avon in his native Warwickshire. We should bear in mind that in Shakespeare's time 'forest' referred primarily

OLIVER   Call him in.                          [*Exit Dennis.*]
  — 'Twill be a good way: and to morrow the
  Wrastling is.                                              100

*Enter Charles.*

CHARLES   Good morrow to your Worship.
OLIVER   Good Monsieur Charles: what's the new News
  at the new Court?
CHARLES   There's no News at the Court, Sir, but
  the old News: that is, the old duke is banish'd          105
  by his younger Brother the new Duke, and three
  or four loving Lords have put themselves into
  voluntary Exile with him, whose Lands and
  Revenues enrich the new Duke, therefore he
  gives them good leave to wander.                         110
OLIVER   Can you tell if Rosalind the Duke's
  Daughter be banish'd with her Father?
CHARLES   O no; for the Duke's Daughter her Cousin
  so loves her, being ever from their Cradles
  bred together, that she would have follow'd             115
  her Exile, or have died to stay behind her;
  she is at the Court, and no less beloved of
  her Uncle than his own Daughter, and never two
  Ladies loved as they do.
OLIVER   Where will the old Duke live?                     120
CHARLES   They say he is already in the Forest of
  Arden, and a many merry Men with him; and there

---

to a tract of land reserved by the Crown for the preservation
and hunting of game. It featured woods, but it often included
pastures and cultivated farmland as well. Cultured members
of Shakespeare's audience would probably have been
reminded of the 'Ardenna woods' that figure in Sir John
Harington's 1591 translation of *Orlando Furioso* ('Roland in
a Fury'), a romantic epic that Lodovico Ariosto completed in
1532. See the note to lines 25–26.

123 **Robin Hood** a legendary figure who was popularized in ballads at least as early as the fourteenth century. *Robin* derives from 'robbing', and Robin Hood and his followers were benign thieves who stole from the rich and gave to the poor. In 1598, shortly before the appearance of *As You Like It*, the Rose Theatre presented two plays that dealt with the life and death of Robin Hood.

125 **fleet the Time carelessly** pass time without cares or duties. Lines 124–26 suggest that Duke Senior is comparable to a shepherd whose sheep 'flock to him' voluntarily and with carefree abandon.

126 **the Golden World** the classical equivalent of the Garden of Eden; an era of pristine harmony and contentment that gave way to the Silver, Bronze, and Iron ages as humanity deteriorated. *Golden* echoes lines 5–7.

128 **Marry** indeed. Compare line 34.

133 **try a Fall** attempt to win a bout.

134 **Credit** respect, reputation as the most redoubtable wrestler of the realm. Charles implies that his continued patronage depends upon his performance.

135 **acquit him well** conduct himself capably, depart clear of shame.

136 **tender** immature; soft and delicate, like the 'tender plant' of Isaiah 53:2. Compare lines 55–57, and see the note to lines 90–91.

137 **loth to foil** unwilling to throw and injure.

140 **withall** Here the word means 'with all this'. Compare I.ii.29.
**stay** prevent. See the note to line 116.

141 **Intendment** intention. Compare *Othello*, IV.ii.204–5.
**brook** bear, tolerate.

143 **Search** seeking, responsibility.

146 **requite** reward, repay. *Requite* echoes *acquit*, line 135.

147 **under-hand** indirect (without the pejorative connotations usual now). It will soon become clear that Oliver's 'means' are 'under-hand' in a way he conceals from Charles.

149 **it is** We would normally say either 'he is' or 'this is'.

151 **Emulator** rival, one who is envious of another. Lines 173–80 make it clear that it is Oliver, not Orlando, who is 'an envious Emulator' of his brother's 'good Parts'. Compare I.ii.251.

they live like the old Robin Hood of England.
They say many young Gentlemen flock to him
every day, and fleet the Time carelessly as                          125
they did in the Golden World.

OLIVER   What, you wrastle to morrow before the new
Duke.

CHARLES   Marry do I, Sir: and I came to acquaint
you with a matter. I am given, Sir, secretly                         130
to understand that your younger Brother
Orlando hath a Disposition to come in disguis'd
against me to try a Fall: to morrow, Sir, I
wrastle for my Credit, and he that escapes me
without some broken Limb shall acquit him well.                      135
Your Brother is but young and tender, and for
your Love I would be loth to foil him, as I
must for my own Honour if he come in: therefore
out of my Love to you, I came hither to acquaint
you withall, that either you might stay him from                     140
his Intendment, or brook such Disgrace well as
he shall run into, in that it is a thing of his
own Search, and altogether against my Will.

OLIVER   Charles, I thank thee for thy Love to me,
which thou shalt find I will most kindly                             145
requite. I had my self notice of my Brother's
Purpose herein, and have by under-hand means
labour'd to dissuade him from it; but he is
resolute. I'll tell thee, Charles, it is the
stubbornest young Fellow of France, full of                          150
Ambition, an envious Emulator of every man's
good Parts, a secret and villainous Contriver
against me his natural Brother: therefore use

---

152   **Parts**   abilities, gifts, accomplishments.

153–   **use thy Discretion**   exercise your own judgement, do as you
54        please. What Oliver advises is the opposite of *Discretion* in
          the sense that relates to discrimination.

154   **had as lief**   would be just as pleased if.

156   **look to't**   be watchful, beware.

157–   **mightily . . . thee**   defeat you by the strength he derives from
58   'grace' (some luck he carries that gives him help from above).
Oliver implies that a victory by Orlando would win him the
'grace' (favour and privilege) that the Duke now accords
Charles, and that Oliver denies even 'his natural Brother' (line
153).

158   **practise**   contrive, intrigue.

160   **Devise**   device, plot.
   **leave thee**   both (a) let you alone, leave you in peace, and (b)
surrender his possession of you (in the manner of an evil spirit
that cannot be exorcized).

161   **indirect**   Oliver means 'treacherous' (line 159).

164   **so . . . villainous**   so steeped in villainy despite his youth. See
the notes to lines 57, 59, 136.

165   **brotherly**   making all the allowances for him that a brother
should. See the notes to lines 91, 99.
   **anathomize**   anatomize (dissect). But here as elsewhere, the
Shakespearean spelling suggests wordplay on 'anathemize'
(anathematize), curse, damn. Compare II.vii.56.

167   **look pale and wonder**   tremble with fright. Compare *Hamlet*,
V.ii.374–75, and *King Lear*, V.iii.231–32.

169   **come to morrow**   Charles means 'come tomorrow [to challenge
me]', but his words can also be construed 'arrive at the
morrow [having survived his bout with me]'. See the second
note to line 99, and compare line 133.

170   **go alone**   walk without assistance. Lines 170–71 will prove
prophetic.

173   **stir**   incite.
   **Gamester**   both (a) athlete, sportsman, and (b) idler. See the
notes to lines 31, 36, 40.

176   **gentle**   both (a) like a gentleman in his bearing, and (b) 'tender'
(line 136).

177   **noble Devise**   the skills and ingenuity characteristic of those of
aristocratic birth. Here Oliver gives *Devise* (intent, creativity)
a positive sense that counters what he told Charles in lines
155–61.

thy Discretion, I had as lief thou didst break
his Neck as his Finger. And thou wert best          155
look to't; for if thou dost him any slight
Disgrace, or if he do not mightily grace
himself on thee, he will practise against thee
by Poison, entrap thee by some treacherous
Devise, and never leave thee till he hath           160
ta'en thy Life by some indirect means or other.
For I assure thee (and almost with Tears I
speak it), there is not one so young, and so
villainous, this Day living. I speak but
brotherly of him, but should I anathomize him       165
to thee as he is, I must blush, and weep, and
thou must look pale and wonder.
CHARLES    I am heartily glad I came hither to you;
if he come to morrow, I'll give him his Payment;
if ever he go alone again, I'll never wrastle        170
for Prize more. And so God keep your Worship.
[OLIVER]    Farewell, good Charles.        *Exit [Charles.]*
– Now will I stir this Gamester. I hope I
shall see an End of him; for my Soul (yet I
know not why) hates nothing more than he. Yet       175
he's gentle, never school'd, and yet learned,
full of noble Devise, of all Sorts enchantingly
beloved, and indeed so much in the Heart of the
World, and especially of my own People, who
best know him, that I am altogether misprised:      180

---

177–   **of all Sorts enchantingly beloved**   adored by all classes of
78     people, as if he had used magical charms to win their
       affection.

179    **People**   followers and servants.

180    **misprised**   mis-apprised, improperly evaluated. Oliver feels that
       he himself is held in low esteem because of the virtues of his
       youngest brother. Later (see IV.iii.122–25) Oliver will admit
       that he has not been 'misprised' by those who consider him
       less lovable than Orlando.

182  **clear all**  take care of everything, acquit me of the discredit I receive when I am cast in the shadow of Orlando's virtues. See the note to line 135.

183  **kindle**  enflame, 'stir' (line 173). Compare III.ii.361, where *kindled* means 'brought forth', 'dropped', or 'given birth to'.
**thither**  there (to the Duke's court for the wrestling match).

183–  **go about**  set myself to executing. Compare *The Winter's Tale*,
84  IV.iv.219–21.

I.ii  This scene takes place on the grounds of Duke Frederick's palace.

1  **Coz**  cousin.

3  **Deer**  dear. But compare I.i.14 and I.iii.33, and see *Hamlet*, II.ii.621, where *Deer* is employed as a royal term of endearment. For related wordplay on *Hart / Heart*, see II.iv.33 and III.ii.263, and compare *Hamlet*, I.v.131.

4  **would . . . merrier**  Rosalind seems to be saying here that she wishes Celia were merry enough that her happiness did not depend on Rosalind's 'Mirth'. Modern editions normally insert an 'I' and render the second clause 'would you yet I were merrier?' Compare II.iv.1–3.

6  **learn**  teach.
**remember**  be mindful of, enjoy. Compare I.i.1, 66–67.

9  **waight**  weight. But here as elsewhere (see line 267), the Shakespearean spelling hints at wordplay on *wait*.

11  **so**  so long as; provided that.

14  **righteously temper'd**  properly controlled (governed), composed (mixed), or durable (like tempered steel). The word 'temper' had various meanings, and it is not clear which of them Celia has in mind here. Here *righteously* means both (a) rightly, correctly, and (b) virtuously, innocently, legitimately (not 'treacherously', as implied in I.iii.45–88).

16  **condition . . . Estate**  state of my circumstances; [melancholy] situation in which I must endeavour to find contentment. *Condition* echoes I.i.46–48.

19  **none**  any. Elizabethan usage permitted double negatives where they are no longer used in standard English.
**like**  likely.
**truly**  I vow to you.

21  **perforce**  by force.

21–22  **render thee again**  return (surrender) to you, make yours again. Celia promises to 'clear all' with Rosalind in a way that will 'acquit' her of any part in, or gain from, Duke Frederick's offence against 'The Courtesy of Nations' (I.ii.182, 135, 48).

but it shall not be so long, this Wrastler
shall clear all. Nothing remains, but that I
kindle the Boy thither, which now I'll go
about.                                         *Exit.*

# Scene 2

### *Enter Rosalind and Celia.*

CELIA    I pray thee, Rosalind, sweet my Coz, be
merry.

ROSALIND    Deer Celia; I show more Mirth than I am
mistress of, and would you yet were merrier:
unless you could teach me to forget a banished              5
Father, you must not learn me how to remember
any extraordinary Pleasure.

CELIA    Herein I see thou lov'st me not with the
full waight that I love thee; if my Uncle thy
banished Father had banish'd thy Uncle the                  10
Duke my Father, so thou hadst been still with
me, I could have taught my Love to take thy
Father for mine; so wouldst thou, if the truth
of thy Love to me were so righteously temper'd
as mine is to thee.                                        15

ROSALIND    Well, I will forget the condition of my
Estate, to rejoice in yours.

CELIA    You know my Father hath no Child but I, nor
none is like to have; and truly when he dies,
thou shalt be his Heir; for what he hath taken             20
away from thy Father perforce, I will render

22   **in Affection**   out of my love for you. Celia insists that her
     'Affection' is 'righteously tempered' – consistent with the laws
     of primogeniture.

23   **turn Monster**   suffer a physical deformity that will warn others
     (from Latin *monere*, from which *Monster* derives) of the
     consequences of a deviation from moral and spiritual
     rectitude.

24   **Rose**   Celia plays on Rosalind's name with an abbreviation that
     distills its essence.

26–27 **devise Sports**   invent diverting entertainments. *Devise* echoes
     I.i.161, 177.

29   **withall**   withal (here meaning both 'with' and 'with all').
     Compare I.i.140.

31   **then**   than. But here as elsewhere, the Folio spelling and
     punctuation permits *then* to function simultaneously in
     something approximating its usual modern sense.

32   **come off again**   emerge from the game. Celia hints at a risqué
     sense of this phrase that would not be compatible with a
     maiden's 'Honour' (chastity); see 2 *Henry IV*, II.iv.51–54,
     where Falstaff commends a bedroom warrior with the virility
     'to come off the Breach, with his Pike bent bravely', and
     *Coriolanus*, I.vi.1–3, where Cominius tells his companions,
     'we are come off / Like Romans, neither foolish in our Stands
     / Nor cowardly in Retire.'

34–35 **good Houswife Fortune**   Dame Fortune was proverbially
     depicted as turning (or in some renderings riding) a Wheel of
     Fortune; Celia's image transforms her into a domestic wife
     plying a spinning wheel. *Houswife* could also refer to a
     'hussy', a woman who bestowed her 'Gifts' on all men
     'equally'. Compare *Hamlet*, II.ii.238–46, where Fortune is
     called a 'Strumpet'.

36   **equally**   justly (as with equal weights on a set of balance scales).

38   **misplaced**   put in the wrong place, bestowed on the wrong
     recipients.
     **bountiful**   Rosalind means both 'generous' and 'liberal' in the
     sense that means 'Libertine' (see II.vii.65–69). She may also
     mean abundant in size.

39   **blind Woman**   Like Justice, Fortune was often depicted as
     blindfolded. For Justice, 'blindness' signified impartiality; for
     Fortune, it connoted the unpredictability of random chance.

thee again in Affection. By mine Honour I will,
and when I break that Oath, let me turn Monster:
therefore, my sweet Rose, my dear Rose, be
merry.                                                                                    25
ROSALIND    From henceforth I will, Coz, and devise
Sports: let me see, what think you of falling
in Love?
CELIA    Marry I prethee do, to make Sport withall:
but love no Man in good Earnest, nor no further             30
in Sport neither, then with safety of a pure
Blush thou mayst in Honour come off again.
ROSALIND    What shall be our Sport then?
CELIA    Let us sit and mock the good Houswife
Fortune from her Wheel, that her Gifts may                   35
henceforth be bestowed equally.
ROSALIND    I would we could do so: for her Benefits
are mightily misplaced, and the bountiful
blind Woman doth most mistake in her Gifts to
Women.                                                                              40
CELIA    'Tis true, for those that she makes Fair, she
scarce makes Honest, and those that she makes
Honest, she makes very Ill-favouredly.

---

39    **mistake**    both (a) err, and (b) mis-take. Compare *Hamlet*,
        III.ii.276, where the Prince upbraids housewives who
        'mistake' their 'Husbands', either by taking their wedding
        vows hypocritically or by taking their 'Benefits' and private
        'Gifts' to other men after they have sworn fidelity to their
        spouses.

41    **Fair**    attractive. The word often meant light-complexioned and
        blond.

42    **scarce**    either (a) hardly, or (b) rarely.
        **Honest**    chaste.

43    **Ill-favouredly**    both (a) unattractive, and (b) unfavourably
        (favouring them with no other 'Gifts' with which to win
        'favour' from those who are drawn to beauty and wealth).
        Celia's remarks will be echoed by the Clown, Touchstone, in
        III.iii.22–40.

44    **Office**   domain, sphere of influence, responsibility.

45–46 **Gifts of the World**   life's circumstances and chances. Rosalind is
        distinguishing between the 'Gifts' one is born with (such as
        beauty 'in the Lineaments of Nature') and those that are
        subject to choice (behaviour, character) in response to the ups
        and downs of worldly fortune.

48    **fall into the Fire**   Celia probably refers to the hell-fire that
        awaits those who yield to worldly temptation and fall victim
        to the fiery lusts of the flesh. But compare II.iii.10–24. *Fall*
        echoes lines 27–28.

49    **flout at**   'mock' (line 34).

51    **Argument**   story, discussion, exchange of repartee. But like *Wit*
        (see IV.i.170–85), *Argument* is frequently a word with genital
        and erotic implications. Both words could also refer to more
        than one kind of 'discourse' (see *Romeo and Juliet*
        II.iii.105–8).

53    **Natural**   a term for idiot. Rosalind plays on the idea that in this
        case 'Nature' is being forced to act unnaturally (in that it
        subverts one of Nature's own gifts, 'Wit' (intelligence or
        potency). 'Naturals' (fools) were said to be well endowed
        physically to compensate for their mental insufficiency (see
        *Twelfth Night*, I.v.1–21, III.i.35–39), and Rosalind alludes to
        that commonplace when she says that the Clown's entry (an
        occurrence attributable to Fortune) proves that 'Fortune is too
        hard for Nature' (more than a match for ordinary 'Nature's
        Wit', and thus able to be its 'cutter off', a cause of its being
        interrupted and emasculated). Compare *King Lear*, I.v.54–55.

55    **Peradventure**   perhaps.

58    **hath**   and hath. An alternative to this reading of the syntax of
        lines 55–60 is to be found in the Second Folio (1632), which
        emends *perceiveth* to *perceiving*.

59    **Whetstone**   a rough-surfaced ('dull') stone used with water to
        sharpen knives and other metal tools. We later learn (see
        II.iv.19) that the Clown's name is Touchstone, referring to a
        black stone used to test the purity of gold or silver by means
        of the streak left when one of those metals was rubbed against
        it.

61    **Wit, whether wander you**   Celia asks Touchstone where
        (whither) he is going, but she uses an expression that usually
        referred to the wandering of one's mind when distracted or
        dysfunctional. *Wander* echoes I.i.109–10.

ROSALIND    Nay now thou goest from Fortune's Office
to Nature's: Fortune reigns in Gifts of the
World, not in the Lineaments of Nature.                              45

*Enter Clown.*

CELIA    No; when Nature hath made a fair Creature,
may she not by Fortune fall into the Fire?
Though Nature hath given us Wit to flout at
Fortune, hath not Fortune sent in this Fool to                       50
cut off the Argument?

ROSALIND    Indeed there is Fortune too hard for
Nature, when Fortune makes Nature's Natural
the cutter off of Nature's Wit.

CELIA    Peradventure this is not Fortune's Work                     55
neither, but Nature's, who perceiveth our
natural Wits too dull to reason of such
Goddesses, hath sent this Natural for our
Whetstone: for always the Dullness of the
Fool is the Whetstone of the Wits. – How                            60
now, Wit, whether wander you?

CLOWN    Mistress, you must come away to your
Father.

CELIA    Were you made the Messenger?

CLOWN    No, by mine Honour, but I was bid to come                  65
for you.

---

64    **Messenger**    In his reply in the next line, Touchstone 'mis-takes'
Celia to mean the arresting officer sent to bring a criminal to
custody.

65–66 **come for you**    call you in. The Clown continues the bawdy
wordplay with a suggestive reminder of another way to 'come
off again' (line 32); in his next speech he reiterates the
firmness of his resolution when he says, 'I'll stand to it' (lines
70–71).

67 **that Oath** Rosalind refers to the phrase 'by mine Honour' (line 65).

70 **naught** nothing; no good, worthless. Compare I.i.17–20, 31–38, and see the note to I.iii.120.

73 **forsworn** guilty of perjury (lying, breaking a vow).

74 **heap** bounty.

76 **I marry** Rosalind means 'Ay, truly' (see the notes to I.i.45, 34), but the sound of what she says provides a reminder of her interest in 'falling in Love' (lines 27–28).
**unmuzzle** Rosalind compares Touchstone's 'Wisdom' to a dog that has been muzzled; she invites him to set it free to 'wander' (line 60) and express itself without restraint.

81 **not** The Clown puns on 'naught' (nothing), lines 68–73, a word that relates to Celia and Rosalind's lack of 'Beards' (line 78), male 'Wits'.

87 **One . . . loves** In I.iii.92 'old Frederick' uses the expression 'upon mine Honour', the topic of lines 65–85.

90 **for Taxation** for taking people to task with your satirical wit. In the Folio printing, lines 88–90 are assigned to Rosalind. The context makes it more plausible to attribute them to Celia, however, and this edition follows other modern texts in transferring them to her.

91–92 **speak . . . foolishly** comment rationally and truthfully upon the follies committed by men reputed to be wise.

93 **By my troth** by my faith, indeed.

94 **Wit** both (a) intelligence, and (b) frank, satirical observation. But Celia may also be referring to a lack of manly prowess in those who have silenced true 'Wit'. Her words remind us of the disparities in the preceding scene, where the weak, cowardly Oliver incites Charles the Wrastler to put down the more vigorous Orlando.

96 **Shew** show, spectacle.
**the Beu** Celia provides an anglicized version of *Le Beau*, a French name meaning 'the handsome' or 'the fine'. The Folio spelling probably reflects the Elizabethan pronunciation.

98 **put on** impose upon. Lines 97–100 continue the erotically playful imagery of the preceding dialogue.

ROSALIND   Where learn'd you that Oath, Fool?

CLOWN   Of a certain Knight, that swore by his
Honour they were good Pancakes, and swore by
his Honour the Mustard was naught: now I'll                    70
stand to it, the Pancakes were naught, and
the Mustard was good, and yet was not the
Knight forsworn.

CELIA   How prove you that in the great heap of
your Knowledge?                                               75

ROSALIND   I marry, now unmuzzle your Wisdom.

CLOWN   Stand you both forth now: stroke your Chins,
and swear by your Beards that I am a Knave.

CELIA   By our Beards (if we had them) thou art.

CLOWN   By my Knavery (if I had it) then I were.          80
But if you swear by that that is not, you are
not forsworn. No more was this Knight swearing
by his Honour, for he never had any; or if he
had, he had sworn it away, before ever he saw
those Pancakes, or that Mustard.                             85

CELIA   Prethee, who is't that thou mean'st?

CLOWN   One that old Frederick your Father loves.

[CELIA]   My Father's Love is enough to honour him
enough; speak no more of him, you'll be
whipp'd for Taxation one of these days.                      90

CLOWN   The more pity that Fools may not speak
wisely, what Wisemen do foolishly.

CELIA   By my troth thou sayest true: for since
the little Wit that Fools have was silenced,
the little Foolery that Wise Men have makes a                95
great Shew. Here comes Monsieur the Beu.

*Enter Le Beu.*

ROSALIND   With his Mouth full of News.

CELIA   Which he will put on us, as Pigeons feed
their Young.

ROSALIND   Then shall we be News-cramm'd.                    100

101–2 **the more marketable**   the heavier, and thus the more appealing to a diner in search of a fat bird for his table.

102 **Boon-iour**   bonjour, good morning. The Folio spelling probably preserves the Elizabethan pronunciation of the word.

105 **Sport**   amusement. Compare lines 26–29.

106 **Colour**   type. Rosalind may be sustaining the pigeon imagery of lines 98–102, with a question about the colour of the birds to be hunted for sport. Another possibility is that she is punning on *Spot*, perhaps as a way of ridiculing Le Beu's pronunciation of *Sport*.

107–8 **How . . . you?**   What do you mean? What kind of reply are you soliciting? Le Beu is trying to figure out what 'Colour' has to do with 'Sport'.

108 **As . . . will**   As your natural 'Wit' prompts you (compare lines 44–61), or as chance inspires you.

110 **decrees**   Many editions emend to 'decree'. But Elizabethan grammar often permitted a third-person plural verb ending in *s*.

111 **laid on with a Trowel**   slapped on thickly, without subtlety or precision (as a bricklayer plops down a batch of mortar). Celia appears to be telling Touchstone that his remark, substituting *Destinies* for *Fortune* in Rosalind's reply, supplies superfluous pseudo-solemnity for what it lacks in wit.

112 **Rank**   Touchstone probably means (a) row (straight line) of bricks, and (b) position, status (as a wit), but in the next line Rosalind interprets the term to mean (c) bad odour. The effect of her interruption is to 'physic' the Clown's 'Rankness' (I.i.91).

113 **loosest**   both (a) releasest, and (b) losest. Compare II.vii.112.

114 **amaze**   astonish.

120 **do**   be enacted.

122 **dead and buried**   Celia pretends to construe 'the End' (line 119) as the funerary epitaph for 'the Beginning' (line 118). *End* echoes I.i.173–74.

124– **an old Tale**   Celia's pokes fun at the fairy-tale opening of Le
25    Beu's story. In fact the story he goes on to tell does have an allegorical quality reminiscent of folklore.

CELIA   All the better: we shall be the more
marketable. – Boon-iour, Monsieur le Beu,
what's the News?

LE BEU   Fair Princess, you have lost much good
Sport.                                                                                    105

CELIA   Sport: of what Colour?

LE BEU   What Colour, Madam? How shall I aunswer
you?

ROSALIND   As Wit and Fortune will.

CLOWN   Or as the Destinies decrees.                                 110

CELIA   Well said, that was laid on with a Trowel.

CLOWN   Nay, if I keep not my Rank.

ROSALIND   Thou loosest thy old Smell.

LE BEU   You amaze me, Ladies: I would have told
you of good Wrastling, which you have lost the                 115
Sight of.

ROSALIND   Yet tell us the manner of the Wrastling.

LE BEU   I will tell you the Beginning: and if it
please your Ladyships, you may see the End,
for the best is yet to do, and here where you                    120
are they are coming to perform it.

CELIA   Well, the Beginning that is dead and buried.

LE BEU   There comes an old Man, and his three Sons.

CELIA   I could match this Beginning with an old
Tale.                                                                                    125

LE BEU   Three proper young Men, of excellent
Growth and Presence.

ROSALIND   With Bills on their Necks: 'Be it known

---

126   **proper**   handsome and well-mannered.
127   **Growth and Presence**   physical size and manly bearing. *Growth*
recalls I.i.14–16, 73–75, 90–92.

128   **Bills**   labels or legal documents. But Rosalind may also be
punning on *bills* in other senses: (a) hedging tools of the sort
carried by peasants, and (b) long-staved pikes of the type used
by watchmen to quell civil disturbances.

129   **by these Presents**  by this present document. Rosalind quotes a formal legal phrase to play on *Presence* (appearance) in line 127.

131   **which Charles**  This phrase is more or less equivalent to 'who'.

133   **that**  so that.
   **of Life in him**  of his survival.

134   **serv'd**  disposed of, dispatched.

136   **Dole**  lamentation, sorrow.

137   **take his part with**  join him in.

139–  **But . . . lost?**  Touchstone's satirical implication is that the
40     calamity Le Beu has just described is anything but 'Sport'. His question is a reminder that Le Beu has yet to provide a satisfactory answer to line 106.

142   **Thus . . . Day**  You have just proved that a person can acquire a new piece of wisdom every day. Touchstone's sarcasm will be seconded by Celia in line 145.

146   **any**  anyone.

147   **broken Music**  Rosalind refers to the sound of ribs breaking, but her phrase derives from musical terminology: 'broken Music' is part-music, written for performance by a number of different instruments or voices. Rosalind's purpose is to contrast 'Wrastling' (line 151) with a more humane 'Sport for Ladies' and gentlemen (line 144).

148   **dotes upon**  desires, is infatuated with.
   **Rib-breaking**  Rosalind may be punning on 'interrupted music-making', with reference to the ribs (the curved pieces of wood) on the body of a lute (whose ribs are 'broken' at the bend in the neck) or on the sides of a violin. She may also be alluding to Genesis 2:21–22, where we read that God took one of Adam's ribs and made a woman; if so, her implication is that 'Rib-breaking' *is* 'Sport for Ladies' (line 144) because it can make a female ('weaker vessel', 1 Peter 3:7) out of a male.

151   **appointed**  designated, scheduled.

153   **sure**  to be sure.

S.D.   **Flourish**  a trumpet fanfare to announce the arrival of an important person (in this case the Duke).

156   **intreated**  beseeched (not to proceed).
   **his . . . Forwardness**  let him suffer the consequences of his heedless youthful audacity. See the notes to I.i.55, 57, 90–91.

unto all men by these Presents.'
LE BEU    The eldest of the three wrastled with      130
    Charles the Duke's Wrastler, which Charles
    in a moment threw him, and broke three of his
    Ribs, that there is little hope of Life in him.
    So he serv'd the second, and so the third.
    Yonder they lie, the poor old Man their Father      135
    making such pitiful Dole over them, that all
    the Beholders take his part with weeping.
ROSALIND    Alas.
CLOWN    But what is the Sport, Monsieur, that the
    Ladies have lost?      140
LE BEU    Why this that I speak of.
CLOWN    Thus men may grow wiser every day. It is
    the first time that ever I heard breaking of
    Ribs was Sport for Ladies.
CELIA    Or I, I promise thee.      145
ROSALIND    But is there any else longs to see
    this broken Music in his Sides? Is there yet
    another dotes upon Rib-breaking? Shall we see
    this Wrastling, Cousin?
LE BEU    You must if you stay here, for here is      150
    the place appointed for the Wrastling, and
    they are ready to perform it.
CELIA    Yonder sure they are coming. Let us now
    stay and see it.

   *Flourish. Enter Duke [Frederick], Lords, Orlando,*
            *Charles, and Attendants.*

DUKE    Come on, since the Youth will not be      155
    intreated, his own Peril on his Forwardness.
ROSALIND    Is yonder the Man?
LE BEU    Even he, Madam.

160 **successfully**  full of success; as if he expects to succeed. Celia's phrasing is a reminder that, though he is 'young' (and thus unable to succeed to the estate bequeathed by law to his older brother), Orlando 'looks successfully' because he has inherited 'the Spirit of [his] Father' (I.i.24).

161 **crept**  come stealthily.

163 **I**  both (a) I [am], and (b) Ay. Compare lines 76, 258. *Leave,* 'permission' (line 164), recalls I.i.110.

166 **Odds**  superiority, advantage. In this speech the Duke describes Charles as if he were a Goliath figure and Orlando a mere David (1 Samuel 17).

167 **fain**  gladly. The Duke's reference to 'the Challenger's Youth', echoing lines 155–60, keeps us mindful of what the youngest of 'de Boys' demonstrated to his 'elder Brother' in I.i.55–65.

169 **move him**  motivate him to change his mind.
170 **hether**  hither. Compare *whether* in I.iii.94.

171 **by**  near. The Duke indicates that he will withdraw so that Celia and Rosalind can speak privately to the poor young man.

174 **attend**  both (a) wait upon, serve, and (b) will listen to.
179 **try him**  put his preeminence to the test. Compare I.i.130–33, I.ii.214.

181 **Proof**  evidence, demonstration. Celia refers to the three sons of the 'old Man' (line 123).

182– **if . . . Eyes**  if you had eyes to perceive yourself [and observe
83    how outmanned you are]. Compare *Julius Caesar*, I.ii.49–60, and *Troilus and Cressida*, III.iii.89–105.

184 **Fear . . . Adventure**  the danger your exploit will expose you to.

185 **a more equal Enterprise**  an endeavour with less overwhelming 'Odds' against it (line 166). *Equal* echoes lines 34–36.

186 **pray**  beseech, entreat.

189 **misprised**  held in low regard. Compare I.i.175–82.

190 **Suit**  request. What Rosalind means in lines 188–91 is that the ladies will beg that the match be called off, thereby taking upon themselves the onus for what would appear to be an act of cowardice if the young man were to request it himself.

CELIA   Alas, he is too young: yet he looks
successfully.                                                      160
DUKE   How now, Daughter, and Cousin: are you
crept hither to see the Wrastling?
ROSALIND   I my Liege, so please you give us
leave.
DUKE   You will take little Delight in it, I can          165
tell you, there is such Odds in the Man: in
pity of the Challenger's Youth, I would fain
dissuade him, but he will not be entreated.
Speak to him, Ladies, see if you can move him.
CELIA   Call him hether, good Monsieur Le Beu.        170
DUKE   Do so: I'll not be by.
LE BEU   Mounsieur the Challenger, the Princess
calls for you.
ORLANDO   I attend them with all Respect and Duty.
ROSALIND   Young Man, have you challeng'd Charles     175
the Wrastler?
ORLANDO   No, fair Princess: he is the general
Challenger, I come but in as others do, to
try with him the Strength of my Youth.
CELIA   Young Gentleman, your Spirits are too bold     180
for your Years. You have seen cruel Proof of
this man's Strength; if you saw your self
with your Eyes, or knew your self with your
Judgement, the Fear of your Adventure would
counsel you to a more equal Enterprise. We        185
pray you for your own sake to embrace your
own Safety, and give over this Attempt.
ROSALIND   Do, young Sir, your Reputation shall
not therefore be misprised: we will make it
our Suit to the Duke, that the Wrastling           190
might not go forward.
ORLANDO   I beseech you, punish me not with your

193    **hard Thoughts** disapproval. Orlando doesn't want Rosalind and Celia to believe that he is merely a rash fool; at the same time he doesn't wish for them to be offended because he declines their kind offer to be of assistance. Here *wherein* appears to mean 'with respect to which'. *Hard* echoes lines 52–54.

196    **foil'd** defeated. See I.i.136–37.

197    **sham'd** humiliated by having lost; disgraced (see I.i.156–59).

198    **gracious** both (a) held in favour and (b) a recipient of Fortune's graces (benefits). In lines 195–99 Orlando's point is that he has nothing to lose.

201    **Injury** injustice (from Latin *juris*, right or justice), harm.

201–  **onely . . . Place** my only function is to occupy a space in the
2     cosmos. For a parallel to lines 201–4, see *All's Well That End's Well*, I.ii.52–69.

203    **supplied** replenished.

206    **eke out** add to, augment.

207–8 **be deceiv'd in** misjudge, underestimate. See lines 180–94.

211    **desirous to lie** intent on taking a position beside, or in union with. Charles's phrasing hints at illicit lust, a desire for incest; what he means, of course, is 'Who is this silly braggart who is so eager to be "dead and buried" (line 122) before he achieves adulthood?'

213    **more modest Working** less overweening and wanton ambition. Orlando is pretending to take literally the sexual implications in line 211. His reply indicates that his 'Will' (a word that can refer both to erotic desire and to the genitalia of either gender) would not presume to seek copulation with 'his Mother Earth'.

216    **entreat** beg and thereby persuade. In lines 215–16 Charles's implication is that it will not be possible for even the Duke to prevail upon Orlando to attempt a second fall. Charles turns out to be correct: the Duke will not 'entreat' Orlando 'to a second'.

216– **mightily persuaded** energetically sought to 'dissuade' (lines
17    165–69).

218    **mean** intend, expect.
       **after** afterwards.

219    **come your ways** come along now; let's proceed.

hard Thoughts, wherein I confess me much guilty
to deny so fair and excellent Ladies any thing.
But let your fair Eyes and gentle Wishes go　　　　　195
with me to my Trial; wherein if I be foil'd,
there is but one sham'd that was never
gracious; if kill'd, but one dead that is
willing to be so. I shall do my Friends no
wrong, for I have none to lament me; the World　　200
no Injury, for in it I have nothing; onely in
the World I fill up a Place, which may be
better supplied when I have made it empty.

ROSALIND　The little Strength that I have, I
would it were with you.　　　　　205

CELIA　And mine to eke out hers.

ROSALIND　Fare you well: pray Heaven I be deceiv'd
in you.

CELIA　Your Heart's Desires be with you.

CHARLES　Come, where is this young Gallant, that　　210
is so desirous to lie with his Mother Earth?

ORLANDO　Ready Sir, but his Will hath in it a
more modest Working.

DUKE　You shall try but one Fall.

CHARLES　No, I warrant your Grace you shall not　　215
entreat him to a second, that have so mightily
persuaded him from a first.

ORLANDO　You mean to mock me after: you should
not have mock'd me before. But come your ways.

ROSALIND　Now Hercules be thy speed, young Man.　　220

---

220　**Hercules**　This mythical demigod was the epitome of strength.
　　　　Among his exploits was his defeat of the seemingly invincible
　　　　Antaeus, a giant wrestler whose strength depended on his
　　　　retaining contact with 'Mother Earth'. Hercules slew Antaeus
　　　　by holding him aloft and strangling him. Compare *The
　　　　Merchant of Venice*, III.ii.53–62, where another maiden prays
　　　　for a Herculean triumph.
　　　　**speed**　help, means of success.

224 **Thunderbolt** Celia alludes to the principal attribute of Zeus, the most powerful of the Greek gods. Her imagery imparts another implication to 'speed' (line 220): instantaneous destruction of Orlando's adversary.

225 **should down** would fall victim to it.

226 **No . . . more** Duke Frederick, seeing his prize wrestler 'down' (line 225), is telling Orlando, 'You shall but try one Fall' (line 214); see the note to line 216.

228 **well breath'd** exercised to the point where I am breathing vigorously.

230 **He . . . Lord** Le Beu's words make it clear that Orlando has 'cut off the Argument' with Charles (lines 49–51); 'the little Wit that Fools have' has been 'silenced' (line 94). Compare lines 264–68.

232 **Liege** lord.

234 **some Man else** some other father.

236 **still** both (a) nevertheless, and (b) always.

237 **Thou shouldst** you would.

240 **thou hadst** This phrase is probably to be elided metrically to 'thou'dst'.

241 **Were I** if I were.
**Coze** Like *Coz* (lines 1, 26), an abbreviation of *Cousin*. Compare line 266.

243 **change** both (a) alter, and (b) exchange.
**that Calling** Orlando means both (a) the name by which I am called, and (b) my role or destiny in life. What he has just achieved fulfils what Orlando said in I.i.73–74. See the notes to I.i.25–26, 50, I.ii.160.

246 **Mind** 'Disposition' (line 251, echoing I.i.132), persuasion.

248 **Tears unto Entreaties** tears to augment my beggings.

251 **rough and envious** coarse and malicious. *Envious* echoes I.i.151, where it refers to a proclivity to vie with others.

CELIA   I would I were invisible, to catch the
strong Fellow by the Leg.                    *Wrastle.*
ROSALIND   O excellent young Man.
CELIA   If I had a Thunderbolt in mine Eye, I can
tell who should down.                        *Shout.*   225
DUKE   No more, no more.
ORLANDO   Yes, I beseech your Grace, I am not yet
well breath'd.
DUKE   How dost thou, Charles?
LE BEU   He cannot speak, my Lord.                      230
DUKE   Bear him away. – What is thy name, young
Man?
ORLANDO   Orlando, my Liege, the youngest Son of
Sir Rowland de Boys.
DUKE   I would thou hadst been Son to some Man else,
The World esteem'd thy Father honourable,          235
But I did find him still mine Enemy.
Thou shouldst have better pleas'd me with this
   Deed
Hadst thou descended from another House:
But fare thee well, thou art a gallant Youth,
I would thou hadst told me of another Father.      240
   *Exit Duke [and all but Rosalind, Celia, and Orlando].*
CELIA   Were I my Father, Coze, would I do this?
ORLANDO   I am more proud to be Sir Rowland's Son,
His youngest Son, and would not change that
   Calling
To be adopted Heir to Frederick.
ROSALIND   My Father lov'd Sir Rowland as his Soul,   245
And all the World was of my Father's Mind.
Had I before known this young Man his Son,
I should have given him Tears unto Entreaties,
Ere he should thus have ventur'd.
CELIA                        Gentle Cousin,
Let us go thank him, and encourage him:            250
My Father's rough and envious Disposition

252 **Sticks me at Heart** pierces to my very soul.

252– **Sir . . . happy** Celia seems to be saying that 'if you adhere to
55   the vows you make in love, you have proven that you fully
     merit your victory as a wrestler.' Most of today's editions
     alter the Folio punctuation adopted here, placing a semicolon
     after *deserv'd* and a comma after *Love*.

256 **Wear . . . me** Rosalind presents Orlando with a token of her
     admiration, probably a chain.
     **out of Suits with Fortune** not favoured by Fortune. Rosalind's
     words can mean (a) no longer wearing Fortune's livery, (b)
     whose requests are not well received by Fortune, and (c)
     whose playing cards are not in the suit that will win Fortune's
     'Hand' (line 257). *Suits* echoes lines 189–91, and it reminds
     us that Rosalind and Orlando are both poor in 'Gifts of the
     World' (lines 45–46).

257 **Hand** both (a) ability, resources, and (b) hand of cards. *Means*
     recalls I.i.147, 161.

259 **better Parts** abilities, qualities, social graces. *Parts* recalls
     I.i.149–53.

260 **thrown down** Having just 'thrown' Charles the Wrastler,
     Orlando now feels overthrown himself, both mentally and
     emotionally. Rosalind continues the wrestling imagery in line
     264. Compare lines 224–25.

261 **Quintine** quintain, a post for use in tilting practice. It
     contained a target (ordinarily in the form of either a shield or
     a human effigy) at the end of a rotating crossbar, and the rider
     sought to hit it squarely with his lance. Orlando now feels like
     such a 'liveless' (lifeless) block of wood. Lines 259–61 are
     probably to be treated as a kind of reverie (a brief soliloquy),
     spoken by Orlando to himself but in such a way that Rosalind
     can hear his voice and think (no doubt wishfully) that he is
     addressing her and Celia. The phrase *stands up* (line 260)
     echoes lines 70–71; see the note to lines 65–66.

263 **would** would like; wishes.

265 **More . . . Enemies** This part-line (with three metrical feet
     rather than the normal five) indicates a pause, a silent 'waight'
     (lines 9, 267) of two heavy feet, during which Rosalind waits
     in vain for Orlando to manage a reply. As it happens, like
     Charles the Wrastler, and like Rosalind, Orlando is
     'overthrown' (lines 264, 269); he 'cannot speak' (lines 230,
     268).

Sticks me at Heart. – Sir, you have well
  deserv'd,
If you do keep your Promises in love;
But justly as you have exceeded all Promise,
Your Mistress shall be happy.
ROSALIND                    Gentleman,                    255
  Wear this for me: one out of Suits with Fortune
  That could give more, but that her Hand lacks
    Means.
  – Shall we go, Coze?
CELIA      I. – Fare you well, fair Gentleman.
ORLANDO  – Can I not say 'I thank you'? My better
  Parts
  Are all thrown down, and that which here
    stands up                                               260
  Is but a Quintine, a mere liveless Block.
ROSALIND  – He calls us back: my Pride fell with
  my Fortunes,
  I'll ask him what he would. – Did you call,
    Sir?
  Sir, you have wrastled well, and overthrown
  More than your Enemies.                                   265
CELIA  – Will you go, Coze?
ROSALIND              Have with you. – Fare you well.
                          *Exit* [*Rosalind with Celia*].
ORLANDO  – What Passion hangs these Waights upon
  my Tongue?
  I cannot speak to her, yet she urg'd Conference.


                    *Enter Le Beu*


O poor Orlando! thou art overthrown:

---

267  **Waights**  both (a) weights, and (b) waits (hesitations).
268  **urg'd Conference**  sought a conversation with me.

270     **Or . . . or**   either . . . or.

       **something weaker**   Orlando probably means two things: (a) a
woman, traditionally referred to as a 'weaker vessel' (see the
note to line 148), and (b) the weaker ('feminine') part of his
own constitution (the emotions, which were to kept
subordinate to the rule of will and reason). Orlando's
phrasing alludes to the notion that 'weaker vessels' are
deficient in male 'things'; see the note to I.iii.120, and
compare lines 68–73, 81–82.

271     **counsaile**   counsel, advise. Compare lines 182–85.

272     **deserv'd**   earned, merited. See lines 252–53.

274     **Condition**   disposition. But in fact a psychological 'condition' is
precisely what Le Beu goes on to describe. Like Oliver, the
Duke is subject to a 'humour' (an irrational and
uncontrollable obsession that subverts the reason and in the
process the senses that supply the reason with its perceptions).
*Condition* echoes line 16.

275     **misconsters**   misconstrues, interprets incorrectly. The Folio
spelling captures the normal emphasis on the second syllable.

276     **humorous**   under the sway of a psychological 'Condition' (line
274), a frenzied mood, that makes him dangerous. By
II.iii.1–28 it will be clear that 'the humorous Duke' (line 8)
has made Orlando's similarly humorous brother even more
hostile than he was before.

277     **suits**   befits. Compare line 256.

       **conceive**   understand, figure out for yourself. Le Beu's indirect
phrasing suggests that in the climate of Duke Frederick's
court, a person has to be careful what he says.

       **then**   both (a) than, and (b) then (after you have drawn your
own inferences). Compare line 31.

281     **Manners**   behaviour, personality.

282     **taller**   This word often means 'sturdier' or 'more valiant', as in
the expression 'Tall Fellow of his Hands' (*The Winter's Tale*,
V.ii.190–95), and it is conceivable that Le Beu is using it in
that sense. What seems more likely, however, is that he means
'higher in stature'. If so, either he is wrong or he has here been
given an incorrect word by the playwright, a scribe, or a Folio
typesetter. Compare the later references to the relative heights
of Celia and Rosalind in I.iii.119 and IV.iii.86–89. Most of
today's editions emend to *smaller*.

285     **whose**   This pronoun refers to both Celia and Rosalind.

Or Charles, or something weaker masters thee.                    270
LE BEU   Good Sir, I do in Friendship counsaile you
    To leave this place. Albeit you have deserv'd
    High Commendation, true Applause, and Love;
    Yet such is now the Duke's Condition,
    That he misconsters all that you have done.                  275
    The Duke is humorous, what he is indeed
    More suits you to conceive, then I to speak of.
ORLANDO   I thank you, Sir; and pray you tell me
        this,
    Which of the two was Daughter of the Duke,
    That here was at the Wrastling?                               280
LE BEU   Neither his Daughter, if we judge by
        Manners,
    But yet indeed the taller is his Daughter,
    The other is Daughter to the banish'd Duke,
    And here detain'd by her usurping Uncle
    To keep his Daughter company, whose Loves                    285
    Are deerer than the natural Bond of Sisters:
    But I can tell you that of late this Duke
    Hath ta'en Displeasure 'gainst his gentle
        Niece,
    Grounded upon no other Argument,
    But that the People praise her for her Virtues,              290
    And pity her, for her good Father's sake;
    And on my Life his Malice 'gainst the Lady
    Will suddenly break forth. Sir, fare you well,
    Hereafter in a better World than this,
    I shall desire more Love and Knowledge of you.               295

---

286   **deerer**   (a) more deer-like in their regality (compare line 3), and
       (b) dearer (closer and more precious).

289   **Argument**   basis, rationale. *Argument* echoes lines 49–51; lines
       287–93 recall I.i.173–84.

293   **suddenly**   both (a) quickly, immediately, and (b) violently.
       Compare *3 Henry VI*, V.v.81–84.

296 **bounden** obliged, beholden. Compare I.i.14–17.

297 **Smother** suffocating smoke. Orlando's expression is a variation of the more modern 'from the frying pan into the fire' (from bad to worse).

**Rosaline** Occasionally the heroine's name is spelled this way in the Folio text. It may result from a compositor's misreading or from an authorial inconsistency; but it is more likely to be an alternate (perhaps less formal and more familiar) pronunciation of Rosalind's name for dramatic purposes. See III.ii.93–118 for another sobriquet for the heroine.

I.iii This scene takes place somewhere in or near the Duke's palace.

1 **Cupid** the blindfolded, childish God of Love. Celia's invocation suggests that the uncommunicative Rosalind is despondent because of her infatuation with another 'liveless Block' (I.ii.261). Compare I.ii.1–28, where Rosalind and Celia both give 'Reasons' (lines 5–9) for their melancholy.

6 **lame . . . Reasons** throw 'Reasons' at my legs until one of them is 'laid up' (line 7).

7 **Then** What Rosalind means is 'if I did that'.
**there were** there would be.

9 **mad** crazed, frenzied. This word is sometimes used to mean 'beside oneself with erotic desire', as in *Othello*, IV.i.243, and *Love's Labour's Lost*, II.i.254–55.
**without any** Rosalind means 'without any reason to be'; but *Reasons* was often pronounced *raisins*, and here it hints at *raisings* (erections), as in *Twelfth Night*, I.v.324–30, III.i.156–63, and *Troilus and Cressida*, II.ii.167–70.

11 **my Child's Father** Rosalind's bold image refers to Orlando and suggests that she has already decided to pursue him until he marries her and they bear offspring. Compare lines 10–11 with *All's Well That Ends Well*, I.i.86–92, where Helena admits, 'I think not on my Father' because 'My Imagination / Carries no Favour in't but Bertram's.'

12 **oh** Here as elsewhere (compare II.iii.2, 3, 14, 56), the Folio's *oh* appears to signify a deeply voiced sigh or moan, as distinguished from the vocative *O* that is addressed to another person in passages such as I.i.43, 112, I.ii.223, 269, I.iii.24, 26, 94, II.i.45, II.iii.16, and II.iv.1, 43.

ORLANDO    I rest much bounden to you: fare you well.

[*Exit Le Beu.*]

– Thus must I from the Smoke into the Smother,
From tyrant Duke unto a tyrant Brother.
But heavenly Rosaline.                                                    *Exit.*

# Scene 3

*Enter Celia and Rosalind.*

CELIA    Why Cousin, why Rosaline: Cupid have mercy,
not a Word?

ROSALIND    Not one to throw at a Dog.

CELIA    No, thy Words are too precious to be cast
away upon Curs, throw some of them at me; come        5
lame me with Reasons.

ROSALIND    Then there were two Cousins laid up,
When the one should be lam'd with Reasons, and
the other mad without any.

CELIA    But is all this for your Father?                            10

ROSALIND    No, some of it is for my Child's Father:
oh how full of Briers is this Working-day
World.

CELIA    They are but Burs, Cousin, thrown upon
thee in holiday Foolery, if we walk not in the        15

---

12–13 **this Working-day World**    Here *Working-day* probably means
both (a) everyday, ordinary (as opposed to holiday, festive),
and (b) subject to what Duke Senior later calls 'the Penalty of
Adam' (II.i.5), the pain and labour visited on mankind as a
consequence of the Fall (Genesis: 3:16–19).

15    **in holiday Foolery**    in the spirit of holiday merriment. In lines
14–17 Celia argues that Rosalind shouldn't take her life's
daily vexations too seriously: they are like the prickly
seedcases that children attach to one another's clothing in
sport. *Thrown* ('cast', line 4) echoes I.ii.264–65, 269–70.

18 **Coat** petticoat.
**these** but these.

20 **Hem them away** Get rid of them by clearing your throat. Celia puns on two other senses: (a) use your sewing needle and make a new hem that eliminates them, and (b) replace them in your heart with 'him' (see line 22). Celia refers to another kind of 'bur', a thickening of the voice, that can be removed with a 'hem', a coughing sound.

24 **take . . . of** are in alliance with [and thus receive the aid of]. *Part* echoes I.ii.135–37, 259–61.

26 **a . . . you** either (a) I have a good wish for you, or (b) may you be granted what you wish to have 'upon you' after you experience a 'Fall' (see the note to lines 26–27).

26–27 **O . . . Fall** Celia plays on wrestling in the sexual sense. She predicts that in time Rosalind will try to 'wrastle' with both Orlando and her 'Affections' (line 23) despite the risk of a 'Fall' (indeed, hoping for the right kind of 'overthrow'). Compare I.ii.26–28, where the 'Sports' Rosalind proposes commence with 'falling in Love'.

27 **despight** despite, defiance.

27–28 **turning . . . Service** sending these witticisms into the ranks of the unemployed, and dismissing them.

33 **deerly** both (a) as one deer loves another, and (b) with deep affection. Compare lines 35, 37, 54, and see I.ii.286.

34 **ensue** follow.

35 **Chase** pursuit (of an argument).

39–40 **deserve well** merit his just deserts (that is, my hate), based on your line of reasoning. *Deserve* echoes I.ii.252–55, 272–75.

45 **dispatch you** remove yourself; be gone.
**with your safest Haste** as quickly as you can do so without any danger to yourself.

46 **Cousin** In Elizabethan English, this word could be applied to any relative, however close or distant.

trodden paths our very Petticoats will catch
    them.
ROSALIND    I could shake them off my Coat, these
    Burs are in my Heart.
CELIA    Hem them away.                                          20
ROSALIND    I would try if I could cry hem and
    have him.
CELIA    Come, come, wrastle with thy Affections.
ROSALIND    O they take the part of a better
    Wrastler than my self.                                      25
CELIA    O, a good Wish upon you: you will try in
    time in despight of a Fall. But turning these
    Jests out of Service, let us talk in good
    Earnest: is it possible on such a Sudden, you
    should fall into so strong a Liking with old       30
    Sir Rowland's youngest Son?
ROSALIND    The Duke my Father lov'd his Father
    deerly.
CELIA    Doth it therefore ensue that you should
    love his Son deerly? By this kind of Chase,      35
    I should hate him, for my Father hated his
    Father deerly, yet I hate not Orlando.
ROSALIND    No faith, hate him not for my sake.
CELIA    Why should I not? doth he not deserve
    well?                                                        40

*Enter Duke [Frederick] with Lords.*

ROSALIND    Let me love him for that, and do you
    love him because I do. Look, here comes the
    Duke.
CELIA    With his Eyes full of Anger.
DUKE    — Mistress, dispatch you with your safest
    Haste,                                                       45
And get you from our Court.
ROSALIND                        Me, Uncle.
DUKE                                     You, Cousin,
    Within these ten Days if that thou beest found

50 **Fault** offence, crime. The literal meaning of *Fault* is 'crack',
and in this line as elsewhere (see IV.i.184–87) the word hints
at Rosalind's desire to 'bear' the carnal 'Knowledge' of her
genital fault. *Knowledge* (a synonym of *acquaintance*, line
52), echoes I.ii.74–75, 294–95, and anticipates II.vii.36–38,
III.ii.213–23, 288–302.

51 **hold Intelligence** have communication, receive information.
Contrast lines 49–56 with the title character's 'To Know my
Deed, / 'Twere best not know my self' in *Macbeth*, II.ii.69–70.

52 **acquaintance** familiarity. In this context Rosalind's phrasing
keeps us mindful of her 'Desires' by echoing the Latin word
for a female 'Fault'; see the note to III.ii.290.

53 **frantic** crazed, seized by a frenzy, 'mad' (line 9).

54 **deer** both (a) dear, and (b) royal (see the notes to line 33 and
I.ii.3). So also in line 70.

55 **unborne** both (a) unborn, and (b) uncarried. Compare II.v.63.

57 **Purgation** clearing themselves of accusations. See I.i.181–82.

58 **Grace** both (a) divine purity, with particular reference to
Christ's role in cleansing mankind by taking on himself the
sins of the world, and (b) royalty (here, the patriotism of the
Duke himself). Compare I.ii.195–99.

61 **whereon . . . depends** on what suspicious behaviour of mine
your mistrust hangs.

66 **Friends** a much stronger word in Elizabethan English than in
modern usage. Here Rosalind means 'relatives', referring to
her father.

67 **my Father was no Traitor** What Rosalind is tactfully not
saying, though lines 63–64 have implied it, is that the
usurping Duke Frederick is himself the realm's principal
traitor. Not only is 'Treason . . . not inherited'; those who
seek to subvert or nullify the legitimacy that is inherited are
by definition 'treacherous' (line 69).

68 **mistake** Rosalind means 'mis-take', misunderstand or wrongly
perceive. Compare I.ii.37–40.

69 **my Poverty** Like her father, and like Orlando (I.ii.199–201),
Rosalind has nothing she can call her own.
**treacherous** Rosalind uses the word in its original sense:
traitorous.

70 **Deer** dear. But see the note to line 54.

So near our public Court as twenty Miles,
Thou diest for it.

ROSALIND          I do beseech your Grace
Let me the Knowledge of my Fault bear with me:          50
If with thy self I hold Intelligence,
Or have acquaintance with mine own Desires,
If that I do not dream, or be not frantic
(As I do trust I am not), then deer Uncle,
Never so much as in a Thought unborne          55
Did I offend your Highness.

DUKE                    Thus do all Traitors,
If their Purgation did consist in Words,
They are as innocent as Grace it self;
Let it suffice thee that I trust thee not.

ROSALIND   Yet your Mistrust cannot make me a
    Traitor;          60
Tell me whereon the Likelihoods depends?

DUKE   Thou art thy Father's Daughter, there's
    enough.

ROSALIND   So was I when your Highness took his
    Dukedom,
So was I when your Highness banish'd him;
Treason is not inherited, my Lord,          65
Or if we did derive it from our Friends,
What's that to me, my Father was no Traitor;
Then, good my Liege, mistake me not so much,
To think my Poverty is treacherous.

CELIA   Deer Sovereign, hear me speak.          70

DUKE   Ay Celia, we stay'd her for your sake,
Else had she with her Father rang'd along.

---

71   **stay'd**   detained, held back. Compare I.i.7–11, 113–16,
         139–43.

72   **rang'd along**   roamed away. The Duke's verb is one that was
         often used to refer to the rovings of domestic animals or
         game, and it serves to remind us that the banished Duke is in
         a rustic setting with none of the amenities – or restrictions –
         of the court. Compare I.i.105–10.

74 **Pleasure**  both (a) wish, preference, and (b) royal will, decree.
**Remorse**  tenderness, pity. Celia's word is the first suggestion in the play that perhaps Duke Frederick may be susceptible to the promptings of compassion.

75 **that time**  at that time, when I was at that age. The phase *too young* echoes I.i.55–57, I.ii.155–60.

77 **still**  always, unceasingly. Compare I.ii.236.

78 **at an instant**  at the very same moment (as if we were linked to one another like Siamese twins).
**eat**  eaten; probably pronounced 'ate'.

79 **Juno's Swans**  The Queen of the Gods was traditionally represented as riding in a chariot drawn by swans.

81 **subtile**  subtle, conniving.
**Smoothness**  placidity, even temper. But what the Duke really means is 'cunning'.

82 **her Patience**  Here the First Folio prints *per*; subsequent editions have adopted the Second Folio's emendation to *her*. It is conceivable, however, that *per Patience* is intended as a pun on the French legal phrase *per pais*, 'by the country', which refers to trial by a jury of one's fellow countrymen, 'People' (line 83) from one's local jurisdiction. In this line *Silence* (a reminder of I.ii.264–68) explains what Duke Frederick means by *Patience*: a willingness to forbear any temptation to utter public complaints about the injustices she and her exiled father are forced to suffer.

84 **robs . . . Name**  bewitches the 'People' and thereby assures that you are 'altogether misprised' (I.i.175–80); compare I.ii.188–89. Here *Name* means 'reputation', social standing.

85 **show**  appear, come across as. Duke Frederick implies that while Rosalind is at court, Celia will be perceived as no more than a dull foil (a dark backdrop) to set off her cousin's bright virtues. Compare *Hamlet*, V.ii.267–69, and *1 Henry IV*, I.ii.216–38. And see Isaiah 14:12–17 for an account of Lucifer (an angel whose name meant 'Bright') and the aspiration that led to an attempt at Duke Frederick's kind of usurpation.

87 **Dombe**  doom, judgement. The Folio spelling hints at authorial wordplay on both *dome* (head) and *dumb* (compare *A Midsummer Night's Dream*, V.i.331–32, where Bottom rhymes *dumbe* and *Tumbe* in the First Quarto printing).

CELIA   I did not then intreat to have her stay,
It was your Pleasure, and your own Remorse,
I was too young that time to value her,                     75
But now I know her; if she be a Traitor,
Why so am I; we still have slept together,
Rose at an instant, learn'd, play'd, eat
together,
And wheresoe'er we went, like Juno's Swans,
Still we went coupled and inseparable.                     80
DUKE   She is too subtile for thee, and her
Smoothness;
Her very Silence, and her Patience,
Speak to the People, and they pity her.
Thou art a Fool, she robs thee of thy Name,
And thou wilt show more bright, and seem more
virtuous,                                                  85
When she is gone: then open not thy Lips,
Firm and irrevocable is my Dombe,
Which I have pass'd upon her, she is banish'd.
CELIA   Pronounce that Sentence then on me, my
Liege,
I cannot live out of her Company.                          90
DUKE   You are a Fool. – You, Niece, provide your
self,
If you out-stay the Time, upon mine Honour,
And in the greatness of my Word, you die.
                                   *Exit Duke &c.*
CELIA   O my poor Rosaline, whether wilt thou go?

---

91   **provide**   prepare, make provision for.

92   **upon mine Honour**   See Touchstone's remarks about this
'Oath' in I.ii.65–92. The compound *out-stay* echoes line 71.

94   **whether**   where, whither; here to be treated metrically as a
one-syllable word.

95 **change** both (a) exchange, and (b) alter. Lines 95–96 echo I.ii.242–44, where Orlando says that he would not change his parentage 'To be adopted Heir to Frederick'.

96 **griev'd** Celia means (a) 'saddened', but in the reply in the next line Rosalind shifts the sense to (b) 'wronged'. Compare line 107, and see I.i.23. *Charge* recalls I.i.3, 70–71.

99 **me his Daughter** The Folio syntax hovers between (a) 'me as his Daughter', and (b) 'me, his Daughter'. Here Celia insists that she meant what she said a moment earlier; see lines 87–90.

101 **am** Celia's unusual, if not ungrammatical, use of the singular verb has the effect of unifying 'thou and I'.

102 **sund'red** divided, broken apart. Elizabethans would probably have heard an echo of the marriage ceremony in the Book of Common Prayer (1559): 'Those whom God hath joined together, let no man put asunder' (a passage derived from Matthew 19:6). See lines 77–80, and compare *A Midsummer Night's Dream*, III.ii.195–216.

104 **fly** flee. *Devise* (plan) echoes I.ii.26–28.

105 **Whether** whither, to where (as in lines 94, 110).

106 **to . . . you** to bear the burden of your change of fortunes alone. In Shakespeare, when the primary meaning of *change* is 'alteration', it tends to imply 'for the worse'; here the word echoes line 95.

108 **this Heaven** As she speaks this phrase, Celia probably points to the sky, which is overcast ('pale') in sympathy with the 'Sorrows' of these young women. The roof above the Globe stage was also referred to as 'the Heaven'.

114 **provoketh** tempts, incites.

115 **mean Attire** humble clothing, that which is worn by the 'poor' peasant classes.

116 **Umber** either earth- or brown-coloured pigment.
**smirch** smear, discolour. Like the 'Fool' her father believes her to be (lines 84, 91), Celia will 'show' even less 'bright' (line 85) in the forest than at court.

118 **stir Assailants** prompt attackers, tempt would-be ravishers.

119 **tall** Rosalind probably means 'lofty in stature', but the 'martial Outside' (line 124) she goes on to describe suggests the senses of *tall* that are associated with 'mannish' courage and strength; see the note to I.ii.282, and compare III.v.118.

Wilt thou change Fathers? I will give thee
   mine:                                        95
I charge thee be not thou more griev'd than I
   am.
ROSALIND   I have more Cause.
CELIA                       Thou hast not, Cousin,
   Prethee be cheerful; know'st thou not the Duke
   Hath banish'd me his Daughter?
ROSALIND                That he hath not.
CELIA   No, hath not? Rosaline lacks then the Love      100
   Which teacheth thee that thou and I am one,
   Shall we be sund'red? shall we part, sweet
     Girl?
   No, let my Father seek another Heir;
   Therefore devise with me how we may fly,
   Whether to go, and what to bear with us,         105
   And do not seek to take your Change upon you,
   To bear your Griefs your self, and leave me out;
   For by this Heaven, now at our Sorrows pale,
   Say what thou canst, I'll go along with thee.
ROSALIND   Why, whether shall we go?         110
CELIA   To seek my Uncle in the Forest of Arden.
ROSALIND   Alas, what Danger will it be to us
   (Maids as we are) to travel forth so far?
   Beauty provoketh Thieves sooner than Gold.
CELIA   I'll put my self in poor and mean Attire,      115
   And with a kind of Umber smirch my Face;
   The like do you, so shall we pass along,
   And never stir Assailants.
ROSALIND             Were it not better,
   Because that I am more than common tall,

120 **all points** both (a) in every respect, and (b) with sharp-pointed weapons. Rosalind is probably alluding to those genital 'points' that distinguish males from females (see *Hamlet*, I.v.123–29, and Sonnet 151, especially lines 7–12). It was a commonplace that a 'weaker vessel' had 'no thing' (or at most an O-thing') and was thus defined by what she lacked; see the note to I.ii.148, and compare *Twelfth Night*, III.iv.327–29.

121 **Curtleaxe** cutlass; a short, curved sword.

122 **Bore-spear** boar-spear, a javelin stout enough to bore through the tough skin of a boar. Like 'A gallant Curtleaxe upon my Thigh', this weapon suggests the 'points' Rosalind is pondering in her 'Heart' (lines 120–22) as she yearns for her 'Child's Father' (line 11).

123 **Lye** lie (an echo of I.ii.210–11). The Folio spelling hints at wordplay on 'lye' (urinate, as in *Macbeth*, II.iii.24–48). Compare *The Merry Wives of Windsor*, II.iii.26–34, 57–64, where the Host ridicules the 'Valour' of 'a Castalion King Urinal' whose 'Mock-water' emerges in combat.

124 **swashing** swashbuckling, swaggering. In *Romeo and Juliet*, I.i.65, this word is spelled *washing*, a reminder of the kind of 'hidden Women's Fear' that can cause 'mannish Cowards' to 'Lye' under the stress of battle (lines 123–26).
**martial** literally, Mars-like; warlike.

125 **mannish** man-like, pretending to be brave.

126 **outface it** put on an outward 'face' (appearance) that masks inward cowardice. See the note to I.i.19–20.
**Semblances** external appearances.

129 **Ganimed** Rosalind's variation on Ganymede, a beautiful boy who served Zeus as cupbearer to the gods.

132 **Celia** Celia's real name means 'Heaven'. The metre calls for the name to be pronounced in this line as a three-syllable word.
**Aliena** alien, other. In the context of the play, this alias means 'outcast', alienated from her father and from the court he has usurped.

133 **assay'd** attempted.

135 **Travail** The original spelling conveys two senses: (a) travel, and (b) hardship, suffering. Compare lines 112–13.

That I did suit me all points like a Man,                          120
A gallant Curtleaxe upon my Thigh,
A Bore-spear in my Hand, and in my Heart,
Lye there what hidden Woman's Fear there will,
We'll have a swashing and a martial Outside,
As many other mannish Cowards have,                                125
That do outface it with their Semblances.

CELIA   What shall I call thee when thou art a Man?

ROSALIND   I'll have no worse a Name than Jove's
   own Page.
   And therefore look you call me Ganimed.
   But what will you be call'd?                                    130

CELIA   Something that hath a reference to my State:
   No longer Celia, but Aliena.

ROSALIND   But Cousin, what if we assay'd to steal
   The clownish Fool out of your Father's Court:
   Would he not be a Comfort to our Travail?                       135

CELIA   He'll go along o'er the wide World with me,
   Leave me alone to woe him. Let's away
   And get our Jewels and our Wealth together,
   Devise the fittest Time, and safest Way
   To hide us from Pursuit that will be made                       140
   After my Flight. Now go in we content
   To Liberty, and not to Banishment.              *Exeunt.*

---

137   **Leave me alone**   leave it to me. Compare lines 112–13. *Devise*
      (line 139) echoes line 104.
      **woe**   woo. But here as elsewhere, the ambiguity in the
      Elizabethan spelling will prove pertinent. Touchstone will
      initially feel that he has exchanged 'Comfort' (line 135) for
      woe ('Adversity', II.i.12) by joining his mistress's flight to the
      forest. See his remarks in III.ii.11–23.

141   **Now go in we content**   now we leave in a state of contentment.

II.i.    Now the play moves to the Forest of Arden. This scene takes place at the camp of Duke Senior, Rosalind's father. The name of Duke Senior's musician, spelled *Amyens* in the opening stage direction and elsewhere, is sometimes rendered *Amiens* in the Folio text (see lines 18, 29) and normally appears in that form in modern editions.

2    **old Custom** Duke Senior probably refers to the habits formed by an extended stay in the forest. But the phrase could also refer to the ancient traditions of pastoral literature. Since classical antiquity, poets and philosophers had praised the low and mean estate of rustic simplicity (see II.iii.66–68 for an allusion to the humility associated with an unpretentious bucolic existence), holding it to be more virtuous and healthy than the life of luxury to be found in courts and cities.

3    **painted Pomp** false grandeur. In Shakespeare 'painting' almost always refers to the use of cosmetics to conceal one's ugliness, disease, age, or vice (see *Hamlet*, III.i.145–50, V.i.203–5); it is thus a metaphor for any form of hypocrisy or deception. 'Pomp' refers to sybaritic splendour, 'Pride', and ceremonious 'Circumstance' (*Othello*, III.iii.344).

4    **envious** malicious and emulous (as in I.i.150–52 and I.ii.251).

5    **feel we not** we are not harmed or distressed by. The Duke does not mean that the forest is free from the discomforts associated with the changing seasons. What he says is that he and his companions welcome 'Adversity' (line 12), misfortune, because it keeps them in touch with reality rather than misleading them with 'Flattery' and blinding them to the 'Peril' (line 4) that smooth-talking is designed to conceal; compare I.iii.81–83.

    **the Penalty of Adam** Genesis 3:16–19 was usually interpreted to mean that decay and death and all the travails of life (including 'the Winter's Wind') were man's punishment for the Fall. *Penalty* recalls I.i.40–41.

7    **churlish Chiding** rude, ungenerous rebuke. Here the stingy-spirited scolding of 'the Winter's Wind' is given special emphasis by the alliterative repetition of the Duke's phonetically imitative *ch* sounds; like the other sibilants (*s* and *sh* whispers) in lines 6–7, they evoke the 'Icy' shivering that occurs when a hissing gust 'bites and blows' upon one's 'Body' (line 8).

10    **Counsellors** trustworthy advisors, as opposed to those who cajole and connive with 'Flattery'.

# ACT II

## Scene 1

*Enter Duke Senior: Amyens, and two or three Lords, like Foresters.*

DUKE SENIOR   Now my Co-mates, and Brothers in
  Exile,
Hath not old Custom made this Life more sweet
Than that of painted Pomp? Are not these Woods
More free from Peril than the envious Court?
Here feel we not the Penalty of Adam,             5
The Seasons Difference, as the Icy Fang
And churlish Chiding of the Winter's Wind,
Which when it bites and blows upon my Body
Even till I shrink with Cold, I smile and say
This is no Flattery: these are Counsellors         10
That feelingly persuade me what I am.
Sweet are the Uses of Adversity,
Which like the Toad, ougly and venomous,

---

11   **feelingly**  both (a) honestly, with genuine feelings, and (b) with
a direct appeal to my own feelings (senses and emotions).
Compare *King Lear*, IV.vi.146–47, where the blinded
Gloucester says he has learned to 'see' himself 'feelingly' as he
stumbles through 'this World' with the wisdom born of
suffering.

12   **Sweet**  delightful, agreeable. So also in line 20.

13   **ougly**  ugly. Here the Elizabethan form of the word seems more
onomatopoeic, and more orthographically apt.

14    **Jewel in his Head**   Duke Senior alludes to the ancient lore that toads were poisonous, but with medicinal nodules in their heads that contained antidotes to their venom. *Jewel* echoes I.iii.137–38.

15    **exempt from public Haunt**   not subject to normal human traffic.

16    **Tongues**   languages, and by extension articulated truths.

18    **change**   both (a) exchange, and (b) alter. Both senses play on *translate* (line 19). Compare I.iii.95, 106.
     **Grace**   both (a) a noble title, and (b) a word that can here mean 'blessed state'. See I.i.157–58.

19    **translate**   Amyens means 'transform', but his image also has to do with 'reading' (construing and explicating) what would normally be interpreted as hardship and finding in it peace and contentment.
     **Stubbornness**   obstinacy, disagreeableness; harshness. Compare I.i.149–50.

20    **Stile**   style, mode of expression (and by extension, way of life and attitude about one's place in the grand scheme of things). Here as elsewhere (compare *Much Ado About Nothing*, V.ii.4–10), the Folio spelling suggests play on the meaning now attached to *stile*, a set of steps over a fence or wall.

22    **irks**   troubles, bothers.
     **dappled Fools**   spotted innocents. Here and in line 40, *Fools* is a term of affection.

23    **Burghers**   city dwellers.
     **desert**   deserted (unpopulated by human beings).

24    **forked Heads**   two-pronged arrows. Duke Senior's reference to antlers suggests the horns of cuckolds, husbands who have been 'goar'd' by their wives and the men they've allowed to 'gore' them. His image anticipates III.iii.48–64.

25    **Haunches goar'd**   hindquarters gored.

26    **Jaques**   normally pronounced as a two-syllable word (usually either 'Jay-kwees' or 'Jay-kes' in modern performances, possibly 'Ya-kes' or 'Yay-kes' in Elizabethan times).
     **grieves at**   both (a) objects to, and (b) weeps at. Compare I.iii.96.

27    **kind**   respect.

29    **To day**   Today. See the second note to I.i.99.

Wears yet a precious Jewel in his Head:
And this our Life exempt from public Haunt,                    15
Finds Tongues in Trees, Books in the running
   Brooks,
Sermons in Stones, and good in every thing.
AMYENS    I would not change it, happy is your Grace
  That can translate the Stubbornness of Fortune
  Into so quiet and so sweet a Stile.                         20
DUKE SENIOR    Come, shall we go and kill us Venison?
  And yet it irks me the poor dappled Fools,
  Being native Burghers of this desert City,
  Should in their own Confines with forked Heads
  Have their round Haunches goar'd.
1 LORD                                      Indeed, my Lord,          25
  The melancholy Jaques grieves at that,
  And in that kind swears you do more usurp
  Than doth your Brother that hath banish'd you.
  To day my Lord of Amiens, and my self,
  Did steal behind him as he lay along                       30
  Under an Oak, whose antic Root peeps out
  Upon the Brook that brawls along this Wood,
  To the which Place a poor sequest'red Stag
  That from the Hunter's Aim had ta'en a Hurt,
  Did come to languish; and indeed, my Lord,                 35

---

31    **antic**    both (a) antique, old, and (b) gnarled, intricately figured.

32    **brawls**    an onomatopoeic word that combines two senses: (a)
      roars like a rioting crowd, and (b) dances vigorously (from the
      French word *branle*). Compare *A Midsummer Night's Dream*,
      II.i.81–87.

34    **ta'en a Hurt**    been 'goar'd (line 25) by an arrow.

35    **languish**    pine in anguish. The 'Groans' (line 36) of the
      wounded stag recall Romans 8:22, where we read that as a
      consequence of the Fall (see the second note to line 5), 'the
      whole creation groaneth and travaileth'.

39 **Cours'd**  chased.

40 **Chase**  pursuit. Compare I.iii.35–36.

41 **marked of**  noted (remarked) by.

42 **exremest Verge**  closest edge (bank). Compare *King Lear*,
IV.vi.25–26, where Edgar tells Gloucester 'you are now
within a Foot / of th' extreme Verge'.

43 **Augmenting it**  supplementing it, adding to it.

44 **moralize**  'translate' (line 19) into 'Tongues', 'Books', and
'Sermons' (lines 16–17).

45 **Similes**  similitudes, comparisons.

46 **for**  as for
**needless**  abundantly supplied; in no need of more water. See
lines 48–49.

47 **Testament**  last will and testament. Compare I.i.1–92.

50 **velvet Friend**  Here *velvet* refers both to the coat of a deer and
to the 'in the velvet' prosperity of the fair-weather 'Friend'
who has abandoned the wounded, 'Bankrupt' stag. Modern
editions normally emend 'Friend' to 'Friends'; but Jaques may
be thinking in particular of the stag's ungrateful heir (lines
47–49, which recall the play's earlier references to
inheritance).

52 **Flux**  both (a) flow, and (b) excess, superfluity (as in lines
46–49).
**Anon**  shortly thereafter.
**careless**  both (a) carefree, and (b) uncaring. Compare
I.i.124–26.

53 **Full of the Pasture**  both (a) well fed, and (b) bounding with
vigour. *Full* continues the emphasis on excess in lines 35–52.

54 **stays**  pauses, stops. Compare I.iii.71, 92.

55 **greazy**  greasy, both (a) well off, 'fat', and (b) soiled with
commerce.

56 **wherefore do**  why should.

57 **broken**  both (a) heartbroken, injured, and (b) 'Bankrupt'.
Compare I.ii.130–49.

58 **invectively**  filled with invective (scornful denunciation).
Compare *Hamlet*, III.ii.283.

The wretched Animal heav'd forth such Groans
That their Discharge did stretch his leathern
   Coat
Almost to bursting, and the big round Tears
Cours'd one another down his innocent Nose
In piteous Chase; and thus the hairy Fool,                         40
Much marked of the melancholy Jaques,
Stood on th' extremest Verge of the swift
   Brook,
Augmenting it with Tears.

DUKE SENIOR              But what said Jaques?
Did he not moralize this Spectacle?

1 LORD   O yes, into a thousand Similes.                   45
First, for his Weeping into the needless
   Stream;
'Poor Deer,' quoth he, 'thou mak'st a Testament
As Worldlings do giving thy Sum of more
To that which had too much.' Then being there
   alone,
Left and abandon'd of his velvet Friend;                          50
''Tis right,' quoth he, 'thus Misery doth part
The Flux of Company.' Anon a careless Herd,
Full of the Pasture, jumps along by him
And never stays to greet him: 'Ay,' quoth
   Jaques,
'Sweep on, you fat and greazy Citizens,                           55
'Tis just the Fashion; wherefore do you look
Upon that poor and broken Bankrupt there?'
Thus most invectively he pierceth through
The Body of Country, City, Court,

---

59   **Body of Country**  Most editors add a *the* before *Country* to
      make this line metrically regular. But it may have been
      intended as a short line (with 'Body of' elided into two
      syllables) – 'pierced through' ('goar'd' metrically, line 25) to
      help emphasize the point of the image.

60    **this our Life**   the 'Life more sweet' (line 2) we've made for ourselves here in the forest.

61    **mere**   both (a) pure, and (b) only (nothing other than).
    **what's worse**   whatever title will label us as even more egregious offenders.

62    **kill them up**   slaughter all of them.

63    **assign'd**   divinely or naturally ordained.

65    **commenting**   moralizing. Here *commenting* is probably to be accented on the second syllable.

67    **cope**   match wits with, encounter.
    **sullen Fits**   seizures of discontent.

68    **Matter**   substance; something interesting to hear and learn from.
    **strait**   straight away, immediately. The Folio spelling, normally reserved now for an adjective that means 'restricted' or 'confined', plays on a related sense of *Fits* (line 67).

II.ii    This scene returns us to the palace of Duke Frederick.

3    **of consent and sufferance in this**   involved in this; among those who have agreed to permit (suffer) this to happen.

5    **Ladies . . . Chamber**   In this line modern editions usually insert parenthetical commas to set off the appositive phrase *her attendants of her Chamber*. Here as elsewhere, Everyman follows the Folio; see the note to I.i.94, and compare line 10.

6    **a-bed**   in bed.

7    **untreasur'd**   unpossessed, unoccupied.

8    **roynish**   coarse or mangy; from the French *rogneux*, 'scurvy'.

9    **wont**   accustomed, disposed.

13    **Parts and Graces**   endowments and gifts, attributes and abilities. *Parts* echoes I.ii.259–61; *Grace* recalls I.i.155–61, I.ii.195–99, I.iii.56–58, II.i.18–20.

14    **sinowy**   sinewy; muscular.

Yea, and of this our Life, swearing that we                    60
Are mere Usurpers, Tyrants, and what's worse,
To fright the Animals and to kill them up
In their assign'd and native dwelling place.

DUKE SENIOR   And did you leave him in this
    Contemplation?

2 LORD   We did, my Lord, weeping and
    commenting                                                 65
Upon the sobbing Deer.

DUKE SENIOR            Show me the place,
I love to cope him in these sullen Fits,
For then he's full of Matter.

1 LORD                  I'll bring you to him strait.

                                        *Exeunt.*


# Scene 2

*Enter Duke [Frederick], with Lords.*

DUKE   Can it be possible that no man saw them?
It cannot be, some Villains of my Court
Are of consent and sufferance in this.

1 LORD   I cannot hear of any that did see
    her,
The Ladies her Attendants of her Chamber
Saw her a-bed, and in the Morning early                        5
They found the Bed untreasur'd of their
    Mistress.

2 LORD   My Lord, the roynish Clown, at
    whom so oft
Your Grace was wont to laugh, is also missing,
Hisperia the Princess' Gentlewoman                             10
Confesses that she secretly o'erheard
Your Daughter and her Cousin much commend
The Parts and Graces of the Wrastler
That did but lately foil the sinowy Charles,

17   **fetch . . . hither** It is not clear whether this clause states the command to be given to Oliver (in which case modern usage would place it in quotation marks), or simply amplifies 'Send to his Brother' (with 'Gallant' and 'Brother' both referring to Oliver), but the former seems the more likely. See III.i.1–12, 15–18. *Gallant* (echoing I.ii.210–11, 239) appears to refer to Orlando; so does *he* in line 18.

18   **If . . . me** Here *he* is usually construed to mean 'Orlando' (assuming that *Gallant* in line 17 refers to Oliver's missing younger brother), but it could also mean Oliver (in accordance with the second reading of line 17); meanwhile *Brother*, usually thought to refer to Oliver, could refer to the middle sibling, Jaques (see I.ii.5–7 and V.iv.159–91), if the Duke is thinking of him as a second keeper for Orlando.

19   **suddenly** immediately. Compare I.ii.292–93.

20   **Inquisition** interrogation, inquiry. But of course this word would have reminded Shakespeare's predominantly anti-Catholic audience of the Spanish Inquisition, and thus have characterized Duke Frederick in terms of the cruel oppression associated with that quest for heretics and traitors. *Search* recalls I.i.142–43.
      **quail** fail as a result of any lack or slackening of effort.

II.iii   This scene takes place in the grounds of Oliver's house.

3   **Memory** living reminder. See the note to I.i.25–26, and compare I.i.66–67, I.ii.6.

4   **make** do. Adam appears to be quoting Oliver and, as it were, speaking in his voice; see I.i.31–38, and compare IV.iii.61.

6   **wherefore** why, to what purpose.

7   **fond to** foolish as to.

8   **bonny Priser** fine, robust prizefighter.
      **humorous** obsessed, tyrannical. Adam means that the Duke is possessed by a 'humour' that blinds him to everything but what his choleric malice allows him to perceive. Compare I.ii.276.

9   **Your Praise** the acclaim your deeds have won you.

11   **Graces** virtues, blessings, 'Lineaments of Nature' (I.ii.46). Compare II.ii.13, and see lines 17–18.

12   **No more do yours** your 'Graces' do no more good for you than theirs do for them.

And she believes where ever they are gone                    15
That Youth is surely in their Company.
DUKE   Send to his Brother, fetch that Gallant
   hither,
If he be absent, bring his Brother to me,
I'll make him find him. Do this suddenly;
And let not Search and Inquisition quail,                     20
To bring again these foolish Runaways.          *Exeunt.*


# Scene 3

*Enter Orlando and Adam, meeting.*

ORLANDO   Who's there?
ADAM   What, my young Master, oh my gentle Master,
   Oh my sweet Master, O you Memory
   Of old Sir Rowland; why, what make you here?
   Why are you virtuous? Why do People love you?            5
   And wherefore are you gentle, strong, and
      valiant?
   Why would you be so fond to overcome
   The bonny Priser of the humorous Duke?
   Your Praise is come too swiftly home before
      you.
   Know you not, Master, to some kind of Men,              10
   Their Graces serve them but as Enemies,
   No more do yours: your Virtues, gentle Master,
   Are sanctified and holy Traitors to you.
   Oh what a World is this, when what is comely

---

13   **sanctified**   'holy'; set apart and kept pure, 'sequest'red' (II.i.33)
      to God.

14   **comely**   becoming, graceful, attractive. In Isaiah 53:2, the
      suffering servant of the Lord, 'a tender plant' (see the note to
      I.i.136), is said to be lacking in 'form' and 'comeliness'.

| 15 | **Envenoms** poisons. Compare II.i.12–14. |
|----|---|
| 18 | **lives** lives as (or 'lives as if he really were'). Most of today's editions insert a semicolon or a full stop after this word. |
| 21 | **Of . . . Father** So different is Oliver from 'the Spirit of' Orlando's 'Father' that Adam cannot bring himself to affirm that Orlando's oldest brother is actually a legitimate son of Sir Rowland de Boys. |
| 23 | **where you use to lie** where you are accustomed to stay. *Burn* recalls I.ii.47–48. In line 22, as in I.ii.218, *means* means 'intends'. |
| 26 | **Practices** stratagems, cunning devices. Compare I.i.158. |
| 27 | **no Place** no home for you. **Butchery** slaughterhouse. |
| 28 | **Abhor it** avoid it; shrink from it. |
| 29 | **whether** whither, where. So also in line 30; compare I.iii.105, 110. |
| 30 | **so** so long as |
| 32 | **boist'rous** violent, uncivil. |
| 32–33 | **enforce . . . Road** become a highwayman and force travellers to yield me the means to live. Orlando's words will prove prophetic; see II.vii.87–135. The reference to begging (line 31) recalls I.i.75–80. |
| 37 | **a diverted Blood** a 'Blood' that has diverged from its natural course, both (a) in Oliver's deviation from the nature of the blood he inherited from his noble father, and (b) in Oliver's surrender to a 'bloody' (murderous) passion that flows in a channel more 'base' (line 32) than that of his bloodline. See the note to I.i.50. |
| 39 | **thrifty Hire** wages accumulated by profitable thrift. |
| 41 | **Service** the ability to continue working as a servant. *Lame* echoes I.iii.5–9. |
| 42 | **unregarded . . . thrown** an unproductive and thus unwanted old man (here a personification of 'Age' itself) cast off like refuse. *Thrown* recalls I.ii.259–70, I.iii.4–6, 14–15. Compare *King Lear*, II.ii.338–39, where Lear discovers that 'Age is unnecessary'. |

Envenoms him that bears it?                                              15
[ORLANDO]   Why what's the matter?
ADAM                                        O unhappy Youth,
   Come not within these Doors: within this Roof
   The Enemy of all your Graces lives
   Your Brother, no, no Brother, yet the Son
   (Yet not the Son, I will not call him Son)                           20
   Of him I was about to call his Father,
   Hath heard your Praises, and this night he
      means
   To burn the Lodging where you use to lie,
   And you within it. If he fail of that
   He will have other Means to cut you off;                             25
   I overheard him, and his Practices.
   This is no Place; this House is but a
      Butchery;
   Abhor it, fear it, do not enter it.
[ORLANDO]   Why whether, Adam, wouldst thou have
      me go?
ADAM   No matter whether, so you come not here.             30
ORLANDO   What, wouldst thou have me go and beg
      my Food,
   Or with a base and boist'rous Sword enforce
   A thievish Living on the common Road?
   This I must do, or know not what to do:
   Yet this I will not do, do how I can,                                35
   I rather will subject me to the Malice
   Of a diverted Blood, and bloody Brother.
ADAM   But do not so: I have five hundred Crowns,
   The thrifty Hire I saved under your Father,
   Which I did store to be my foster Nurse                              40
   When Service should in my old Limbs lie lame,
   And unregarded Age in Corners thrown.

43–44 **he ... Sparrow**  Adam alludes to such passages as Psalm 147:9 ('He giveth to the beast his food, and to the young ravens which cry'), Matthew 10:29 ('Are not two sparrows sold for a farthing? and one of them shall not fall on the ground without your Father') and Luke 12:24 ('Consider the ravens: for they neither sow nor reap; which neither have storehouse nor barn; and God feedeth them: how much more are ye better than the fowls?'). Compare Job 38:41 and Luke 12:6.

44  **providently**  both (a) with the foresight to supply one's needs in good time, and (b) providentially, with divine grace (unmerited favour).

47  **lusty**  healthy, robust.

49  **rebellious Liquors**  strong drink that subverts one's health.

50–51 **unbashful ... Debility**  proud and immodest brows, unashamed of the licentious pursuits that enslave a man to lust and disable him with venereal disease. Here as in I.iii.137 *woe* means 'woo' but suggests the woe that ensues.

53  **kindly**  benign and natural (like the honest 'Chiding' of II.i.7), in keeping with its 'kind'.

57  **constant**  both (a) unchanging, reliable, and (b) faithful.

**antique World**  Orlando's phrasing links Adam to the Edenic Adam before the Fall of Man; it also evokes the classical Golden Age (see I.i.121–26; II.i.1–20). *Antique* echoes II.i.31.

58  **Meed**  reward. Here *sweat* means 'sweated'.

60  **Promotion**  advancement, selfish gain. Compare *The Winter's Tale*, I.ii.352–57.

61  **choke ... up**  'come slack of former Services' with 'weary Negligence' (*King Lear*, I.iii.10, 13), stifling any further inclination to be helpful.

65  **In lieu of**  in return for (literally, to replace).
**Pains and Husbandry**  efforts at cultivation, attentive gardening. Orlando's tree image, recalling II.i.16, 29–35, and anticipating IV.iii.99–122, alludes to such New Testament passages as Matthew 7:15–20, where Jesus says that 'A good tree cannot bring forth evil fruit, neither can a corrupt tree bring forth good fruit'. Compare III.ii.121–88, 250–53, 276–78.

66  **come thy ways**  come along now. Compare I.ii.219.

Take that, and he that doth the Ravens feed,
Yea providently caters for the Sparrow,
Be comfort to my Age: here is the Gold,                        45
All this I give you, let me be your Servant,
Though I look old, yet am I strong and lusty;
For in my Youth I never did apply
Hot and rebellious Liquors in my Blood,
Nor did not with unbashful Forehead woe                        50
The Means of Weakness and Debility,
Therefore my Age is as a lusty Winter,
Frosty, but kindly. Let me go with you,
I'll do the Service of a younger Man
In all your Business and Necessities.                          55
ORLANDO   Oh good old Man, how well in thee appears
The constant Service of the antique World,
When Service sweat for Duty, not for Meed:
Thou art not for the Fashion of these Times,
Where none will sweat, but for Promotion,                      60
And having that do choke their Service up,
Even with the Having. It is not so with thee:
But poor old Man, thou prun'st a rotten Tree,
That cannot so much as a Blossom yield,
In lieu of all thy Pains and Husbandry,                        65
But come thy ways, we'll go along together,
And ere we have thy youthful Wages spent,
We'll light upon some settled low Content.
ADAM   Master go on, and I will follow thee
To the last Gasp with Truth and Loyalty,                       70

---

68    **light upon**   alight upon, come across.
      **settled**   peaceful, harmonious.
      **low Content**   humble way of life that will provide contentment.
          Compare I.iii.115, 141–42.

71    **seventy** Here and in line 73 the Folio text reads 'seauentie'; since the early eighteenth century editors have emended to 'seventeen', on the assumption that Adam, now approaching eighty, has spent his entire working life in the de Boys household (see lines 73–74). However, *seventy* accords more readily with *Week* (line 74), here measured in decades rather than days.

74    **Week** In this passage *Week* is used metaphorically (as a synecdoche that means either 'time' or 'year'). No doubt the word choice was dictated by the need to find a rhyme for 'seek' in line 73.

76    **not . . . Debtor** not owing anything to my master for my upkeep, even if I'm 'in Corners thrown' (line 42) once I've outlived my usefulness.

II.iv    This scene takes place in the Forest of Arden.

S.D.    **Rosaline for Ganimed** Rosalind disguised as Ganimed.
    **alias Touchstone** This is the play's first reference to the Clown's name.

1    **merry** Most of today's editions emend to *weary*. But the context suggests that, like Duke Senior, Rosalind either finds 'Adversity' to be 'Sweet' (II.i.12) or is trying to maintain that she does. Her responsibility, paralleling that of Orlando in II.vi, is to be strong enough to 'comfort the weaker Vessel' (line 6), Celia. Despite the question mark at the end of this sentence, Rosalind's tone is probably more exclamatory than interrogative. Lines 1–3 echo I.ii.1–27.

4    **disgrace** shame humiliate. See I.ii.195–99 and II.iii.10–24.

6    **Weaker Vessel** As noted at I.ii.148 and I.iii.120, this term for 'woman' derives from 1 Peter 3:7.

6–7    **Doublet and Hose** the tight-fitting jacket and breeches worn by gentlemen in Elizabethan England. Here Rosalind's phrase stands metonymically for 'Man's Apparel' (line 5) and signifies masculinity; by the same token, *Petty-coat* (line 8) means 'women's clothing' and signifies femininity.

7    **show it self courageous** maintains a brave demeanour.

8    **Petty-coat** petticoat. Here the Folio spelling (which yields the meaning 'small coat') reinforces the implication that Rosalind is both larger and stronger than the petite Celia. Compare I.iii.16, III.ii.358.

From seventy years till now almost fourscore
Here lived I, but now live here no more.
At seventy years many their Fortunes seek,
But at fourscore it is too late a Week,
Yet Fortune cannot recompense me better          75
Than to die well, and not my Master's Debtor.

*Exeunt.*

# Scene 4

*Enter Rosaline for Ganimed, Celia for Aliena,*
*and Clown, alias Touchstone.*

ROSALIND   O Jupiter, how merry are my Spirits?
CLOWN   I care not for my Spirits, if my Legs were
not weary.
ROSALIND   I could find in my Heart to disgrace
my Man's Apparel, and to cry like a Woman: but          5
I must comfort the weaker Vessel, as Doublet
and Hose ought to show it self courageous to
Petty-coat; therefore Courage, good Aliena.
CELIA   I pray you bear with me, I cannot go no
further.          10
CLOWN   For my part, I had rather bear with you
than bear you: yet I should bear no Cross if

---

9    **bear with me**   grant me your patient forbearance, forgive my
     lack of endurance.

12   **bear no Cross**   The Clown plays on 'bear with' (tolerate), 'bear'
     (carry), and 'Cross'. *Cross* can mean (a) burden, (b) affront,
     insult, or injury, (c) affliction, and (d) a penny with a cross
     stamped on it. The expression 'bearing a cross' normally
     alluded to Jesus (and to such passages as Matthew 10:38), but
     it also referred to one who put up with 'crosses' (insults)
     without defending his honour by retaliating.

16  **I now**   both (a) I, now, and (b) Ay, now.
**the more Fool I**   The Clown means that in addition to his professional role as a court jester, he is now a real fool.

17  **When . . . place**   Touchstone's words echo what Adam has told Orlando in II.iii.27–28.

18  **Travellers**   Touchstone is probably playing on *travailers*, those who are faced with adversity (see I.iii.135). His words thus offer yet another variation (this one meant ironically) on the idea that a bit of hardship builds wisdom and character (compare II.i.1–17). *Content* echoes II.iii.66–68.

19  **Touchstone**   This is the play's first spoken reference to the Clown by this name. It may well be that it was only at this point that Shakespeare decided upon a sobriquet for him. See the note to I.ii.59.

33  **hartily**   both (a) like an ardent hart (male deer), and (b) heartily, with all your heart. See the note to I.ii.3, and compare III.ii.261–63.

34  **Folly**   Having heard Touchstone's reflections on two kinds of folly (see the note to line 16), we now hear reference to a third: the irrational behaviour of those subject to love-melancholy, the humour of being in love.

35  **run**   charge headlong, rush rashly. Touchstone mimics *run into* in lines 54–55.

38  **Wearing**   both (a) wearing out, and (b) wearying. Compare lines 1–10.

40  **broke from Company**   sequestered yourself. Compare I.ii.130–49, I.iii.87–90, II.i.29–57.

44  **searching of**   probing. *Searching* echoes II.ii.20–21.
**their Wound**   the 'Hurt' (II.i.34) of Silvius, Corin, and all the lovers whose symptoms have been enumerated in lines 25–43. This reading, based on an emendation of the First Folio's *they would*, derives from the Second Folio. Most of today's editions adopt *thy wound*, the phrasing Nicholas Rowe introduced in his collected edition of 1709.

45  **by hard Adventure**   by painful chance. *Adventure* echoes I.ii.182–85; *hard* recalls I.ii.52–54, 192–94.

I did bear you, for I think you have no Money
in your Purse.

ROSALIND   Well, this is the Forest of Arden.   15

CLOWN   I, now am I in Arden, the more Fool I:
when I was at home I was in a better place,
but Travellers must be content.

*Enter Corin and Silvius.*

ROSALIND   Ay, be so good Touchstone. Look you,
who comes here, a young Man and an old in   20
solemn Talk.

CORIN   That is the way to make her scorn you still.

SILVIUS   Oh Corin, that thou knew'st how I do love
her.

CORIN   I partly guess: for I have lov'd ere now.

SILVIUS   No, Corin, being old, thou canst not guess,   25
Though in thy Youth thou wast as true a Lover
As ever sigh'd upon a Midnight Pillow:
But if thy Love were ever like to mine,
As sure I think did never Man love so,
How many Actions most ridiculous   30
Hast thou been drawn to by thy Fantasy?

CORIN   Into a thousand that I have forgotten.

SILVIUS   Oh thou didst then never love so hartily,
If thou rememb'rest not the slightest Folly
That ever Love did make thee run into,   35
Thou hast not lov'd.
Or if thou hast not sat as I do now,
Wearing thy Hearer in thy Mistress' Praise,
Thou hast not lov'd.
Or if thou hast not broke from Company,   40
Abruptly as my Passion now makes me,
Thou hast not lov'd.
O Phebe, Phebe, Phebe.                    *Exit.*

ROSALIND   Alas poor Shepherd, searching of their
Wound,
I have by hard Adventure found mine own.   45

47–48 **broke . . . Smile**   Touchstone appears to be describing a
        punishment for his 'Sword' that befits the 'Curtleaxe upon' his
        'Thigh' (see I.iii.119–26), if that weapon has been 'coming
        a-night to Jane Smile' (copulating with a compliant nocturnal
        companion). *Coming* recalls I.ii.30–32, and *Stone* (a word for
        'testicle', as in *Romeo and Juliet*, I.iii.53) echoes II.i.17.
        Compare Adam's remarks in II.iii.50–51.

49     **Batler**   a laundry club used to beat clothes in the wash.

50     **chopp'd**   chapped, rough.

52     **Peascod**   peapod; here referring to the entire pea plant. Peasant
        youths gave their sweethearts peascods in the belief that this
        would keep the maids faithful to them.

53     **Cods**   individual peapods, with a reminder of (a) the scrotum,
        and (b) the codpiece (the bag or flap covering the crotch in
        male breeches).

55     **strange Capers**   extraordinary escapades. The 'weeping Tears'
        in line 54 echo II.i.35–49.

57     **mortal in Folly**   both (a) subject to 'the Penalty of Adam'
        (II.i.5), and thus subject to the ageing process that leads to
        death, and (b) inconstant, irrational, and subject to the
        promptings of appetite and the passions. Here *Folly* hints at
        sexual licence, a sense related to the 'Fool' tradition noted at
        I.ii.53.

58     **ware**   aware. In the next line Touchstone puns on 'wary' and
        'beware'. Lines 59–60 can be construed in various ways,
        among them (a) I shall never be aware of (and thus beware)
        my 'Wit' (my 'Sword' and 'Stones', and the 'Capers' they
        prompt me to) until I feel the pain it inflicts on me when I
        stumble because of it, and (b) I shall never pay heed to my
        'Wit' (reason, wisdom) until it intrudes itself upon my
        consciousness and forces me to attend its counsel. See
        I.ii.47–113. For other 'Shin' references, see *Romeo and Juliet*,
        I.ii.50–54, and *Love's Labour's Lost*, III.i.73–149.

62     **upon my Fashion**   along lines that parallel my own. *Fashion*
        echoes I.i.1–2, II.i.55–56, II.iii.59–62.

67     **Clown**   rustic. Like Jaques, but in a different sense, Touchstone
        calls out to a shepherd he regards as 'a Fool i'th' Forest'
        (II.vii.12).

69     **Else**   otherwise.

70     **even**   evening. It is now after noon.

CLOWN   And I mine: I remember when I was in love,
  I broke my Sword upon a Stone, and bid him
  take that for coming a night to Jane Smile,
  And I remember the kissing of her Batler, and
  the Cow's Dugs that her pretty chopp'd Hands      50
  had milk'd; and I remember the wooing of a
  Peascod instead of her, from whom I took two
  Cods, and, giving her them again, said with
  weeping Tears, 'Wear these for my sake.' We
  that are true Lovers run into strange Capers;    55
  but as all is mortal in Nature, so is all
  Nature in Love mortal in Folly.
ROSALIND   Thou speak'st wiser than thou art ware
  of.
CLOWN   Nay, I shall ne'er be ware of mine own Wit,
  till I break my Shins against it.                60
ROSALIND   Jove, Jove, this Shepherd's Passion
            Is much upon my Fashion.
CLOWN   And mine, but it grows something stale
  with me.
CELIA   I pray you, one of you question yond Man,   65
  If he for Gold will give us any Food,
  I faint almost to death.
CLOWN               – Holla; you Clown.
ROSALIND   Peace, Fool, he's not thy Kinsman.
CORIN                              Who calls?
CLOWN   Your Betters, Sir.
CORIN                 Else are they very wretched.
ROSALIND   Peace, I say; good even to you, Friend.  70
CORIN   And to you, gentle Sir, and to you all.
ROSALIND   I prethee, Shepherd, if that Love or Gold

73    **desert**   uninhabited. Compare II.i.23.
      **Entertainment**   'Hospitality' (line 83).

75    **Travail**   both (a) travel, and (b) labour. See I.iii.135, and
      compare line 18.

76    **Succour**   help, aid.

80    **do not shear the Fleeces that I graze**   do not get the wool
      (profit) from the sheep I tend.

81    **churlish**   disagreeable, tight-fisted. Compare II.i.6–7.
      *Disposition* recalls I.ii.251.

82    **wreaks**   recks (reckons), concerns himself.

84    **Coate**   cote, 'Cottage' (line 93).
      **Bounds of Feed**   'Pasture' (line 93), land on which he is
      permitted to graze his sheep.

85    **Sheep-coat**   sheepcote, shepherd's cottage.

88    **in my Voice**   on my authority (limited though it is).

89    **What**   who; what kind of person.

90    **Swain**   peasant lover (Silvius).
      **erewhile**   a short while ago.

91    **cares for**   turns his mind to, is inclined to.

92    **stand with Honesty**   is consistent with honest dealings.

94    **have to pay for it of us**   receive what you need to pay for it
      from us.

95    **mend**   augment, improve. *Place* echoes lines 17, 73.

96    **waste**   spend, pass.

97    **Assuredly**   certainly, without doubt.

98    **upon Report**   after you have heard and learned more.

99    **this . . . Life**   a shepherd's existence. Corin's phrasing recalls
      II.i.60. *Soil* (land) can also refer to the soiling (dirtying) of
      oneself and one's clothing by manual labour. Compare
      III.ii.42–90.

100    **Feeder**   servant, shepherd. Compare lines 72–88.

101    **right suddenly**   immediately. *Suddenly* echoes II.ii.18.

Can in this desert place buy Entertainment,
Bring us where we may rest our selves, and feed:
Here's a young Maid with Travail much
      oppress'd,                                                75
And faints for Succour.
CORIN                       Fair Sir, I pity her,
And wish for her sake more than for mine own,
My Fortunes were more able to relieve her:
But I am Shepherd to another Man,
And do not shear the Fleeces that I graze.                    80
My Master is of churlish Disposition,
And little wreaks to find the way to Heaven
By doing Deeds of Hospitality.
Besides his Coate, his Flocks, and Bounds of
      Feed
Are now on sale, and at our Sheep-coat now,                  85
By reason of his Absence there is nothing
That you will feed on: but what is, come see,
And in my Voice most welcome shall you be.
ROSALIND   What is he that shall buy his Flock and
      Pasture?
CORIN   That young Swain that you saw here but
      erewhile,                                              90
That little cares for buying any thing.
ROSALIND   I pray thee, if it stand with Honesty,
Buy thou the Cottage, Pasture, and the Flock,
And thou shalt have to pay for it of us.
CELIA   And we will mend thy Wages: I like this
      place,                                                 95
And willingly could waste my Time in it.
CORIN   Assuredly the thing is to be sold:
Go with me, if you like upon Report
The Soil, the Profit, and this kind of Life,
I will your very faithful Feeder be,                         100
And buy it with your Gold right suddenly.
                                        *Exeunt.*

II.v    We now move to a different part of the forest. The song that
        opens the scene is to be performed by Amyens (Amiens); there
        is no stage direction, but the dialogue in lines 9–39 specifies
        him as the singer.

3–4     **turn . . . Throat**   adapt his own tune to that of the bird singing
        overhead.

6–8     **Here . . . Weather**   The song repeats the major theme of Duke
        Senior's speech in II.i.1–17. It also presents the forest as a
        refuge for those who must beware of a more hostile 'Enemy'
        (see II.iii.10–28). *Winter* echoes II.iii.52–53.

10      **melancholy**   gloomy, sombre. See II.i.26, 41, where Amyens's
        companion is called 'the melancholy Jaques'.

15      **ragged**   rough, raspy.

19      **Stanzo**   stanza. This word, newly imported from Italy, was still
        associated with affectation.

20      **What you will**   Amyens's reply, repeating the subtitle of
        *Twelfth Night*, is a paraphrase of *As You Like It*.

21–22   **Nay . . . nothing**   I have no real interest in their identities (what
        they are called); they are not in debt to me. Jaques alludes to
        the practice whereby those who borrowed money signed their
        names in the lender's account book. Compare II.iii.75–76.
        *Care for* echoes II.iv.90–91.

23      **then**   either (a) then (meaning 'later'), or (b) than. Compare
        I.ii.277.

26      **Complement**   compliment; compliance with decorum, polite
        manners.

27      **Dog-apes**   baboons. Jaques refers to the effusive bowing and
        scraping of creatures who are in the habit of imitating
        ceremonial forms.

28      **hartily**   both (a) in a hartlike fashion (compare II.iv.33), and (b)
        with his heart and nothing else.

29–30   **beggarly Thanks**   verbal expressions of gratitude (like those of
        a beggar who has just received alms from me), but nothing
        beyond that.

30      **and**   if.

# Scene 5

*Enter Amyens, Jaques, and Others.*

SONG

> *Under the green wood Tree,*
> *who loves to lie with me,*
> *And turn his merry Note*
> *unto the sweet Bird's Throat,*
> *Come hither, come hither, come hither:*    5
> *Here shall he see*
> *no Enemy*
> *But Winter and rough Weather.*

JAQUES    More, more, I prethee more.

AMYENS    It will make you melancholy, Monsieur    10
Jaques.

JAQUES    I thank it: more, I prethee, more, I can
suck Melancholy out of a Song, as a Weasel
sucks Eggs. More, I prethee, more.

AMYENS    My Voice is ragged, I know I cannot please    15
you.

JAQUES    I do not desire you to please me, I do
desire you to sing. Come, more, another
Stanzo: call you 'em Stanzos?

AMYENS    What you will, Monsieur Jaques.    20

JAQUES    Nay, I care not for their Names, they owe
me nothing. Will you sing?

AMYENS    More at your Request, then to please my
self.

JAQUES    Well then, if ever I thank any Man, I'll    25
thank you: but that they call Complement is
like th' Encounter of the two Dog-apes. And when a
Man thanks me hartily, me thinks I have given
him a Penny, and he renders me the beggarly
Thanks. — Come sing; and you that will not,    30
hold your Tongues.

32–33 **cover the while**    set the table as I sing.

34    **look**    look for, seek.

36    **disputable**    given to philosophical discourse. But Jaques may also mean 'argumentative, prone to initiate debates'. Jaques asserts in his next sentence that he is inclined to keep his own thoughts to himself. The play provides scant support for such a claim. Compare II.i.67–68.

38    **warble**    sing. Jaques alludes to the bird imagery in lines 3–4.

40    **Who . . . shun**    whoever aspires to nothing more than 'settled low Content' (II.iii.66–68).

41    **live i'th' Sun**    expose himself to the sun and the elements with no roof over his head, trusting to Providence for sustenance. Compare II.iii.43–45.

42    **Seeking . . . eats**    foraging for his food (rather than growing or buying it), like the birds referred to in II.iii.43–44.

43    **pleas'd with what he gets**    happy with whatever he gleans for a given day, and with no desire to hoard more than he needs.

48    **Note**    both (a) tune, and (b) topic.

49    **in despight of my Invention**    either (a) in spite of my lack of artistic creativity, or (b) in defiance of my poetic powers. *Despight* recalls I.iii.26–27.

53    **turn Ass**    become a fool [by shunning 'Ambition', line 40, and taking leave of 'his Wealth and Ease' line 54, like Duke Senior, his companion Lords, and Rosalind, Celia, Orlando, and Adam].

55    **a . . . please**    to obey an unyielding 'humour' (see the notes to I.ii.274, 276). *Stubborn* recalls II.i.18–20.

56    **Ducdame**    This word is probably best explained as equivalent, both in metre (duc-dá-me) and in significance, to 'Come hither' (line 44) in the verse that Jaques is parodying. Whether it is adapted from an actual language, however, is anything but certain; scholars have found in it garbled versions of Latin, Italian, French, Gaelic, and Cymric phrases. Jaques's song presents a satirical version of the pastoral message in the original lyric; for the speaker in Jaques's ditty the only reason a person would leave 'Wealth and Ease' for 'Winter and rough Weather' is a 'stubborn Will' that makes him an 'Ass' rather than a wise man in search of rustic content. At the beginning of III.ii Touchstone expresses similar scepticism about the virtues of the simple life. Compare the Fool's comments in *King Lear*, II.ii.251–69.

AMYENS   Well, I'll end the Song. Sirs, cover the
   while, the Duke will drink under this Tree;
   he hath been all this Day to look you.
JAQUES   And I have been all this Day to avoid him:                    35
   He is too disputable for my Company. I think
   of as many Matters as he, but I give Heaven
   thanks, and make no Boast of them. Come, warble,
   come.

SONG *Altogether here.*

   *Who doth Ambition shun,*                                          40
      *and loves to live i'th' Sun,*
   *Seeking the Food he eats,*
      *and pleas'd with what he gets,*
   *Come hither, come hither, come hither,*
         *Here shall he see*                                          45
            *no Enemy*
   *But Winter and rough Weather.*

JAQUES   I'll give you a Verse to this Note, that
   I made yesterday in despight of my Invention.
AMYENS   And I'll sing it.                                            50
   Thus it goes:

   *If it do come to pass*
      *that any Man turn Ass,*
   *Leaving his Wealth and Ease*
      *a stubborn Will to please,*                                    55
   *Ducdame, ducdame, ducdame:*
         *Here shall he see,*

58    **gross**   palpable, obvious.

59    **And if**   if.

61    **Invocation**   summoning of spirits.

61–62 **to . . . Circle**   As he speaks these words, Jaques reminds his companions that they are arrayed in a circle around him. As an actor he also alludes to the circular amphitheatres in which dramatic performances took place in Athenian Greece. By so doing he informs the audiences in Shakespeare's own 'Wooden O' (see the note to V.iv.218) that they too are 'Fools' (gullible listeners) at his command. Compare V.iii.10.

63    **rail against**   upbraid, reproach. Compare I.i.65, where Orlando tells a 'first borne' that he has 'rail'd on' himself.

63–64 **the first borne of Egypt**   Jaques alludes to Exodus 12:29–33 and 16:2–3. After God struck down all the 'first borne' (first born and thus first carried) of the Egyptians, the Pharaoh allowed the captive Israelites to leave the country; once the Israelites discovered how hard their lot was in the wilderness, however, they began murmuring against Moses and wishing that they had died along with the Egyptians. Jaques is now murmuring about his travails in the Forest of Arden. But his words also remind us that a first-born duke is now in this modern wilderness (where Jaques 'rails against' his usurpation, II.i.60–63), and that he will soon be joined by two other first-borns (Celia and Rosalind) and by a younger brother (Orlando) who is fleeing the tyranny of yet another first-born (Oliver). Compare I.i.48–51.

65    **Banket**   banquet; a light dessert course of fruits, wine, and sometimes cheeses and sweetmeats.

II.vi   This scene takes place elsewhere in the forest.

1    **Deer**   dear. Compare I.iii.54, 70. The beginning of this scene echoes that of II.iv; for other parallels, see *King Lear*, IV.vi and V.ii.

2–3   **Here . . . Grave**   Calculate the length and width of the hole required for my burial. Compare *Romeo and Juliet*, III.iii.64–70.

4    **Heart**   courage (a word that derives from *cor*, the Latin word for 'heart').

6    **uncouth**   both (a) unknown, unfamiliar, and (b) uncivilized.

9    **Conceit**   mental state, conception (of your condition).

> gross Fools as he,
> And if he will come to me.

AMYENS    What's that 'Ducdame'?                              60
JAQUES    'Tis a Greek Invocation, to call Fools
   into a Circle. I'll go sleep if I can: if I
   cannot, I'll rail against all the first borne
   of Egypt.
AMYENS    And I'll go seek the Duke, his Banket is        65
   prepar'd.                                              *Exeunt.*

# Scene 6

*Enter Orlando and Adam.*

ADAM    Deer Master, I can go no further: O I die
   for Food. Here lie I down, and measure out my
   Grave. Farewell, kind Master.
ORLANDO    Why how now, Adam? No greater Heart
   in thee: live a little, comfort a little, cheer          5
   thy self a little. If this uncouth Forest
   yield any thing savage, I will either be Food
   for it, or bring it for Food to thee. Thy
   Conceit is nearer Death than thy Powers. For
   my sake be comfortable, hold Death a while at          10
   the Arm's end: I will here be with thee
   presently, and if I bring thee not something
   to eat, I will give thee leave to die. But if

---

10    **comfortable**    comforted, at ease.

12    **presently**    shortly.

13    **leave**    permission. Compare I.i.110, I.ii.163–64.

14    **Mocker of**   one who scorns or has no appreciation for. Compare I.ii.34–36, 218–19.

15    **Well said**   well done. Adam has given some indication that he is now feeling more cheerful.
     **cheerly**   of good cheer; optimistic.

17    **bleak**   inhospitable. Adam's situation is a consequence of the bleak heir whose 'churlish Disposition' (II.iv.81) has driven both Orlando and himself into 'the bleak Air' as exiles. Compare *Timon of Athens*, IV.iii.218–20.

19    **Desert**   unfrequented place (probably not a barren locale in the modern sense). See II.iv.73. *Dinner* refers to the midday meal.

II.vii   We return to the site of II.v, in the Forest of Arden. Modern editions normally supplement the Folio stage direction with 'A table set out.' But in all likelihood the table set in II.v (according to lines 32–33) has simply remained on the stage during the brief intervening scene. The Duke and his companions probably enter carrying food and drink, but there is no indication that anyone begins eating in this scene until after line 171.

2    **no where**   both (a) in no place, and (b) in no way.
     **find him like a Man**   discover him in the form of a man.

5    **compact of Jars**   patched together out of a jumble of discords.
     **Musical**   The Duke uses the term as a metaphor for inner harmony. *Merry* (line 4) recalls II.iv.1–3.

6    **Discord in the Spheres**   The crystalline spheres that were thought to revolve around the Earth (providing 'orbs' for the stars and planets) were believed to emit an ethereal music too refined in its concord (harmony) for mortal ears to hear. For a more extended treatment of 'sweet Harmony' and of the 'Affections dark' that can be expected from 'The Man that hath no Music in himself', see *The Merchant of Venice*, V.i.54–88.

9    **what a Life is this**   what kind of life is this? Compare II.iv.99.

10    **woe**   woo, entreat. Compare II.iii.50.

11    **look merrily**   appear cheerful. *Merrily* ('Cheerly', II.vi.15, 20) echoes line 4.

12    **a Fool i'th' Forest**   What excites Jaques is the fact that a court jester would be found so far from the court. See II.iv.67.

13    **motley**   a reference to the particoloured costume of professional clowns.

thou diest before I come, thou art a Mocker of
my Labour. Well said, thou look'st cheerly, and          15
I'll be with thee quickly: yet thou liest in
the bleak Air. Come, I will bear thee to some
Shelter, and thou shalt not die for lack of a
Dinner, if there live any thing in this Desert.
Cheerly, good Adam.                          *Exeunt.*   20

## Scene 7

*Enter Duke Senior and Lord[s],
like Outlaws.*

DUKE SENIOR  I think he be transform'd into a
      Beast,
  For I can no where find him like a Man.
I LORD  My Lord, he is but even now gone
      hence,
  Here was he merry, hearing of a Song.
DUKE SENIOR  If he, compact of Jars, grow Musical,    5
  We shall have shortly Discord in the Spheres:
  Go seek him, tell him I would speak with him.

*Enter Jaques.*

I LORD  He saves my Labour by his own Approach.
DUKE SENIOR  Why how now, Monsieur, what a Life
      is this
  That your poor Friends must woe your Company?        10
  What, you look merrily.
JAQUES  A Fool, a Fool: I met a Fool i'th' Forest,
  A motley Fool (a miserable World),
  As I do live by Food, I met a Fool,

15     **bask'd . . . Sun**   This phrase echoes II.v.40–41, 107–10.

16     **rail'd . . . Terms**   upbraided Fortune's injustices to good effect. Compare I.ii.34–60, II.v.62–64.

17     **good set Terms**   the conventional ways of describing Fortune's attributes. See the note to line 40.

19     **Call . . . Fortune**   Jaques alludes to the traditional view that those who rely on Fortune's favour for their happiness will eventually discover, to their pain, that they have been foolish to do so. Compare II.i.1–20, and see II.v.40–63.

20     **Dial**   either a portable sundial or a watch.
          **Poke**   carrying bag.

21     **lack-lustre**   sober, without a twinkle.

23     **wags**   goes, passes. But 'wags' also suggests a tail ('Tale', line 28), a term that often refers to the male member. In Latin, the word for *tail* is *penis*; see the note to line 66.

28     **thereby hangs a Tale**   a proverbial expression that normally means 'there's a lesson attached to this'. In the present context, the 'Tale' (tail) is identical with an overripe fruit, and that is precisely the 'moral' (line 29) of the Fool's meditation on the inevitability of decay and death. Compare II.iii.63–65. Here *Hour* probably puns on *whore*, and *rot* alludes to syphilis.

29     **moral**   'moralize' (II.i.43–44).

30     **Chanticleer**   a conventional name for a rooster, most familiar from Chaucer's 'Nun's Priest's Tale' in *The Canterbury Tales*.

32     **sans**   French for 'without'.

34     **Wear**   acceptable apparel (fashion) for these 'miserable' times. *Onely* (only) recalls I.ii.201; compare line 44.

38     **the Gift to know it**   both (a) the grace (wit, intelligence) to recognize their own beauty, and (b) any 'Gift' they demand from a 'Courtier' who seeks 'to know it' (to 'know' their youth and charm carnally). Compare I.ii.34–60, where Rosalind and Celia bandy words about how 'Fortune' dispenses her 'Gifts', and see the note to I.iii.50.

39     **remainder Biscuit**   leftover hardtack. A 'dry' brain preserved a good memory, and housed a dry wit. Compare *Twelfth Night*, I.iii.73–80.

Who laid him down, and bask'd him in the Sun,                          15
And rail'd on Lady Fortune in good Terms,
In good set Terms, and yet a motley Fool.
'Good morrow, Fool,' quoth I. 'No Sir,' quoth
     he,
'Call me not Fool till Heaven hath sent me
     Fortune,'
And then he drew a Dial from his Poke,                                 20
And looking on it, with a lack-lustre Eye,
Says, very wisely, 'It is ten a' clock:
Thus may we see,' quoth he, 'how the World
     wags.
'Tis but an Hour ago, since it was nine,
And after one Hour more, 'twill be eleven,                             25
And so from Hour to Hour, we ripe, and ripe,
And then from Hour to Hour, we rot, and rot,
And thereby hangs a Tale.' When I did hear
The motley Fool, thus moral on the Time,
My Lungs began to crow like Chanticleer,                               30
That Fools should be so deep contemplative:
And I did laugh, sans Intermission,
An Hour by his Dial. Oh Noble Fool.
A worthy Fool: Motley's the onely Wear.
DUKE SENIOR   What Fool is this?                                       35
JAQUES   O worthy Fool: one that hath been a
     Courtier
And says 'If Ladies be but young and fair,
They have the Gift to know it.' And in his
     Brain,
Which is as dry as the remainder Biscuit

40 **strange Places** both (a) hidden cupboards, and (b) peculiar and often marvellous topics of discourse. The word 'places' (commonplace or 'good set Terms', line 17) is a direct translation of the Greek word *topoi* ('topics'). The 'strange Places' in the Fool's brain correspond to the 'mangled Forms' of his deliberately 'motley' discourse (lines 13, 42–43).

41 **Observation** both (a) notes from experience, and (b) lore.

41–42 **he vents / In mangled Forms** The professional fool disguised his wisdom as folly (and protected himself from censure) by mingling pithy observations with apparent nonsense. See Viola's remarks about a 'Fellow' who is 'wise enough to play the Fool' in *Twelfth Night*, III.i.66–74.

44 **Suit** request, but with a pun on 'costume'. Another pun on apparel occurs in the next line with *weed* (a play on 'clothing' and 'weed out'). Compare I.ii.188–91, 255–57, 276–77, and I.iii.118–20.

46 **rank** both (a) overly abundant, and (b) diseased. See I.i.90–92, I.ii.112–13.

48 **Withall** with all, in addition (to my 'motley Coat', line 43).
**Charter** licence (liberty) to range freely. *Wind* recalls II.i.5–11.

50 **galled** rubbed, irritated. Here *Folly* refers to the Fool's satirical words, gestures, and actions, often designed to parody the foibles and vices of his audience.

55 **Seem . . . Bob** Most of today's editions add 'Not to' at the beginning of this line to repair deficiencies in both sense and metre. That provides what might seem to be the proper meaning; unfortunately it also makes 'If not' awkward at the end of the line. One way of construing lines 53–55 as they stand in the Folio (a way that yields a reading compatible with that which results from the standard emendation) is: 'He who knows himself to have been aptly struck by the Fool's jibe acts "foolishly", pretending not to be wise enough to know what has happened even though he inwardly feels the sting.' Like II.i.59, this line may be metrically defective (with one foot bobbed off, so to speak, to produce an iambic tetrameter).

56 **Folly** both (a) irrational behaviour, and (b) surrender to lust (see the note to II.iv.56–57, and compare *Twelfth Night*, III.i.35–41).
**anathomiz'd** both (a) anatomized, and (b) anathemized (damned). Compare I.i.165–67.

After a Voyage, he hath strange Places cramm'd                    40
With Observation, the which he vents
In mangled Forms. O that I were a Fool,
I am ambitious for a motley Coat.
DUKE SENIOR   Thou shalt have one.
JAQUES                                    It is my onely Suit,     45
Provided that you weed your better Judgements
Of all Opinion that grows rank in them,
That I am wise. I must have Liberty
Withall, as large a Charter as the Wind,
To blow on whom I please, for so Fools have:
And they that are most galled with my Folly,                      50
They most must laugh. 'And why, Sir, must they
    so?'
The Why is plain as Way to Parish Church:
He that a Fool doth very wisely hit
Doth very foolishly, although he smart,
Seem senseless of the Bob. If not,                                55
The Wise-man's Folly is anathomiz'd
Even by the squand'ring Glances of the Fool.
Invest me in my Motley: give me leave
To speak my Mind, and I will through and
    through
Cleanse the foul Body of th' infected World,                      60
If they will patiently receive my Medicine.

---

57   **squand'ring Glances**   random, seemingly wasteful, scattershot
        hits.

58   **invest**   dress, outfit, 'suit' (line 44).
        **leave**   liberty, licence. Compare II.vi.13.

60–61 **Cleanse . . . Medicine**   purge the diseased 'World' of its
        infection if its inhabitants will 'patiently' (passively and
        uncomplainingly) allow themselves to be my patients. See
        I.iii.82, and compare the medical imagery in I.i.26–27, 90–92,
        II.i.12–14, 58–59, II.iii.45–53, 63–65, II.vii.64–69. *Mind*
        recalls I.ii.245–46.

63    **Counter** a small metal disc to be used in calculations. Jaques's question is an expression employed in wagering; the bet he stakes is of no more value than a counterfeit coin. Compare *The Tempest*, II.i.21–26, for a similar exchange. Here *for a Counter* can also mean 'for a reply or counter-argument', either Jaques's or Duke Senior's; compare V.iv.83–85.

65    **Libertine** a person given to excessive 'Liberty' (line 47, recalling I.iii.141–42), loose, ungoverned behaviour. The Duke's 'Counter' (rebuttal) suggests that Jaques lacks the moral discipline to sit in judgement on the vices of others.

66    **brutish Sting** animal lust (based on an analogy between a bee's sting and a male's genital 'tail'), the stimulus of desire.

67    **imbossed** swollen.
   **headed Evils** headstrong diseases that, like infected boils, have come to a head. Duke Senior implies that Jaques is an undisciplined and unmanageable carrier of venereal disease.

68    **Licence . . . Foot** a 'Wit' that has been chartered to wander wherever it wishes (see the notes to I.ii.51, 53, 61, 76, and II.vii.48). *Foot* plays on the French verb *fourtre* (copulate), as in *The Merry Wives of Windsor*, II.i.118–25, where Pistol warns Ford to watch his wife because 'Thieves do foot by Night', and in *Henry V*, III.iv.54–63, where Princess Katherine expresses shock over '*Le Foot et le Count*'. Compare *King Lear*, III.ii.31–34, III.iv.99–103.

71    **tax** take to task and thus offend. In lines 70–72 Jaques's point is that 'Pride' (ostentatious display) is so rampant as to be virtually universal. Since everyone is guilty, then, no one in particular should feel singled out for attack. Compare I.ii.88–90, and see lines 85–87.
   **private Party** particular person. Jaques hints at what Troilus refers to as his 'private Part' in *Troilus and Cressida*, II.ii.124, and at the 'Pride' (line 70) of arousal as Shakespeare describes it in Sonnet 151, lines 10–12.

73    **Till . . . ebb** to the point where the very means of ostentation have become exhausted and thus ebb. *Weary* echoes II.iv.3. *Means* (playing on *Main*, a word for both the 'Sea' and the land that seems to recede or 'ebb' at high tide) recalls I.ii.257 and II.iii.25, 51.

DUKE SENIOR    Fie on thee. I can tell what thou
   wouldst do.
JAQUES    What, for a Counter, would I do but good?
DUKE SENIOR    Most mischievous foul Sin, in chiding
   Sin:
  For thou thy self hast been a Libertine,          65
  As sensual as the brutish Sting it self,
  And all th' imbossed Sores, and headed Evils,
  That thou with Licence of free Foot hast
   caught,
  Wouldst thou disgorge into the general World.
JAQUES         Why who cries out on Pride,     70
  That can therein tax any private Party:
  Doth it not flow as hugely as the Sea,
  Till that the weary very Means do ebb.
  What Woman in the City do I name
  When that I say the City Woman bears      75
  The Cost of Princes on unworthy Shoulders?
  Who can come in, and say that I mean her,
  When such a one as she, such is her Neighbour?
  Or what is he of basest Function,
  That says his Bravery is not on my Cost,     80

---

75–76 **the City . . . Shoulders**    Here *Cost of* can mean 'wealth
     equivalent to that of', with the implication that citizens' wives
     are 'unworthy' of the luxurious apparel normally associated
     only with those of royal station. But Jaques may also be
     referring to the 'Cost' (expenditures and diseases) to the
     'Princes' when 'the City Woman bears' them sexually. See the
     note to line 38.

79    **of basest Function**    of the most menial occupation.

80    **Bravery**    both (a) fancy apparel, and (b) brazenly lavish
     lifestyle.
     **on my Cost**    costing me anything; any of my business.

81–82 **but ... Speech** who doesn't thereby show that his 'Folly' (unwise or irresponsible behaviour) is a perfect fit for the vice my words are criticizing. *Suits* echoes lines 44–47, 58.

82 **Mettle** spirit, merit. Jaques may be punning on *metal*, with particular reference to the touchstone used to test metals for purity. See the note to I.ii.59.

84 **do him right** correctly diagnose the aspect of him that is 'infected' (line 60).

85 **free** untainted by disease or folly. Compare line 69, where *free* means 'unrestrained'.

87 **come** Modern editions usually emend this verb to *comes*. But it may be that, seeing Orlando enter with his sword drawn, Jaques assumes that other robbers will be entering right behind him.

88 **Forbear** abstain (cease eating). So also in line 97.
**eat none** eaten none.

89 **Necessity be serv'd** Need (here personified) be given its share of food.

90 **Of ... of?** What kind of fowl produced this strutting, audacious rooster?

91 **bolden'd** emboldened, made 'rude' (line 92) and aggressive.

92 **rude** rustic, uncivilized. Compare II.iii.31–34.

93 **That ... Empty** that you seem so lacking in courtesy. *Empty* frequently means 'famished' in Shakespeare, and that sense is pertinent here; compare I.ii.201–3, and see *The Taming of the Shrew*, IV.i.191, *2 Henry VI*, III.i.247–49, *3 Henry VI*, I.i.270–72, and *Romeo and Juliet*, V.iii.37–39.

94–95 **the ... Distress** the sharp pricking of the 'Distress' that results from desperation over a stomach 'bare' of food. *Point* recalls I.iii.119–20, and *thorny* echoes *brutish Sting* (line 66).

95 **Shew** show, display.

96 **in-land bred** born and reared in a cultivated setting. *In-land* is perhaps best understood by its opposite, *outlandish* (rustic, unexposed to proper manners), a concept implicit in the reference to *Outlaws* in the stage direction that opens this scene. *Bred* recalls I.i.1–14, 113–16; *smooth* echoes I.iii.81–83.

97 **some Nurture** a degree of education. Orlando's modesty about his 'Nurture' recalls I.i.1–27.

Thinking that I mean him, but therein suits
His Folly to the Mettle of my Speech,
There then, how then, what then, let me see
    wherein
My Tongue hath wrong'd him. If it do him right,
Then he hath wrong'd himself: if he be free,                    85
Why then my Taxing like a Wild-goose flies
Unclaim'd of any Man. But who come here?

*Enter Orlando.*

ORLANDO    Forbear, and eat no more.
JAQUES                        Why I have eat none yet.
ORLANDO    Nor shalt not, till Necessity be serv'd.
JAQUES    – Of what kind should this Cock come of?        90
DUKE SENIOR    Art thou thus bolden'd, Man, by thy
    Distress?
Or else a rude Despiser of good Manners,
That in Civility thou seem'st so Empty?
ORLANDO    You touch'd my Vein at first, the thorny
    Point
Of bare Distress hath ta'en from me the Shew              95
Of smooth Civility: yet am I in-land bred,
And know some Nurture. But forbear, I say,
He dies that touches any of this Fruit,
Till I and my Affairs are answered.
JAQUES    And you will not be answer'd with Reason,       100
I must die.
DUKE SENIOR    What would you have? Your Gentleness
    shall force,

---

100    **And**    if.

102    **Gentleness**    both (a) gentility (the bearing and manners
        associated with 'gentle' birth and breeding), and (b) tender,
        peaceful behaviour. In lines 102–3 Duke Senior plays on the
        paradox that gentleness is more forceful than force in this
        situation. Compare I.i.20–23, 45–48, 175–78, II.iii.5–6.

108 **Countenance** appearance, face. This word recalls I.i.17–20.

110 **Desert inaccessible** remote, unpopulated wilderness. *Desert* echoes II.vi.17–19.

111 **melancholy** sombre. Compare II.v.10–14.

112 **Loose and neglect** waste and spend carelessly. *Loose* (both 'lose' and 'loose', release) recalls I.ii.113.
**creeping** slow-moving, stealthy. Compare I.ii.161.

113 **better** happier, more prosperous. Compare II.iv.68–69, and see line 120.

114 **knoll'd** knell'd, tolled.

115 **sate** sat.

118 **Enforcement** compulsion. Here Orlando uses the term paradoxically, to mean 'persuasion', the opposite of what *force* normally implies. He plays on what Duke Senior has said in lines 102–3; compare lines 124–26.

119 **blush** visibly express my embarrassment and remorse for my shameful intrusion.

123 **engend'red** conceived, given birth to.

124 **in Gentleness** with the ease and etiquette expected in a civilized society [and thus without any need to use or fear coercion or violence].

125 **upon Command** at your request, for the asking [as if you had demanded it by 'strong Enforcement', line 118].

127 **forbear** abstain from (as in line 88).

131 **suffic'd** given sufficient food.

132 **weak** debilitating, enfeebling. Orlando's analogy between old Adam and a tender 'Fawn' (line 128) recalls what Rosalind has said in II.iv.4–8; compare the deer Imagery in I.ii.3, II.i.21–65, II.iv.33, II.v.27–30.

More than your Force move us to Gentleness.
ORLANDO    I almost die for Food, and let me have it.
DUKE SENIOR    Sit down and feed, and welcome to our
 Table.                                                                                105
ORLANDO    Speak you so gently? Pardon me, I pray
 you,
 I thought that all things had been Savage here,
 And therefore put I on the Countenance
 Of stern Commandment. But what e'er you are
 That in this Desert inaccessible,                                          110
 Under the Shade of melancholy Boughs,
 Loose and neglect the creeping Hours of Time:
 If ever you have look'd on better Days,
 If ever been where Bells have knoll'd to
  Church,
 If ever sate at any Good Man's Feast,                                115
 If ever from your Eyelids wip'd a Tear,
 And know what 'tis to pity, and be pitied,
 Let Gentleness my strong Enforcement be,
 In the which Hope, I blush, and hide my Sword.
DUKE SENIOR    True is it, that we have seen better
 Days,                                                                                   120
 And have with holy Bell been knoll'd to Church,
 And sat at Good Men's Feasts, and wip'd our
  Eyes
 Of Drops that sacred Pity hath engend'red:
 And therefore sit you down in Gentleness,
 And take upon Command, what Help we have      125
 That to your Wanting may be minist'red.
ORLANDO    Then but forbear your Food a little
 while,
 Whiles (like a Doe) I go to find my Fawn,
 And give it Food. There is an old poor Man
 Who after me, hath many a weary Step              130
 Limp'd in pure Love: till he be first suffic'd,
 Oppress'd with two weak Evils, Age and Hunger,
 I will not touch a bit.
DUKE SENIOR   Go find him out,

134 **waste** consume. Compare II.iv.95–96.

135 **Comfort** care, provision. Compare II.vi.9–10. Orlando's thanks recall II.v.25–30.

136 **we are not all alone unhappy** we are not the only ones in the world who are unfortunate.

137 **Theatre** Duke Senior alludes to one of the most popular rhetorical *topoi* (see the note to line 40) of the Renaissance, the ancient commonplace known as *theatrum mundi* (the notion that the world is like a theatre).

138 **then** Here the primary sense is 'than'; but as in I.ii.31 and II.v.23, 'then' can be pertinent too.

139 **All . . . Stage** This clause is a variation on the Latin motto, *Totus mundus agit histrionem* ('the whole world plays the actor'), which adorned the Globe playhouse from the time it opened in mid-1599.

140 **merely Players** nothing more than actors. Compare *Macbeth*, V.v.24–28.

142 **Parts** roles. Compare II.ii.13, and line 155.

144 **Mewling** crying (like a cat's meowing). *Creeping* (crawling), line 146, echoes line 112.

148 **woeful** both (a) 'woo-full' (compare line 10), replete with devices to woo his lady, and (b) doleful (begging her to pity his love-woes, as in II.iv.25–45 and III.v.1–34).

150 **strange Oaths** exotic forms of swearing. Compare 'strange Places' (line 40).
**bearded like the Pard** mustachioed like a leopard or panther. *Bearded* recalls I.ii.77–80.

151 **Jealous in Honour** zealous in guarding against any slights on his reputation.
**sudden** impulsive, rash; swift to retaliate violently. Compare I.ii.292–93, II.iv.100.

152 **Bubble** Jaques's description of 'reputation' emphasizes how ephemeral one's credit for 'Honour' (line 151) can be. Compare Iago's dismissal of 'Reputation' as 'an idle and most false Imposition; oft got without Merit, and lost without Deserving', in *Othello*, II.iii.271–73.

And we will nothing waste till you return.
ORLANDO   I thank ye, and be blest for your good
  Comfort.                                    [*Exit*]   135
DUKE SENIOR   Thou seest we are not all alone
  unhappy:
  This wide and universal Theatre
  Presents more woeful Pageants then the Scene
  Wherein we play in.
JAQUES                    All the World's a Stage,
  And all the Men and Women merely Players;                140
  They have their Exits and their Entrances,
  And one Man in his Time plays many Parts,
  His Acts being seven Ages. At first the Infant,
  Mewling and puking in the Nurse's Arms.
  Then the whining School-boy with his Satchel            145
  And shining Morning Face, creeping like Snail
  Unwillingly to School. And then the Lover,
  Sighing like Furnace, with a woeful Ballad
  Made to his Mistress' Eyebrow. Then a Soldier,
  Full of strange Oaths, and bearded like the
    Pard,                                                  150
  Jealous in Honour, sudden, and quick in Quarrel,
  Seeking the Bubble Reputation
  Even in the Canon's Mouth. And then the Justice,
  In fair round Belly, with good Capon lin'd,
  With Eyes severe, and Beard of formal Cut,              155

---

153   **the Canon's Mouth**   both (a) the jaws of the law (canon) itself,
      notwithstanding its prohibitions against private duelling, and
      (b) the barrel of a cannon that is set to discharge its lethal
      ammunition. Compare the *Cannon* / *Canon* pun in *Hamlet*,
      I.ii.132, where in the Second Quarto text the title character
      complains that 'the Everlasting' has 'fix'd / His Cannon
      'gainst seal Slaughter'. Also see *King Lear*, III.iv.8–10.

154   **Capon**   a rooster castrated and fattened for eating. See the note
      to I.ii.102.

156 **Saws** proverbial sayings, 'sententious' remarks (V.iv.65–66).
**modern Instances** everyday examples of the wisdom in 'wise
Saws'.

158 **Pantaloon** the tight-trousered old man of Italian *commedia
dell'arte*. In this description, the *s*-sounds imitate the old
wheezer's 'Whistles' (line 163).

160 **well sav'd** probably a reference to the 'tightness' of his 'Pouch'
(line 159) or moneybag. Compare the old 'Miser' whom
Touchstone evokes in V.iv.60–64.

161 **Shank** leg, and particularly the calf.

163 **his** either (a) his (referring to the 'pantaloon') or (b) its
(referring to 'Voice'). The usual Elizabethan forms for our
pronoun *its* were *it* and *his*.

164 **History** story; chronicle, narrative.

165 **mere Oblivion** either (a) total forgetfulness (if this phrase refers
to senility), or (b) complete obliteration from 'Remembrance',
I.i.66–67 (if this phrase refers to a decaying corpse). *Mere*
recalls I.ii.261 and II.i.61; *strange* (odd), line 164, echoes line
150.

166 **Sans** French for 'without' (as in line 32).

167 **venerable Burthen** time-honoured burden. Cultivated
Elizabethan playgoers would have seen a parallel between
Orlando, with his weary old servant on his shoulders, and
Aeneas carrying his father Anchises out of the flaming ruins of
Troy in Book II of Virgil's *Aeneid*. The entry of old Adam
provides an amusing illusttration of Jaques's 'Last Scene of
all' (line 163), but it also suggests that 'Age' need not be
'unregarded' (II.iii.42): like Orlando, Duke Senior rewards
Adam's gentleness and generosity with reverence and
hospitality.

168 **And let him feed** In all likelihood, the six-syllable blank space
between this and the next line of verse is designed to supply a
pause for Orlando to set Adam down at the table. *Feed* echoes
II.iv.72–102, where Corin wishes he could provide for Celia,
Rosalind's charge, in a way that parallels Duke Senior's offer
of 'Comfort' (line 135) here.

169 **for him** for his sake, on his behalf.

171 **fall to** begin eating.

Full of wise Saws, and modern Instances,
And so he plays his Part. The sixt Age shifts
Into the lean and slipper'd Pantaloon,
With Spectacles on Nose, and Pouch on Side,
His youthful Hose well sav'd, a World too wide,                160
For his shrunk Shank, and his big manly Voice,
Turning again toward childish treble Pipes,
And Whistles in his Sound. Last Scene of all,
That ends this strange eventful History,
Is second Childishness, and mere Oblivion,                    165
Sans Teeth, sans Eyes, sans Taste, sans
    every thing.

*Enter Orlando with Adam.*

DUKE SENIOR   Welcome: set down your venerable
    Burthen,
And let him feed.
ORLANDO   I thank you most for him.
ADAM                                    So had you need,
I scarce can speak to thank you for my self.                  170
DUKE SENIOR   Welcome, fall to: I will not trouble
    you
As yet to question you about your Fortunes.
— Give us some Music, and good Cousin, sing.

---

173   **Music**   Duke Senior probably calls for non-vocal harmony, no
      doubt supplied by a lute, and perhaps accompanied in some
      performances by additional instruments. In all likelihood,
      'good Cousin' is addressed to Amyens, as in II.v, and no
      doubt his fingers play the strings while his voice intones the
      song.

174    **Winter Wind**    Once again we are reminded that Arden
       represents not the perpetual spring of the Golden Age (as
       suggested in I.i.126) but the 'adversity' of biting cold weather.
       Compare lines 47–51.

177    **keen**    sharp. Lines 174–79 parallel *King Lear*, I.iv.289–303 and
       III.ii.1–24.

179    **rude**    uncivilized, with wordplay on (a) discourteous (as with
       rude words) and (b) foul (not sweetened for polite company),
       rather than clean and 'well breath'd' (I.ii.228). Compare line
       92. Here *rude* plays on *rood*, the holy cross (see the note to
       II.iv.12) that symbolizes both 'Man's Ingratitude' (line 176)
       and the 'green Holly' (line 180) of God's grace. See *Hamlet*,
       III.iv.13.

180    **green Holly**    As an evergreen, the holly symbolizes a sturdiness
       of character that is proof against the winter's 'Breath'. The
       word *holly* was a variant on *holy* – which was often
       pronounced the same way, a fact preserved in today's
       pronunciation of *holiday*, *Holyroodhouse* (the royal palace in
       Edinburgh), and *Hollywood* (a name that can be construed as
       a reference to the 'holy wood' of the 'rood') – and this led, no
       doubt, to its association with the Christmas season.

181    **fayning**    The Folio spelling conveys the meanings of both (a)
       faining (longing, wishful thinking), and (b) feigning
       (pretending, deceiving). Compare III.iii.18–30.
       **mere Folly**    either (a) nothing more than infatuation (foolishly
       misplaced affection), or (b) unmitigated lust (see the first note
       to line 56).

185    **nigh**    near (that is, deep, 'nigh' to the bone).

186    **Benefits forgot**    favours unregistered or unappreciated by those
       who have neglected to manifest their gratitude. Compare lines
       165, 175–76, 188–89, and see II.v.25–30.

187    **warp**    disfigure, turn to ice.

189    **rememb'red not**    not thanked or valued. See *Hamlet*,
       IV.v.177–79, where Ophelia says, 'There's Rosemary, that's
       for Remembrance', and echoes all the play's other
       exhortations to 'remember'.

196    **Effigies**    image, resemblance.

SONG

> Blow, blow, thou Winter Wind,
> Thou art not so unkind                                           175
>     as Man's Ingratitude.
> Thy Tooth is not so keen
> Because thou art not seen,
>     although thy Breath be rude.
> Heigh ho, sing heigh ho, unto the green Holly,                   180
> Most Friendship is fayning, most Loving, mere
>     Folly:
>         Then heigh ho, the Holly,
>         This Life is most jolly.

> Freeze, freeze, thou bitter Sky,
> That dost not bite so nigh                                       185
>     as Benefits forgot:
> Though thou the Waters warp,
> Thy Sting is not so sharp
>     as Friends rememb'red not.
> Heigh ho, sing heigh ho unto the green Holly,                    190
> Most Friendship is fayning, most Loving, mere
>     Folly:
>         Then heigh ho, the Holly,
>         This Life is most jolly.

DUKE SENIOR   If that you were the good Sir
    Rowland's Son,
  As you have whisper'd faithfully you were,                       195
  And as mine Eye doth his Effigies witness,

197 **limn'd**   painted, depicted.
  **living**   surviving. The alliteration in the phrase 'limn'd and
    living' links past and present in sound as well as in sense. And
    it provides another witness to what Orlando has referred to as
    'the Spirit of my Father, which I think is within me'
    (I.i.24–25). Duke Senior's manner of identifying himself – in
    itself a certification of both his values and his virtues – recalls
    I.ii.231–52, where the usurping Duke Frederick and the
    legitimate Duke Senior are contrasted in terms of their
    attitudes towards 'the good Sir Rowland' (see line 194).

199 **Residue of your Fortune**   remainder of your story.

201 **right**   truly. Compare 'right suddenly' in II.iv.101.

Most truly limn'd, and living in your Face,
Be truly welcome hither: I am the Duke
That lov'd your Father, the Residue of your
    Fortune
Go to my Cave, and tell me. – Good Old Man,        200
Thou art right welcome, as thy Master is.
– Support him by the Arm. – Give me your Hand,
And let me all your Fortunes understand.        *Exeunt.*

III.i   This scene takes place in the palace of Duke Frederick.

2       **were . . . Mercy** if the larger half of me were not composed of mercy. In due course this line will prove prophetic; see V.iv.160–73.

3–4     **I . . . present** I would not look elsewhere for an object or reason for revenge, knowing that you are here for the punishing. Compare II.ii.16–18.

4       **look to it** see that it is done. Compare I.i.155–56, where Oliver uses the same warning in his remarks to Charles the Wrastler.

6       **with Candle** looking into every dark corner. Duke Frederick's expression is probably an allusion to Luke 15:8, where Jesus says, 'What woman having ten pieces of silver, if she lose one piece, doth not light a candle, and sweep the house, and seek diligently till she find it?' Ironically, the biblical context pertains to a search with a quite different purpose than the kind Duke Frederick has in mind. When she finds the silver and rejoices, the woman in the parable illustrates one of Jesus' teachings about divine grace: 'Likewise, I say unto you, there is joy in the presence of the angels of God over one sinner that repenteth' (Luke 15:10). Eventually Duke Frederick's reference to this passage will prove pertinent in ways that he and Oliver have no way of anticipating at this point.

7       **turn** both (a) return, and (b) direct, bend.

10      **Worth seizure** that is, everything you have that is of sufficient value to repay our efforts to claim it.

11      **quit . . . Mouth** acquit yourself by means of your brother's testimony [that you are innocent of involvement in my daughter's escape]. *Quit* recalls *acquit*, I.i.133–35, and *clear*, I.i.181–82. *Mouth* (voice) echoes II.vii.151–53.

12      **think against thee** suspect you of having committed.

14      **knew my Heart** were acquainted with my true sentiments. Compare I.i.175–80, I.ii.251–52, I.iii.18–19, 122, II.iv.4–5.

15      **More Villain thou** Even the reprobate Duke Frederick can see that Oliver's 'defence' is actually an offence even worse than the crime he stands accused of. See the notes to I.iii.74, III.ii.2, 6.

15–18   **Well . . . going** These lines are probably addressed to an attendant, ordering him to evict Oliver, who is the sole heir to Sir Rowland's 'House and Lands'. See the notes to II.ii.17, 18.

# ACT III

## Scene 1

*Enter Duke [Frederick], Lords, and Oliver.*

DUKE    Not see him since? Sir, Sir, that cannot be:
But were I not the better part made Mercy,
I should not seek an absent Argument
Of my Revenge, thou present. But look to it,
Find out thy Brother wheresoe'er he is,          5
Seek him with Candle: bring him dead or living
Within this twelvemonth, or turn thou no more
To seek a Living in our Territory.
Thy Lands and all things that thou dost call
    thine,
Worth seizure, do we seize into our Hands,       10
Till thou canst quit thee by thy Brother's
    Mouth
Of what we think against thee.
OLIVER    Oh that your Highness knew my Heart in this:
I never lov'd my Brother in my Life.
DUKE    More Villain thou. Well, push him out of Doors,    15

16   **of such a nature**   of the appropriate type (that is, functionaries whose job is to handle these evictions).

17   **Make an Extent**   draw up a writ of extent (a legal document to appraise a piece of property to its full value before turning it over to the party in whose behalf it is being seized, normally for debt).

18   **expediently**   speedily.
**turn him going**   send him on his way. *Turn* echoes lines 7–8.

III.ii   This scene returns us to the Forest of Arden. III.ii could be treated as a ten-line scene, since the stage seems to be momentarily cleared after Orlando's departure; but the Folio editors, who did mark brief scenes in II.ii, II.vi, III.i, and IV.ii, chose not to do so here. Perhaps Corin and the Clown enter before Orlando's exit is concluded.

1   **Hang there**   Orlando attaches a sheet of paper to a tree (probably represented by one of the pillars on the theatre stage).
**in witness of**   as a testimony to. *Witness* echoes II.vii.194–98.

2   **thrice crowned Queen of Night**   Orlando addresses the goddess referred to as 'triple Hecate' in the Epilogue to *A Midsummer Night's Dream*: as Goddess of the Moon she reigned as Cynthia, Phoebe, or Luna; on Earth she manifested herself as Diana the Huntress; and in Hades she was known as either Hecate or Proserpina.

3   **pale Sphere above**   the Moon. In her personae as Cynthia and as Diana, the 'Queen of Night' was revered as the Goddess of Chastity and the patroness of virgins.

4   **Thy Huntress' Name**   Orlando refers to Rosalind. What he doesn't realize, of course, is that she will soon be 'hunting' him.
**sway**   both (a) rule, control, and (b) cause to swing, veer, or tilt.

6   **character**   inscribe, write (using the characters of the alphabet).

10   **unexpressive**   inexpressible, indescribable. Orlando's description of Rosalind is a reminder of the 'unexpressive' (inarticulate) wrestlers of I.ii.230, 259–77.

13   **in respect of**   with regard to.

15   **naught**   literally, nothing; here, both (a) worthless, and (b) naughty, wicked. See lines 34–90, and compare I.i.37–38.

And let my Officers of such a nature
Make an Extent upon his House and Lands:
Do this expediently, and turn him going.        *Exeunt.*

# Scene 2

*Enter Orlando.*

ORLANDO    Hang there, my Verse, in witness of my
    Love.
    — And thou, thrice crowned Queen of Night,
        survey
    With thy chaste Eye, from thy pale Sphere
        above,
    Thy Huntress' Name, that my full Life doth
        sway.
    — O Rosalind, these Trees shall be my Books,              5
    And in their Barks my Thoughts I'll character,
    That every Eye which in this Forest looks
    Shall see thy Virtue witness'd every where.
    — Run, run, Orlando, carve on every Tree
    The fair, the chaste, and unexpressive She.              10
                                        *Exit.*

*Enter Corin and Clown.*

CORIN    And like you this Shepherd's Life, Master
    Touchstone?
CLOWN    Truly, Shepherd, in respect of it self, it
    is a Good Life; but in respect that it is a
    Shepherd's Life, it is naught. In respect that              15
    it is Solitary, I like it very well: but in

17   **Private**   both (a) lonely, and (b) given to privation
      (deprivation), like the life of a private, a common soldier.
      Compare II.vii.70–71.
      **Vild**   vile.

20   **tedious**   boring, wearisome.
      **Spare**   sparing, lacking in luxury.

23   **Stomach**   appetite.
      **Philosophy**   wisdom, intellectual sophistication.

25–33 **No . . . Kindred**   Having just heard Touchstone describe the
      obvious differences between country life and court life, Corin
      responds with a set of equally obvious definitions of everyday
      phenomena. *Means* echoes II.vii.73; *Content* recalls
      II.iv.16–18; *Fire* harks back to I.ii.47–48 and II.iii.16–24.

32–33 **complain of good Breeding**   bemoan his lack of good genes
      ('Nature') or education ('Art'). Corin's words recall what
      Orlando has told Adam and Oliver in I.i.1–78; *Breeding*
      echoes II.vii.96.

33   **dull**   unintelligent (lacking in a trainable 'Nature'). *Wit* (lines
      31–33) recalls II.iv.39–60.

34   **a natural Philosopher**   Touchstone's mock-solemn
      commendation refers to either (a) a philosopher of Nature
      (that is, a student of science), or (b) a 'natural' (idiot)
      attempting to be a philosopher; see the note to I.ii.53. He
      probably admires Corin's ability to 'philosophize' in a mode
      that compares favourably to Touchstone's own parody of
      learned discourse.

38   **I hope**   both (a) I hope you are wrong, and (b) I exhibit hope,
      the state of those who trust in God's grace and expect to enter
      Heaven. The opposite of hope, despair, is the unpardonable
      sin that assures damnation. For hope as a Christian virtue, see
      Romans 8:24–25 ('we are saved by hope') and 1 Corinthians
      13:13.

39–40 **like . . . side**   like a half-baked egg, with only the side that has
      been exposed to heat edible. Touchstone's point is that, for all
      his 'natural' qualities, Corin lacks the courtly cultivation that
      would make him a complete 'Philosopher'.

42–45 **Why . . . Damnation**   Touchstone's 'logic' in this speech
      depends on his deliberately confusing two senses of *good*: (a)
      socially 'correct', and (b) morally 'right'.

46   **parlous State**   perilous condition (your soul in danger of
      perdition unless you repent). Compare IV.i.201–2.

respect that it is Private, it is a very Vild
Life. Now in respect it is in the Fields, it
pleaseth me well: but in respect it is not in
the Court, it is tedious. As it is a Spare                    20
Life, look you, it fits my Humour well: but as
there is no more Plenty in it, it goes much
against my Stomach. Hast any Philosophy in
thee, Shepherd?

CORIN   No more, but that I know the more one Sickens,   25
the worse at Ease he is: and that he that wants
Money, Means, and Content is without three good
Friends. That the Property of Rain is to wet,
and Fire to burn. That good Pasture makes fat
Sheep; and that a great cause of the Night is         30
lack of the Sun; that he that hath learned no
Wit by Nature, nor Art, may complain of good
Breeding, or comes of a very dull Kindred.

CLOWN   Such a one is a natural Philosopher. Wast
ever in Court, Shepherd?                              35

CORIN   No truly.

CLOWN   Then thou art damn'd.

CORIN   Nay, I hope.

CLOWN   Truly thou art damn'd, like an ill roasted
Egg, all on one side.                                40

CORIN   For not being at Court? your Reason.

CLOWN   Why, if thou never wast at Court, thou never
saw'st good Manners: if thou never saw'st good
Manners, then thy Manners must be wicked, and
Wickedness is Sin, and Sin is Damnation. Thou        45
art in a parlous State, Shepherd.

47 **whit** bit.

50–51 **you . . . Hands** you do not greet one another at court without kissing hands. *Mockable* echoes II.vi.13–15.

52 **uncleanly** insanitary, unhygienic. Compare lines 71–72.

54 **Instance** supporting example, proof.
**briefly** both (a) quickly, and (b) concisely.

55 **Ewes** female sheep.

56 **Fells** fleeces. *Greasy* recalls II.i.55–57; *sweat* (lines 57–59) echoes II.iii.56–61.

61 **hard** rough, calloused. Compare II.iv.44–45.

65 **Surgery** medical care. Tar was often used to cover and soothe sore spots.

67 **Civet** a musky perfume derived from the secretions of a civet cat's anal glands.

68–69 **Thou . . . Flesh** You corpse (food for worms) in comparison with a healthy embodiment of humanity. Touchstone is probably playing on a bawdy sense for both *Worm's-meat* and *Piece of Flesh*. Compare *Romeo and Juliet*, I.i.31–32, where 'Piece of Flesh' refers to the male member, and see *Much Ado About Nothing*, IV.ii.86–90, where the asinine Dogberry hints at that sense without realizing that he is encouraging his listeners to 'suspect' his 'Place' (line 80).

70 **perpend** pay attention, consider. But Touchstone is probably punning on another Latin sense: 'hang' (with the same implications as in II.vii.28) like a tail of 'worm's-meat' (line 68) from a civet cat's rear (see the note to line 67).

70–71 **of . . . Birth** of an even lower 'Kindred' (line 34). *Baser* echoes II.vii.79 and recalls II.iii.31–33; *uncleanly* echoes line 52.

71 **Flux** overflow, secretion. Compare II.i.51–52.

73 **rest** rest my case; cease trying to match your wits. In the next line Touchstone uses the word to mean 'be content to remain', and thereby accuses Corin of a spiritual sloth that can result in damnation; see 1 Thessalonians 5:1–13, where the Apostle Paul says 'let us not sleep' but 'let us watch and be sober' lest we be caught unawares on 'the day of the Lord'.

CORIN   Not a whit, Touchstone. Those that are good
Manners at the Court are as ridiculous in the
Country as the Behaviour of the Country is most
mockable at the Court. You told me you salute       50
not at the Court, but you kiss your Hands;
that Courtesy would be uncleanly if Courtiers
were Shepherds.

CLOWN   Instance, briefly: come, Instance.

CORIN   Why are we still handling our Ewes, and      55
their Fells you know are greasy.

CLOWN   Why, do not your Courtiers Hands sweat?
and is not the Grease of a Mutton as wholesome
as the Sweat of a Man? Shallow, shallow. A
better Instance, I say: come.                        60

CORIN   Besides, our Hands are hard.

CLOWN   Your Lips will feel them the sooner. Shallow
again: a more sounder Instance, come.

CORIN   And they are often tarr'd over with the
Surgery of our Sheep: and would you have us        65
kiss Tar? The Courtier's Hands are perfum'd
with Civet.

CLOWN   Most shallow, Man: thou Worm's-meat in
respect of a good Piece of Flesh indeed. Learn
of the Wise and perpend: Civet is of a baser        70
Birth than Tar, the very uncleanly Flux of a
Cat. Mend the Instance, Shepherd.

CORIN   You have too Courtly a Wit for me, I'll rest.

CLOWN   Wilt thou rest damn'd? God help thee,

75 **make Incision in thee** cure you by a medicinal cut. Touchstone alludes to what Corin has said in lines 64–66; he implies that unless he receives 'Surgery', Corin is a lost 'Sheep' (see Isaiah 53:6 and Matthew 18:11–14). Compare *The Merchant of Venice*, II.i.5–7.

76 **raw** both (a) diseased or sore (with play on the sense that means, 'cut open', with an exposed wound), and (b) uncultivated, untaught (here, unredeemed and uncatechized).

77 **true Labourer** both (a) legitimately employed, trustworthy, industrious workman, and (b) member of the spiritually elect who 'labour among you' and eschew sleep and drunkenness in 'the hope of salvation' (1 Thessalonians 5:12, 6–8). See the notes to lines 38, 73.

78 **get** obtain (by honest means), buy.
   **envy** both (a) emulate, and (b) harbour malice about. Compare II.i.3–4.

80 **content with my Harm** able to accept my own troubles and pains with 'Patience' (I.iii.82); *content* echoes line 27.

81 **Pride** instead of vanity or selfishness, Corin means self-satisfaction, pleasure. Compare II.vii.70–71.

82 **simple** This could mean (a) naive, unintended, but Touchstone treats it as a word meaning (b) unmitigated, absolute.

83 **offer** undertake.

84 **get your Living** earn your wages. Touchstone alludes to line 78 and uses *get* in a way that hints at the sense that means 'beget' (see *Othello*, I.iii.189, where Brabantio says he'd 'rather to adopt a Child than get it').

85 **Bawd to a Bellwether** procurer (pimp) for the male sheep who wears the shepherd's bell as the leader of the flock.
   **betray** undermine the chastity of.

86 **crooked-pated** Touchstone refers to the horns that make the ram a cuckold (here, a male whose previous partners have betrayed him with infidelity).

88–89 **the . . . Shepherds** even the Devil holds shepherds in too much contempt to admit them into his domain.

90 **else** otherwise.
   **scape** escape [damnation].

93 **Western Inde** the West Indies.

shallow Man. God make Incision in thee, thou　　　　75
art raw.

CORIN　Sir, I am a true Labourer: I earn that I
eat, get that I wear, owe no man Hate, envy no
man's Happiness; glad of other men's Good,
content with my Harm; and the greatest of my　　80
Pride is to see my Ewes graze, and my Lambs suck.

CLOWN　That is another simple Sin in you, to bring
the Ewes and the Rams together, and to offer
to get your Living by the Copulation of Cattle;
to be Bawd to a Bellwether, and to betray a　　85
She-Lamb of a twelvemonth to a crooked-pated
old cuckoldly Ram, out of all reasonable Match.
If thou beest not damn'd for this, the Divel
himself will have no Shepherds, I cannot see
else how thou shouldst scape.　　　　　　　90

CORIN　Here comes young Master Ganimed, my new
Mistress's Brother.

*Enter Rosalind.*

ROSALIND *From the East to Western Inde,*
　　　　*no Jewel is like Rosalinde,*
　　　　　*Her Worth, being mounted on the Wind,*
　　　　　*through all the World bears Rosalinde.*　　95
　　　　*All the Pictures fairest lin'd*
　　　　　*are but black to Rosalinde;*
　　　　*Let no face be kept in mind*
　　　　　*but the fair of Rosalinde.*　　　　100

---

97　**lin'd**　either (a) drawn with lines ('limn'd', II.vii.197), or (b)
　　　　'painted' with lines of verse. In this passage the Folio's
　　　　*Rosalinde* signifies a long-*i* pronunciation for rhyming
　　　　purposes.

98　**to**　compared to.

100　**fair**　light-complexioned (as opposed to 'black', line 98).

101  **eight years together**  for eight consecutive years without ceasing.

102  **Dinners**  main midday meals.

103–4  **it . . . Market**  Touchstone compares the jog-trot of Orlando's verse to that of a 'rank' (line, procession, as in the formula 'rank and file') of farm women carrying butter to market. *Rank* recalls I.ii.111–13, II.vii.44–47.

106  **For a Taste**  both (a) to give you a taste of my talent, and (b) to put my rhyming skill to a test (compare *King Lear*, I.ii.47–49, for another use of *Taste* in the sense that means 'test').

107  **Hart, Hind**  male and female deer. Compare I.i.20, and see the note to I.ii.3.

109  **after kind**  both (a) act like one of its own kind, and (b) seek one of its own kind. *Cat* echoes lines 71–72; *kind* recalls II.vii.90.

111  **lin'd**  padded for warmth; but *lin'd* also means 'covered' or 'stuffed' sexually. *Winter'd* (prepared for winter) echoes II.vii.174–93.

113  **sheaf**  gather cut stalks of grain into bundles (sheaves).

114  **Cart**  Touchstone refers to a farm cart, but his image also calls to mind the carts used to expose whores to public shame. See *The Taming of the Shrew*, I.i.48–55.

115  **sowrest**  both (a) sourest, and (b) sorest (with a bawdy suggestion that Rosalind's 'Rind' has been 'lin'd' so thoroughly that it has been rubbed 'raw', lines 111, 75–76). Compare *The Merchant of Venice*, V.i.306–7, where Gratiano says he'll 'fear no other thing / So sore as keeping safe Nerissa's Ring'.

118  **Prick**  both (a) the thorn of a rosebush, and (b) the male member (as in *Romeo and Juliet*, I.iv.25–31, II.iii.21–23, 119–20). Touchstone is no doubt playing on a sense of *Nut* that refers to the *glans penis*, the head or 'Bob' (II.vii.55) at the end of a male 'Bable' (bauble); see *Romeo and Juliet*, II.iii.100. The Clown mocks Orlando's naive verses on love with a series of worldly jests on lust.

119  **false Gallop**  tedious canter. Touchstone derides the monotonously regular trot of Orlando's verses.

123  **Truly . . . Fruit**  Surely this is a 'false' tree (line 119), because the 'Fruit' it 'yields' is corrupt. See the note to II.iii.65, and compare lines 250–53.

CLOWN   I'll rime you so, eight years together;
  Dinners, and Suppers, and Sleeping Hours
  excepted. It is the right Butter-women's Rank
  to Market.

ROSALIND   Out, fool.                                                    105

CLOWN   For a Taste.
>        If a Hart do lack a Hind,
>            let him seek out Rosalinde;
>        If the Cat will after kind,
>            so be sure will Rosalinde.                                  110
>        Wint'red Garments must be lin'd,
>            so must slender Rosalinde:
>        They that reap must sheaf and bind,
>            then to Cart with Rosalinde.
>        Sweetest Nut hath sowrest Rind,                                 115
>            such a Nut is Rosalinde.
>        He that sweetest Rose will find
>            must find Love's Prick, and Rosalinde.

  This is the very false Gallop of Verses, why
  do you infect your self with them?                                    120

ROSALIND   Peace, you dull Fool, I found them on a
  Tree.

CLOWN   Truly the Tree yields bad Fruit.

124–  **I'll graff ... Medler**   Medlars are apple-like fruit that are slow
28    to ripen and are usually eaten only on the verge of rotting; by
      grafting Touchstone onto 'that Tree' (line 123), Rosalind will
      produce medlars that are rotten ('spoiled') before they mature,
      sexually experienced, if not diseased, before they are half
      developed. *Medler* puns on 'Meddler', one who mingles pro-
      miscuously with other wantons and meddles lustfully with
      women's 'Medlers' (vulvas); see *Romeo and Juliet*, II.i.33–38.
      *Country* plays on a vulgar English word for the female
      'Medler'; see the reference to 'Country Matters' in *Hamlet*,
      II.ii.122.

128   **right Virtue**   true mettle proper quality. *Right* echoes line 103
      and recalls II.vii.201.

129   **said**   *spoken.*

130   **let ... judge**   leave it to the forest to determine. Touchstone
      implies that Nature, rather than human wisdom, can best
      evaluate the validity of Rosalind's remarks. In time 'the
      Forest' will function as a 'judge' of all the 'Fruit' that falls
      within its bounds.

133   **this Desert**   Both logic and metre call for the insertion of an *a*
      before *Desert*, and most of today's editions supply the missing
      article. But in view of Celia and Roalind's remarks about
      Orlando's 'lame' verses (lines 172–80), it is conceivable that
      the 'Effect defective' in this line 'comes by Cause' (*Hamlet*,
      II.ii.101) and was intentional. Compare *unpeopled* (rather
      than *unpeople'd*) in line 134, and see the note to line 174.

135   **Tongues**   utterances. Compare I.i.62–65, I.ii.267, II.i.16,
      II.v.30–31, II.vii.83–84.

136   **civil**   civilized, characteristic of the city rather than of wild
      forests. Compare II.vii.91–96.

137   **Some**   some [sayings] about.

138   **erring**   both (a) wandering, meandering, and (b) error-prone.

139   **Span**   both (a) the distance between the tips of the thumb and
      little finger of an outspread hand, and (b) a spang, buckle.

140   **buckles in**   holds, encloses.
      **his Sum of Age**   a person's lifetime.

143   **Bows**   boughs (here spelled to rhyme with 'Vows'). Compare
      II.vii.11. This line may be punning on *Bows* meaning
      'curtsies'.

ROSALIND   I'll graff it with you, and then I shall
   graff it with a Medler: then it will be the          125
   earliest Fruit i'th' Country, for you'll be
   rotten ere you be half ripe, and that's the
   right Virtue of the Medler.
CLOWN   You have said: but whether wisely or no,
   let the Forest judge.                              130

   *Enter Celia reading a Writing.*

ROSALIND   Peace, here comes my Sister reading,
   stand aside.                          [*They withdraw.*]
CELIA   *Why should this Desert be?*
      *for it is unpeopled? No:*
   *Tongues I'll hang on every Tree,*                  135
      *that shall civil Sayings show.*
   *Some, how brief the Life of Man*
      *runs his erring Pilgrimage,*
   *That the Stretching of a Span*
      *buckles in his Sum of Age.*                     140
   *Some of violated Vows,*
      *'twixt the Souls of Friend and Friend:*
   *But upon the fairest Bows,*
      *or at every Sentence End,*
   *Will I Rosalinda write,*                           145
      *teaching all that read to know*
   *The Quintessence of every Sprite*
      *Heaven would in little show.*

---

144   **at . . . End**   at the conclusion of each saying. *Sentence* (which
      here means *sentence's*) derives from the Latin *sententia*, a
      maxim or gem of wisdom.

147   **Sprite**   spirit, here rhyming with *write*.

148   **in little show**   exemplify in a little epitome (microcosm) of the
      whole.

149 **charg'd** commanded.

151 **wide enlarg'd** distributed throughout the universe. *Graces* (endowments, gifts, blessings) recalls II.iii.11, 18.

152 **presently distill'd** soon thereafter extracted into a concentrated liquid.

153 **Helen's . . . Heart** the beauty but not the infidelity of Helen of Troy. Here *his* can be construed to mean 'its' (see the note to II.vii.163), but it is difficult to make that pronoun refer to either 'Helen's' or 'Cheek'. Most of today's editions follow Nicholas Rowe (1709) and emend to *her*. For the reasons outlined in note 133, Everyman retains the Folio reading.

155 **Atalanta** a swift-footed maiden who promised to marry anyone who could out-race her; eventually she lost to Hippomenes when she stopped to pick up three apples of the Hesperides, which he had craftily dropped in her path. Atalanta's 'better Part' is probably a reference to her ability to 'fleet the Time carelessly as they did in the Golden World' (I.i.125–26); compare 'Parts', in II.ii.13. But Orlando's phrasing hints at a 'better' bodily 'Part'; see lines 294–95.

156 **Lucrecia** Lucretia, a chaste Roman matron who killed herself after being raped. A youthful Shakespeare narrated her story in 1594 in his poem *Lucrece*.

158 **By Heavenly Synod** as the result of a council of the Gods (or a benign conjunction of the 'stars' in astrological terms).

160 **Touches** traits, attributes.
   **pris'd** prized; appraised, valued. This word can also have other meanings, among them (a) seized, taken by force, and (b) grasped, pried, as by an implement that supplies leverage.

161 **would** willed, saw to it.

162 **live and die** Orlando's phrasing hints at the 'rise and fall' of a man's 'Flesh' in the 'Affairs' of 'Love' (Sonnet 151). See the note to IV.i.100.

164 **Homily** sermon (compare II.i.17). As Rosalind steps forth from hiding, she likens Celia to a loquacious priest who bores his 'Parishioners' (congregation).

165 **withal** with. *Patience* (line 166) recalls I.iii.82–83.

167 **How . . . Friends** How is it that you are all here? Please excuse us and leave us here alone, friends. Apparently Celia is surprised to see that Rosalind, who has just stepped out of

Therefore Heaven Nature charg'd
    that one Body should be fill'd                    150
With all Graces wide enlarg'd,
    Nature presently distill'd
Helen's Cheek, but not his Heart,
    Cleopatra's Majesty,
Atalanta's better Part,                               155
    sad Lucrecia's Modesty.
Thus Rosalind of many Parts
    by Heavenly Synod was devis'd,
Of many Faces, Eyes, and Hearts,
    to have the Touches dearest pris'd.               160
Heaven would that she these Gifts should have,
    and I to live and die her Slave.

ROSALIND   O most gentle Jupiter, what tedious
Homily of Love have you wearied your
Parishioners withal, and never cried, 'Have          165
Patience, good People.'

CELIA   How now, back, Friends. – Shepherd, go off
a little. – Go with him, Sirrah.

CLOWN   Come, Shepherd, let us make an honourable
Retreat, though not with Bag and Baggage, yet        170
with Scrip and Scrippage.          *Exit [with Corin].*

CELIA   Didst thou hear these Verses?

hiding to deliver lines 163–66, is accompanied by Corin
('Shepherd') and Touchstone ('Sirrah', a form of address to a
social inferior). Celia may be punning on *back-friends* (a
reading found in some editions), which meant 'false friends'
(the kind who attack you from the rear or talk behind your
back).

169–   **make ... Scrippage** retire with a semblance of dignity, not
71     with all of our possessions (our heavy bags and their contents)
       but nevertheless with what we carry ('Scrippage') in our
       'Scrips' (pouches), here a fool's wallet and a shepherd's
       pouch. Touchstone compares himself and Corin to an army
       that has suffered some losses but has been able to retreat in
       time to avoid an ignominious rout or surrender.

174 **Feet** metrical feet. Rosalind is correct to note that many of 'the Feet were lame' and 'stood lamely in the Verse' (lines 178–80). See line 133, which requires an inserted syllable before *Desert* to make it metrical, and line 147, where *Quintessence* needs to be accented, not on the third syllable, but on the first and third. Several of the trochaic tetrameter lines that Celia has read have 'more too' (line 173), extra unstressed syllables at the beginning (lines 147, 157–62).

184– **seven ... came** Rosalind alludes to the proverbial expression
85 'nine days' wonder'. Her point is that she had already consumed seven days' worth of wonder contemplating the verses she has found.

186 **Palm** This tropical or semi-tropical tree is one of the play's many indications that 'Arden' is meant to connote an imaginative, exotic setting, rather than a northern European clime. In rural dialect *palm* could mean 'willow', but that is not likely to be the tree Rosalind refers to.

187 **since ... Rat** since I was an Irish rat in the time of Pythagoras (the Greek philosopher who believed that souls transmigrated from one creature to another in a sequence of reincarnations).

189 **Trow ... this?** Do you know who has done this?

191 **And** yes, and he has.

192 **change you Colour?** Celia's question implies that Rosalind's cheeks have turned red with blushing or white with shock.

194– **it is ... encounter** Celia varies (indeed reverses) a proverbial
96 expression: 'Friends may meet, but mountains never greet.' Her point is that if Rosalind is so imperceptive as not to know that Celia is referring to Orlando, it will prove harder to bring these two 'Friends' together than to move mountains. Compare Matthew 17:20, where Jesus says, 'If ye have faith as a grain of mustard seed, ye shall say unto this mountain, Remove hence to yonder place; and it shall remove; and nothing shall be impossible unto you.' *Hard* echoes line 61; compare lines 333–37. See the note on *encounter* at IV.iii.182.

199– **petitionary Vehemence** eager begging, fervent importunity.
200

203 **out of all Hooping** beyond all (a) embracing, and (b) exclaiming (whooping). Compare *Coriolanus*, IV.v.60 ('Hoop'd out of Rome') and *The Winter's Tale*, IV.iv.414, where *hope* is usually emended to *hoop* in 'hope his Body more with thy Embraces'.

ROSALIND   O yes, I heard them all, and more too,
   for some of them had in them more Feet than
   the Verses would bear.                                            175
CELIA   That's no matter: the Feet might bear the
   Verses.
ROSALIND   Ay, but the Feet were lame, and could
   not bear themselves without the Verse, and
   therefore stood lamely in the Verse.                             180
CELIA   But didst thou hear without wondering how
   thy Name should be hang'd and carved upon
   these Trees?
ROSALIND   I was seven of the nine Days out of the
   Wonder, before you came: for look here what I                    185
   found on a Palm Tree. I was never so be-rim'd
   since Pythagoras' Time that I was an Irish Rat,
   which I can hardly remember.
CELIA   Trow you who hath done this?
ROSALIND   Is it a Man?                                             190
CELIA   And a Chain that you once wore about his
   Neck: change you Colour?
ROSALIND   I prethee who?
CELIA   O Lord, Lord, it is a hard Matter for
   Friends to meet; but Mountains may be remov'd                    195
   with Earthquakes, and so encounter.
ROSALIND   Nay, but who is it?
CELIA   Is it possible?
ROSALIND   Nay, I prethee now, with most petitionary
   Vehemence, tell me who it is.                                    200
CELIA   O wonderful, wonderful, and most wonderful
   wonderful, and yet again wonderful, and that
   out of all Hooping.

204   **Complection**   complexion, 'Disposition' (line 206). Compare III.iv.53, and see the note to III.v.116.

205   **caparison'd**   outfitted (like a horse with its ceremonial trappings).

206   **Disposition**   emotional makeup. Compare II.iv.81. *Doublet and Hose* (set of male garments) recalls II.iv.4–8 and anticipates lines 232–33.

207   **is a South Sea of Discovery**   is equivalent to the time and effort it would take to send an expedition to the South Seas.

210   **powre**   pour. But here as elsewhere (see *Macbeth*, I.iii.98, I.v.28, and IV.i.18), the Elizabethan spelling permits wordplay on power. Compare V.i.45.

214   **Tidings**   news. Rosalind puns on *tide*, here one that contains 'too much' water to be accommodated; compare lines 211–12 with lines 173–74 and with II.i.47–52.

215   **a Man in your Belly**   Celia translates Rosalind's drinking metaphor into a metaphor about copulation, conception, and pregnancy. Compare I.iii.10–11. *Manner* (line 216) recalls I.ii.117.

221   **be thankful**   express gratitude for God's blessing. Compare II.viii.135, 169–70.
      **stay**   either (a) await, or (b) 'delay' (line 222). Compare I.iii.71. *Beard* (lines 217–23) recalls II.vii.150, 155, and anticipates V.iv.225–31.

222–  **the . . . Knowledge of his Chin**   the identity of the man who owns
23    his chin. Rosalind's phrasing hints suggestively at carnal knowledge; compare lines 213–15. *Knowledge* recalls I.iii.50 and II.vii.36–38.

227   **the . . . Mocking**   to hell with this teasing. *Mocking* recalls II.vi.13–15.

227–  **speak . . . Maid**   speak seriously, like an honest fellow maiden.
28    Here *sad* means 'sober or serious'.

233   **Doublet and Hose**   'Man's Apparel' (II.iv.5, echoed in line 245). Compare lines 204–6.

234   **Wherein**   in what [kind of clothing].

235   **makes**   does. Compare II.iii.4.

239   **Gargantua's Mouth**   the mouth of the giant in Rabelais's *Gargantua and Pantagruel* (1552); on one occasion he gobbles up five men in a single serving.

ROSALIND    Good my Complection, dost thou think,
though I am caparison'd like a Man, I have a                205
Doublet and Hose in my Disposition? One Inch
of Delay more is a South Sea of Discovery. I
prethee tell me who is it quickly, and speak
apace. I would thou couldst stammer, that thou
might'st powre this conceal'd Man out of thy           210
Mouth, as Wine comes out of a narrow-mouth'd
Bottle: either too much at once, or none at
all. I prethee take the Cork out of thy Mouth,
that I may drink thy Tidings.

CELIA    So you may put a Man in your Belly.            215

ROSALIND    Is he of God's making? What manner of
Man? Is his Head worth a Hat? Or his Chin
worth a Beard?

CELIA    Nay, he hath but a little Beard.

ROSALIND    Why God will send more, if the Man will     220
be thankful. Let me stay the Growth of his
Beard, if thou delay me not the Knowledge of
his Chin.

CELIA    It is young Orlando, that tripp'd up the
Wrastler's Heels, and your Heart, both in an           225
Instant.

ROSALIND    Nay, but the Divel take Mocking: speak
sad Brow, and true Maid.

CELIA    I'faith, Coz, 'tis he.

ROSALIND    Orlando?                                    230

CELIA    Orlando.

ROSALIND    Alas the Day, what shall I do with my
Doublet and Hose? What did he when thou saw'st
him? What said he? How look'd he? Wherein went
he? What makes he here? Did he ask for me?             235
Where remains he? How parted he with thee? And
when shalt thou see him again? Answer me in
one Word.

CELIA    You must borrow me Gargantua's Mouth first:
'tis a Word too great for any Mouth of this            240

241–
43   **To say . . . Cathechism**   Celia notes that Rosalind's rapid-fire questions are like the 'Particulars' (individual items) in a catechism (a summary of the principles of the Christian faith), many of whose questions could be answered with a simple 'yes' or 'no'. See the note to IV.i.201–2.

242   **then**   Celia means 'than', but 'then' (therefore) can also yield an awkward but relevant sense. Compare II.vii.138.

247   **Atomies**   the tiniest particles of matter, such as the motes in a beam of light.

248   **Propositions**   problematic queries.

249   **my finding him**   how I came across him. *Taste* echoes line 106 and recalls II.vii.166. The picture Celia presents in lines 250–51 harks back to II.i.29–32 and looks forward to IV.iii.99–108.

249–
50   **with good Observance**   in such a way as to savour it (as an appetizer) with your full attention. Compare II.vii.38–42.

253   **Fruit**   Rosalind's image recalls Touchstone's 'bad Fruit' image in line 123 and Orlando's 'rotten Tree' image in II.iii.63. And in the context of Celia's reference to catechism and Rosalind's reference to Jove (often used in Shakespeare as a metaphor for the Christian God), it also echoes Matthew 7:17–20; see the note to II.iii.65.

256   **along**   at full length, supine.

256–
57   **wounded Knight**   Courtly lovers were conventionally referred to as wounded by Cupid's arrow.

259   **Ground**   both (a) the earth, and (b) the background for such a 'Sight' (as in a painting). See the note to I.iii.85.

260   **Holla**   whoa; a cry to halt a horse.

261   **curvets unseasonably**   leaps friskily ahead of its master's wishes, at a time when it should be stationary.
  **furnish'd**   accoutred, apparelled and equipped.

263   **Hart**   a play on (a) deer, and (b) heart. Compare II.iv.33, II.vii.128–33, and see lines 107–8.

264   **Burthen**   either (a) the bass undersong to a melody, or (b) the repeated refrain. In either case, Celia is saying that she would like to 'sing' (tell her tale) without Rosalind's burdening her with accompaniment. Compare II.vii.167, IV.ii.14, and see lines 343–45.

Age's Size. To say Ay and No, to these
Particulars, is more then to answer in a
Catechism.

ROSALIND    But doth he know that I am in this
Forest, and in Man's Apparel? Looks he as                           245
freshly as he did the day he wrastled?

CELIA    It is as easy to count Atomies as to resolve
the Propositions of a Lover: but take a Taste
of my finding him, and relish it with good
Observance. I found him under a Tree like a                         250
dropp'd Acorn.

ROSALIND    It may well be call'd Jove's Tree, when
it drops forth Fruit.

CELIA    Give me Audience, good Madam.

ROSALIND    Proceed.                                               255

CELIA    There lay he stretch'd along like a wounded
Knight.

ROSALIND    Though it be pity to see such a Sight,
it well becomes the Ground.

CELIA    Cry 'Holla' to the Tongue, I prethee: it                 260
curvets unseasonably. He was furnish'd like
a Hunter.

ROSALIND    O ominous, he comes to kill my Hart.

CELIA    I would sing my Song without a Burthen,
thou bring'st me out of Tune.                                     265

ROSALIND    Do you not know I am a Woman, when I
think, I must speak: Sweet, say on.

*Enter Orlando and Jaques.*

CELIA    You bring me out. Soft, comes he not here?

---

268    **You bring me out**    Celia again plays on *out of Tune* (line 265);
she probably means both (a) 'you distract me from my
purpose, and make me forget the part I've prepared for this
performance', (b) 'you put me out of patience'.

271    **lief**   gladly. Compare I.i.154.

272    **Fashion'**   fashion's. See II.iv.61–62.

273    **Society**   company. Compare II.i.49–57.

274    **God buy**   God be with, goodbye to. Jaques may also be punning on the other sense of *buy* (purchase); compare I.i.77–78, II.iv.72–73, 89–91, 97–101.

277    **mar**   disfigure, harm. This word echoes I.i.31–38.

279    **moe**   more.

280    **ill-favouredly**   unfavourably. Compare I.ii.43.

282    **just**   just so, correct. *Pleasing* (line 284) recalls II.v.15–24, 40–59, II.vii.44–49, III.ii.18–20.

288    **pretty**   clever, quaint. *Heart* (line 287) echoes line 263; compare lines 224–26.

290    **conn'd . . . Rings**   Jaques probably means 'memorized the love posies (pretty verses) engraved on their rings'. But it also seems possible that he uses *conn'd* in a way that anticipates the modern sense (cheated or seduced pliable 'wives'), by way of wordplay on 'cony-catch' (see the note to line 360). Jaques probably employs this phrase with bawdy innuendo. Shakespeare frequently uses *ring* to refer to the female genitalia (see the quotation from *The Merchant of Venice* in the note to line 115), and *conned* and *acquainted*, which echo *cunnus*, the Latin word for the female pudendum, both hint at carnal knowledge; see the notes to lines 124–26, 222–23. *Acquainted* recalls I.i.129–30, 138–40, I.iii.51–56.

291–    **right painted Cloath**   with clichés drawn directly from the
92      pictures and trite mottoes on stained cloths (inexpensive substitutes for hanging tapestries). Compare II.i.1–3.

295    **Atalanta's Heels**   By comparing Orlando's wit to the heels of a fleet-footed maiden, Jaques may be hinting that Orlando is cowardly. But it seems more likely that he is suggesting that, like Atalanta, Orlando can be outwitted and will thus lose the race. See line 155. *Wit* (line 294) echoes lines 31–33, 73.
       **Will you**   if you will, if it please you. Lines 295–97 recall I.ii.34–96, II.i.43–66, II.v.62–64, II.vii.12–87.

296    **rail**   declaim, complain. Compare II.v.62–64.

298    **Breather**   living, breathing person.

299    **Faults**   flaws, offences (literally, cracks, imperfections).

301    **change**   both (a) exchange, and (b) alter. Compare II.i.18, III.ii.192.

ROSALIND  'Tis he, slink by, and note him.

JAQUES  I thank you for your Company, but good          270
faith I had as lief have been my self alone.

ORLANDO  And so had I: but yet for Fashion' sake
I thank you too, for your Society.

JAQUES  God buy you, let's meet as little as we
can.                                                                          275

ORLANDO  I do desire we may be better Strangers.

JAQUES  I pray you mar no more Trees with writing
Love-songs in their Barks.

ORLANDO  I pray you mar no moe of my Verses with
reading them ill-favouredly.                                     280

JAQUES  Rosalind is your Love's Name?

ORLANDO  Yes, just.

JAQUES  I do not like her Name.

ORLANDO  There was no thought of pleasing you when
she was christen'd.                                                   285

JAQUES  What Stature is she of?

ORLANDO  Just as high as my Heart.

JAQUES  You are full of pretty Answers: have you
not been acquainted with Goldsmiths' Wives,
and conn'd them out of Rings?                              290

ORLANDO  Not so: but I answer you right painted
Cloath, from whence you have studied your
Questions.

JAQUES  You have a nimble Wit; I think 'twas made
of Atalanta's Heels. Will you sit down with          295
me, and we two will rail against our Mistress
the World, and all our Misery.

ORLANDO  I will chide no Breather in the World but
my self, against whom I know most Faults.

JAQUES  The worst Fault you have is to be in love.    300

ORLANDO  'Tis a Fault I will not change, for your
best Virtue: I am weary of you.

303 **Fool** Jaques means Touchstone (see II.vii.12–61), the professional court fool, but he plays on the more usual sense that can apply to 'you' (Orlando) or to himself (see lines 305–9). Compare lines 105, 121–22.

305–6 **look . . . him** Orlando alludes to Narcissus, who fell in love with his own reflection in a pond and pined away. Orlando's implication is that Jaques is not only a fool but a victim of self-love.

309 **Cipher** the figure zero. Orlando reduces Jaques to nothing. Compare *The Winter's Tale*, I.ii.6–9, and see lines 15–18 of the Prologue to *Henry V*.

314–15 **saucy Lackey** sassy, impudent page.

315 **under that Habit** in that disguise. *Habit* normally means 'apparel' or 'uniform'; here it has the metaphorical meaning of 'manner' (a role to 'play'). Compare II.vii.139–66.
**Knave** cheeky servant (with play on 'boy' and 'villain', the other common senses).

316 **Forester** forest-dweller or officer of the forest (see the note to I.i.121–22).

317 **would you** is your will. Compare I.ii.263, II.vii.102.

319 **time o' Day** time as measured by the position of the sun.

323 **detect** spy out, disclose. *Groaning* (line 322) recalls II.i.35–38.

327 **divers** diverse, different. The phrase *swift Foot* (line 325) echoes lines 294–95.

329 **ambles withal** moves unhurriedly with. *Withal* echoes line 165.

333 **Marry** truly (as in I.ii.76).

335 **solemniz'd** made official in a formal ceremony.

336 **Se'ennight** week.
**hard** hard to take, uncomfortable for the rider. But here and in line 333 Rosalind's 'hard Thoughts' (I.ii.193) also hint at another kind of 'Length' (line 337) that occupies the mind of the eager maid while Time slowly conveys her from her engagement day to her wedding night. See the note to I.ii.53, and compare lines 194–95.

338 **Who . . . withal?** With whom does Time amble?

JAQUES   By my troth, I was seeking for a Fool,
   when I found you.

ORLANDO   He is drown'd in the Brook, look but in,        305
   and you shall see him.

JAQUES   There I shall see mine own Figure.

ORLANDO   Which I take to be either a Fool, or a
   Cipher.

JAQUES   I'll tarry no longer with you, farewell,        310
   good Signior Love.

ORLANDO   I am glad of your Depature: adieu, good
   Monsieur Melancholy.                    [*Exit Jaques.*]

ROSALIND   – I will speak to him like a saucy
   Lackey, and under that Habit play the Knave        315
   with him. – Do you hear, Forester?

ORLANDO   Very well: what would you?

ROSALIND   I pray you, what is't a' Clock?

ORLANDO   You should ask me what Time o' Day:
   there's no Clock in the Forest.                    320

ROSALIND   Then there is no true Lover in the Forest,
   else sighing every Minute and groaning every
   Hour would detect the lazy Foot of Time as
   well as a Clock.

ORLANDO   And why not the swift Foot of Time? Had        325
   not that been as proper?

ROSALIND   By no means, Sir; Time travels in divers
   Paces with divers Persons. I'll tell you who
   Time ambles withal, who Time trots withal, who
   Time gallops withal, and who he stands still        330
   withal.

ORLANDO   I prethee, who doth he trot withal?

ROSALIND   Marry he trots hard with a young Maid,
   between the Contract of her Marriage, and the
   Day it is solemniz'd: if the Interim be but a        335
   Se'ennight, Time's Pace is so hard, that it
   seems the Length of seven Year.

ORLANDO   Who ambles Time withal?

339 **a . . . Latin** an ignorant cleric who knows so little that he is incapable of performing a lengthy marriage service. See lines 333–37, and compare III.iii.65–108.

340 **Gout** a disease caused by an excess of uric acid in the blood. It often settles in the big toe, where it turns 'lame' even the 'Feet' of 'a rich Man' (see line 178).

341 **sleeps . . . study** has no difficulty sleeping because his inability to 'study' makes it unnecessary for him to burn the midnight oil, and because his ignorance makes him free of the cares and worries that can keep the thoughtful awake.

344 **wasteful** ruinous, consumptive; disposing one to grow 'lean' by wasting away from long hours of impoverished and therefore famishing dedication to 'Learning'. *Wasteful* recalls II.vii.133–34; *Burthen* echoes lines 264–65.

345 **Penury** poverty. Compare I.i.40–41. *Tedious* echoes lines 19–20, 163–65.

349 **softly** both quietly and slowly.

353 **Term** session. The legal year was divided into quarterly terms. The 'Vacation' was the interval between terms. *Term* echoes II.vii.16–17.

355 **pretty** delicate, attractive. Orlando's question suggests that despite her male 'Habit' (line 315), she hasn't completely obscured her feminine charms.

357 **Skirts** outskirts, here playing on 'Fringe'. *Petticoat* (line 358) recalls II.iv.4–8.

360 **Cony** rabbit. But Rosalind's reply also carries a suggestive undertone: *Cony* often refers to a female 'rabbit' who is willing to be caught, and the word itself echoes a bawdy synecdoche for such a female; see the note to line 290.

361 **kindled** born (a verb used in relation to rabbits). But the more usual meaning, 'set aflame', is also relevant to the state of excitation that Rosalind is struggling to keep under control. Compare I.i.182–84.

362 **something finer** somewhat more refined (cultivated).

363 **purchase** obtain.
**removed** remote from civilized society. Compare lines 194–96.

365 **religious** holy, attached to a religious order.

366 **inland man** a man accustomed to the city or the court. *Inland* recalls II.vii.96–97.

ROSALIND    With a Priest that lacks Latin, and a
rich Man that hath not the Gout: for the one                    340
sleeps easily because he cannot study, and the
other lives merrily because he feels no Pain;
the one lacking the Burthen of lean and
wasteful Learning, the other knowing no
Burthen of heavy tedious Penury. These Time                    345
ambles withal.

ORLANDO    Who doth he gallop withal?

ROSALIND    With a Thief to the Gallows: for though
he go as softly as Foot can fall, he thinks
himself too soon there.                                        350

ORLANDO    Who stays it still withal?

ROSALIND    With Lawyers in the Vacation: for they
sleep between Term and Term, and then they
perceive not how Time moves.

ORLANDO    Where dwell you, pretty Youth?                      355

ROSALIND    With this Shepherdess my Sister: here
in the Skirts of the Forest, like Fringe upon
a Petticoat.

ORLANDO    Are you native of this place?

ROSALIND    As the Cony that you see dwell where she            360
is kindled.

ORLANDO    Your Accent is something finer than you
could purchase in so removed a Dwelling.

ROSALIND    I have been told so of many: but indeed
an old religious Uncle of mine taught me to                    365
speak, who was in his Youth an inland man, one

367 **Courtship** Rosalind puns on (a) court life, and (b) courting.

369 **Lectors** lectures. Compare lines 163–66.

370 **touch'd** tainted.

370– **giddy Offences** sins causing or committed because of
71 'giddiness' (dizziness inconstancy, flightiness, lack of
self-control or self-discipline).

371 **tax'd** criticized, taken to task. Compare II.vii.70–71, 84–87.

374 **laid . . . Women** both (a) burdened women with (one meaning
of *charge* being 'load'), and (b) accused women of (bringing a
formal 'charge' or indictment against them).

375 **principal** foremost.

376 **like** as like. *Fault* echoes lines 288–89.

380 **Physic** medical powers, remedies. Compare I.i.90–92. Lines
380–81 echo Matthew 9:12 ('They that be whole need not a
physician, but they that are sick') and Luke 4:23 ('Physician,
heal thyself'). *Cast* recalls Matthew 7:6 ('Give not that which
is holy unto the dogs, neither cast ye your pearls before
swine . . .').

382 **abuses** misuses, mars (lines 277–80).

385 **forsooth** in truth, to be sure.
**defying** slighting, insulting, challenging. Rosalind implies that
Orlando 'abuses' her 'Name' as well as the 'Barks' upon
which it is carved. Most of today's editions adopt the Second
Folio's emendation to *deifying*; that verb conveys Orlando's
intention. But what Rosalind suggests is that the man who
'haunts the Forest' is guilty of taking her name in vain,
audaciously degrading rather than dignifying it with his
unauthorized publicizing of it.

386 **Fancy-monger** seller of 'Fancy' (love). *Monger* tends to have
salacious connotations in Shakespeare (see *Fishmonger* in
*Hamlet*, II.ii.178, and *Flesh-monger* in *Measure for Measure*,
V.i.325–26), and Rosalind hints playfully at such
implications.

387 **good Counsel** sound advice. Compare I.ii.180–85, 271–72.
Like *Cony* (line 360), *Counsel* provides an aural reminder of
the 'better Part' (line 155) that Rosalind is eager to bestow
(see lines 213–15).

that knew Courtship too well, for there he
fell in love. I have heard him read many
Lectors against it, and I thank God I am not
a Woman to be touch'd with so many giddy            370
Offences as he hath generally tax'd their
whole Sex withal.

ORLANDO   Can you remember any of the principal
Evils that he laid to the charge of Women?

ROSALIND   There were none principal, they were    375
all like one another as half Pence are, every
one Fault seeming monstrous, till his Fellow-
fault came to match it.

ORLANDO   I prethee recount some of them.

ROSALIND   No: I will not cast away my Physic, but  380
on those that are sick. There is a man haunts
the Forest, that abuses our young Plants with
carving 'Rosalind' on their Barks; hangs Odes
upon Hawthorns, and Elegies on Brambles; all
(forsooth) defying the Name of Rosalind. If I      385
could meet that Fancy-monger, I would give him
some good Counsel, for he seems to have the
Quotidian of Love upon him.

ORLANDO   I am he that is so Love-shak'd, I pray
you tell me your Remedy.                            390

ROSALIND   There is none of my Uncle's Marks upon
you: he taught me how to know a Man in Love,
in which Cage of Rushes I am sure you are not
Prisoner.

---

388   **Quotidian**   an ague (such as a malarial fever) that caused daily
(continual) attacks of shivering, making one feel 'Love-shak'd'
(line 389).

391   **Marks**   symptoms, signs of the disease.

393   **Cage of Rushes**   basket or enclosure made of rush stalks (pithy
grass-like plants growing near water). Rosalind is probably
alluding to the custom of country lovers exchanging rings
woven of rushes.

397 **blew** blue (perhaps with wordplay on the past tense of *blow*, bloom or swell).

398 **unquestionable** reticent or irritable; not given to conversation, and not responsive to inquiries.

400–1 **having in Beard** being in possession of a beard. *Beard* recalls lines 216–23.

401 **Younger Brother's Revenue** another reference to the fact that younger brothers were often so poorly provided for that they were left to fend for themselves. See I.i.1–54, I.ii.192–203.

402–3 **Bonnet unbanded** hat without a band. *Hose* echoes lines 232–33.

405 **careless Desolation** the 'lean', 'sunken', and 'wasteful' demeanour (lines 333–34, 396–97) of a man so desperate and destitute that he is 'careless' (II.vii.112).

406 **rather** instead.
**Point-device** outfitted with every point (tie-lace) in place. Compare *Twelfth Night*, II.v.172–73.

407 **Accoutrements** accoutrements, apparel.

407–8 **loving your self . . . other** suffering self-love rather than love of another. Not seeing any of the traditional signs of a lover's self-neglect, Rosalind concludes that Orlando must suffer from the opposite problem. Here, as in II.v.23, *then* can mean both (a) than and (b) then. So also in line 412.

413 **apter** more willing, more readily moved.

414 **still** always.

415 **Consciences** both (a) conscious awareness, and (b) moral senses. In Shakespeare's time *conscience* often meant what later became known as 'consciousness'. In lines 413–15 Rosalind's phrasing is erotically suggestive. *Consciences* plays on the Latin-derived vulgar term for a woman's 'good Counsel' (see the note to line 387, and compare Sonnet 157, where *Conscience* refers to carnal knowledge); *Points* carries phallic implications (see *Hamlet*, I.v.126–27); and *give the Lie* (accuse of falsehood) can refer to permitting a man to enjoy the pleasures of a 'Lie' (copulative 'encounter', line 196), as in *Othello*, IV.i.28–37, and *Macbeth*, II.iii.24–48. Compare I.ii.210–11.

416 **sooth** faith, truth. Compare line 385.

417 **admir'd** wondered at, worshipped.

ORLANDO   What were his Marks?                              395

ROSALIND   A lean Cheek, which you have not; a
blew Eye and sunken, which you have not; an
unquestionable Spirit, which you have not; a
Beard neglected, which you have not (but I
pardon you for that, for simply your having        400
in Beard is a Younger Brother's Revenue). Then
your Hose should be ungarter'd, your Bonnet
unbanded, your Sleeve unbutton'd, your Shoe
untied, and every thing about you demonstrating
a careless Desolation. But you are no such        405
Man; you are rather Point-device in your
Accoustrements, as loving your self, then
seeming the Lover of any other.

ORLANDO   Fair Youth, I would I could make thee
believe I love.                                            410

ROSALIND   Me believe it? You may as soon make her
that you love believe it, which I warrant she
is apter to do, then to confess she does. That
is one of the Points in the which Women still
give the Lie to their Consciences. But in good     415
sooth, are you he that hangs the Verses on the
Trees, wherein Rosalind is so admir'd?

ORLANDO   I swear to thee, Youth, by the white Hand
of Rosalind, I am he, that unfortunate he.

ROSALIND   But are you so much in love, as your Rimes    420
speak?

ORLANDO   Neither Rime nor Reason can express how
much.

ROSALIND   Love is merely a Madness, and I tell

---

422   **Rime nor Reason**   This alliterative pairing was already
proverbial by Shakespeare's time. For other instances of it
compare *The Comedy of Errors*, II.ii.49–50, *Love's Labour's
Lost*, I.ii.110–11, and *The Merry Wives of Windsor*,
V.v.127–33.

425 **deserves** it deserves.
   **a dark House** the typical treatment for the violently insane, confinement in an unlit chamber. Compare *Twelfth Night*, V.i.345–49.

428 **ordinary** widespread, unexceptional.

429 **I profess** I make a profession of.
   **Counsel** good advice. See the note to line 387.

433 **woe** woo. Compare II.vii.10.

434 **moonish** half-lunatic, subject to the changeable moods induced by the moon.
   **grieve** both (a) complain, and (b) mourn, weep. Compare II.i.26.

435 **effeminate** weak, frail (see *Hamlet*, I.ii.146), 'changeable'.
   **liking** affectionate.

436 **fantastical** subject to wild and unpredictable whims and fantasies.
   **apish** as whimsical and imitative as an ape.

437– **for . . . thing** manifesting some signs of every emotional state,
39    but not remaining true (constant) to any of them. Compare *Twelfth Night*, II.iv.72–78.

440 **Cattle of this Colour** stupid and easily led beasts of this type. *Colour* echoes line 192 and recalls I.ii.106–8.

441 **entertain him** welcome him graciously. Compare II.iv.72–74.

442 **forswear him** swear off him, reject him. See I.ii.67–85.

443 **drave** drove.

445– **forswear . . . Monastic** withdraw from the world's affairs and
46    live in a purely monastic cell. Shakespeare often presents the life of a monk or a nun as the primary alternative to married love. In the opening scene of *A Midsummer Night's Dream* Hermia is told that she must either wed the man her father favours or face a choice between execution and a life confined to 'chaunting faint Hymns to the cold fruitless Moon'. Rosalind's words anticipate V.iv.162–73.

446 **meerly** merely. The Folio spelling may involve wordplay on *meer*, an alternate spelling for both *more* and *mare*, one of whose meanings is 'a kind of throw in wrestling' (see I.ii.259–70). Compare *Antony and Cleopatra*, III.xiii.9, where *meered* puns on both *mare* and *mere*, and III.vii.7–9, where *merely* plays on *Mares* and means 'mare-ly' (in an effeminate, mare-like manner).

you, deserves as well a dark House, and a Whip,                    425
as Madmen do: and the reason why they are not
so punish'd and cur'd, is that the Lunacy is so
ordinary that the Whippers are in love too.
Yet I profess curing it by Counsel.

ORLANDO   Did you ever cure any so?                               430

ROSALIND   Yes one, and in this Manner. He was to
imagine me his Love, his Mistress: and I set
him every day to woe me. At which time
would I, being but a moonish Youth, grieve, be
effeminate, changeable, longing, and liking,                     435
proud, fantastical, apish, shallow, inconstant,
full of Tears, full of Smiles; for every
Passion something, and for no Passion truly
any thing, as Boys and Women are for the most
part Cattle of this Colour; would now like him,                  440
now loathe him; then entertain him, then
forswear him; now weep for him, then spit at
him; that I drave my Suitor from his mad Humour
of Love to a living Humour of Madness, which
was to forswear the full Stream of the World,                    445
and to live in a Nook meerly Monastic. And
thus I cur'd him, and this way will I take

448 **Liver** the seat of the obsessive passions.
**sound** healthy, whole.

448– **as clean as a sound Sheep's Heart** As 'free' of vice or disease
49 (see II.vii.85–87) as the healthy, wholesome innards of a
sheep that is 'clean' enough for sacrificial rituals (see Numbers
28:3, where the lambs to be offered must be 'without spot').
Rosalind associates the Sheep with cleanness because of the
whiteness of its fleece. Her language echoes Isaiah 1:18,
'Come now, and let us reason together, saith the Lord: though
your sins be as scarlet, they shall be as white as snow; though
they be red like crimson, they shall be as wool.' In lines
448–50 *Spot* (impurity or blemish) alludes to a number of
biblical passages that depict sinners as spotted; see *Othello*,
III.iii.424, and compare Jeremiah 13:23, Hebrews 9:14, and 2
Peter 3:14.

453 **Coat** cote, cottage. Compare II.iv.84–94.

457 **shew** show. Compare II.vii.95.

458 **by the way** as we walk.

III.iii We now move to another setting in the Forest of Arden.

2 **Goats** In the previous scene Rosalind has spoken of sheep. The
reference to Audrey's goats is probably meant to echo
Matthew 25:31–33, where Jesus compares himself to a
shepherd who divides his sheep from his goats.

4 **Features** Audrey misunderstands Touchstone; she may think
he said 'faitors' (cheats), or she may assume that he is
referring to 'features' an 'honest' (chaste) woman (line 17)
shouldn't know about.
**warrant** guard, secure. Compare IV.i.82.

7 **capricious** Touchstone uses this word in its original sense
(deriving from the Italian word *capro*, he-goat), which meant
'goatish' and thus frisky, if not lascivious. He alludes to Ovid
(Publius Ovidius Naso, 47 BC–AD 17) as the author of a witty
love manual (the *Ars Amatoria*), and associates him with an
animal proverbial for lechery.
**honest** both (a) truth-telling, and (b) virtuous. Touchstone
probably plays ironically on a third sense, (c) chaste, that
contradicts what he implies by *capricious*. See lines 24–40,
and compare I.ii.37–43.

8 **Gothes** Goths. But as the Folio spelling makes clear, the word
was pronounced in a way that echoed *goats*. Ovid was exiled
to live among the Getae (Goths), and complained that his
works were not understood by these barbarians.

upon me to wash your Liver as clean as a sound
Sheep's Heart, that there shall not be one
Spot of Love in't.                                                                    450

ORLANDO   I would not be cur'd, Youth.

ROSALIND   I would cure you, if you would but call
me Rosalind, and come every day to my Coat, and
woe me.

ORLANDO   Now, by the faith of my Love, I will;      455
tell me where it is.

ROSALIND   Go with me to it, and I'll shew it you;
and by the way, you shall tell me where in the
Forest you live. Will you go?

ORLANDO   With all my Heart, good Youth.              460

ROSALIND   Nay, you must call me Rosalind. – Come
Sister, will you go?                                        *Exeunt.*


# Scene 3

*Enter Clown, Audrey, and Jaques.*


CLOWN   Come apace, good Audrey, I will fetch up
your Goats, Audrey. And how, Audrey, am I the
Man yet? Doth my smple Feature content you?

AUDREY   Your Features, Lord warrant us: what
Features?                                                                   5

CLOWN   I am here with thee, and thy Goats, as the
most capricious Poet honest Ovid was among
the Gothes.

9    **ill inhabited**  ill-housed, lodged in humble, poor, or
     inappropriate surroundings. It is not clear whether Jaques is
     (a) sympathizing with Touchstone as a man of learning who is
     forced to live among the ignorant, (b) agreeing with his
     statement about Ovid's privation in similar circumstances, (c)
     generalizing about such situations and relating them to his
     own state, or (d) commenting on the way 'Knowledge' is
     abused by the uses to which Touchstone puts it in his pun on
     *Goats* and *Gothes*. Compare III.ii.221–23, and see I.i.1–78,
     II.iii.2–28, for a parallel description of Orlando's lot in life.

10   **Jove . . . House**  In Book VIII of the *Metamorphoses* Ovid
     describes a visit by the disguised Jove and Mercury to the
     cottage of a peasant couple, Philemon and Baucis.

12   **seconded**  assisted, supported, backed up. *Wit* echoes
     III.ii.294–95.
     **forward**  eager, forthcoming, teachable.

14   **great . . . Room**  a large bill for the use of a small room in an
     inn (or metaphorically, a terrible if not mortal accounting for
     a trifling peccadillo). See the note to III.v.81.

19   **faining**  both (a) longing, desiring, and (b) feigning (which
     could mean either lying or relying on the powers of the
     imagination). Compare II.vii.181, 191.

26   **feign**  pretend, lie.

28   **hard-favour'd**  ugly (literally, rough-featured). Compare
     I.ii.41–43, III.iii.279–80.

29   **Honesty**  both (a) truth-telling, and (b) chastity.

29–30 **Honey . . . Sugar**  a cloying sweetness (that is, 'too much of a
     good thing', IV.i.130–31). Touchstone is probably speaking
     tongue-in-cheek here, because while his words imply that
     'Honesty' makes 'Beauty' all the sweeter (as a more intense
     form of the same substance), he indicates elsewhere that, for a
     man who is reluctant to risk the bonds of matrimony, a
     'Beauty' that is *not* 'coupled to' Honesty is sweeter than one
     that is.

31   **material**  'full of Matter' (II.i.67–68), 'worthy' (II.vii.34).

32   **fair**  Audrey probably means both (a) blonde, and (b) attractive.
     But *fair* could also mean (a) unspotted, pure, and (b) neat and
     clean (the opposite of *foul*, line 34), and Audrey's words
     could be construed to mean that she hopes to be made
     'honest' (respectable, decent, honourable) by becoming a
     lawfully married wife.

JAQUES    O Knowledge ill inhabited, worse than
Jove in a thatch'd House.                                                  10
CLOWN    When a man's Verses cannot be understood,
nor a man's good Wit seconded with the forward
Child, Understanding, it strikes a man more
dead than a great Reckoning in a little Room:
truly, I would the Gods had made thee poetical.         15
AUDREY    I do not know what Poetical is. Is it
honest in Deed and Word: is it a true thing?
CLOWN    No truly: for the truest Poetry is the most
faining, and Lovers are given to Poetry; and
what they swear in Poetry, may be said as                20
Lovers, they do feign.
AUDREY    Do you wish then that the Gods had made
me Poetical?
CLOWN    I do truly: for thou swear'st to me thou
art honest. Now if thou wert a Poet, I might          25
have some hope thou didst feign.
AUDREY    Would you not have me honest?
CLOWN    No truly, unless thou wert hard favour'd:
for Honesty coupled to Beauty, is to have Honey
a sauce to Sugar.                                                           30
JAQUES    A material Fool.
AUDREY    Well, I am not fair, and therefore I pray
the Gods make me honest.
CLOWN    Truly, and to cast away Honesty upon a foul

---

34–36 **Truly ... Dish**    Touchstone appears to be seconding Audrey's
wish that 'the Gods' rather than he make Audrey 'honest'
(lines 32–33); 'to cast away Honesty' (holy matrimony) on
such a wench would be like throwing pearls before swine (see
the notes to III.ii.380, V.iv.62–64).

35 **Slut** either (a) a slattern, a slovenly woman, or (b) a whore
(with the words *foul* and *unclean* meaning either 'physically
unkempt' or 'morally depraved', depending on the pertinent
sense).

**Meat** food (not restricted to meat in the modern sense).

38 **foul** (a) untidy, or (b) plain, if not ugly. Apparently thinking
that *Slut* refers only to a loose woman, Audrey rejects any
application of that term to herself. Her reply echoes such
formulaic expressions of jocular deprecation as 'I am the
youngest of that Name, for fault of a Worse' (*Romeo and
Juliet*, II.iii.129–30) and, 'So like you, 'tis the worse' (*The
Winter's Tale*, II.iii.94–96).

42 **Mar-text** The Vicar's name suggests that he is too inept to get
the 'text' (the Scriptures and the liturgy) right. Sir Oliver
corresponds to Rosalind's 'Priest that lacks Latin' (III.ii.339),
and he is just the kind of 'Gothic' (ignorant) cleric that
Touchstone is looking for to help him spend his exile among
the goats as pleasurably as possible. *Mar* recalls such
Elizabethan Puritan writings as the anonymous 'Marprelate
Tracts' of the 1580s; as in I.i.34–36 (compare II.ii.277–80), it
plays on *marry*.

45 **couple** join. It is probably significant that Touchstone does not
say 'marry'. *Couple* plays on *Copulation* (see lines 80–87) and
echoes III.ii.29–30.

46 **fain** gladly (as in I.ii.167).

49 **stagger** waver, hesitate, become weak at the knees. *Heart* puns
on 'hart' (male deer). Compare III.ii.263, 287, 447–50.

51 **Horn-beasts** Touchstone refers to Audrey's goats. But the
reference to horns reminds him of the 'odious' (hateful) kind
of horns that adorn the brows of a cuckold (a man whose
wife is not 'honest'). See the note to line 86.

53 **Many . . . Goods** Touchstone quotes a proverb that meant
'Many a man is unaware of how prosperous he really is.' He
is probably alluding to the idea that his wife is one of his
'Goods' (see *The Taming of the Shrew*, III.ii.233, where
Petruchio says, 'She is my Goods, my Chattels') and hinting
that a cuckold 'knows no end' of his wife carnally because her
'end', though endlessly available to other men, is only rarely
open to her feckless spouse.

Slut were to put good Meat into an unclean                    35
Dish.

AUDREY    I am not a Slut, though I thank the Gods I
am foul.

CLOWN    Well, praised be the Gods, for thy Foulness;
Sluttishness may come hereafter. But be it, as                40
it may be, I will marry thee: and to that end
I have been with Sir Oliver Mar-text, the
Vicar of the next Village, who hath promis'd
to meet me in this place of the Forest, and to
couple us.                                                    45

JAQUES    I would fain see this Meeting.

AUDREY    Well, the Gods give us Joy.

CLOWN    Amen. A Man may, if he were of a fearful
Heart, stagger in this Attempt: for here we
have no Temple but the Wood, no Assembly but             50
Horn-beasts. But what though? Courage. As
Horns are odious, they are necessary. It is
said 'Many a Man knows no end of his Goods.'
Right: many a Man has good Horns, and knows no
end of them. Well, that is the Dowry of his              55

---

54–55 **knows no end of them**    Touchstone probably means both (a) is
subject to an unlimited number of cuckoldings, and (b) can
find no way to be rid of them (either the horns on his
forehead or the horns of tumescence that torment his crotch).
The figurative horns on a cuckold's brow correspond to the
hidden horns (erections) of a man who is perpetually horny,
unable to find relief for his mounting desires. For *Horn* as a
term for the *penis erectus*, see *The Two Gentlemen of Verona*,
I.i.70–80, and *Love's Labour's Lost*, IV.i.113–21.

55    **Dowry**    wedding gift (technically, the property a wife brought
to a marriage as part of the contract between the husband and
the bride's father).

56–57 **Horns . . . alone** It is not clear whether Touchstone means (a) that only poor (wealthless) men are subject to cuckoldry, (b) that with 'Horns' alone for a 'Dowry', all men are left 'poor' (impoverished and pitiable) by marriage, (c) that the man whose wife gives him only horns is left alone to be scorned by those who have a happier fate, or (d) that only 'Men' (as opposed, say, to 'Deer') are subject to the infidelity that puts horns on their heads.

58 **Rascal** both (a) a young, lean deer, and (b) a scoundrel. In this line *Deer* (stag) can also mean 'dear' (sweetheart). See the note to I.ii.3, and compare II.vi.1 and IV.i.54.

59 **Single** unattached, unwed.

63 **Defence** both fencing 'skill' and armour. Touchstone probably refers to the walls surrounding a town (lines 159–62); he may be thinking of the type of fortification known as 'horn-work'. His image is interesting, because 'a walled Town' suggests what John Milton was later to call a 'cloistered virtue', a well-guarded female chastity; compare *King Lear*, V.iii.75–76, where the salacious Regan offers 'the Walls' of her body to Edmund, and *All's Well That Ends Well*, I.i.119–80, where Parolles tells Helena that women are foolish to 'barricade' their 'Virginity'.
**Skill** an ability to defend oneself (as with swordsmanship).

64 **to want** both (a) to be lacking in defence, and (b) to have one's sexual needs totally unmet. By sophistry, Touchstone has just metamorphosed something 'odious' (the cuckold's horns) into something 'honourable' and 'noble' (a strong defence).

66 **you . . . met** we are happy to see you here. Compare line 75.
**dispatch us** both (a) couple us, and (b) do it with dispatch.

67–68 **or . . . Chapel** Sir Oliver provides no answer to this question, probably because he has no chapel.

70 **on gift of any Man** Touchstone does not want a woman who has belonged to another man. Above all, he is unwilling to have her father present her, because he has no desire for a legitimate wedding.

75 **'ild** yield (reward, bless).

76 **your last Company** the last time we were together (II.vii).

77 **even . . . here** We're merely taking care of a trifling matter here. The 'Toy' (nothing) the clown has 'in hand here' is also Audrey.

Wife, 'tis none of his own getting; Horns,
even so poor Men alone. No, no, the Noblest
Deer hath them as huge as the Rascal. Is the
Single Man therefore blessed? No, as a wall'd
Town is more worthier than a Village, so is                    60
the Forehead of a Married Man more honourable
than the bare Brow of a Bachelor: and by how
much Defence is better than no Skill, by so
much is a Horn more precious than to want.

*Enter Sir Oliver Mar-text.*

Here comes Sir Oliver. – Sir Oliver Mar-text,                  65
you are well met. Will you dispatch us here
under this Tree, or shall we go with you to
your Chapel?
OLIVER   Is there none here to give the Woman?
CLOWN   I will not take her on gift of any Man.                70
OLIVER   Truly she must be given, or the Marriage
is not lawful.
JAQUES   Proceed, proceed: I'll give her.
CLOWN   Good even, good Master What-ye-call't: how
do you, Sir, you are very well met. God 'ild                   75
you for your last Company, I am very glad to
see you, even a Toy in hand here, Sir. Nay,
pray be cover'd.
JAQUES   Will you be married, Motley?

---

78   **be cover'd**   Touchstone probably means 'put your hat back on'
     (assuming that the person being addressed – either Jaques or
     Sir Oliver – has deferentially removed a head covering to
     show respect). But it is conceivable that Touchstone is
     instructing Audrey to cover her head for church, in
     accordance with 1 Corinthians 11:4–6, or to cover a bodily
     part that is immodestly exposed; compare V.i.18–19 and
     V.iv.71–72.

79   **Motley**   Jaques's epithet for the Clown echoes II.vii.12–61.

80    **Bow**   the rounded collar of the yoke. Compare III.ii.143.

81    **Curb**   bridle. Like the 'Bells' attached to a falcon's legs, a curb is a means of controlling an animal.

82    **bill**   'kiss', caress or nibble another with their bills (beaks). Touchstone depicts 'Desires' as a restraint upon a man's freedom to roam (see the note to line 80), a shackle that binds and domesticates him in 'Wedlock'.

84    **Breeding**   both (a) bloodline, and (b) nurture, education. Compare III.ii.31–33.

85    **under . . . Beggar**   in the woods liked a person of no means or cultivation. Compare 2 *Henry VI*, IV.ii.53–54, where we hear that the rude Jack Cade was born 'under a Hedge'. Rosalind will echo Jaques's reference to a 'Bush' and a 'Beggar' in her epilogue to the prenuptial ceremonies that conclude the play; see V.iv.209–18.

86–87 **can tell you what Marriage is**   probably both (a) knows what marriage is, and (b) can instruct you in the responsibilities of married life. Jaques refers to the portions of the 'Solemnization of Matrimony' in which the minister describes why God 'instituted' the 'honourable estate' of marriage; Shakespeare and his audience would have known this liturgy in the form codified by the 1559 Book of Common Prayer.

88    **Wainscot**   wood panelling. In lines 87–90 Jaques is probably punning on *parnel*, a wanton wench, especially one who serves as a priest's concubine. Compare *Antony and Cleopatra*, IV.xii.20–21, where Antony complains that 'The Hearts / That pannelled me at Heels, to whom I gave / Their Wishes, do dis-Candy, melt their Sweets / On blossoming Caesar'. Here *warp* can mean both (a) become crooked or curved, and (b) deviate from its proper course, alter for the worse. See lines 91–95.

91–92 **I am not . . . another**   I am not sure that I would not rather be married by him than by another. *Mind* recalls II.vii.58–61.

93    **like**   likely.

96    **counsel thee**   'tell you what Marriage is' (lines 86–87). *Counsel* recalls III.ii.428.

98    **Bawdry**   sin; unchastity.

104   **Wind**   wend, go. The Folio spelling, *winde*, suggests a long-*i* pronunciation. Touchstone appears to be doing variations on a song that was popular in the 1590s.

CLOWN    As the Ox hath his Bow, Sir, the Horse his          80
   Curb, and the Falcon her Bells, so Man hath
   his Desires, and as Pigeons bill, so Wedlock
   would be nibbling.

JAQUES    And will you (being a Man of your Breeding)
   be married under a Bush like a Beggar? Get you          85
   to Church, and have a good Priest that can tell
   you what Marriage is. This Fellow will but
   join you together as they join Wainscot, then
   one of you will prove a shrunk Panel, and like
   green Timber, warp, warp.          90

CLOWN    I am not in the mind, but I were
   better to be married of him than of another,
   for he is not like to marry me well: and not
   being well married, it will be a good Excuse
   for me hereafter, to leave my Wife.          95

JAQUES    Go thou with me, and let me counsel thee.

[CLOWN]    – Come, sweet Audrey.
   We must be married, or we must live in Bawdry.
   – Farewell, good Mastter Oliver: Not
      *O sweet Oliver,*          100
      *O brave Oliver,*
    *Leave me not behind thee,*
   but
      *Wind away,*
      *Be gone I say;*          105
    *I will not to Wedding with thee.*

OLIVER    'Tis no matter; ne'er a fantastical Knave
   of them all shall flout me out of my Calling.

                    *Exeunt.*

---

107    **ne'er** both (a) never, and (b) not (compare *nary* in colloquial
    American English).
   **fantastical** frivolous. Compare III.ii.435.

108    **flout** jeer, scorn.
   **Calling** vocation as a priest.

III.iv  This scene returns us to the place in the forest appointed for Rosalind's meeting with Orlando.

1  **Never**  do not. Compare III.iii.107.

2  **grace**  both (a) wisdom, and (b) disposition, virtue, character. Compare III.ii.150–51.

4  **cause**  reason, justification. In this line *cause* carries a sense that overlaps with *case*, another word that derives from the same root, *causa*, in Latin. Here as in V.iv.214–16 (where Rosalind asks, 'What a Case am I in then . . . ?'), the heroine's phrasing is a reminder of her own case (situation), and of the case (costume) in which she hides the genital case that marks her gender. For *case* as a word for the pudendum, see *The Merry Wives of Windsor*, IV.i.59–74, and compare *Romeo and Juliet*, II.iii.50–60, III.iii.84–90. In lines 5–6 Celia authorizes her companion to 'weep' like the 'weaker vessel' she is beneath the disguise that represents her as 'a Man' (line 3); see the notes to I.ii.148, I.iii.120, II.iv.6.

7  **dissembling**  deceiving. Rosalind probably means that Orlando's hair is reddish brown ('Chestnut', lines 12–13), like that traditionally associated with Judas Iscariot. *Colour* recalls III.ii.439.

9  **Marry**  truly. This expression originated as an oath on the Virgin Mary. Compare III.ii.333. Here, as in I.ii.76, *Marry* provides a reminder of the matrimonial sense in III.iii.71–98; see the note to III.ii.42.

9–10  **his Kisses . . . Children**  Celia alludes to the fact that when Judas betrayed Jesus he identified him to his captors by kissing him (Luke 22:47–48).

13  **onely**  only (here with a hint at 'one-ly' as an adjective alluding to an upright, virile 'one'). Compare II.vii.34, 44, and see Genesis 2:24 (quoted in Matthew 19:3–6 and Ephesians 5:30–33), where we are told that a man and his wife shall be 'one flesh'. Celia's words in lines 12–13 echo II.vii.34.

15  **holy Bread**  either (a) bread blessed by a priest and distributed after the Eucharist to noncommunicants, or (b) sacramental communion bread.

16  **cast Lips**  Here *cast* involves a play on *chaste*, often spelled *chast* in Shakespeare; and the lips so described are (a) cast in the form of Diana's lips, or (b) cast off by Diana (compare III.iii.34–36).

# Scene 4

*Enter Rosalind and Celia.*

ROSALIND   Never talk to me, I will weep.

CELIA   Do, I prethee, but yet have the grace to
consider, that Tears do not become a Man.

ROSALIND   But have I not cause to weep?

CELIA   As good Cause as one would desire, therefore          5
weep.

ROSALIND   His very Hair is of the dissembling
Colour.

CELIA   Something browner than Judas's. Marry his
Kisses are Judas's own Children.                              10

ROSALIND   I'faith his Hair is of a good Colour.

CELIA   An excellent Colour: your Chestnut was ever
the onely Colour.

ROSALIND   And his Kissing is as full of Sanctity
as the Touch of holy Bread.                                  15

CELIA   He hath bought a pair of cast Lips of Diana:
a Nun of Winter's Sisterhood kisses not more
religiously, the very Ice of Chastity is in
them.

ROSALIND   But why did he swear he would come this          20
Morning, and comes not?

CELIA   Nay certainly there is no Truth in him.

ROSALIND   Do you think so?

CELIA   Yes, I think he is not a Pick-purse, nor

---

17   **Nun of Winter's Sisterhood**   This phrase can mean (a) a nun
who became a sister in the cold of winter, or (b) a nun of the
coldest (most self-denying, 'bloodless') order possible. Celia's
point is that Orlando's kisses are so lacking in illicit passion
as to be nun-like in their chastity. See the note to
III.ii.445–46.

24   **Pick-purse**   petty thief, pickpocket.

25 **verity** faithfulness, truth.

26 **concave** hollow, and thus empty of sincerity and fidelity.
Compare *Julius Caesar*, I.i.50–53.
**covered Goblet** With its dome-like cover on, a goblet was like
a sphere. *Covered* echoes III.iii.77–78; *Nut* (line 27) recalls
III.ii.115–16.

29 **in** Celia means 'in love'. She may also be hinting at 'in' in a
copulative sense. The word 'downright' in the next line would
fit a man's posture in such a situation. Compare *Measure for
Measure*, III.i.395–97, where Lucio expresses doubt that the
icy Angelo was 'made by Man and Woman, after this
downright way of Creation'.

35 **Tapster** server who draws ale from a cask at an inn or tavern.

36 **Reckonings** accountings, in two senses: (a) a tavern bill, and
(b) an account or story of one's love. Compare III.iii.11–14.
**attends** waits; is in attendance to (as part of the retinue of
those who serve or are loyal to).

39 **Question** exploratory conversation. Compare V.iv.167–70,
and see the note to III.ii.398.

40 **of as good as he** Rosalind's phrase would probably have struck
the Duke as pleasantly cheeky; hence his laughter. He has not
recognized the young 'swain' as his daughter in disguise. But
see V.iv.26–27.

44 **brave** Celia uses the word to mean 'putting on a bold, dashing
front', displaying splendid bravado. Compare II.vii.79–80.

46 **bravely** courageously. Celia's sarcasm includes puns on two
senses of *breaks*: (a) forswears (disavows his 'Oaths',
promises), and (b) splits or shatters (see lines 47–49), referring
to the lance of a jousting knight.
**travers** traverse; awry, at a glancing angle.
**athwart** against, crossing.

47 **puisny** puny (from the French *puis né*, later born), unskilled.

49 **Goose** a proverbially clumsy and silly bird. In lines 44–51
Celia is probably suggesting that Orlando is a braggart and a
whoremonger, the kind of 'Youth' who 'mounts' another
'Goose' (a loose woman, such as the whorish 'Winchester
Goose' of *1 Henry VI*, I.iii.53, and *Troilus and Cressida*,
V.iii.53), and gets a broken (dysfunctional) genital 'Staff'
(afflicted by the swollen groin that was also known as
'Winchester Goose') for his 'Folly'.

a Horse-stealer, but for his verity in Love I                        25
do think him as concave as a covered Goblet,
or a Worm-eaten Nut.

ROSALIND   Not true in Love?

CELIA   Yes, when he is in, but I think he is not
in.                                                                  30

ROSALIND   You have heard him swear downright he
was.

CELIA   'Was' is not 'is': besides, the Oath of a
Lover is no stronger than the Word of a
Tapster, they are both the confirmer of false          35
Reckonings. He attends here in the Forest on
the Duke your Father.

ROSALIND   I met the Duke yesterday, and had much
Question with him. He ask'd me of what
Parentage I was; I told him of as good as he,          40
so he laugh'd and let me go. But what talk we
of Fathers, when there is such a Man as
Orlando?

CELIA   O that's a brave Man, he writes brave
Verses, speaks brave Words, swears brave Oaths,        45
and breaks them bravely, quite travers athwart
the Heart of his Lover, as a puisny Tilter,
that spurs his Horse but on one side, breaks
his Staff like a noble Goose; but all's brave
that Youth mounts, and Folly guides. Who comes         50
here?

---

49–50 **But . . . guides**   But every ride seems 'brave' (spirited, virile)
           that is mounted by 'Youth' (the audacity of inexperience) and
           directed by 'Folly' (the rashness of unbridled exuberance and
           passion). *Folly* recalls II.vii.181: compare II.iv.33–36, 54–57.

148

54    **Who**  Modern usage would call for *Whom* in this context.

55    **proud**  haughty, arrogant. Compare line 59, and see
      I.ii.242–44, 262, II.vii.70–71, III.ii.80–81, 436.

56    **Mistress**  both (a) object of adoration, and (b) ruler. Poor
      Silvius would love to make Phebe his 'Mistress' in a
      matrimonial or erotic sense, but that meaning of the word is
      painfully inapplicable here.
      **Well**  even so; that's correct.

57    **Pageant**  display, brief dramatic entertainment.

58    **pale Complexion**  Lovers were proverbially pale because of the
      sighs they emitted. It was thought that a person lost a drop of
      blood with every sigh. *Complexion* recalls III.ii.204.

61    **remove**  follow (move ourselves from here to there). Compare
      III.ii.194–96, 362–63. *Mark* (observe) echoes III.ii.391–408.

64    **busy Actor**  Rosalind probably means that as she watches, she
      will be performing the lovers' parts vicariously in her own
      heart. As it turns out, she proves to be 'busy' in an even more
      active sense. Puck speaks, and responds, in similar fashion in
      *A Midsummer Night's Dream*, III.i.80–81.

III.v  This scene follows immediately in an adjacent part of the forest.

1     **Phebe**  The name of Silvius's 'Mistress' is a variation on *Phoebe*
      (from the Greek *Phoibos*), the Goddess of the Moon in Greek
      myth. Also known as *Cynthia* (*Kynthia*) and Artemis in
      Greek, she corresponded to the Roman huntress Diana; see
      the note to III.iv.16. Phebe's 'Scorn', her 'proud Disdain'
      (III.iv.59), is a comic reflection of her immortal namesake's
      vigorously defended chastity. In IV.i, Rosalind will treat
      Orlando to her own version of what a man should expect
      when he submits his will to that of an untamed mistress. The
      name *Silvius* plays on both *silver*, the colour of the moon (as
      noted in *Love's Labour's Lost*, IV.iii.33–35, and elsewhere),
      and *silvanus*, the Latin word for 'a wood').

4     **hard**  unfeeling, calloused. *Hard* recalls III.ii.333–37.

5     **Falls**  lets fall.
      **humbled**  both (a) bowed (to the chopping block), and (b)
      penitent.

*Enter Corin.*

CORIN    Mistress and Master, you have oft inquir'd
  After the Shepherd that complain'd of Love,
  Who you saw sitting by me on the Turf,
  Praising the proud disdainful Shepherdess                    55
  That was his Mistress.
CELIA                Well: and what of him?
CORIN    If you will see a Pageant truly play'd
  Between the pale Complexion of true Love
  And the red Glow of Scorn and proud Disdain,
  Go hence a little, and I shall conduct you                   60
  If you will mark it.
ROSALIND            O come, let us remove,
  The Sight of Lovers feedeth those in love.
  Bring us to this Sight, and you shall say
  I'll prove a busy Actor in their Play.            *Exeunt.*


# Scene 5

*Enter Silvius and Phebe.*

SILVIUS    Sweet Phebe, do not scorn me, do not,
    Phebe,
  Say that you love me not, but say not so
  In bitterness. The common Executioner,
  Whose Heart th' accustom'd sight of Death
    makes hard,
  Falls not the Axe upon the humbled Neck,                      5

6    **But first begs** without first begging. Lines 3–6 echo *Richard II*, V.iii.113–21, where the Duke of York tells the new king Henry IV to 'say "Pardonne moy" ' as he executes the treacherous Aumerle, and Aumerle's mother urges the king to 'Speak Pardon as 'tis current in our Land' because 'The chopping French we do not understand'.

7    **bloody Drops** both (a) drops of blood, and (b) the dropping to the ground of bloody heads.

9    **fly** run away from.
    **for** because.

11    **'Tis probable** a neatly phrased idea, to be sure, and highly credible. Celia's heavy irony echoes III.ii.288.

13    **coward Gates** fearful eyelids.
    **Atomies** specks of dust. Compare III.ii.247–48.

14    **Murtherers** murderers. Lines 1–14 parallel *Twelfth Night*, II.i.37–38, where Antonio tells Sebastian, 'If you will not murther me for my Love, let me be thy Servant.'

17    **counterfeit to swound** pretend to swoon; *swound* rhymes with *wound* in the previous line. Phebe's words anticipate a real swoon that Rosalind will attempt to pass off as a counterfeit; see IV.iii.166–83.

22    **Rush** pithy aquatic plant. See III.ii.391–94.

23    **Cicatrice** normally, a scar; here a small indentation ('Impressure', impression). Here *capable* means 'capacious' receptive.

24    **some moment** for a brief period.

25    **darted** shot like a dart (a short arrow).

27    **do Hurt** cause pain. Compare II.i.34.
    **deer** dear, but perhaps with wordplay on 'doe'. Compare III.iii.58.

28    **as** Silvius probably means (a) 'as I hope'; but another sense turns out to be pertinent, (b) 'inasmuch as'.

29    **Fancy** love's infatuation. Compare *A Midsummer Night's Dream*, II.i.161–64, where Cupid's 'fiery Shaft' misses its target and an 'Imperial Vot'ress' passes on 'In Maiden Meditation, Fancy-free'.

30–31  **Then . . . make** Silvius's words will soon prove applicable to the visible 'Wounds' that a higher 'Love's keen Arrows make'; see IV.iii.128–57, and compare lines 15–16, 20, III.ii.250–57.

But first begs Pardon: will you sterner be
Than he that dies and lives by bloody Drops?

*Enter Rosalind, Celia, and Corin.*

PHEBE  I would not be thy Executioner,
  I fly thee, for I would not injure thee:
  Thou tell'st me there is Murder in mine Eye,          10
  'Tis pretty sure, and very probable,
  That Eyes that are the frail'st and softest
    things,
  Who shut their coward Gates on Atomies,
  Should be called Tyrants, Butchers, Murtherers.
  Now I do frown on thee with all my Heart,          15
  And if mine Eyes can wound, now let them kill
    thee.
  Now counterfeit to swound, why now fall down,
  Or if thou canst not, oh for Shame, for Shame,
  Lie not, to say mine Eyes are Murtherers.
  Now shew the Wound mine Eye hath made in thee,    20
  Scratch thee but with a Pin, and there remains
  Some Scar of it; lean upon a Rush,
  The Cicatrice and capable Impressure
  Thy Palm some moment keeps; but now mine Eyes,
  Which I have darted at thee, hurt thee not,        25
  Nor I am sure there is no Force in Eyes
  That can do Hurt.
SILVIUS          O deer Phebe,
  If ever (as that ever may be near)
  You meet in some fresh Cheek the power of
    Fancy,
  Then shall you know the Wounds invisible        30
  That Love's keen Arrows make.

---

31    **keen**  sharp, painful. Corin alludes to the commonplace that
        love is ignited by a shot from the bow of Cupid, the God of
        Love. Compare *Hamlet*, III.ii.269–75, where Ophelia calls the
        ribald Prince 'keen' and he says, 'It would cost you a
        Groaning to take off mine Edge.' *Mocks* (line 33) echoes
        III.ii.227.

36 **insult** vaunt over your victim, like a triumphing warrior with no pity or civility.

39 **Than . . . Bed** What Rosalind means is that Phebe has no beauty to illuminate the world. Compare II.ii.5–7. *Candle* recalls III.i.6, and echoes Matthew 5:14–15; Rosalind's implication is that, despite her vanity, Celia is anything but 'the light of the world'.

42–43 **the ordinary . . . Sale-work** Nature's most common and inexpensive ready-made merchandise.

43 **'Od's my little Life** God save my trivial life. *'Od's* echoes I.ii.166.

44 **tangle** entangle as in a net. Here *means* means 'intends'; in line 41 it means 'signifies'.

47 **bugle** dark, inky, like black beads. Compare *The Winter's Tale*, IV.iv.226. Rosalind emphasizes that Phebe is not 'fair'; see the note to I.ii.41, and compare Sonnets 127, 130, and *Love's Labour's Lost*, III.i.201–12.

48 **to your Worship** to worship you. Rosalind puns on 'your Worship' as a title of respect; see I.i.93, 101, 171.

49 **wherefore** why.
**follow** both (a) trail behind, pursue, and (b) attend, wait upon, adhere to obediently.

50 **foggy South** the moisture-bearing south wind.
**puffing** sighing breathlessly. Most editions substitute a question mark for the comma that concludes this line in the Folio. In the original printing, Rosalind doesn't pause long enough for her question to register fully, because she is intent on making the point that occupies lines 51–52.

51 **properer** more attractive and seemly. Compare I.ii.126–27 and III.ii.325–26.

53 **ill-favour'd** (a) ugly, (b) unfavoured (unloved and uncared for), and (c) badly behaved. Compare III.ii.279–80.

54 **Glass** mirror. Compare III.ii.303–9.

PHEBE                              But till that Time
  Come not thou near me: and when that Time
    comes,
  Afflict me with thy Mocks, pity me not,
  As till that Time I shall not pity thee.
ROSALIND   And why, I pray you? who
    might be your Mother,                                          35
  That you insult, exult, and all at once
  Over the Wretched? what though you have no
    Beauty
  (As, by my faith, I see no more in you
  Than without Candle may go dark to Bed),
  Must you be therefore proud and pitiless?                 40
  Why what means this? why do you look on me?
  I see no more in you than in the ordinary
  Of Nature's Sale-work? – 'Od's my little Life,
  I think she means to tangle my Eyes too.
  – No, faith, proud Mistress, hope not after
    it,                                                              45
  'Tis not your inky Brows, your black silk Hair,
  Your bugle Eyeballs, nor your Cheek of Cream
  That can entame my Spirits to your Worship.
  – You foolish Shepherd, wherefore do you
    follow her
  Like foggy South, puffing with Wind and Rain,             50
  You are a thousand times a properer Man
  Than she a Woman. 'Tis such Fools as you
  That makes the World full of ill-favoured
    Children:
  'Tis not her Glass, but you that that flatters her,

55 **more proper** to be more appealing. Compare lines 51–52. Lines 54–56 parallel *Julius Caesar*, I.ii.51–68, and *Troilus and Cressida*, III.iii.89–102.

56 **Lineaments** features (literally, lines).
  **show her** make her appear to be.

59 **friendly** friend-like, in a friendly manner.

60 **Sell . . . Markets** Rosalind returns to the merchandising metaphor of lines 42–43; her advice to Phebe is not to wait for a better 'Offer' (line 61).

61 **Cry the man Mercy** ask your suitor to forgive you.

62 **Foul** In this line the word has three shades of meaning: (a) ugly, (b) unmannerly, and (c) ill-natured, unfair (unjust). See III.iii.32–40, and compare *Macbeth*, I.i.9–10.

64 **together** without interruption. Compare III.ii.101.

66 **Foulness** both (a) ugliness, and (b) ill-tempered, scoffing 'Scorn' (III.iv.59). Compare III.iii.32–40, where Touchstone admits that he has 'fall'n in love with' Audrey's 'Foulness', and see II.vii.58–64.

67–70 **And she'll . . . Words** Rosalind addresses these words to Silvius.

69 **sauce** Rosalind probably means something like the modern term 'sass'. But she also has a culinary metaphor in mind: she will season her words with a bitter sauce. Compare III.ii.314–16, III.iii.28–30. *Bitter* echoes lines 1–3 and recalls II.vii.184–86.

73 **falser than Vows made in Wine** Rosalind implies that she is incapable of fidelity and therefore not to be loved. But of course her real meaning is that she is not the man Phebe takes her to be. On the Elizabethan stage, the irony of her statement would have had an even deeper dimension: the performer playing Rosalind playing Ganimed was a male actor (no actresses were permitted in London's public playhouses until the 1660s), with the consequence that in this case two layers of falseness added up to the semblance of an underlying truth. *Falser* echoes III.ii.119–20, III.iv.33–36. Line 73 anticipates what Rosalind will say in her epilogue; see V.iv.209–16.

75 **Tuft** cluster.
  **hard by** adjacent, nearby.

And out of you she sees her self more proper                       55
Than any of her Lineaments can show her.
— But Mistress, know your self, down on your
    Knees
And thank Heaven, fasting, for a Good Man's
    Love;
For I must tell you friendly in your Ear,
Sell when you can, you are not for all Markets.                    60
Cry the man Mercy, love him, take his Offer,
Foul is most foul, being foul to be a Scoffer.
— So take her to thee, Shepherd, fareyouwell.
PHEBE   Sweet Youth, I pray you chide a Year
    together,
I had rather hear you chide than this Man woo.                     65
ROSALIND   He's fall'n in love with your Foulness.
— And she'll fall in love with my Anger. If it
be so, as fast as she answers thee with
frowning Looks, I'll sauce her with bitter
Words. — Why look you so upon me?                                  70
PHEBE   For no ill Will I bear you.
ROSALIND   I pray you do not fall in love with me,
For I am falser than Vows made in Wine;
Besides, I like you not. If you will know my
    House,
'Tis at the Tuft of Olives, here hard by.                          75

76    **ply her hard**   press her with all your vigour [to 'look on' you 'better', line 77, and see you for the proper man you are]. *Hard* echoes lines 4, 75.

79    **abus'd**   Rosalind's primary meaning is 'deceived'; but the more usual modern sense of the word is also appropriate to how Silvius's 'Sight' (what he sees in Phebe) has been mistreated. Compare III.ii.381–83.

81    **Dead Shepherd**   Phebe quotes a dead shepherd within the world of the play; but many Elizabethans would have recognized the 'Saw' (saying) she quotes as a line from Christopher Marlowe's *Hero and Leander* (published in 1598, though probably circulated privately for several years prior to that date). Many believe that Touchstone's reference to 'a great Reckoning in a little Room' (III.iii.14) is an allusion to the quarrel over a tavern bill that led to Marlowe's murder in a Deptford inn in 1593.
    **I . . . might**   I discover the forcible truth of the proverb you coined. *Saw* echoes II.vii.156.

87    **Grief in Love**   both (a) grievances (complaints) owing to love, and (b) 'sorrow' from unrequited love. Compare III.iii.433.

89    **extermin'd**   terminated, banished.

91    **were**   would be.
    **Covetousness**   Phebe picks up on 'neighbourly' in line 90 and alludes to the Tenth Commandment ('Thou shalt not covet thy neighbour's house, . . . nor any thing that is thy neighbour's', Exodus 20:17).

95    **erst**   before. *Irksome* (annoying) recalls II.i.22–25.

100    **Poverty of Grace**   lack of favour. *Poverty* recalls I.iii.67–69; *Grace* echoes I.iii.56–58 and III.iv.2.

102    **glean the broken Ears**   pick up the leftover scraps of grain. *Broken* echoes I.i.133–35, I.ii.130–49, II.i.56–57, II.iv.40–48, III.iv.44–49.

103    **loose**   let drop. Silvius continues the reaping metaphor of the previous sentence; so also with 'scatt'red' in line 104. *Scatter'd Smile* (line 104) recalls II.vii.57, where Jaques refers to 'the squand'ring Glances of the Fool'.

105    **yerewhile**   a while earlier; *yere* is a frequent variant of *ere*.

107    **Bounds**   fields, pastures. See II.iv.84.

— Will you go, Sister? — Shepherd, ply her
  hard.
— Come, Sister. — Shepherdess, look on him
  better,
And be not proud; though all the World could
  see,
None could be so abus'd in Sight as he.
— Come, to our Flock.    *Exit [with Celia and Corin].*   80
PHEBE   Dead Shepherd, now I find thy Saw of might,
'Who ever lov'd that lov'd not at first Sight?'
SILVIUS   Sweet Phebe.
PHEBE               Hah: what say'st thou, Silvius?
SILVIUS   Sweet Phebe, pity me.
PHEBE   Why I am sorry for thee, gentle Silvius.   85
SILVIUS   Where ever Sorrow is, Relief would be:
If you do sorrow at my Grief in Love,
By giving Love your Sorrow and my Grief
Were both extermin'd.
PHEBE   Thou hast my Love, is not that neighbourly?   90
SILVIUS   I would have you.
PHEBE             Why that were Covetousness.
Silvius, the Time was that I hated thee;
And yet it is not that I bear thee Love,
But since that thou canst talk of Love so well,
Thy Company, which erst was irksome to me,   95
I will endure; and I'll employ thee too.
But do not look for further Recompense
Than thine own Gladness, that thou art employ'd.
SILVIUS   So holy, and so perfect is my Love,
And I in such a Poverty of Grace,   100
That I shall think it a most plenteous Crop
To glean the broken Ears after the Man
That the main Harvest reaps; loose now and then
A scatt'red Smile, and that I'll live upon.
PHEBE   Know'st thou the Youth that spoke to me
  yerewhile?   105
SILVIUS   Not very well, but I have met him oft,
And he hath bought the Cottage and the Bounds

108     **Carlot**   peasant. The word derives from 'carl', a variant of
        'churl'. Compare III.v.81–83.

110     **peevish**   This word normally meant 'silly' or 'quirky'. Here,
        though, the context suggests that it also anticipates the
        modern sense: 'crotchety', 'disagreeable'. Lines 111–12 recall
        III.ii.284–85.

113     **pretty**   handsome, attractive, delicate.

114     **proud**   haughty, as in III.iv.55. Compare lines 40, 45, 78.
        **becomes him**   makes him all the more appealing. Compare
        I.i.75–76, 83–84, III.ii.258–59, III.iv.2–3.

115     **proper**   handsome, manly. See line 55.

116     **Complexion**   This word often meant 'disposition' and referred
        to the balance of one's humours; here, though, it seems to
        refer to the youth's appearance. Compare III.ii.204–6,
        III.iv.57–61.

118     **tall**   high in stature. See the note to I.iii.119.

123     **mingled Damask**   a combination of red and white, as in the
        damask rose.

124     **mark'd**   observed, noted. This verb echoes III.iv.60–61.

125     **In Parcels**   part by part. *Cause* (line 128) echoes III.iv.4–6 and
        recalls I.iii.96–97, III.ii.30–31.

129     **what had he to do**   what business did he have.

130     **black**   the opposite of 'fair' (light-complexioned, and thus
        beautiful, as noted in I.ii.41 and III.iii.33). See the note to line
        47, and compare Sonnet 130.

131     **am rememb'red**   recall. Compare II.iv.33–36, II.vii.187–89.

133     **all one**   all the same. Phebe's words keep us aware that she is
        eager to be 'all one' – both 'even' (see V.iv.18, 25) and 'one
        flesh' (see the notes to I.iii.102, III.iv.13) – with the object of
        her infatuation.
        **Omittance is no Quittance**   To have omitted a reply is not the
        same thing as to have forgiven the wrongs he did me. Phebe
        alludes to the legal doctrine that one does not renounce a
        claim for damages or debt merely by failing to assert it at the
        outset. *Quittance* recalls I.i.144–46 and III.i.11.

134     **tanting**   taunting. Phebe's phrasing hints at *tantalizing*
        (provocatively suggesting favours that are being withheld for
        now) and indicates that she will pretend to be throwing a
        tantrum.

That the old Carlot once was Master of.
PHEBE   Think not I love him, though I ask for him,
  'Tis but a peevish Boy, yet he talks well,                    110
  But what care I for Words? yet Words do well
  When he that speaks them pleases those that
     hear.
  It is a pretty Youth, not very pretty,
  But sure he's proud, and yet his Pride becomes
     him;
  He'll make a proper Man. The best thing in him    115
  Is his Complexion: and faster than his Tongue
  Did make Offence, his Eye did heal it up.
  He is not very tall, yet for his Years he's tall;
  His Leg is but so so, and yet 'tis well;
  There was a pretty Redness in his Lip,              120
  A little riper; and more lusty red
  Than that mix'd in his Cheek; 'twas just the
     Difference
  Betwixt the constant Red, and mingled Damask.
  There be some Women, Silvius, had they mark'd
     him
  In Parcels as I did, would have gone near          125
  To fall in love with him; but for my part
  I love him not, nor hate him not; and yet
  Have more cause to hate him than to love him,
  For what had he to do to chide at me?
  He said mine Eyes were black, and my Hair black,   130
  And, now I am rememb'red, scorn'd at me.
  I marvel why I answer'd not again,
  But that's all one: Omittance is no Quittance.
  I'll write to him a very tanting Letter,

136  **strait**  straight, immediately. See the note to II.i.68.

138  **passing short**  surpassingly curt. *Bitter* echoes lines 69–70.

And thou shalt bear it, wilt thou, Silvius?                    135
SILVIUS   Phebe, with all my Heart.
PHEBE                          I'll write it strait:
The Matter's in my Head, and in my Heart,
I will be bitter with him, and passing short.
Go with me, Silvius.                    *Exeunt.*

IV.i   This scene takes place near the sheepcote in the forest.

4      **it** 'Melancholy' (line 3, echoing III.ii.312–13). *Acquainted* (line 2) recalls III.ii.288–90.

6      **abhominable** inhuman, grotesque. Elizabethans thought that this word derived from the latin *ab* (away from) and *homine* (man). Alluding to 'the Golden Mean', a Greek aesthetic and philosophical principle that had been codified in Aristotle's *Nicomachean Ethics*, Rosalind tells Jaques that excessive 'Sadness' (line 21, recalling I.i.5) is just as reprehensible, just as distorting for human nature, as excessive levity (a 'Laughing' humour, line 4).

7      **modern** ordinary, daily. Compare II.vii.156.
       **Censure** judgement (here registering disapproval, the kind of judgement that is now common for this word).

8      **sad** serious (not necessarily sorrowful).

9      **Post** a block of wood, normally in an upright position (as in a fence), and thus a metaphor for a person who is content to stand and 'say nothing' (line 8). Compare *The Two Gentlemen of Verona*, I.i.156, where 'worthless Post' combines this sense with 'Messenger', a meaning that is also relevant to what Jaques has just said.

11     **Emulation** envy of one's learned betters. Compare I.i.149–53.

12     **fantastical** caused by an overactive imagination in the service of a self-indulgent artistic temperament. Compare III.iii.107–8.

13     **proud** arch. See III.v.14.
       **ambitious** zealous in pursuit of honour. See Jaques's portrait of military ambition in II.vii.149–53, and compare the Prince's praise of Fortinbras's 'Spirit, with divine Ambition puff'd' in *Hamlet*, IV.iv.46.

14     **politic** crafty and calculating.

15     **nice** coy, overly refined, affected; fastidiously delicate.

17     **compounded . . . Simples** composed of a number of individual ingredients.

# ACT IV

## Scene 1

*Enter Rosalind and Celia, and Jaques.*

JAQUES   I prethee, pretty Youth, let me be better
aquainted with thee.

ROSALIND   They say you are a melancholy Fellow.

JAQUES   I am so: I do love it better than Laughing.

ROSALIND   Those that are in extremity of either                    5
are abhominable Fellows, and betray themselves
to every modern Censure, worse than Drunkards.

JAQUES   Why, 'tis good to be sad and say nothing.

ROSALIND   Why then 'tis good to be a Post.

JAQUES   I have neither the Scholar's Melancholy,                  10
which is Emulation, nor the Musician's, which
is fantastical, nor the Courtier's, which is
proud, nor the Soldier's, which is ambitious,
nor the Lawyer's, which is politic, nor the
Lady's, which is nice, nor the Lover's, which                     15
is all these: but it is a Melancholy of mine
own, compounded of many Simples, extracted
from many Objects, and indeed the sundry

---

18   **Objects**   Normally 'simples' were extracted from medicinal
plants; Jaques's metaphorical ones derive from his
'Observations' (in accordance with the pattern Jaques
describes in II.vii.38–42) as he sifts the 'sundry' (manifold)
'Experience' (line 27) he has collected for 'Contemplation'
('Rumination') in his 'Travels' – both his journeys and the
arduous 'travail' (line 30) they have imposed upon him.

19–20 **which . . . Rumination**   which by frequent meditation. The Folio text has an *in* before this phrase. Modern editions normally retain the *in* but emend *by* to *my*.

20–21 **a most humorous Sadness**   a sobriety dominated by the melancholic humour (thought to be the result of an excess of black bile). *Humorous* recalls II.iii.8, III.ii.20–21, 443–46.

23–24 **sold . . . Men's**   both (a) exchanged your own land holdings for money to travel to lands owned by others, and (b) sold your own country short to admire the beauties and customs of foreign countries (see lines 35–40). Rosalind alludes to two New Testament passages: (a) the story in Luke 18:18–23, where Jesus tells a rich young ruler to 'sell all that thou hast, and distribute unto the poor, and thou shalt have treasure in heaven' (a narrative parodied in *Othello*, I.iii.386–89), and (b) the question Jesus poses in Mark 8:36 when he asks, 'For what shall it profit a man, if he shall gain the whole world, and lose his own soul?' (a teaching that underlies *Macbeth*, III.i.59–68, and will turn out to be a theme central to the conversions that occur in *As You Like It*).

25–26 **to have rich Eyes and poor Hands**   to be rich in perception but poor in possessions.

30    **travail**   both (a) travel, and (b) labour. See the note to line 18, and compare II.iv.75. *Merry* (line 29) recalls I.ii.1–27, II.iv.1–3.

33    **buy**   both (a) be with, and (b) purchase. Compare III.ii.274–75, another instance in which Jaques may be punning on the usual 'Goodbye' formula.
     **and**   if. So also in lines 42, 55.

33–34 **blank Verse**   unrhymed iambic pentameter, the normal medium of elevated discourse in Shakespeare's plays. Jaques's remark suggests that he wishes to have nothing to do with the change in tone introduced by Orlando. As it happens, Orlando's greeting is the only line of blank verse in the scene, which remains 'rustic' and 'informal'.

35    **Traveller**   both (a) traveller, and (b) travailer. Rosalind plays on 'Monsieur Melancholy', a nickname she overheard in III.ii.312–13.

36    **lisp**   speak with a foreign affectation.
     **disable**   demean, disparage.

38    **Nativity**   birth, here a synecdoche for 'place of birth' or native country.

Contemplation of my Travels, which by often
Rumination wraps me in a most humorous          20
Sadness.

ROSALIND   A Traveller: by my faith you have great
Reason to be sad. I fear you have sold your
own Lands to see other Men's: then to have
seen much, and to have nothing, is to have rich          25
Eyes and poor Hands.

JAQUES   Yes, I have gain'd my Experience.

*Enter Orlando.*

ROSALIND   And your Experience makes you sad. I
had rather have a Fool to make me merry than
Experience to make me sad, and to travail for          30
it too.

ORLANDO   Good Day, and Happiness, dear Rosalind.

JAQUES   Nay then God buy you, and you talk in blank
Verse.

ROSALIND   Farewell, Monsieur Traveller: look you          35
lisp, and wear strange Suits, disable all the
Benefits of your own Country, be out of love
with your Nativity, and almost chide God for
making you that Countenance you are, or I will
scarce think you have swam in a Gundello.          40

[*Exit Jaques.*]

— Why how now, Orlando, where have you been

---

39   **Countenance**   identifying appearance (to disclose your
        'Nativity', line 38). Compare II.vii.108–9.

40   **Gundello**   gondola. Travellers who had been to Venice tended
        to be even more affected and supercilious than those who had
        toured elsewhere.

42–43 **and . . . Trick**  if you treat me to another device such as this
 (deceiving me into thinking you'd be here at a given time and
 then showing up late).

44  **more**  again.

46  **of my Promise**  of when I pledged to be here.

49  **thousand**  thousandth.

51–52 **hath . . . Shoulder**  has tapped him casually and lightly on the
 shoulder in the manner of an arresting officer.

52–53 **but . . . Heart hole**  but I'll guarantee that he has a 'hole' where
 his 'Heart' should be [since he shows no sign of having had
 his heart pierced by Cupid's arrow]. To a theatre audience
 Rosalind's concluding phrase could be heard as *Heart-whole*
 (heart uninjured), a sense reflected in the usual modern
 emendation, and one that conveys much the same implication
 as the Folio reading. *Deer* (line 54) recalls III.iii.58, III.v.27.

56  **lief**  gladly. Compare III.ii.271. In line 55, as in lines 33, 68,
 and 75, *and* means 'if'.

58  **I**  Ay. But 'I [had]' is another possible reading. Compare
 II.iv.16, and see lines 126, 140.

60  **Joincture**  jointure; the estate a husband settled on his wife at
 marriage to provide for her in case he died before she did.
 Compare III.iii.55–56, where Touchstone speaks similarly
 about 'the Dowry of' a man's 'Wife'.

61  **Destiny**  predestined fate. Compare *Othello*, III.iii.267–71,
 where the title character says that the 'Forked Plague' (a
 forehead branched with 'Horns', line 64) is 'Destiny
 unshunnable, like Death'. For similar references to cuckolding
 as something to which 'Great Ones' are 'Fated' see *All's Well
 That Ends Well*, I.iii.64–67, *The Merchant of Venice*,
 III.i.81–82, and *Troilus and Cressida*, V.i.69–70. *Destiny*
 recalls I.ii.104–10; *Snail* (lines 56–58) echoes II.vii.145–47.

64  **fain**  pleased, obliged. Compare I.ii.166–68.

65  **beholding**  beholden, indebted.

66  **armed in his Fortune**  already supplied with the 'Destiny' (line
 61) he would otherwise have to wait for. Rosalind's use of
 *armed* recalls Touchstone's 'Defence' imagery in III.iii.58–64.

66–67 **prevents the Slander of his Wife**  anticipates, if not forestalls,
 the mark of slander (public disgrace, shame) that his wife
 would otherwise have to give him (the horns of a cuckold).

all this while? you a Lover? and you serve me
such another Trick, never come in my Sight
more.

ORLANDO   My fair Rosalind, I come within an Hour        45
of my Promise.

ROSALIND   Break an Hour's Promise in Love? he
that will divide a Minute into a thousand
Parts, and break but a part of the thousand
part of a Minute in the Affairs of Love, it        50
may be said of him that Cupid hath clapp'd
him o'th' Shoulder, but I'll warrant him
Heart hole.

ORLANDO   Pardon me, deer Rosalind.

ROSALIND   Nay, and you be so tardy, come no more        55
in my Sight, I had as lief be woo'd of a Snail.

ORLANDO   Of a Snail?

ROSALIND   I, of a Snail: for though he comes
slowly, he carries his House on his Head; a
better Joincture I think than you make a        60
Woman. Besides, he brings his Destiny with
him.

ORLANDO   What's that?

ROSALIND   Why Horns: which such as you are fain
to be beholding to your Wives for. But he comes        65
armed in his Fortune, and prevents the Slander
of his Wife.

ORLANDO   Virtue is no Horn-maker: and my Rosalind
is virtuous.

ROSALIND   And I am your Rosalind.        70

72    **Leer** smile (here signifying Rosalind's countenance, facial complexion). Celia alludes to the fact that Rosalind has darkened her skin in assuming the 'person' of Ganimed; but she also refers to the demeanour of the real Rosalind, who 'is no Horn-maker' (line 68), rather than that of the sceptical male she counterfeits as a worldly-wise page. *Pleases* (line 71) echoes III.v.111–12.

74    **holi-day** both (a) holiday, festive, and (b) holy-day (alluding to the wedding day she hopes is forthcoming). Compare I.iii.14–15, II.vii.180. *Humour* (mood, disposition) echoes lines 19–21; *like* (likely) recalls III.iii.93. In line 75 *and* means 'if'.

76    **very** true, real.

79    **gravell'd** impeded, at a loss for 'Matter' (thoughts to utter). This figurative term appears to refer either to (a) being choked or smothered, as by 'gravel' in the throat (compare *Othello*, II.i.198–99), or (b) getting stuck or running aground in sand and gravel.

81    **out** out of things to say, having forgotten the words they'd prepared. Compare III.ii.264–65, 268.
      **spit** expectorate as a 'Shift' (line 83) to restore their confidence, memory, or concentration. Compare *The Taming of the Shrew*, III.i.40, where Lucentio tells a fumbling lute player to 'Spit in the Hole, Man, and tune again'.

82    **warn** protect and bless. In this phrase *warn* is a variant of *warrant*, 'secure' or 'assure', as in III.iii.4; compare *A Midsummer Night's Dream*, V.i.323, where the First Quarto prints 'God warnd us'.

83    **cleanliest Shift** quickest, politest, and most sanitary device (makeshift).

85    **Entreaty** pleading.

86    **new Matter** a new set of exchanges. Rosalind probably uses 'Matter' in the sense of rhetorical *topoi*; see the note to II.vii.40.

87    **out** Orlando probably means 'out of matter' or 'out of suit'. See the note to line 81.

89    **Marry** truly. Compare III.iv.9–10.

CELIA   It pleases him to call you so: but he hath a
Rosalind of a better Leer than you.

ROSALIND   Come, woo me, woo me: for now I am in a
holi-day Humour, and like enough to consent.
What would you say to me now, and I were your          75
very, very Rosalind?

ORLANDO   I would kiss before I spoke.

ROSALIND   Nay, you were better speak first, and
when you were gravell'd, for lack of Matter,
you might take occasion to kiss: very good              80
Orators, when they are out, they will spit,
and for Lovers, lacking (God warn us) Matter,
the cleanliest Shift is to kiss.

ORLANDO   How if the Kiss be denied?

ROSALIND   Then she puts you to Entreaty, and there     85
begins new Matter.

ORLANDO   Who could be out, being before his beloved
Mistress?

ROSALIND   Marry that should you if I were your
Mistress, or I should think my Honesty ranker          90
than my Wit.

ORLANDO   What, of my Suit?

---

90    **ranker**   more corrupt, diseased. See II.vii.44–47, and compare
III.ii.103–4, and IV.iii.79–81. Rosalind pretends to take *out*
(line 87) in a sexual sense. What she means in lines 89–91 is
that her 'Honesty' (chastity) would not think of allowing
Orlando to be 'in'. In all likelihood, *Wit* (line 91) involves
sexual wordplay as well. Rosalind uses it here to refer to
mental quickness; but by lines 176–79 it is clear that the word
has the same genital implications that 'Will' often does. See
the notes to I.ii.51, 53, and compare III.iii.11–15.

93–94 **out of your Suit**   Having rejected any implication that this phrase might mean 'undressed' (or at least having one's 'Wit' exposed) in line 93, Rosalind now suggests that it means either (a) 'denied' (line 84), your plea rejected, or (b) out of countenance, dumbfounded (as noted at lines 81, 87). *Suit* (which picks up on line 92) recalls II.vii.42–47.

100   **by Attorney**   by proxy (by appointing someone else to die for you). *Die* (lines 99–100) recalls the exchanges on 'Murther' in III.v.1–14. One meaning of *die* is 'achieve orgasm', and Orlando's phrasing suggests that if he cannot have Rosalind he will 'die' alone, in his own 'Person'. See the note to III.ii.162.

102   **all this Time**   Biblical interpreters of Shakespeare's day had calculated the age of the earth as less than six thousand years.

103   *videlicet*   Latin for 'namely', 'that is'.
      **Love Cause**   Latinate legal terminology for 'a case of love'. See the note to III.iv.4, and compare III.v.124–29.

104   **Troilus**   a faithful Trojan lover who gave his all for Criseyde.

105   **Grecian Club**   Rosalind makes Troilus's death more crude and undignified than her sources presented it; in Chaucer's *Troilus and Criseyde* the hero is killed by the spear of Achilles. The phrase *Grecian Club* hints at the genital 'Club' of the mightiest 'Grecian' in classical mythology. For other references to 'Hercules' Club' see *Love's Labour's Lost*, I.iii.181–83, V.i.136–51, V.ii.588–93, and *Much Ado About Nothing*, II.i.262–64, III.iii.140–48.
      **die**   Rosalind probably means by pining for love; but here as in lines 99–100 *die* could also refer to orgasm, and that too would fit Troilus's story. Not long after he completed *As You Like It*, Shakespeare produced his own treatment of this story in *Troilus and Cressida*.

106   **Patterns**   exemplars, models, paradigms.

107   **Leander**   Another 'pattern' of faithful love, Leander swam nightly from Abydos to Sestos, where his sweetheart Hero lived in a tower; one night in a storm the light that guided Leander went out and he drowned. Once again, Rosalind debunks what she pretends to consider a sentimental interpretation of the 'facts' of the case, in lines 107–13. For other Shakespearean treatments of Leander, see *The Two Gentlemen of Verona*, I.i.20–35, III.i.117–20, *Much Ado About Nothing*, V.ii.25–37, and *A Midsummer Night's Dream*, V.i.198–99.

ROSALIND   Not out of your Apparel, and yet out of
your Suit: am not I your Rosalind?

ORLANDO   I take some joy to say you are, because      95
I would be talking of her.

ROSALIND   Well, in her Person, I say I will not
have you.

ORLANDO   Then in mine own Person, I die.

ROSALIND   No faith, die by Attorney: the poor      100
World is almost six thousand years old, and in
all this Time there was not any Man died in
his own Person (*videlicet*) in a Love Cause.
Troilus had his Brains dash'd out with a
Grecian Club, yet he did what he could to die      105
before, and he is one of the Patterns of Love.
Leander, he would have liv'd many a fair year
though Hero had turn'd Nun, if it had not been
for a hot Midsummer-night; for, good Youth, he
went but forth to wash him in the Hellespont,      110
and being taken with the Cramp, was drown'd,
and the foolish Chroniclers of that Age found
it was Hero of Cestos. But these are all Lies:

---

108   **though ... Nun**   even if his sweetheart had forsaken love and
entered a convent. Compare *A Midsummer Night's Dream*,
I.i.62–90.

110   **went ... him**   went out merely to bathe himself.

112   **found**   determined that. Rosalind is probably mocking legal
terminology again, in the sense that a judge or jury 'finds' a
defendant guilty or not guilty. In this case, she says, the
coroner's jury foolishly blamed Hero or Love for a death that
was actually caused by nothing more romantic than a cramp.

113   **Cestos**   the Folio spelling for Sestos. *Worms* (line 114) echoes
III.ii.68–69, III.iv.25–27.

116   **right**   correct, actual. Compare III.ii.128, 291.

117   **protest**   testify, declare. *Mind* recalls III.iii.91–92.

120   **coming-on**   receptive, indeed flirtatiously suggestive.
      *Disposition* echoes III.ii.204–6.

126   **I**   both (a) I [will], and (b) Ay. Compare lines 58, 140.

128   **good**   Orlando understands 'Ganimed' to mean 'virtuous' in
      moral terms; lines 130–31 make it clear that Rosalind is
      employing a virile sense that means 'satisfying' and 'potent'.

131   **good thing**   Rosalind plays on the sexual meaning of 'thing'
      (here the male member). See the notes to I.ii.270 and
      IV.i.185–86.

137   **have to Wife**   Celia echoes the phrasing in the marriage
      ceremony of the Elizabethan Book of Common Prayer, where
      the priest says 'Wilt thou have this woman to thy wedded
      wife . . . ?'

140   **I**   either (a) Ay, or (b) 'I' (quoting Orlando's reply).

145   **your Commission**   If Rosalind is addressing Orlando (the usual
      interpretion of line 145), she means 'your authority for taking
      her, since there is no one here to give her away (commit her to
      you)'. On the other hand, if Rosalind is speaking to Celia (and
      the *you* and *thee* pronouns in lines 145–46 would seem to
      imply a shift of address), her meaning is 'your authority to
      perform weddings'. In either case, this moment echoes the
      'crisis' that Touchstone faced in III.iii.69–98, in an earlier
      mock-wedding.

147   **There's . . . Priest**   What Rosalind means is that, like an
      over-eager girl, she has said 'I will' before the priest has asked
      her if she accepts Orlando for her husband.

148–  **a . . . Actions**   a woman's impulses prompt her to act more
49    swiftly than a man's 'Thought' would. Compare II.ii.204–6,
      266–67, where Rosalind speaks with similar deprecation
      about the irrationality, passion, rashness, and physical frailty
      of 'a Woman'.

152   **possess'd her**   both (a) made her yours by your vows, and (b)
      consummated those vows in bed.

Men have died from time to time, and Worms
have eaten them, but not for Love.                                    115
ORLANDO   I would not have my right Rosalind of this
Mind, for I protest her Frown might kill me.
ROSALIND   By this Hand, it will not kill a Fly.
But come, now I will be your Rosalind in a
more coming-on Disposition: and ask me what          120
you will, I will grant it.
ORLANDO   Then love me, Rosalind.
ROSALIND   Yes faith will I, Fridays and Saturdays,
and all.                                                              125
ORLANDO   And wilt thou have me?
ROSALIND   I, and twenty such.
ORLANDO   What sayest thou?
ROSALIND   Are you not good?
ORLANDO   I hope so.
ROSALIND   Why then, can one desire too much of a       130
good thing? — Come Sister, you shall be the
Priest, and marry us. — Give me your Hand,
Orlando. — What do you say, Sister?
ORLANDO   Pray thee marry us.
CELIA   I cannot say the Words.                                      135
ROSALIND   You must begin, 'Will you, Orlando.'
CELIA   Go to: 'Will you, Orlando, have to Wife this
Rosalind?'
ORLANDO   I will.
ROSALIND   I, but when?                                              140
ORLANDO   Why now, as fast as she can marry us.
ROSALIND   Then you must say, 'I take thee, Rosalind,
for Wife.'
ORLANDO   I take thee, Rosalind, for Wife.
ROSALIND   I might ask you for your Commission,        145
but I do take thee, Orlando, for my Husband.
There's a Girl goes before the Priest, and
certainly a Woman's Thought runs before her
Actions.
ORLANDO   So do all Thoughts, they are wing'd.          150
ROSALIND   Now tell me how long you would have
her, after you have possess'd her?

155 **woe** woo. But see the note to I.iii.137, and compare III.ii.432.
Here *April* refers to a spring-like freshness, a youthful vitality,
in contrast with the age and wintry storminess of *December*.
In lines 156–57 *May* signifies the merriment that accompanies
warm and mild weather; when *the Sky changes* (for the
worse, as noted in I.iii.106, II.i.18, III.ii.192, 301–2), those
who reflect it become moody, dark, and hostile.

158– **Barbary Cock-pigeon** Rosalind refers to the male of a species
59 of pigeon imported from Asia (not Africa, as the name would
suggest); it had long been proverbial for its jealousy of the
hen-pigeon. *Cock* recalls II.vii.90.

160 **against Rain** when it can tell that rain is coming. Here *against*
means both (a) in anticipation of, and (b) in opposition to or
defiance of.
 **new-fangled** fascinated with novelty.

161 **giddy** unstable, capricious. Compare III.ii.369–72.

162– **Diana in the Fountain** Rosalind may be referring to the
63 weeping heroine in a popular romance, *Diana* (1559), by the
Portuguese writer Jorge de Montemayor. Shakespeare drew
on it as a source for several of his comedies. It has also been
suggested that Rosalind is thinking about a sculpted goddess
Diana in a decorative fountain. *Diana* echoes III.iv.16.

164 **Hyen** hyena, an animal whose bark sounds like a laugh.
*Dispos'd* (echoing line 120) frequently means *merry* or
'playful', as in *Love's Labour's Lost*, II.i.247, V.ii.465; here
*merry* recalls lines 28–30 and plays on *marry* ('wed', line
156).

167 **By my Life** Rosalind's oath provides a witty reminder that her
life and Ganimed's are one and the same.

168 **wise** prudent, rational, self-controlled. Compare II.vii.44–57.

170 **Make** make fast, close tight.

171 **Wit** cunning, here referring to her will to be free of restraint.
See the notes to lines 90, 93–94.

172 **Casement** part of a hinged window. The repetitions of *out*
(lines 170–74) echo lines 80–94.

173 **stop** block off, stop up.

ORLANDO    For ever and a Day.

ROSALIND    Say a Day, without the Ever: no, no,
Orlando, Men are April when they woe, December          155
when they wed; Maids are May when they are
Maids, but the Sky changes when they are Wives.
I will be more jealous of thee than a Barbary
Cock-pigeon over his Hen, more clamorous than
a Parrot against Rain, more new-fangled than           160
an Ape, more giddy in my Desires than a Monkey.
I will weep for nothing, like Diana in the
Fountain, and I will do that when you are
dispos'd to be merry; I will laugh like a Hyen,
and that when thou art inclin'd to sleep.              165

ORLANDO    But will my Rosalind do so?

ROSALIND    By my Life, she will do as I do.

ORLANDO    O but she is wise.

ROSALIND    Or else she could not have the Wit to
do this: the wiser, the waywarder. Make the            170
Doors upon a Woman's Wit, and it will out at
the Casement; shut that, and 'twill out at the
Key-hole; stop that, 'twill fly with the Smoke
out at the Chimney.

ORLANDO    A Man that had a Wife with such a Wit,      175
he might say, 'Wit, whether will't?'

ROSALIND    Nay, you might keep that Check for it,

---

176    **Wit, whether will't?**    Orlando alludes to the same proverb
quoted by Celia in I.ii.61, 'Wit, whether wander you?' But in
this context, the phrase gives 'Wit' a meaning that refers to
something other than a mind that cannot remain focused for
long enough to complete a thought. Rosalind is describing a
'Wit' with a will of its own; for *Will* as a word that can refer
both to erotic desire and to the genitalia, see Sonnets 135–36.

177    **Check**    rebuke, restraint. Rosalind may also be alluding to the
term for a chess move that puts an opponent's King at risk.

178 **Wive's**  wife's. In Shakespeare a final *s* turns an unvoiced *f* to a voiced *v* whether the resulting word-form is a simple plural or a possessive in modern English.

180 **Wit**  Here the two uses of the word mean (a) quick-thinking ingenuity, and (b) a woman's wantonness (with a genital sense of 'Wit' implicit in the second implication).

182 **Marry**  indeed. Here as elsewhere (see line 89), this word alludes ironically to the matrimonial sense to be found, for example, in lines 131–34.

183 **take**  capture, seize, apprehend. But here and in line 184, *take* also hints at the copulative sense.

184 **her Tongue**  her ability to speak. *Tongue* often has sexual implications (as in II.i.217 of *The Taming of the Shrew*), and here it suggests the kind of male 'Answer' (line 183) a female 'Question' seeks to 'make her Fault' (see the notes to lines 170, 185–86). For the genital senses of 'Question' and 'Answer' see *All's Well That Ends Well*, II.ii.15–16, where the Countess agrees with the Clown that 'that's a bountiful Answer that fits all Questions'.

185– **make . . . Occasion**  excuse her wrongdoing by saying that she
86 was busy on an errand for her husband. Here *Fault* refers to a sexual misdeed; but the word frequently refers to the female genitalia as well. A 'fault' is literally a crack or fissure; it thus relates to the Elizabethan commonplace that the female anatomy has a genital deficiency (either 'an O-thing' or 'a no-thing'). *Fault* recalls I.iii.50, III.ii.298–99, 375–78.

187 **breed . . . Fool**  both (a) rear it the way a fool would, and (b) train it to be a fool. *Breed* echoes III.iii.84

188 **these**  the next. So also in line 190.

190 **deer**  dear (but with the same ambiguity as in line 54).

192 **Dinner**  the main midday meal, as in II.vi.19.

194 **go your ways**  be on your way. Compare II.iii.66.

195 **prove**  turn out to be.

197 **'Tis but one cast away**  I'll just be another abandoned lover. The phrase *cast away* echoes III.iii.34–36 and III.iv.16.

198 **so come Death**  Rosalind's concern that she will die without Orlando echoes lines 97–118.

200 **Troth**  faith, truth.

till you met your Wive's Wit going to your
Neighbour's Bed.

ORLANDO    And what Wit could Wit have, to excuse        180
that?

ROSALIND    Marry to say she came to seek you there:
you shall never take her without her Answer,
unless you take her without her Tongue. O that
Woman that cannot make her Fault her Husband's        185
Occasion, let her never nurse her Child her
self, for she will breed it like a Fool.

ORLANDO    For these two Hours, Rosalind, I will
leave thee.

ROSALIND    Alas, deer Love, I cannot lack thee two        190
Hours.

ORLANDO    I must attend the Duke at Dinner, by two
a' clock I will be with thee again.

ROSALIND    Ay, go your ways, go your ways, I knew
what you would prove, my Friends told me as        195
much, and I thought no less. That flattering
Tongue of yours won me: 'tis but one cast away,
and so come Death. Two o'clock is your Hour.

ORLANDO    Ay, sweet Rosalind.

ROSALIND    By my Troth, and in good Earnest, and        200
so God mend me, and by all pretty Oaths that

---

201–    **by all . . . dangerous**  Rosalind is probably thinking of Jesus'
2          admonitions against swearing in Matthew 5:33–37, where he
          says, 'Swear not at all . . . But let your communication be,
          Yea, yea; Nay, nay.'

201    **mend**  regenerate, preserve.
       **pretty**  both (a) eloquently phrased and (b) inoffensive, polite,
       genteel. Compare III.ii.288, III.v.11, 113.

202 **dangerous** blasphemous, and thus imperilling the soul of the person who utters them. Compare III.ii.42–90.

**iot** jot; from the Greek letter 'iota' and (like other words that now begin with *j*) probably pronounced with a *y*-sound by some speakers in Shakespeare's time.

203 **behind your Hour** later than the time you pledge.

204 **pathetical** miserable.

205 **hollow** empty of sincerity. Compare *concave*, III.iv.26.

207 **gross** both (a) large, and (b) unworthy.

208 **Censure** judgement (here meaning 'condemnation', as in line 7).

210 **Religion** faith, devotion.

**then** than. But here as in III.ii.407–12, 'then' can also provide a kind of sense.

212–13 **Time . . . try** Rosalind alludes to the proverb 'Time tries all things.' Here *try* means 'put to the test' in a judicial trial. *Justice* means 'judge' or 'magistrate'.

214 **Offenders** lawbreakers, evildoers. See the note to IV.iii.133.

215 **simply** absolutely, completely.

**misus'd our Sex** abused the reputation of our gender.

216 **prate** idle chatter. *Doublet and Hose* recalls III.ii.233.

217–18 **what . . . Nest** Celia alludes to the proverb 'It is a foul bird that fouls [defiles] its own nest.' *Shew* (show) echoes III.v.20.

220 **Fathom** fathoms. A fathom is a measure of six feet.

221 **sounded** both (a) plumbed for depth, and (b) expressed.

222 **unknown Bottom** unfathomable depth. Celia offers another reading of the phrase in the next line. Rosalind's wording echoes *A Midsummer Night's Dream*, IV.i.208–21, a burlesque of 1 Corinthians 2:9–10, where the Apostle Paul says that 'Eye hath not seen, nor ear heard, neither have entered into the heart of man, the things which God hath prepared for them that love him'. In the 1557 Geneva Bible, Elizabethans would have gone on to read that 'God hath opened them unto us by his Sprite, for the Spirite searcheth all things, yea, the bottom of Goddes secrets.'

are not dangerous, if you break one iot of
your Promise, or come one Minute behind your
Hour, I will think you the most pathetical
Break-promise, and the most hollow Lover, and                    205
the most unworthy of her you call Rosalind,
that may be chosen out of the gross Band of
the Unfaithful: therefore beware my Censure,
and keep your Promise.

ORLANDO   With no less Religion, then if thou wert            210
indeed my Rosalind: so adieu.

ROSALIND   Well, Time is the old Justice that
examines all such Offenders, and let Time try:
adieu.                                        *Exit [Orlando].*

CELIA   You have simply misus'd our Sex in your               215
Love-prate: we must have your Doublet and Hose
pluck'd over your Head, and shew the World what
the Bird hath done to her own Nest.

ROSALIND   O Coz, Coz, Coz: my pretty little Coz,
that thou didst know how many Fathom deep I                   220
am in love. But it cannot be sounded: my
Affection hath an unknown Bottom, like the Bay
of Portugal.

CELIA   Or rather Bottomless, that as fast as you
pour Affection in, it runs out.                              225

ROSALIND   No, that same wicked Bastard of Venus,
that was begot of Thought, conceiv'd of Spleen,
and borne of Madness, that blind rascally Boy,

---

227   **begot of**   impregnated by. *Thought* (here referring to 'Desire' or
        'Longing', or perhaps Melancholy') echoes lines 147–50.
      **Spleen**   the organ regarded as seat of the impulsive passions
        (love, anger, laughter), and thus of waywardness (line 170) or
        caprice.

228   **borne of**   either (a) given birth by (if 'Madness' is to be
        construed as either a mother or a midwife), or (b) carried by
        (with 'Madness' functioning either as pregnant mother-to-be
        or as nurse).

229 **abuses**  both (a) deceives, and (b) misuses, as in line 79. In this speech Rosalind refers to Cupid, whom she reduces to a 'wicked Bastard' of the Goddess of Love (lines 226–28), fathered by 'Thought' (wishful thinking) under the influence of 'Spleen', and 'borne of Madness'. Rosalind is saying that she feels like the victim of an irrational power that has enslaved her.

230 **out**  out of use ('blind', line 228, or at least blindfolded). *Out* echoes lines 170–74, and anticipates lines 231–32.

**deep**  both (a) deep (submerged 'in love'), and (b) deeply, earnestly.

232 **Shadow**  a shady place in keeping with the dark mood of love-melancholy.

233 **till he come**  until he returns. But Rosalind's 'sigh' (which recalls II.iv.27) also hints at the kind of 'Groaning' (III.ii.322) that lasts till a man has 'come' in the sense implied in *Hamlet*, III.ii.269–75 (see the quotation in the note to III.v.31, and compare lines 196–98 and V.ii.35–37).

IV.ii  This scene takes place elsewhere in the forest. It provides an interlude to cover the two hours that elapse while Orlando eats dinner with Duke Senior.

2 **Dear**  Here and in lines 5, 11, this word can mean either 'deer' (stag, as in II.i.29–63) or 'dear', here a sweetheart who has 'died . . . for Love' (IV.i.114–15), either figuratively (see the second note to IV.i.105) or literally, perhaps at the hands of a horn-mad, Othello-like cuckold. *Dear* echoes IV.i.190.

5–6 **Dear's Horns . . . Victory**  Jaques proposes a ritual whereby the 'Roman Conqueror' who has killed a deer will be honoured with a trophy that will mark him, not as a triumphant warrior, but as a weak fool whose 'Dear' has made him an object of scorn. The 'Roman' reference is probably an allusion to Julius Caesar's famous 'Veni, vidi, vici' (I came, I saw, I conquered), a boast (see V.ii.35–37) that was often used facetiously in Shakespeare's time to describe sexual conquests. The deer's horns echo the story of Actaeon, a hunter who surprised Diana and her maidens while they were bathing, and whose punishment was to have horns spring from his brow; mistaking him for a stag, Actaeon's hunting dogs tore him to pieces. Ovid tells the story in Book III of the *Metamorphoses*. *Branch*, alluding to the laurel wreath that signified 'Victory' in Greek and Roman antiquity, can also refer to the antlers atop a stag's brows; see the note to IV.i.61. *Horns* recalls III.iii.48–64, IV.i.55–70.

that abuses every one's Eyes, because his own
are out, let him be judge, how deep I am in                    230
love. I'll tell thee, Aliena, I cannot be out
of the Sight of Orlando: I'll go find a Shadow,
and sigh till he come.

CELIA   And I'll sleep.                              *Exeunt.*


# Scene 2

*Enter Jaques and Lords, Foresters.*

JAQUES   Which is he that killed the Dear?
LORD   Sir, it was I.
JAQUES   Let's present him to the Duke like a
Roman Conqueror, and it would do well to set
the Dear's Horns upon his Head, for a Branch            5
of Victory; have you no Song, Forester, for
this purpose?
LORD   Yes sir.
JAQUES   Sing it: 'tis no matter how it be in Tune,
so it make Noise enough.                    *Music.*   10


SONG

*What shall he have that kill'd the Dear?*
*His Leather skin, and Horns to wear:*

---

6   **Forester**   warden of the forest and its game. Compare III.ii.316.
It may well be that Amyens, or the actor who plays him in
other scenes, is the officer who will sing the verses that follow.
Compare II.vii.173–93.

13–14 **bear / this Burthen**   sing this refrain (the lines that follow). It appears likely that one member of the party sings the first four lines of the song, with the rest joining in for the chorus that begins with line 15. *Burthen* recalls II.vii.167, III.ii.264–65, 343–45.

15   **Take thou no Scorn**   do not consider yourself disgraced.

16   **Crest**   both (a) an ornament atop a helmet, and (b) a heraldic device on a coat of arms. *Crest* can also refer to the comb of a rooster, and thus to the red strip atop a fool's cap. By implication, then, the 'conqueror' being satirically celebrated in this song has been labelled a coxcomb (see *Othello*, V.ii.226, where Aemilia calls the deceived Moor a 'murd'rous Coxcomb' and a 'Fool') who has inherited his 'Horn', as if by 'Destiny' (IV.i.61), from both his 'Father' and his 'Father's Father' (line 17–18). See II.vii.90, IV.i.158–59.
  **borne**   both (a) carried (see lines 14, 18), and (b) born. Compare IV.i.228.

19   **lusty**   The usual meaning of this adjective is 'vigorous', 'hearty'. Here it may also carry implications of 'lustful' (the cuckold's horns symbolizing the tumescent male member of a husband whose sex drive has been frustrated). See the note to III.iii.54–55.

IV.iii   This scene returns us to where Rosalind and Celia await the return of Orlando.

2   **And here much Orlando**   And look how much Orlando we see!

3   **warrant**   assure. Compare IV.i.82.

3–4   **with . . . Brain**   This adverbial phrase can relate either to Celia's warranting (line 3) or to Orlando's departure to sleep (lines 4–5).

5   **sleep**   Celia's witty anticlimax (the verb one would expect here is 'hunt' or 'war' or something equally active) is probably meant to cheer up Rosalind by making her laugh. See the note to III.ii.147. The reference to 'Bow and Arrows' evokes the traditional image of Cupid; see I.iii.1–2, IV.1.47–53.

7   **this**   Silvius refers to a letter, which he hands to Rosalind as he speaks.

9   **waspish Action**   fierce manner. See the note to III.v.134.

11   **Tenure**   tenor, import; literally, 'holding' (matter contained).

Then sing him home, the rest shall bear
  this Burthen.
Take thou no Scorn to wear the Horn,          15
It was a Crest ere thou wast borne,
Thy Father's Father wore it,
And thy Father bore it,
The Horn, the Horn, the lusty Horn,
Is not a thing to laugh to Scorn.     Exeunt.  20

# Scene 3

*Enter Rosalind and Celia.*

ROSALIND  How say you now, is it not past two
a' clock? And here much Orlando.

CELIA  I warrant you, with pure Love, and troubled
Brain, he hath ta'en his Bow and Arrows, and
is gone forth to sleep. Look who comes here.     5

*Enter Silvius.*

SILVIUS  My Errand is to you, fair Youth.
My gentle Phebe did bid me give you this:
I know the Contents, but as I guess
By the stern Brow, and waspish Action
Which she did use, as she was writing of it,     10
It bears an angry Tenure. Pardon me,
I am but as a guiltless Messenger.

13   **Patience her self** Rosalind personifies an attribute as a goddess, here one who would react in a manner that goes against her very nature.
**startle** be shocked.

14   **Swaggerer** one who threatens revenge like a 'Challenger' (line 32), rather than turning the other cheek (see Matthew 5:38–48) with passive forbearance, and thereby remaining 'guiltless' (line 12) and passive in the face of treatment that demeans his honour.
**bear this, bear all** if I put up with this, I'll put up with anything.

15   **fair** beautiful. See the note to III.v.130.

16   **and that** and says that. *Proud* recalls III.v.114.

17   **as rare as Phoenix** unique. The phoenix was a mythical Arabian bird of which only one lived at a time; she was said to live for half a millennium, whereupon she would die in a flame and give birth to a new bird who would spring from her ashes.
**'Od's my Will** as God directs my will. Compare III.v.43.

18   **Hare** large, solitary relative of the rabbit. Compare the imagery in III.ii.359–61.

19   **Well . . . well** Here *well* functions as an interjection roughly equivalent to 'Aha! Now I see!'

20   **Device** invention, composition. Compare I.i.155–61, 175–77, I.ii.26–27, I.iii.104, 139–41.

21   **protest** vow, testify under oath. See IV.i.117.

23   **turn'd into the Extremity of Love** (a) sent off on a wild-goose chase because of the severity of your infatuation, and (b) transformed into an epitome of the folly (lack of moderation or measure) that love induces. *Extremity* recalls II.i.42 and IV.i.5–6.

25   **Freestone-colour'd** the colour of greyish-yellow sandstone. *Leathern* ('hard', III.ii.61, and thick-skinned), line 24, echoes IV.ii.11–12.

27   **Huswive's Hand** a hand made coarse from doing a housewife's chores. *Huswive's* recalls I.ii.34–36; see the note to IV.i.178.

28   **invent** conceive and compose. See line 20.

29   **Hand** both (a) handwriting, and (b) 'Invention', handiwork. Rosalind puns on yet another sense of 'Hand'; see lines 24–27.

ROSALIND   Patience her self would startle at this
   Letter,
And play the Swaggerer, bear this, bear all:
She says I am not fair, that I lack Manners,        15
She calls me proud, and that she could not
   love me
Were Man as rare as Phoenix. 'Od's my Will,
Her Love is not the Hare that I do hunt,
Why writes she so to me? Well, Shepherd, well,
This is a Letter of your own Device.        20
SILVIUS   No, I protest, I know not the Contents,
   Phebe did write it.
ROSALIND        Come, come, you are a Fool,
And turn'd into the Extremity of Love.
I saw her Hand, she has a leathern Hand,
A Freestone-colour'd Hand; I verily did think        25
That her old Gloves were on, but 'twas her
   Hands;
She has a Huswive's Hand, but that's no matter;
I say she never did invent this Letter,
This is a Man's Invention, and his Hand.
SILVIUS   Sure it is hers.        30
ROSALIND   Why, 'tis a boisterous and a cruel
   Stile,
A Stile for Challengers; why, she defies me,
Like Turk to Christian. Women's gentle Brain

---

31    **Stile**  style, both (a) handwriting (referring to the formation of
       the letters in Phebe's script), and (b) rhetorical style, mode of
       discourse. Rosalind may also be alluding to the sense of *Stile*
       (steps over a fence or wall) that relates to pride, here the
       ambition of a social-climbing shepherdess who aspires to a
       higher station than the humble Silvius can give her. Compare
       Audrey's 'Desire to be a Woman of the World' (V.iii.4–5).
       *Stile* recalls II.i.18–20.

34  **giant rude**  as savage as if it had originated with primordial giants, such as the Titans who stormed Olympus in a rebellion against Zeus. Compare *Hamlet*, IV.v.123–24. V.i.262–70, 289–96, V.ii.75–80. Lines 33–34 echo *The Merchant of Venice*, IV.i.187–89.

35  **Ethiop**  both (a) black (see line 15), and (b) pagan, savage. Compare *A Midsummer Night's Dream*, III.ii.257, and see *Pericles*, II.iii.20, where a knight bears a 'Shield' with the 'Device' of 'a black Ethiope reaching at the Sun'.

36  **Countenance**  appearance, manner. Compare IV.i.38–39.

37  **So please you**  if you don't mind; if it pleases you to do so.

39  **Phebes**  Rosalind verbs Phebe's name as if it epitomized cruel tyranny. Her implication is that Phebe is treating 'Ganimed' just as high-handedly as she has treated poor Silvius.

40  **Are . . . turn'd?**  This question alludes to the doctrine of God's incarnation in Christ, the 'good Shepherd' of John 10:11–17; compare Isaiah 40:11, 53:6–7. See note 44.

42  **rail**  attack, berate. Rosalind is using this term ironically, of course. Compare III.ii.295–97.

44  **thy Godhead laid a part**  having set aside your divinity and assumed human form. Phebe's phrasing recalls Philippians 2:5–8, where 'Christ Jesus' is said to have surrendered 'the form of God' in order to be 'made in the likeness of men'. In this line the Folio spelling, *a part*, mirrors the concept behind what is rendered as a single word today.

50  **Eyne**  a 'poetic' and somewhat affected plural for *eye*, here used for rhyming purposes.

53  **in mild Aspect**  with a friendly, gentle manner.

54  **chid**  chided, scolded.

55  **Prayers**  pleas for my affection. Compare I.ii.186.

56  **He**  Phebe refers to Silvius, her messenger.

58  **by him seal up thy Mind**  reply (reveal your 'Mind' or thoughts) by giving him a sealed letter to bring back to me (so that he will remain unaware of the content of the messages he is carrying). In this line *seal* is to be treated metrically as a two-syllable word. *Mind* echoes IV.i.116–17.

59  **Kind**  nature (kind of person).

Could not drop forth such giant rude
   Invention,
Such Ethiop Words, blacker in their Effect        35
Than in their Countenance. Will you hear the
   Letter?
SILVIUS   So please you, for I never heard it yet:
Yet heard too much of Phebe's Cruelty.
ROSALIND   She Phebes me: mark how the Tyrant
   writes.
> *Art thou God, to Shepherd turn'd?*        40
> *That a Maiden's Heart hath burn'd.*
Can a Woman rail thus?
SILVIUS   Call you this Railing?
ROSALIND
> *Why, thy Godhead laid a part,*
> *Warr'st thou with a Woman's Heart?*        45
Did you ever hear such Railing?
> *Whiles the Eye of Man did woo me,*
> *That could do no Vengeance to me.*
Meaning me a Beast.
> *If the Scorn of your bright Eyne*        50
> *Have Power to raise such Love in mine,*
> *Alack, in me what strange Effect*
> *Would they work in mild Aspect?*
> *Whiles you chid me, I did love,*
> *How then might your Prayers move?*        55
> *He that brings this Love to thee*
> *Little knows this Love in me:*
> *And by him seal up thy Mind,*
> *Whether that thy Youth and Kind*
> *Will the faithful Offer take*        60

61    **make**   Phebe probably means 'do' (see I.i.31, II.iii.4) as well as 'make'. Compare IV.i.170–71, 185–86.

63    **study how to die**   try to figure out the best way to expire, whether by pining away or by committing suicide. Compare IV.i.188–98 and IV.ii.1, 11. *Study* recalls III.ii.291–93, 338–42.

65    **Alas . . . Shepherd**   Celia's implication is that, for Silvius, Phebe's words are even worse than 'Chiding'. In the speech that follows, Rosalind chides Celia for her 'Pity' and then Silvius for his timidity and submissiveness. If he is 'guiltless' (see the note to line 14), she implies, he is also gilt-less, lacking in the gold-plating (mettle, armour) to defend himself; see the notes to III.v.1 and III.iii.63.

68    **play false Strains**   both (a) produce discordant notes on you, and (b) 'play false' with you (deceive and misuse you). The Prince of Denmark uses a similar metaphor when he accuses Rosencrans and Guildenstern of trying to play on him like a recorder in *Hamlet*, III.ii.378–402.

70–71  **tame Snake**   a creature so abject that people feel free to walk all over you. See the note to line 109.

72    **charge**   command. Compare I.iii.96, III.ii.373–74.

73    **have**   receive, take (see the note to IV.i.183).

74–75  **not a Word**   not a word of protest from you.

77    **in the Purlews**   within the purlieus (confines).

78    **Sheep-coat**   sheepcote, shepherd's cottage, as in II.iv.85.

79    **neighbour Bottom**   next dale (shallow valley). *Bottom* echoes IV.i.219–25.

80    **rank of Oziers**   row of willows.

81    **Left**   left behind, passed.

82    **doth keep it self**   is unoccupied.

84    **If . . . Tongue**   if my eye may benefit from the description another's 'Tongue' (language, words) provided me. *Tongue* recalls I.i.62–65, I.ii.267, II.i.16, II.v.30–31, II.vii.83–84, III.ii.135–36, 260–61, III.v.115–17, IV.i.182–84, 196–97.

86    **Years**   age, as in I.ii.181, III.v.118.

87    **female Favour**   feminine face and features. *Fair* (light-complexioned) echoes line 15.
        **bestows himself**   carries himself in manner and dress.

*Of me, and all that I can make,*
*Or else by him my Love deny,*
*And then I'll study how to die.*

SILVIUS   Call you this Chiding?
CELIA   Alas poor Shepherd.                                          65
ROSALIND   Do you pity him? No, he deserves no
   Pity. – Wilt thou love such a Woman? what, to
   make thee an Instrument, and play false Strains
   upon thee? not to be endur'd. Well, go your way
   to her (for I see Love hath made thee a tame        70
   Snake), and say this to her: that if she love
   me, I charge her to love thee; if she will not,
   I will never have her, unless thou intreat for
   her. If you be a true Lover hence, and not a
   Word; for here comes more Company.   *Exit Silvius.*   75

*Enter Oliver.*

OLIVER   Good morrow, Fair Ones: pray you, if you
   know,
   where in the Purlews of this Forest stands
   A Sheep-coat fenc'd about with Olive-trees.
CELIA   West of this place, down in the neighbour
   Bottom
   The rank of Oziers, by the murmuring Stream        80
   Left on your right hand, brings you to the
      place:
   But at this Hour the House doth keep it self,
   There's none within.
OLIVER   If that an Eye may profit by a Tongue,
   Then should I know you by Description,
   Such Garments and such Years: 'the Boy is          85
      fair,
   Of female Favour, and bestows himself

88    **ripe Sister**   older sister. *Ripe* recalls II.vii.26–28 and
       III.ii.123–28. Here *low* means 'short' (see the note to I.ii.282).

89    **browner**   of an 'umber' complexion (see I.iii.115–16).

94    **Napkin**   handkerchief. See line 98.

102   **Chewing . . . Fancy**   ruminating on bittersweet love (because of
       the mixed messages Rosalind had given him during their last
       meeting). Compare IV.i.10–21. *Sweet* recalls II.i.12–20; *bitter*
       echoes III.v.137–38.

103   **aside**   to one side.

104   **mark**   note. Compare line 39, and see III.v.124.

105   **Under an old Oak**   This description recalls II.i.29–63, III.ii.123,
       and III.ii.250–51, and it suggests that we are to be alert to
       symbolic details in a narrative that is more allegorical (moral
       and spiritual in its import) than realistic. *Object* echoes
       IV.i.10–21.

107   **A . . . Hair**   The 'old man' described here accords well with the
       'old tree' he lies under. Both suggest the unregenerate biblical
       'old man, which is corrupt according to the deceitful lusts'
       (Ephesians 4:22). In line 136 we learn that Oliver is here
       describing himself, and in a way that can only be read as
       figurative.

109   **A green and guilded Snake**   Oliver's description recalls
       traditional representations of Envy, such as the one in the
       pageant of the Seven Deadly Sins in Book I of Edmund
       Spenser's *The Faerie Queene* (1590). There we are told that in
       Envy's 'bosome secretly there lay / An hatefull Snake, the
       which his taile uptyes / In many folds, and mortall sting
       implyes.' Spenser also describes Envy in a way that aptly fits
       the Oliver we have met earlier in the play: 'every good to bad
       he doth abuse'. We shall soon be shown that 'Love hath made
       . . . a tame Snake' (lines 70–71) not only of Oliver's 'Threats'
       (line 110) but of Orlando's older brother himself. See the note
       to III.v.30–31. The Folio's *guilded* (gilded, glistening with
       gold) plays on both (a) guileful and (b) guilty. See the note to
       line 65, and compare *Macbeth*, II.ii.52–54, and *Hamlet*,
       I.iii.130.

113   **indented**   undulating, slithering; in a pattern that resembles the
       tooth-like, zigzagging borders of legal indentures (contracts of
       parchment divided so as to permit later matching, if
       necessary, to certify the validity of two or more copies).

Like a ripe Sister; the Woman low
And browner than her Brother.' Are not you
The Owner of the House I did enquire for?                    90
CELIA    It is no Boast, being ask'd, to say we are.
OLIVER    Orlando doth commend him to you both,
    And to that Youth he calls his Rosalind,
    He sends this bloody Napkin; are you he?
ROSALIND    I am: what must we understand by this?       95
OLIVER    Some of my Shame, if you will know of me
    What Man I am, and how, and why, and where
    This Handkercher was stain'd.
CELIA                              I pray you tell it.
OLIVER    When last the young Orlando parted from
        you,
    He left a Promise to return again                       100
    Within an Hour, and pacing through the Forest,
    Chewing the Food of sweet and bitter Fancy,
    Lo what befell: he threw his Eye aside,
    And mark what Object did present it self
    Under an old Oak, whose Bows were moss'd
        with Age
    And high Top bald with dry Antiquity.                   105
    A wretched ragged Man, o'ergrown with Hair,
    Lay sleeping on his Back; about his Neck
    A green and guilded Snake had wreath'd it self,
    Who with her Head nimble in Threats approach'd          110
    The opening of his Mouth; but suddenly
    Seeing Orlando, it unlink'd it self
    And with indented Glides did slip away
    Into a Bush, under which Bush's Shade

115    **with ... dry**   famished, because her infant cubs have drunk all the milk she can produce to nourish them. See line 127, where the lioness is depicted as 'suck'd and hungry'.

116    **couching**   crouching alertly. The lioness is probably meant to symbolize Wrath, a co-mate of Envy in the pageant of the Seven Deadly Sins. In *The Faerie Queene*, after we learn about the attributes of Envy, we read that 'him beside rides fierce revenging Wrath, / Upon a Lion, loth for to be led.'

118    **royal Disposition**   Oliver suggests that the most regal 'Beast' in the animal kingdom is too noble to attack a defenceless foe or scavenge on a dead creature. *Disposition* echoes IV.i.119–21.

123    **render him**   describe him as. Compare I.ii.20–22.

128    **purpos'd so**   intended to 'leave him there' (line 126).

129    **Kindness**   compassion, the fellow-feeling that derives from Orlando's 'Kind' or 'Nature' (line 130), as distinguished from the envy and vengeful wrath of his 'most unnatural' older brother (line 123).

130    **just Occasion**   Oliver means that Orlando would have had justice as well as personal 'Revenge' on his side if he had simply left his wicked brother to the fate he deserved. *Occasion* recalls IV.i.184–87.

132    **Hurtling**   sudden tumult, 'Noise' (IV.ii.10).

133    **miserable Slumber**   Oliver's description suggests not only his physical and psychological condition, but his spiritual state as an 'old man' given over so completely to the 'spirit of slumber' (Romans 11:8) that he is in mortal danger of losing his soul. In passages such as Matthew 25:5 and 1 Thessalonians 5:6–7, slumber is associated with a spiritual lethargy that will prove fatal unless one awakens and dons the spirit of the 'new man' (Colossians 3:9–10) before it is too late. In the liturgical 'General Confession' of the 1559 Book of Common Prayer, the congregation was instructed to pray 'O Lord, have mercy upon us miserable offenders.' This passage would have resonated with Elizabethan playgoers not only here but in IV.i.212–14.

A Lioness, with Udders all drawn dry,                                      115
Lay couching Head on Ground, with Catlike
   Watch
When that the sleeping Man should stir: for
   'tis
The royal Disposition of that Beast
To prey on nothing that doth seem as dead.
This seen, Orlando did approach the Man,                                   120
And found it was his Brother, his elder
   Brother.
CELIA   O I have heard him speak of that same
   Brother,
And he did render him the most unnatural
That liv'd amongst Men.
OLIVER                      And well he might so do,
For well I know he was unnatural.                                          125
ROSALIND   But to Orlando: did he leave him there
Food to the suck'd and hungry Lioness?
OLIVER   Twice did he turn his Back, and purpos'd
   so:
But Kindness, nobler ever than Revenge,
And Nature stronger than his just Occasion,                                130
Made him give Battle to the Lioness,
Who quickly fell before him, in which Hurtling
From miserable Slumber I awak'd.
CELIA   Are you his Brother?
ROSALIND                      Was't you he rescu'd?
CELIA   Was't you that did so oft continue to kill
   him?                                                                    135

136    'Twas I but 'tis not I    Oliver's description of his 'Conversion'
         (line 137) echoes the Apostle Paul's account of his own
         spiritual renewal: 'I am crucified with Christ: nevertheless I
         live; yet not I, but Christ liveth in me . . . who loved me, and
         gave himself for me' (Galatians 2:20). Oliver has been
         transformed from an 'old man' (see the note to line 107) to a
         'new man, which after God is created in righteousness and
         true holiness' (Ephesians 4:22–24, paralleled by Colossians
         3:9–11). The phrase *sweetly tastes* (line 138) echoes line 102.

139    **for**   as for.
         **bloody Napkin**   The bloody handkerchief functions as a token
         of Orlando's second Herculean exploit in the play. In the first,
         by defeating Charles the Wrastler, he won the heart of
         Rosalind. In the second, by proving himself to be 'his
         brother's keeper' (see the notes to I.i.9, 21, 47–48, 91, 99)
         and thereby preventing a recurrence of the Cain and Abel
         story, he has won the heart of Oliver. In the process, he has
         re-enacted certain aspects of the sacrifice of Christ.
         **By and by**   I'll tell you about that shortly, but first I need to
         finish the rest of my narrative.

141    **Tears . . . bath'd**   our tales to each other had been immersed in
         tears. Oliver describes a scene in which the weeping brothers
         exchanged their stories ('Recountments'). But the way he
         depicts the 'Tears' suggests that they here serve a baptismal
         function, washing away the old nature that had made Oliver
         'wretched' (line 107) and permitting him to 'walk in newness
         of life' (see Romans 6:1–10).

144    **fresh Array**   clean apparel to replace the 'ragged' garments
         Oliver brought into the forest with him. Like the 'white
         raiment' of Revelation 3:18, Oliver's new clothes are meant to
         symbolize a new spirit. Compare *King Lear*, IV.vii.19–21,
         where the storm-chastened monarch is 'array'd' in 'fresh
         Garments'.
         **Entertainment**   welcome, hospitality. Compare II.iv.72–74,
         III.ii.439–42.

151    **Brief . . . him**   To sum up briefly, I restored him to
         consciousness. *Wound* recalls III.v.30–31.

152    **small space**   short interval.

OLIVER   'Twas I: but 'tis not I. I do not shame
  To tell you what I was, since my Conversion
  So sweetly tastes, being the thing I am.
ROSALIND   But for the bloody Napkin?
OLIVER                                By and by:
  When from the first to last betwixt us two                    140
  Tears our Recountments had most kindly bath'd,
  As how I came into that desert Place,
  I'brief he led me to the gentle Duke,
  Who gave me fresh Array, and Entertainment,
  Committing me unto my Brother's Love,                         145
  Who led me instantly unto his Cave,
  There stripp'd himself, and here upon his Arm
  The Lioness had torn some Flesh away,
  Which all the while had bled; and now he
    fainted,
  And cried in fainting upon Rosalind.                          150
  Brief, I recover'd him, bound up his Wound,
  And after some small space, being strong at
    Heart,
  He sent me hither, Stranger as I am,
  To tell this Story, that you might excuse

---

154   **this Story**   A narrative that may now be summed up as an
        account of how Oliver, so given over to Envy and Wrath that
        he was in danger of being destroyed by those vices, was
        rescued by a younger brother who had to overcome the
        temptation to 'revenging Wrath' himself before he could bring
        himself to act in accordance with the promptings of
        'Kindness' (line 129). Having been delivered by his 'Brother's
        Love' (line 145), Oliver is now on an errand that proves him
        to have been transformed from a would-be fratricide, an
        unregenerate Cain, into his 'brother's keeper' in a sense quite
        different from that described in the speech with which
        Orlando opened the play. See the notes to line 139 and to
        III.ii.130.
    **excuse**   exonerate him for, acquit him of responsibility for.
        *Broken* (line 155) echoes III.v.102.

156  **Died**  dyed. But the Folio spelling also suggests that the handkerchief has undergone a symbolic death, a crucifixion, that corresponds to what has happened to Orlando and, by extension, to Oliver. See the notes to lines 139, 141.

158  **how now**  Celia's expression of alarm is explained in line 159, which makes it clear that Rosalind has 'fainted' (line 149) in reciprocation of Orlando's 'swoon'.

167  **counterfeited**  pretended, faked. Compare III.v.17, and see line 182.

170  **Complexion**  both (a) appearance (Rosalind's bloodless features), and (b) physiological and psychological condition (Rosalind's temporary loss of the proper balance among her humours). See the note to III.v.115–16. Rosalind's swoon is a much deeper version of the 'overthrow' she experienced in I.ii in response to Orlando's first heroic exploit. If her initial 'Fall' (I.iii.27) was prompted primarily by Orlando's demonstration of physical prowess, her second has been prompted primarily by Orlando's manifestation of an even greater measure of physical and spiritual strength.

171  **Passion of Earnest**  genuine surrender to the emotions. Oliver's phrasing offers yet another reminder of the Passion of Christ: his agony in the Garden of Gethsemane and his suffering on the Cross. See the notes to lines 139, 141, 156.

180  **excuse**  forgive, accept his excuse. See the note to line 154.

181  **devise something**  compose a suitable written 'Answer' (line 179). *Devise* echoes line 20.

182  **commend my Counterfeiting to him**  tell him how convincingly I pretended to faint. Rosalind's phrasing is a reminder that she remains eager to 'commend' her 'Counterfeiting' to Orlando in a conjugal sense. See *Romeo and Juliet*, II.iii.50–55, where *Counterfeit* puns on 'counter' (see the note to III.ii.290) and 'fit' to suggest a copulative linkage of genitalia. Compare *encounter* (see III.ii.194–95), a word that means 'in-count-'er' in *Troilus and Cressida*, III.iii.217–19.

His broken Promise, and to give this Napkin,                    155
Died in this Blood, unto the Shepherd Youth,
That he in Sport doth call his Rosalind.
CELIA   Why how now, Ganimed, sweet Ganimed.
OLIVER   Many will swoon when they do look on Blood.
CELIA   There is more in it. — Cousin Ganimed.                  160
OLIVER   Look, he recovers.
ROSALIND   I would I were at home.
CELIA                               We'll lead you thither.
— I pray you will you take him by the Arm.
OLIVER   Be of good Cheer, Youth: you a Man?
You lack a Man's Heart.
ROSALIND                       I do so, I confess it.            165
Ah Sirrah, a body would think this was well
counterfeited, I pray you tell your Brother
how well I counterfeited: heigh ho.
OLIVER   This was not Counterfeit, there is too
great Testimony in your Complexion that it                      170
was a Passion of Earnest.
ROSALIND   Counterfeit, I assure you.
OLIVER   Well then, take a good Heart, and
counterfeit to be a Man.
ROSALIND   So I do: but i'faith I should have been             175
a Woman by right.
CELIA   Come, you look paler and paler: pray you
draw homewards. — Good Sir, go with us.
OLIVER   That will I: for I must bear Answer back
How you excuse my Brother, Rosalind.                            180
ROSALIND   I shall devise something: but I pray you
commend my Counterfeiting to him. Will you
go?                                              *Exeunt.*

V.i   We now move to the part of the forest where the shepherds perform their labours.

2   **gentle**   kind, tender, frail. Audrey is now anxious to become 'gentle' (a respectable member of the gentry) in a social sense. See the note to IV.iii.31.

4–5   **for . . . Saying**   despite what the fastidious Jaques said [when he intervened to forestall the marriage ceremony in III.iii].

7   **lays**   who lays.

8   **I**   either 'I' (if Audrey stammers, perhaps nervously) or 'Ay'. Compare IV.i.140, and see lines 25, 31.

8–9   **Interest in me**   claim on me.

11   **Meat**   solid food (not limited to 'meat' in the usual modern sense).
    **Clown**   William is a real clown (country bumpkin); Touchstone only pretends to be one in keeping with his profession as a court jester; his words echo what Jaques has said in II.vii.12–44, and what Touchstone himself has implied in II.iv.67.

12   **good Wits**   Touchstone refers to his sophisticated intelligence, of course, but his phrasing recalls what Rosalind has suggested about 'good' genital 'Wits' in IV.i.125–31; see the notes to IV.i.171, 176, 180.

13   **answer for**   be judged for (referring to reprehensible behaviour). See the note to IV.i.184.
    **shall be flouting**   can't stop ourselves from scoffing at others. Compare I.ii.49–51, III.iii.107–8.

16   **God ye**   God give you.

18   **Cover thy Head**   William, acknowledging Touchstone as one of his betters, has taken off his hat as a sign of deference. See the note to III.iii.78. Here as in line 2, Touchstone uses *gentle* in a way that is probably to be construed as condescending. William is 'gentle' in the sense that means 'tame' (IV.iii.70–71): too meek and uncomprehending to be able to imagine a self-assertive act such as retaliation for an insult.

22   **ripe**   mature. Compare IV.iii.88.

24   **borne**   both (a) born, and (b) carried (as in IV.ii.16).

25   **I**   both (a) I [was], and (b) Ay. Compare line 31.

# ACT V

## Scene 1

*Enter Clown and Audrey.*

CLOWN   We shall find a Time, Audrey, patience,
gentle Audrey.

AUDREY   Faith the Priest was good enough, for all
the old Gentleman's Saying.

CLOWN   A most wicked Sir Oliver, Audrey, a most                    5
vile Mar-text. But Audrey, there is a Youth
here in the Forest lays claim to you.

AUDREY   I, I know who 'tis: he hath no Interest
in me in the World. Here comes the Man you
mean.                                                              10

*Enter William.*

CLOWN   It is Meat and Drink to me to see a Clown.
By my troth, we that have good Wits have much
to answer for; we shall be flouting; we cannot
hold.

WILLIAM   Good ev'n, Audrey.                                       15

AUDREY   God ye good ev'n, William.

WILLIAM   And good ev'n to you, Sir.

CLOWN   Good ev'n, gentle Friend. Cover thy Head,
cover thy Head: nay prethee be cover'd. How
old are you, Friend?                                               20

WILLIAM   Five and twenty, Sir.

CLOWN   A ripe Age. Is thy name William?

WILLIAM   William, Sir.

CLOWN   A fair Name. Wast borne i'th' Forest here?

WILLIAM   I Sir, I thank God.                                      25

29     **but so, so**   Touchstone plays on the paradox that if 'so, so' is 'good', it nevertheless remains 'so so' (mediocre, of indifferent value).

31     **pretty Wit**   William probably means 'a fine mind' or an 'aptitude for clever repartee'. But his words could also be construed as a boast about his 'pretty Piece of Flesh' (*Romeo and Juliet*, I.i.30–32); see the note to IV.i.90. *Pretty* recalls IV.i.1, 201, 219.

33–34   **'The . . . Fool'**   This proverb has an ancient lineage. It echoes the teachings of Socrates, and it is probably related as well to such New Testament passages as I Corinthians 3:18–19, 'If any man among you seemeth to be wise in this world, let him become a fool, that he may be wise. For the wisdom of this world is foolishness with God.' The more sophisticated members of Shakespeare's audience would also have associated the notion of wise folly with Desiderius Erasmus's *In Praise of Folly* (1509).

35     **Heathen Philosopher**   Whether Touchstone is burlesquing a particular philosopher is difficult to tell, but his description of the sage's 'wisdom' suggests that he may be thinking of Epicurus, popularly associated with a life committed to pleasure-seeking.

41     **learned**   literate.

43     **To . . . have**   Touchstone states a tautology (defining a thing in terms of itself or in terms of something identical with itself), but as usual he does so with a solemnity designed to impress and intimidate the ignorant. Unlike Corin, who proves a good match for the Clown's cleverness in III.ii.1–90, William is easily awed.

44     **Figure in Rhetoric**   What Touchstone describes is the most elementary common sense. He does manage a rhetorical figure, however, if 'filling the one' is intended as a sexual metaphor.

45     **powr'd**   poured. But see the note to III.ii.210.

47     **consent**   agree (arrive at a consensus).
       **ipse**   Latin for 'he himself'. Throughout this scene, Touchstone pokes fun at the rhetorical excesses of John Lyly's *Euphues* (1578) and the 'euphuistic' (excessively balanced and self-consciously artificial) style it made faddish.

51–52   **the Vulgar**   the idiom of the unlearned, the 'Boorish' or 'Common' people (lines 53–54).

CLOWN   'Thank God': a good Answer. Art rich?

WILLIAM   'Faith Sir, so, so.

CLOWN   'So, so' is good, very good, very excellent
good: and yet it is not, it is but so, so. Art
thou wise?                                                                30

WILLIAM   I Sir, I have a pretty Wit.

CLOWN   Why, thou say'st well. I do now remember a
Saying: 'The Fool doth think he is wise, but
the Wiseman knows himself to be a Fool.' The
Heathen Philosopher, when he had a desire to                35
eat a Grape, would open his Lips when he put
it into his Mouth, meaning thereby that Grapes
were made to eat, and Lips to open. You love
this Maid?

WILLIAM   I do, Sir.                                                     40

CLOWN   Give me your Hand: art thou learned?

WILLIAM   No Sir.

CLOWN   Then learn this of me: 'To have, is to have.'
For it is a Figure in Rhetoric, that Drink
being powr'd out of a Cup into a Glass, by                    45
filling the one, doth empty the other. For all
your Writers do consent, that *ipse* is he: now
you are not *ipse*, for I am he.

WILLIAM   Which he, Sir?

CLOWN   He, Sir, that must marry this Woman.                  50
Therefore you Clown, abandon (which is in the
Vulgar, 'leave') the Society (which in the Boorish,

53 **Company** Rosalind has used this term in IV.iii.75.

56 **to wit** namely; to state the matter another way.

59 **Bastinado** cudgelling, beating with a short, heavy club.
  **Steel** a sword.
  **bandy** exchange blows.

60 **in Faction** either (a) in a spirit of contention, or (b) in league
  with others of my party.
  **o'er-run thee with Police** either (a) outstrip you with policy
  (cunning intrigues), or (b) overwhelm you with the forces of
  civil order. The most common modern sense of *police* dates
  from the late eighteenth and early nineteenth centuries.

64 **rest you merry** keep you hearty (healthy).

65 **Our . . . Mistress** Ganimed (Rosalind) and Aliena (Celia).

67 **Trip** Step on it!
  **I attend** I hear you, and will wait upon their will. Compare
  I.ii.174, IV.i.192.

V.ii This scene takes place in the forest near the sheepcote.

2 **like her** take a fancy to her, find her attractive. *Acquaintance*
  recalls IV.i.1–2; compare lines 6–9.

4 **graunt** grant your wish and consent to accept you.

5 **persever to enjoy her** maintain your efforts until you win her
  hand in marriage.

6–7 **Neither . . . question** Do not question the dizzying speed of it.
  *Giddiness* echoes IV.i.161.

7 **the Poverty of her** the fact that she has no dowry to bestow on
  her husband. Oliver has no way of knowing that 'Aliena' is
  really the daughter of Duke Frederick. Nor does he have any
  way of knowing that by the end of the play the Duke's own
  actions will reduce her to 'Poverty' in any event. For the 'new'
  Oliver, who has resolved to be 'poor in spirit' (Matthew 5:3)
  and adopt the life of a 'Shepherd' (lines 11–15), Aliena's
  'Poverty' will present no obstacle. In her he will have his Celia
  (Heaven), and will need no other worldly possessions. But see
  the note to V.iv.176. *Poverty* recalls I.iii.67–69, III.v.99–103.

is 'Company') of this Female (which in the Common,
is Woman); which together is, abandon the Society of
this Female, or Clown, thou perishest; or, to thy better    55
Understanding, diest; or, to wit, I kill thee, make
thee away, translate thy Life into Death, thy Liberty
into Bondage. I will deal in Poison with thee,
or in Bastinado, or in Steel; I will bandy with
thee in Faction, I will o'er-run thee with Police;    60
I will kill thee a hundred and fifty ways,
therefore tremble and depart.

AUDREY   Do, good William.

WILLIAM   God rest you merry, Sir.                    *Exit.*

*Enter Corin.*

CORIN   Our Master and Mistress seeks you: come    65
away, away.

CLOWN   Trip, Audrey, trip, Audrey. – I attend, I
attend.                                          *Exeunt.*

# Scene 2

*Enter Orlando and Oliver.*

ORLANDO   Is't possible, that on so little
Acquaintance you should like her? that, but
Seeing, you should love her? And Loving, woo?
and Wooing, she should graunt? And will you
persever to enjoy her?                                5

OLIVER   Neither call the Giddiness of it in
question; the Poverty of her, the small
Acquaintance, my sudden Wooing, nor sudden
Consenting. But say with me, I love Aliena;
say with her, that she loves me, consent with    10
both, that we may enjoy each other. It shall

14    **estate upon you** settle on you, bequeath to you.

16    **You have my Consent** Orlando agrees to give the bride away in the marriage ceremony (a request Oliver has made in lines 9–11). Neither of them knows that her father is still alive.

17    **to morrow** tomorrow. But the Folio orthography also permits the meaning 'directed to the morrow (the bright future that awaits you)'. Compare II.i.29, and see lines 48, 52, 55, 76, 82, 120, 122, 124, 126.

18    **all's** all of his (so abbreviated in the Folio text, probably to imitate colloquial speech).

19    **my Rosalind** Orlando means 'the young man I'm pretending is my Rosalind'. He little realizes that what he says is literally true.

20    **Brother** brother-in-law. 'Ganimed' is speaking here as the brother of 'Aliena'; see III.ii.131, 355–58. Meanwhile in her own person Rosalind is speaking as the future wife of Oliver's brother, not as the brother of Oliver's future wife.

21    **Sister** Oliver joins with Orlando in treating 'Ganimed' as if 'he' were really Rosalind.

22    **grieves** saddens. Compare III.ii.432–36.

30    **sound** swoon (here pronounced 'soond'). Compare IV.i.219–23.

32    **I** Ay. But *I* could also mean 'I [was told about you]'. Compare V.i.25, 31.

33    **where you are** where you are coming from; that is, what you mean (the instant infatuation of Oliver and Aliena).

36    **thrasonical** boastful. Rosalind's adjective derives from the name of a braggart soldier, Thraso, in the *Eunuchus*, a comedy by the Roman writer Terence (190–155 BC). *Rams* (line 35) echoes III.ii.82–87.

37    **overcome** overcame. See the notes to IV.i.233 and IV.ii.5–6, and for similar treatments of Caesar's 'Brag' compare *Love's Labour's Lost*, IV.i.68–80, *2 Henry IV*, IV.iii.44–46, and *Cymbeline*, III.i.22–24. Shakespeare's preference for *overcome* or *overcame*, rather than *conquered*, is probably due to his desire to pun on the copulative sense of 'over-came'. See the note to lines 43–44.

be to your good: for my Father's House, and
all the Revenue that was old Sir Rowland's,
will I estate upon you, and here live and die
a Shepherd.                                                                15

*Enter Rosalind.*

ORLANDO   You have my Consent. Let your Wedding
be to morrow: thither will I invite the Duke and
all's contented Followers. Go you, and prepare
Aliena; for look you, here comes my Rosalind.
ROSALIND   God save you, Brother.                              20
OLIVER   And you, fair Sister.                        [*Exit*]
ROSALIND   Oh my dear Orlando, how it grieves me to
see thee wear thy Heart in a Scarf.
ORLANDO   It is my Arm.
ROSALIND   I thought thy Heart had been wounded        25
with the Claws of a Lion.
ORLANDO   Wounded it is, but with the Eyes of a
Lady.
ROSALIND   Did your Brother tell you how I
counterfeited to sound when he shew'd me          30
your Handkercher?
ORLANDO   I, and greater Wonders than that.
ROSALIND   O, I know where you are. Nay, 'tis
true: there was never any thing so sudden,
but the Fight of two Rams, and Caesar's            35
thrasonical Brag of 'I came, I saw, and
overcome.' For your Brother and my Sister no
sooner met, but they look'd; no sooner look'd,
but they lov'd; no sooner lov'd, but they
sigh'd; no sooner sigh'd, but they asked one       40

41    **Reason**   cause, explanation. *Reason* was often pronounced
      'raison' in Shakespeare's time, and it thus invited wordplay on
      *raising*; see the second note to I.iii.9, and compare
      II.vii.100–1, IV.i.22–23. Here it hints at the heightening
      desire of a couple who are rushing up the 'Stairs' to
      consummation.

43    **Degrees**   steps.

43–44 **pair . . . Marriage**   Rosalind may be thinking of a stile (steps
      leading over a fence or wall, here a platform that suggests the
      high altar). See the note to IV.iii.31, and compare *Much Ado
      About Nothing*, V.ii.1–10, where Benedick and Margaret
      exchange bawdy puns on *Stile/Style, Stairs*, and *come over
      me*.

44    **incontinent**   both (a) immediately, and (b) unable to restrain
      (contain) themselves.

46    **Wrath**   here used as a synonym for 'fury', an uncontrollable
      frenzy.

46–47 **will together**   both (a) will the same thing, to get their erotic
      and genital wills together (see the note to IV.i.176), and (b)
      will be together.

47    **Clubs cannot part them**   When civil disturbances broke out in
      Elizabethan England, the Watch (the volunteer guard) used
      clubs to part the combatants and restore order. *Clubs* echoes
      IV.i.105.

49    **bid**   invite.
      **the Duke**   Duke Senior.
      **Nuptial**   wedding.

53    **by how much**   to that extent.

55–56 **serve your Turn**   meet your need. Rosalind's phrase hints at a
      sense of *Turn* that means 'trick', an erotic encounter.
      Compare *Antony and Cleopatra*, II.v.57–58, where a
      messenger tells the Egyptian queen that her paramour is now
      'bound unto Octavia'; when asked 'For what good Turn?' he
      replies 'For the best Turn i'th' Bed.' For similar wordplay on
      *Turn*, see *Titus Andronicus*, II.i.95–97, and *Othello*,
      IV.i.256–58.

57    **by Thinking**   by imagining and pretending only. Compare the
      remarks on *Thought* in IV.i.147–50, 226–33.

58    **weary you**   try your patience. *Weary* recalls II.iv.1–3,
      II.vii.72–73, 129–31, III.ii.163–66, 302.

another the Reason; no sooner knew the Reason,
but they sought the Remedy; and in these
Degrees have they made a pair of Stairs to
Marriage, which they will climb incontinent,
or else be incontinent before Marriage; they                    45
are in the very Wrath of Love, and they will
together. Clubs cannot part them.

ORLANDO    They shall be married to morrow: and I
will bid the Duke to the Nuptial. But O, how
bitter a thing it is, to look into Happiness                    50
through another man's Eyes: by so much the
more shall I to morrow be at the height of
Heart-heaviness, by how much I shall think my
Brother happy in having what he wishes for.

ROSALIND    Why then to morrow I cannot serve your             55
Turn for Rosalind?

ORLANDO    I can live no longer by Thinking.

ROSALIND    I will weary you then no longer with
idle Talking. Know of me then (for now I speak
to some Purpose) that I know you are a                          60
Gentleman of good Conceit. I speak not this,
that you should bear a good Opinion of my
Knowledge; insomuch I say, I know you are;

---

60    **to some Purpose**    earnestly, and with the power to make my
          words good. *Purpose* echoes I.i.146–49, IV.iii.128.

61    **of good Conceit**    (a) of sound mind, of intelligence, and (b) of
          integrity.

63    **insomuch . . . are**    I say so much because I know you are a man
          of good judgement. *Knowledge* recalls III.ii.221–23,
          III.iii.9–10.

64–66 **neither . . . me**   nor do I seek any more of your esteem than is needed to persuade you that if you trust me it will be to your own benefit. Here *to grace me* means 'to elevate myself in your opinion'; compare III.v.100.

68   **strange**   wondrous and mysterious.

69   **Magitian**   magician. The same Folio spelling appears in line 80 and in V.iv.33. In this line *profound* refers to an 'Art' (skill in magic) so 'deep' that 'it cannot be sounded' (IV.i.220–21).

70   **not damnable**   not dealing with the powers of Hell. Compare IV.i.201–2.

71–72 **your . . . out**   your bearing and manner proclaim.

73   **Straights**   straits; constraints, circumstances. The Folio spelling suggests that Aliena is now being 'driven' in a 'straight' line to the destiny her seemingly wayward 'Fortune' has had in store for her all along. Compare II.i.68, III.v.136.

75   **inconvenient**   untoward, unfitting. The Latin roots of *convenient* mean 'coming together'; see the notes to III.ii.290, IV.i.120.

77   **humane**   The Elizabethan spelling combines the modern senses for both 'human' and 'humane'. Here 'Ganimed' is emphasizing that the Rosalind he plans to produce will not be a spirit (a demonic apparition, as in *Macbeth*, IV.i.) but an ordinary mortal.
     **Danger**   risk of doing anything evil or damnable. See the note to line 70.

78   **in sober Meanings**   in all seriousness.

79   **tender deerly**   hold dear, take good care of. Rosalind will soon 'tender' (hand over) her life 'deerly' (like a submissive doe to the hart who has hunted her and captured her). Compare IV.i.190, and see III.ii.107–8, 263.

82   **to morrow**   both (a) tomorrow, and (b) to the morrow (the future you seek). See the note to line 17, and compare lines 48, 120–26.

86   **done me much Ungentleness**   acted toward me in a way that is very improper for a gentleman. Here *Ungentleness* means 'unkindness' or 'discourtesy'. See the notes to V.i.2, 18, and compare lines 88–89.

87   **shew**   show. But here as in III.v.20, the Folio spelling permits wordplay on *'schew*, an aphetic form of *eschew* (treat with contempt, spurn).

neither do I labour for a greater Esteem than
may in some little measure draw a Belief from          65
you, to do your self good, and not to grace me.
Believe then, if you please, that I can do
strange things. I have since I was three year
old convers'd with a Magitian, most profound
in his Art, and yet not damnable. If you do          70
love Rosalind so near the Heart as your Gesture
cries it out, when your Brother marries Aliena,
shall you marry her. I know into what Straights
of Fortune she is driven, and it is not
impossible to me, if it appear not inconvenient          75
to you, to set her before your Eyes to morrow,
humane as she is, and without any Danger.

ORLANDO  Speak'st thou in sober Meanings?

ROSALIND  By my Life I do, which I tender deerly,
though I say I am a Magitian. Therefore put          80
you in your best Array, bid your Friends: for
if you will be married to morrow, you shall;
and to Rosalind if you will.

*Enter Silvius and Phebe.*

Look, here comes a Lover of mine, and a Lover
of hers.          85

PHEBE  Youth, you have done me much Ungentleness,
To shew the Letter that I writ to you.

ROSALIND  I care not if I have: it is my Study
To seem despightful and ungentle to you.

---

88  **Study**  intent, purposeful endeavour. This word echoes
     IV.iii.63.

89  **despightful**  spiteful, unpleasant.

90    **followed**   both (a) pursued, and (b) attended obediently, as by a worshipful disciple. See I.i.115–16, II.iii.69–70, III.v.49–50, and compare such New Testament passages as Matthew 16:24, where Jesus says 'If any man will come after me, let him deny himself, and take up his cross, and follow me.'

93    **all made**   composed entirely.

98    **Faith and Service**   fidelity and adherence to duty. See the note to line 90.

103    **Fantasy**   fancy, imagination.

104    **Passion**   both (a) loving devotion and (b) self-sacrifice (see the note to IV.iii.171).

105    **Observance**   attentiveness. Compare II.vii.38–42.

107    **Trial**   willingness to endure even the most trying circumstances, seeing them as mere tests of one's Job-like 'Patience' and 'Purity'.

115    **Why do you speak too**   why do you too say.

116    **To . . . hear**   Orlando's reply answers the question 'who' rather than 'why', and many editors therefore assume that the previous line should read 'Whom do you speak to . . .'. But it seems more likely that Orlando simply makes a logical leap from 'why' to 'who', on the assumption that 'Ganimed' will understand him to be saying, '[I too speak these words because I speak] to her that is not here. . . .'

118    **Howling . . . Moon**   Some commentators have suggested that Rosalind specifies 'Irish' here because of a 1598 rebellion in which Ireland challenged the hegemony of England, and thus of Queen Elizabeth (sometimes represented as the 'Moon' in contemporary iconography because, like the Goddess of that heavenly body, she was a chaste virgin). Compare *A Midsummer Night's Dream*, V.ii.1–2, where Puck says, 'Now the hungry Lion roars, / And the Wolf beholds the Moon'.

118–   **– I . . . Commands**   Rosalind addresses each sentence to a
29    different person or group: Silvius, Phebe, All, Phebe, Orlando, Silvius, Orlando, Silvius, and All. Rosalind's final sentence echoes such New Testament passages as John 15:14 ('Ye are my friends, if ye do whatsoever I command you') and Matthew 28:19–20 (Jesus' final commission to his disciples).

120    **altogether**   all together, in unison. Compare II.v.39.

You are there followed by a faithful Shepherd,                    90
Look upon him, love him: he worships you.

PHEBE   Good Shepherd, tell this Youth what 'tis
  to love.

SILVIUS   It is to be all made of Sighs and Tears,
And so am I for Phebe.

PHEBE   And I for Ganimed.                                        95

ORLANDO   And I for Rosalind.

ROSALIND   And I for no Woman.

SILVIUS   It is to be all made of Faith and Service,
And so am I for Phebe.

PHEBE   And I for Ganimed.                                        100

ORLANDO   And I for Rosalind.

ROSALIND   And I for no woman.

SILVIUS   It is to be all made of Fantasy,
All made of Passion, and all made of Wishes,
All Adoration, Duty, and Observance,                             105
All Humbleness, all Patience, and Impatience,
All Purity, all Trial, all Observance:
And so am I for Phebe.

PHEBE   And so am I for Ganimed.

ORLANDO   And so am I for Rosalind.                               110

ROSALIND   And so am I for no Woman.

PHEBE   If this be so, why blame you me to love
  you?

SILVIUS   If this be so, why blame you me to love
  you?

ORLANDO   If this be so, why blame you me to love
  you?

ROSALIND   Why do you speak too, 'why blame you me
  to love you'.                                                  115

ORLANDO   To her, that is not here, nor doth not
  hear.

ROSALIND   Pray you no more of this, 'tis like the
Howling of Irish Wolves against the Moon. — I
will help you if I can. — I would love you if
I could. — To morrow meet me altogether. — I             120
will marry you, if ever I marry Woman, and I'll

124     **content you**   satisfy you, make you content. *Content* echoes *contented* (line 18) and recalls III.ii.80, III.iii.3.

126     **As . . . meet**   Because you love Rosalind, be present for this get-together.

V.iii     The setting remains in the forest near the sheepcote.

4     **dishonest**   unchaste, sinful. Compare III.iii.7, 24–40.

4–5     **a Woman of the World**   Audrey probably means 'a married woman'. It was not unusual to speak of getting married as 'going to the world', probably to distinguish the matrimonial state from the cloistered life of the nun (shut off from the world). But it may be that Audrey also thinks that marrying Touchstone will make her 'worldly' (perhaps because he will take her out of the simple life of the forest and expose her to the ways of the Court). See the notes to IV.iii.31, V.i.2, and V.ii.7, and compare *Much Ado About Nothing*, II.i.333–34, where Beatrice says, 'Thus goes every one to the World but I'. *World* anticipates V.iv.169–70.

10     **sit . . . middle**   The Second Page alludes to a well-known rhyme, 'Hey diddle diddle, fool in the middle'. Compare II.v.61–62. The phrase *for you* means 'game', 'at your service', 'available for you'.

11     **clap . . . roundly**   launch into it directly, circumventing any preliminaries.

12     **Hauking**   an onomatopoeic word for throat-clearing. *Spitting* recalls IV.i.80–81.

13     **onely**   only. Compare lines 19, 25, 31, 37 and see the note to line 19.

14–15   **in a Tune**   in one [the same] tune. The Second Page's phrasing suggests 'in a plot or conspiracy'; compare *Much Ado About Nothing*, IV.ii.33–34, where Dogberry says that Conrade and Borachio, malefactors who are being interrogated, 'are both in a Tale'.

15     **like two Gipsies on a Horse**   either (a) together, in unison, or (b) one after the other, in a canon (round). The song that follows was printed in Thomas Morley's *First Book of Ayres* (1600), and the music survives in a manuscript that also appears to derive from Morley. What is rendered in this and in other modern editions as the final stanza is printed in the First Folio as if it were to be combined with the first stanza.

be married to morrow. – I will satisfy you, if
ever I satisfied Man, and you shall be married
to morrow. – I will content you, if what pleases
you contents you, and you shall be married          125
to morrow. – As you love Rosalind, meet. – As
you love Phebe, meet. – And as I love no Woman,
I'll meet. So fare you well: I have left you
Commands.
SILVIUS   I'll not fail, if I live.                 130
PHEBE   Nor I.
ORLANDO   Nor I.                              *Exeunt.*

# Scene 3

*Enter Clown and Audrey.*

CLOWN   To morrow is the joyful Day, Audrey,
to morrow will we be married.
AUDREY   I do desire it with all my Heart: and I
hope it is no dishonest Desire to be a Woman
of the World? Here come two of the banish'd      5
Duke's Pages.

*Enter two Pages.*

1 PAGE   Well met, honest Gentleman.
CLOWN   By my troth well met: come, sit, sit, and
a Song.
2 PAGE   We are for you, sit i'th' middle.         10
1 PAGE   Shall we clap into't roundly, without
Hauking or Spitting, or saying we are Hoarse,
which are the onely Prologues to a bad Voice.
2 PAGE   I'faith, i'faith, and both in a
Tune like two Gipsies on a Horse.                  15

17 **With . . . nonino** Like other refrains in songs of the period, these words probably have no meaning. But given the agricultural imagery of the lyrics, *hey* and *ho* may be meant to evoke the hay that flourishes in a 'Field' that has been cultivated with a hoe; compare *Twelfth Night*, III.i.140–42, where Viola replies to a speech about how to 'reap' a 'Harvest' with the words 'Westward hoe'.

18 **corn Field** field of grain. Only later did 'corn' come to mean maize (sweet corn).

19 **pretty Ring Time** fine, apt time to exchange rings of betrothal and matrimony. Here 'Ring Time' is also the season for a male who is in his lusty 'Prime' (line 36) to seek the 'pretty Ring' of a responsive 'Lass'; for 'Ring' as a term for the female pudendum, see *The Merchant of Venice*, V.i.306–7. In this line *onely* plays on *one*, a figure whose upright posture in both the Arabic and Roman numeral systems can stand for the erect male 'Horn' (see the notes to III.iii.54–55 and III.iv.13). *Pretty* echoes V.i.31.

22 **Between the Acres of the Rye** on the strips of unploughed land that separate the cultivated rows of the ryefield.

24 **These . . . lie** In this line 'Country-folks' carries the same suggestiveness as 'Country Copulatives' (V.iv.58), 'Sweet Lovers' who are inclined to 'lie' in erotic embraces; see the notes to I.ii.211 and III.ii.414, and compare the use of *lie* in the song that commences Act II, Scene v.

28 **Carol** song.

30 **a . . . Flower** a human life, though as beautiful and fragrant as a 'Flower', is also as fragile as a flourishing blossom, and as limited in duration.

34 **And therefore take the present Time** and therefore take advantage of the brief time available to you. The 'moral' of this lovely lyric is *carpe diem* (a Latin phrase meaning 'seize the day'): youth is as brief as a 'Flower' in 'the Prime' and must be enjoyed before it fades.

36 **For . . . Prime** Love reaches its apogee, and most fully reaps the rewards of its efforts, when it is 'crowned with the Prime': (a) garlanded with a 'Branch of Victory' (IV.ii.5–6) that has been woven of springtime flora (one sense of *Prime* being 'Spring'), and (b) consummated while both lovers are 'prime' (ruttish, as in the phrase 'prime as Goats, as hot as Monkeys', *Othello*, III.iii.393) and in their primes (their height of vitality).

## SONG

*It was a Lover, and his Lass,*
  *With a hey, and a ho, and a hey nonino,*
*That o'er the green corn Field did pass,*
  *In Spring Time, the onely pretty Ring Time.*
*When Birds do sing, hey ding a ding, ding:*                    20
*Sweet Lovers love the Spring.*

*Between the Acres of the Rye,*
  *With a hey, and a ho, and a hey nonino,*
*These pretty Country-folks would lie,*
  *In Spring Time, the onely pretty Ring Time.*               25
*When Birds do sing, hey ding a ding, ding:*
*Sweet Lovers love the Spring.*

*This Carol they began that Hour,*
  *With a hey, and a ho, and a hey nonino:*
*How that a Life was but a Flower,*                            30
  *In Spring Time, the onely pretty Ring Time.*
*When Birds do sing, hey ding a ding, ding:*
*Sweet Lovers love the Spring.*

*And therefore take the present Time,*
  *With a hey, and a ho, and a hey nonino,*                   35
*For Love is crowned with the Prime,*
  *In Spring Time, the onely pretty Ring Time.*
*When Birds do sing, hey ding a ding, ding:*
*Sweet Lovers love the Spring.*

CLOWN   Truly, young Gentlemen, though there was           40

41–42 **the Note . . . Untuneable**   the performance of it was lacking in melodious beauty.

43   **kept Time**   maintained the proper rhythm and harmony (with *Time*, here synonymous with 'tune'). Compare *Twelfth Night*, 99–101, and *Hamlet*, III.i.161–62.

44   **lost not our Time**   The Page's words are essentially a repetition of 'we kept Time'; but in their rephrasing they reiterate the message of the song itself (let those of us who are young lose not 'our Time' in the prime).

45   **Time lost**   Time wasted. Touchstone is not willing to grant that there is any 'Matter' (meaning, substance) in a song so 'foolish'. *Matter* (line 41) recalls II.i.67–68, IV.i.78–86.

46   **buy**   both (a) purchase, and (b) be with. See the notes to III.ii.274, IV.i.33. *Mend* (repair), line 47, echoes II.iv.95, III.ii.72, IV.i.201.

V.iv   This scene takes place near the sheepcote in the forest.

1   **Boy**   Ganimed (Rosalind).

4   **fear they hope**   are afraid that they are merely indulging in wishful thinking. Lines 3–4 echo the exchange in Mark 9:23–24 where Jesus tells the father of a demon-possessed child that 'If thou canst believe, all things are possible to him that believeth. And straightway the father of the child cried out and said with tears, Lord, I believe; help thou mine unbelief.' Compare *The Winter's Tale*, V.iii.93–94, where Paulina tells Leontes, 'It is requir'd / You do awake your Faith'.

5   **whiles our Compact is urg'd**   while what we have all agreed to is reaffirmed. In this phrase *urg'd* means 'asserted', 'set out for ratification'. *Compact* (agreement) is to be accented on the second syllable.

7   **bestow her on Orlando**   give her to Orlando in marriage. Compare III.iii.69–98, IV.i.145–46. *Bestow* recalls I.ii.34–36, IV.iii.86–89.

8   **had . . . her**   Duke Senior's pledge will prove to be more than an idle 'hope' (line 4).

9   **have**   accept, marry.

12   **Hour after**   the following hour. Here *Hour* is to be treated metrically as a two-syllable word. Phebe hopes that she will 'die' carnally 'the Hour after' she marries 'Ganimed'; see the notes to IV.ii.1, IV.iii.63, 156.

no great Matter in the Ditty, yet the Note was
very untuneable.

1 PAGE   You are deceiv'd, Sir, we kept Time,
we lost not our Time.

CLOWN   By my troth yes: I count it but Time lost      45
to hear such a foolish Song. God buy you, and
God mend your Voices. – Come, Audrey.      *Exeunt.*


# Scene 4

*Enter Duke Senior, Amyens, Jaques, Orlando,*
*Oliver, Celia.*

DUKE SENIOR   Dost thou believe, Orlando, that the
Boy
Can do all this that he hath promised?

ORLANDO   I sometimes do believe, and sometimes do
not,
As those that fear they hope, and know they
fear.

*Enter Rosalind, Silvius, and Phebe.*

ROSALIND   Patience once more, while our Compact
is urg'd:                                                                  5
You say, if I bring in your Rosalind,
You will bestow her on Orlando here?

DUKE SENIOR   That would I, had I Kingdoms to give
with her.

ROSALIND   And you say you will have her, when I
bring her?

ORLANDO   That would I, were I of all Kingdoms King.   10

ROSALIND   You say, you'll marry me, if I be willing.

PHEBE   That will I, should I die the Hour after.

17    **Though ... thing**   Silvius little realizes that to 'have' Phebe in a union that would make them 'one flesh' (Genesis 2:24, quoted in Ephesians 5:28–33) would be 'one thing' with a 'Death' (see the notes to III.ii.162, IV.i.100, V.iv.12) that would 'make all this Matter even' (line 18). *Thing* recalls IV.i.130–31 and anticipates lines 117–18.

18    **to make all this Matter even**   to even out all the difficulties in this complicated set of circumstances, to bring about 'a more equal Enterprise' (I.iii.185).

25    **To make these Doubts all even**   to resolve your questions and fears (another sense of *Doubts* that echoes lines 3–4) in these matters, to bring about the kind of 'Mirth' (conjugal joy) that occurs 'When Earthly Things made even / atone together' (lines 117–18). To 'make . . . even' is to level all distinctions, to create the balance and harmony that obtains when all accounts are equal, and to smooth the way to atonement (at-one-ment).

26    **I do remember**   I am reminded. The irony in Duke Senior's remark is that, though he doesn't realize it, he does 'remember'. See the note to III.iv.40, and compare III.v.131, V.i.32–34.

27    **lively Touches**   sprightly, living characteristics. *Touches* recalls III.ii.160.
     **Favour**   appearance, demeanour. Compare IV.iii.86–88.

30    **Forest borne**   rustic, a native of the 'Forest', which has 'borne' (nurtured) him from the day he was 'born' here. *Borne* echoes IV.ii.16.

31    **Rudiments**   fundamentals. But here the first syllable plays on 'rude' (rustic, crude) in a sense appropriate to the forest setting.

32    **desperate Studies**   Here *desperate* probably means 'perilous to the soul'; compare *dangerous* (IV.i.201–2, echoed in V.ii.77) and *damnable* (V.ii.70). Those who delved in the magical arts were usually thought to be engaging in traffic with evil spirits, who were assumed to have the power to drive the soul to despair (beyond hope of redemption), as illustrated by Christopher Marlowe's *Doctor Faustus* (1592).

ROSALIND    But if you do refuse to marry me,
  You'll give your self to this most faithful
    Shepherd.
PHEBE    So is the Bargain.                                    15
ROSALIND    You say that you'll have Phebe if she
    will.
SILVIUS    Though to have her and Death were both
    one thing.
ROSALIND    I have promis'd to make all this Matter
    even.
  Keep your Word, O Duke, to give your
    Daughter,
  You yours, Orlando, to receive his Daughter;          20
  Keep you your Word, Phebe, that you'll marry
    me,
  Or else refusing me to wed this Shepherd;
  Keep your Word, Silvius, that you'll marry her
  If she refuse me, and from hence I go
  To make these Doubts all even.                        25
                          *Exeunt Rosalind and Celia.*
DUKE SENIOR    I do remember in this Shepherd Boy
  Some lively Touches of my Daughter's Favour.
ORLANDO    My Lord, the first time that I ever saw
    him
  Me thought he was a Brother to your Daughter:
  But my good Lord, this Boy is Forest borne,           30
  And hath been tutor'd in the Rudiments
  Of many desperate Studies, by his Uncle,
  Whom he reports to be a great Magitian,

34 **Obscured in the Circle** hidden within the bounds. But the word *obscured* (literally, shadowed) reinforces the idea that this mysterious 'Magician' has been dealing with 'dark spirits'. Meanwhile *Circle* alludes to the magic confinement into which magicians sought to draw demonic spirits. The implication of Orlando's words is that Ganimed's 'Uncle' works his magic throughout the forest, which thus becomes a potent conjuring field not unlike the island where a later Shakespearean character (Prospero) will practise his art in *The Tempest*. In lines 218–19 Rosalind herself will lay claim to the conjuring powers of a thespian wonder-worker. *Magitian* echoes V.ii.69, 80.

35 **sure another Flood toward** certainly another Noahic deluge in the offing. Jaques is being facetious, but there are ways in which the forest setting functions like the ark that preserved a remnant of life from the Flood (Genesis 6–9) that cleansed the world and gave a corrupt mankind a fresh start.

37 **pair . . . Beasts** Jaques compares Touchstone and Audrey to the animals, 'two and two of all flesh' and 'male and female of all flesh' (Genesis 7:15–16), who boarded Noah's ark.

38 **Tongues** languages. Compare IV.iii.84–85. Jaques aludes to another biblical narrative (Genesis 11:1–9), this one about the punishment visited on human presumption when God descended on the hubristic Tower of Babel (a word meaning 'confusion') to 'confound the language of all the earth' and turn into babble the words of those who tried to communicate with the speakers of other 'Tongues'. *Fools* echoes the song alluded to in V.iii.2 and the jest Jaques plays in II.v.61–62.

41 **Motley-minded** with a mind like the patchwork of jester's costume. Compare III.iii.7–8, and see *Twelfth Night*, I.v.60–63, where the clown Feste insists 'I wear not Motley in my Brain'.

44–45 **put . . . Purgation** put me to a trial that will allow me to clear myself of any suspicion that attaches to my name. Compare *Hamlet*, III.ii.329–32, where *Purgation* carries an additional sense that refers to medical procedures such as cathartics and bleeding to rid the body of disease.

45 **trod a Measure** taken my turn at courtly dances.

46 **flatter'd a Lady** used flattery to beguile a lady of her favours.
**politic** crafty, underhanded. See IV.i.10–16, V.i.60–61.

*Enter Clown and Audrey.*

Obscured in the Circle of this Forest.

JAQUES   There is sure another Flood toward, and          35
these Couples are coming to the Ark. Here
comes a pair of very strange Beasts, which in
all Tongues are call'd Fools.

CLOWN   Salutation and Greeting to you all.

JAQUES   Good my Lord, bid him welcome. This is the     40
Motley-minded Gentleman that I have so often
met in the Forest: he hath been a Courtier, he
swears.

CLOWN   If any man doubt that, let him put me to
my Purgation. I have trod a Measure, I have          45
flatt'red a Lady, I have been politic with my
Friend, smooth with mine Enemy, I have undone
three Tailors, I have had four Quarrels, and
like to have fought one.

JAQUES   And how was that ta'en up?          50

CLOWN   'Faith we met, and found the Quarrel was
upon the seventh Cause.

JAQUES   How seventh Cause? – Good my Lord, like this
Fellow.

DUKE SENIOR   I like him very well.          55

---

47   **smooth**   flattering, deceptively amiable. Compare I.iii.81–83,
II.vii.94–96.
**undone**   ruined financially (probably by ordering apparel and
not paying for it).

50   **ta'en up**   resolved without a duel, settled or intercepted before
it led to combat.

52   **Cause**   case (category of, or reason for, taking offence). See the
note to III.iv.4, and compare I.iii.97, III.ii.30–31; also see the
note to line 69.

56    **God . . . like**  God yield you, sir, I bear the same good wishes to you. But Touchstone's wording also suggests 'I want you to like me.' Compare III.iii.75–76.

57    **press in**  intrude myself. Touchstone's phrase hints at sexual assertiveness.

58    **Country Copulatives**  rustic couples. But both words also have bawdy implications; see the notes to III.ii.290 and V.iii.24, and compare II.i.58–59, III.ii.47–50, 124–28, IV.i.35–40. The grammatical meaning of *Copulatives*, weak verbs that link subjects with predicate complements, is pertinent to the kind of 'Marriage' Touchstone seeks.
    **forswear**  unswear, disavow or disregard the oath one has sworn.

59    **Blood breaks**  passion causes me to break my vows. See the note to I.i.50.

60    **ill-favoured thing**  both (a) an unattractive woman (compare III.v.52–53), and (b) a 'thing' (object of erotic attention, as noted at line 17) that no one favours (prefers) but those who favour it in all 'ill' (evil, lustful) fashion.

61    **a poor Humour**  a trifling, if not debasing, whim, founded on a lust for 'a Toy in hand' (III.iii.77). *Humour* recalls IV.i.74.

62–64  **rich . . . Oyster**  Touchstone implies that though Audrey is 'ill-favour'd' (line 60), as 'poor' (impoverished, unkempt) as a miser's dwelling and as 'foul' (ugly, dirty) as an oyster, her 'Honesty' (see III.iii.6–45) makes her as precious as a pearl.

65–66  **swift and sententious**  quick-witted and full of wise 'sentences' ('Saws', II.vii.156).

67    **Fool's Bolt**  Touchstone pick up on 'swift' in line 65 and alludes to the proverb 'A Fool's bolt [arrow] is soon shot.' His implication is that a foolish person (who probably has only one bolt, if that, in his quiver) utters his opinion too early and too hastily and thus renders any further comment worthless ('shot' – like a 'shotten Herring', *1 Henry IV*, II.iv.140–42, a fish that has discharged its roe at spawning time and is now weak and emaciated).

68    **dulcet Diseases**  sweet afflictions. Touchstone implies that his 'sentences' (wise sayings) are little more than minor ailments. But his phrasing also hints at the venereal diseases a 'Fool' risks by shooting his 'Bolt' in 'dulcet' pastimes. See the notes on fools and folly at I.ii.53. II.vii.56.

CLOWN    God'ild you, Sir, I desire you of the like.
I press in here, Sir, amongst the rest of the
Country Copulatives to swear, and to forswear,
according as Marriage binds and Blood breaks.
A poor Virgin, Sir, an ill-favour'd thing, Sir,                    60
but mine own, a poor Humour of mine, Sir, to
take that that no man else will: rich Honesty
dwells like a Miser, Sir, in a poor House, as
your Pearl in your foul Oyster.

DUKE SENIOR    By my faith, he is very swift, and           65
sententious.

CLOWN    According to the Fool's Bolt, Sir, and such
dulcet Diseases.

JAQUES    But for the seventh Cause. How did you
find the Quarrel on the seventh Cause?                          70

CLOWN    Upon a Lie, seven times remov'd – bear
your Body more seeming, Audrey – as thus,
Sir. I did dislike the Cut of a certain Courtier's
Beard. He sent me Word, if I said his Beard
was not cut well, he was in the mind it was:               75
this is call'd the Retort Courteous. If I sent
him Word again, it was not well cut, he would

---

69    **Cause**  Here the word is used in a way that parallels the legal
sense, a sense also evident in *find* (to arrive at a judgement
through legal proceedings). See the note to line 52.

72    **more seeming**  in a more seemly fashion. Apparently Audrey's
posture is not yet that of a woman of the world. See the note
to III.iii.78.

73–74 **Cut . . . Beard**  length or shape of a courtly gentleman's 'Beard'
(a word that recalls I.ii.77–85, II.vii.155, III.ii.216–23,
395–400). Touchstone's instance makes it clear that to
challenge a 'Courtier's Beard' is to question his virility, his
standing as a man of valour and honour. Compare *Hamlet*,
II.ii.454–55, 608–17.

75    **in the mind**  disposed to think; of the opinion. *Mind* recalls
IV.iii.58.

79 **Quip Modest** ironically deferential reply. Lines 76–78 echo
   IV.i.71 and recall III.ii.284–85.

80 **disabled** called into question. Compare IV.i.35–37. *Churlish*
   (disagreeable) recalls II.iv.81.

83 **Reproof Valiant** brave rebuke.

85 **Countercheck** contradiction. Compare II.vii.63.

86 **Circumstantial** conditional, subject to qualification by
   circumstances.
   **Direct** without mitigating or qualifying conditions.

90–91 **give . . . Direct** tell me in no unqualified terms that I was lying.
   The phrase 'Lie Direct' hints at another sense of 'Lie' (see the
   note to V.iii.24) and at four related senses of 'Direct': (a)
   directly, immediately, (b) straight, upright (see the note to
   V.iii.20), (c) plain, naked, and (d) aimed or pointed forward.
   In similar fashion *Countercheck* (line 85) echoes English
   derivatives of the Latin word *cunnus* (see the note to V.iii.24),
   and *Circumstantial* (line 90) suggests both 'circling around
   before taking a stance' and 'standing in a circle'; compare
   *Romeo and Juliet*, II.i.23–29, and *Othello*, III.iii.395–98.

91 **measur'd Swords** compared the lengths of our swords (to
   assure that neither side had an unfair advantage) in
   preparation for fighting. Here as elsewhere, *swords* are
   indicators of more than one kind of male weapon; compare
   *Romeo and Juliet*, I.i.1–67, 75–81, II.iii.7–40, 153–69,
   III.i.1–138. *Measur'd* recalls II.vi.1–3.

93 **nominate** name, enumerate.

95–96 **O . . . Manners** Touchstone satirizes volumes such as Vincent
   Saviolo's *Practice of the Sword and Dagger* (1594) and Sir
   William Segar's *Book of Honour and Arms* (1590), which
   catalogued 'the nature and diversity of lies' and instructed
   gentlemen about when and how to respond in keeping with
   the 'Terms of Honour' (*Hamlet*, V.ii.258). To 'quarrel in
   Print' was to adhere precisely to the rules of etiquette, to go
   'by the Book'; compare *Romeo and Juliet*, I.iv.225.

103 **All these you may avoid** You may get away with all these
   'degrees' of quarrelling without having to duel.

105 **Justices** 'elder Maisters of known Honour' (*Hamlet*, V.ii.260),
   respected arbiters of disputes in the 'good Manners' (line 96)
   that govern aristocratic male decorum. Here as in line 50,
   *take up* means 'resolve or settle'.

send me Word he cut it to please himself: this
is called the Quip Modest. If again, it was not
well cut, he disabled my Judgement: this is          80
call'd the Reply Churlish. If again it was not
well cut, he would answer I spake not true:
this is call'd the Reproof Valiant. If again,
it was not well cut, he would say I lie: this
is call'd the Countercheck Quarrelsome. And so       85
to Lie Circumstantial, and the Lie Direct.

JAQUES   And how oft did you say his Beard was not
well cut?

CLOWN   I durst go no further than the Lie
Circumstantial: nor he durst not give me the         90
Lie Direct. And so we measur'd Swords, and
parted.

JAQUES   Can you nominate in order now, the Degrees
of the Lie?

CLOWN   O Sir, we quarrel in Print, by the Book,     95
as you have Books for good Manners. I will
name you the Degrees. The first, the Retort
Courteous; the second, the Quip Modest; the
third, the Reply Churlish; the fourth, the
Reproof Valiant; the fift, the Countercheck          100
Quarrelsome; the sixt, the Lie with
Circumstance; the seventh, the Lie Direct.
All these you may avoid, but the Lie Direct;
and you may avoid that too, with an If. I knew
when seven Justices could not take up a              105
Quarrel, but when the Parties were met
themselves, one of them thought but of an

108    **as**  for example.

110    **much Virtue in If**  This witty phrase relates not only to the use of hypothetical language to resolve disputes, but more generally to the role that 'supposing' (assuming, pretending, experimenting with various guises and postures) plays in *As You Like It* as a whole. It might be said, indeed, that 'If' and 'as you like it' (as you would have it be) are near-synonyms. And if 'If is the onely Peace-maker', it is appropriate that 'supposing' should figure so prominently in a dramatic action whose final cause is peace-making. The *onely* (only) in this sentence echoes V.iii.13–37, and as in line 19 it hints at the 'one-ly', phallic aggressiveness of 'noble swelling Spirits / That hold their Honours in a wary Distance' (*Othello*, II.iii.54–55) and require 'the onely Peacemaker' to keep them from fighting one another.

112    **at any thing**  at everything he says and does. *Thing* echoes line 17 and anticipates lines 117–18.

113–  **Stalking-horse**  either a real horse or a decoy by means of which
14    a hunter, using it as cover, stalks his game and gets within shooting range. In lines 113–15 Duke Senior means that Touchstone's 'Folly' (his pretence that he is a real fool) is merely the pretext ('Presentation') that allows him to penetrate the defences of his satirical targets. See the notes to lines 67, 68. *Wit* (line 115) figures in Duke Senior's imagery as an intellectual weapon (see the notes to lines 67, 91). But here as elsewhere, *Wit* can also function as genital 'Bolt'; compare IV.i.167–87, V.i.29–31, 55–57.

117    **made even**  resolved, settled, 'taken up.' See the notes to lines 18, 25. The 'Earthly Things' in this line refer to every aspect of this world, including the genital 'things' that come 'together' in matrimony. See the notes to IV.i.128, 131.

118    **atone together**  become 'at one' (the root meaning of *atone*). These words are spoken by the God of Marriage, whose role is to make a man and a woman 'one flesh' (see the note to III.v.133). Compare *Antony and Cleopatra*, II.ii.101–4, where Mecenas seeks to 'atone' Antony and Octavius.

121    **hether**  hither, as in I.ii.170.

If; as 'If you said so, then I said so': and
they shook Hands, and swore Brothers. Your If
is the onely Peace-maker: much Virtue in If.                    110
JAQUES   Is this not a rare Fellow, my Lord? He's
as good at any thing, and yet a Fool.
DUKE SENIOR   He uses his Folly like a Stalking-
horse, and under the Presentation of that he
shoots his Wit.                                                 115

> *Enter Hymen, Rosalind, and Celia.*
> *Still Music.*

HYMEN   *Then is there Mirth in Heaven,*
　　　*When Earthly Things made even*
　　　　　*atone together.*
　　　*Good Duke, receive thy Daughter,*
　　　*Hymen from Heaven brought her,*                          120
　　　　　*Yea brought her hether,*
　　　*That thou might'st join his Hand with his,*
　　　*Whose Heart within his Bosom is.*

---

122   **his Hand with his**   the hand of 'thy Daughter' (line 119) with
that of her husband-to-be Orlando. Compare III.iii.69–73.
Virtually all modern editions emend the first *his* to *her*. But
even if Rosalind now emerges, for the first time in Arden, in
female attire, Hymen may be deliberately referring to her with
a masculine pronoun, to hint that 'Earthly Things' can only be
'made even' when 'Ganimed' and 'Rosalind' are seen to 'atone
together' in the 'busy Actor' (III.iv.64) whose 'Wit' underlies
'the Presentation' of both characters (lines 113–15).

124 **my self**  For the first time since she arrived in the forest, Rosalind is now speaking in her own person. It may be that it is only as 'he' speaks lines 124–25 that 'Ganimed' removes 'his' clothing (line 122) to disclose the 'her' the 'Good Duke' (lines 120, 119) and his future son-in-law will recognize as Rosalind; see the note to line 122. In this speech Rosalind's first line is to her father, and her second is to Orlando. In lines 130–32 she addresses Duke Senior, Orlando, and Phebe.

126 **If there be Truth in Sight**  if what our eyes tell us can be believed. We should note that both Duke Senior and Orlando (in line 127) use the hypothetical 'If'. Within the world of the play, there is now 'Truth in Sight'; but of course this is because of the provisional nature of the theatre that encloses the play. One of its conditions is that the audience suspend disbelief long enough to accept the 'Presentation' (line 114) by means of which a male actor can 'be' Duke Senior's 'Daughter' (line 126) as well as the resourceful page Ganimed.

133 **bar Confusion**  prohibit any chaotic medley of incompatible elements. *Bar* recalls I.i.20–23. A good deal of the 'Confusion' now to be eliminated relates to the ambiguity of lines 122–23, a passage whose enigmatic pronouns reflect the problematic identity of Rosalind/Ganimed. See the notes to lines 122, 124.

135 **strange Events**  astonishing outcomes. Hymen's phrasing captures the essence of the play's 'Conclusion' (a word that means both 'ending' and 'coming together'). The things that have occurred in the forest are 'strange' in at least two senses: (a) they seem to violate the laws of probability (and thus expectation), and (b) they are mysterious, beyond easy comprehension. The fact that Hymen's own presence is unexplained is integral to the numinous (seemingly supernatural) quality of the moment. Is Hymen really a god whom Rosalind has managed to conjure into the magic circle of the forest, or is he merely a 'forester' she has commissioned to 'present' the deity? All we know is that 'Reason' cannot completely undo this 'Wonder' (line 146). *Strange* echoes lines 36–38 and recalls II.iv.54–55, II.vii.40–41, 149–50, 163–65, IV.i.35–38, IV.iii.50–53, V.ii.29, 37, 67–68.

137 **Bands**  both (a) bonds, and (b) wedding bands (rings). Compare line 150.

139 **no Cross shall part**  shall be divided by no disagreements, obstacles, or other troubles.

ROSALIND   To you I give my self, for I am yours.
– To you I give my self, for I am yours.                                125
DUKE SENIOR   If there be Truth in Sight, you are
   my Daughter.
ORLANDO   If there be Truth in Sight, you are my
   Rosalind.
PHEBE   If sight and Shape be true,
        Why then my Love adieu.
ROSALIND   I'll have no Father, if you be not he;              130
– I'll have no Husband, if you be not he;
– Nor ne'er wed Woman, if you be not she.
HYMEN   Peace ho: I bar Confusion,
        'Tis I must make Conclusion
            Of these most strange Events.                      135
        Here's eight that must take Hands,
        To join in Hymen's Bands,
            If Truth holds true Contents.
        You and you, no Cross shall part;
        – You and you, are Hart in Hart;                        140
        – You, to his Love must accord,
        Or have a Woman to your Lord.
        – You and you, are sure together,
        As the Winter to fowl Weather.

---

140   **Hart in Hart**   two harts (noble deer) whose hearts are conjoined
      in 'Truth' (both honesty and fidelity), line 138, and 'Love',
      line 140. This phrase echoes lines 122–23; see the note to
      I.ii.3, and compare I.i.175–80, I.ii.251–52, I.iii.18–19,
      II.iv.33, II.vi.1–5, III.i.1–5, III.ii.149–60, 263, 286–87,
      446–50, III.iii.48–49, III.iv.44–49, III.v.137, IV.iii.40–45,
      164–65, 173–74, V.ii.22–28.

143   **fowl Weather**   both (a) foul (inclement) weather, and (b) the
      kind of weather fit for fowl of your feather. *Fowl* recalls
      IV.i.215–18, V.iii.20–21, and *foul* echoes III.v.66; compare
      *The Tempest*, II.i.124–25, for another pun on 'foul' and 'fowl
      Weather'.

146   **That . . . diminish**   that Reason (rational 'Questioning', line
      145) may reduce the sway of 'Wonder' (amazement).

149   **Juno's Crown**   the crowning achievement of the Goddess of
      Marriage. *Crown* echoes V.iii.36.

150   **Boord**   board (table filled with food). The 'Bond' (union)
      depicted here is reinforced by the four alliterative *B*'s in this
      line.

151   **peoples**   populates, disseminates offspring in. Compare *Much
      Ado About Nothing*, II.iii.257–58, where a bachelor who has
      ridiculed wedlock rationalizes his new matrimonial 'Humour'
      by citing the biblical injunction for Adam and his descendants
      to 'Be fruitful, and multiply, and replenish the earth, and
      subdue it'. According to the reform-minded Benedick, who
      now believes the shrewish Beatrice to be in love with him, 'the
      World must be peopled'.

155   **O my deer Niece**   Duke Senior greets Celia. *Deer* (deer) recalls
      V.ii.79.

156   **Daughter welcome**   as welcome as my own daughter. Here
      *Even* can function both as an adverb (in this case an
      intensifier comparable to 'indeed') and as an adjective
      meaning 'equal' and modifying *Daughter*. See the notes to
      lines 18, 25.

158   **Thy Faith . . . combine**   Your fidelity ('Faith') joins ('doth
      combine') my love ('Fancy') to you. Phebe addresses this
      speech to Silvius, whose 'Virtue' will at last be rewarded
      (compare line 195). *Fancy* recalls III.v.27–31, IV.iii.102.

S.D.  **2 Brother**   Jaques de Boys (as we know from I.i.5).

163   **resorted to**   gathered in.
      **Worth**   both (a) wealth, standing, and (b) worthiness. See
      I.i.104–26 and II.i.1–20, and compare II.vii.33–36, III.i.9–12,
      III.ii.93–100, 216–18, III.iii.59–62.

164   **Address'd a mighty Power**   led an army to the forest. See the
      note to III.ii.130.

165   **in . . . Conduct**   under his own command.
      **purposely to take**   with the purpose of taking.

166   **put . . . Sword**   execute him on the spot.

168   **an old Religious Man**   a hermit belonging to a religious order.
      *Religious* echoes III.ii.364–68, IV.i.208–11; *Skirts* (line 167)
      recalls III.ii.357.

— Whiles a Wedlock Hymn we sing,
Feed your selves with Questioning:                                    145
That Reason, Wonder may diminish
How thus we met, and these things finish.

SONG

*Wedding is great Juno's Crown,*
  *O blessed Bond of Boord and Bed;*                              150
*'Tis Hymen peoples every Town,*
  *High Wedlock then be honoured;*
*Honour, high Honour and Renown*
*To Hymen, God of every Town.*

DUKE SENIOR   O my deer Niece, welcome thou art
  to me,                                                                          155
Even Daughter welcome, in no less Degree.
PHEBE   I will not eat my Word, now thou art mine,
Thy Faith my Fancy to thee doth combine.

*Enter Second Brother.*

2 BROTHER   Let me have audience for a
  Word or two:
I am the second Son of old Sir Rowland,                           160
That bring these Tidings to this fair Assembly.
Duke Frederick hearing how that every Day
Men of great Worth resorted to this Forest,
Address'd a mighty Power, which were on foot
In his own Conduct, purposely to take                             165
His Brother here, and put him to the Sword:
And to the Skirts of this wild Wood he came,
Where, meeting with an old Religious Man,

169–  **was . . . World**  was so reoriented in his spirit that he
70    abandoned both his project and his usurped dukeship to
      sequester himself from the secular world and devote his life to
      religion. Here *World* has the New Testament sense
      exemplified in 1 John 2:15–16, 'Love not the world, neither
      the things that are in the world. . . . For all that is in the
      world, the lust of the flesh, and the lust of the eyes, and the
      pride of life, is not of the Father, but is of the world.' It recalls
      I.i.124–26, 175–80, I.ii.44–46, 201–3, 235–36, 294–95,
      I.iii.12–13, 136, II.iii.14–15, 56–58, II.vii.13, 23–28, 58–69,
      160–61, III.ii.95–96, 295–97, 443–46, III.v.52–53, 78–79,
      IV.i.99–103, 216–18, V.i.8–9, V.iii.3–5. *Converted* echoes
      IV.iii.135–38. In line 169, *Question* (conversation, here
      perhaps in a query-and-answer form similar to that of a
      catechism) echoes line 145 and recalls II.iv.65–66,
      II.vii.171–72, III.ii.288–93, 397–98, III.iv.38–39, V.ii.6–9.

172   **to him**  to Duke Senior. Modern editions normally emend this
      phrase to 'to them' (the other exiled lords). But restoring the
      lords' 'Lands' would appear to be a task that is left to Duke
      Senior; he seems to be promising to discharge that
      responsibility in lines 180–83.

174   **I do engage my Life**  I pledge, with my life as security.

175   **Thou . . . Wedding**  you bring a splendid present to honour
      your brothers' wedding.

176   **one**  Oliver, whose seized lands (see III.i.1–12) will now be
      returned to him. Presumably Orlando's older brother will
      now be excused from the pledge he made in V.ii.9–15. See the
      note to V.ii.7, and compare line 197 below.
      **the other**  Orlando, who will now become the heir to the
      dukedom as the husband of the restored Duke Senior's
      daughter.

178   **do those Ends**  complete those tasks. Duke Senior refers
      primarily to the wedding ceremonies to be conducted.

179   **begot**  conceived, given life. Compare I.i.59–62, IV.i.226–28.

180   **every**  every one.

181   **shrew'd**  cursed (beshrewed); 'churlish' (II.i.7), shrewishly
      disagreeable.

183   **Measure . . . States**  legal extent of their previous holdings and
      titles. Compare lines 45, 91–92, and 187, and see II.vi.2–3,
      V.ii.64–66.

After some Question with him, was converted
Both from his Enterprise, and from the World,                    170
His Crown bequeathing to his banish'd Brother,
And all their Lands restor'd to him again
That were with him exil'd. This to be true,
I do engage my Life.
DUKE SENIOR          Welcome, young Man.
Thou offer'st fairly to thy Brothers' Wedding:                   175
To one his Lands withheld, and to the other
A Land it self at large, a potent Dukedom.
First, in this Forest, let us do those Ends
That here were well begun, and well begot:
And after, every of this happy Number                            180
That have endur'd shrew'd Days, and Nights with
     us,
Shall share the good of our returned Fortune,
According to the Measure of their States.
Mean time, forget this new-fall'n Dignity,
And fall into our Rustic Revelry.                                185
– Play Music, and you Brides and Bride-grooms
     all,
With Measure heap'd in Joy, to th' Measures
     fall.

184  **new-fall'n Dignity**   newly descended honour and 'Fortune' (line
      182). Duke Senior's compound adjective suggests that the
      blessings that have been 'returned' to him and his companions
      are like 'Mercy' (divine grace), which 'droppeth as the gentle
      Rain from Heaven' (*The Merchant of Venice*, IV.i.187–88).
      *Fall'n* plays on *fall* (lines 185, 187) and recalls I.ii.47–48,
      I.iii.26–31, III.ii.347–50, III.v.17, 66–73, 124–26.

187  **Measure**   both (a) a measuring device and (b) moderation. See
      the notes to IV.i.6 and IV.ii.23.
      **Measures**   both (a) dance measures (graceful motions), and (b)
      musical measures (harmonious cadences).

188  **by your patience**  if you will please forgive a question from me. *Patience* anticipates line 195 and recalls I.iii.81–83, III.ii.163–66, IV.iii.13, V.i.1–2, V.ii.103–7, V.iv.5.

189  **put . . . Life**  donned the habit of a new 'Religious Man' (line 168); see the notes to IV.iii.107, 136, 141.

190  **thrown into Neglect the pompous Court**  decided to throw away all the luxury of court life. Compare II.i.1–17. *Neglect* recalls II.vii.109–12, III.ii.395–401.

192  **Convertites**  recent converts. See the note to lines 169–70.

193  **Matter**  substance, wisdom. Compare II.i.67–68, III.ii.176–77, 194–95, IV.i.78–86, V.iii.40–46, V.iv.18.

194  **You**  Jaques addresses Duke Senior. In the lines that follow, he appears to address, in turn, Orlando, Oliver, Silvius, and Touchstone (though it is possible that line 196 is addressed to Oliver, and line 197 to Orlando). Jaques's bequests are delivered with something like the tone and authority of a priest bestowing a benediction; and there is the clear implication that he will be the next to 'put on a Religious Life'.

197  **great Allies**  high-placed relatives by blood or by marriage. If Jaques addresses Oliver, he is referring to himself, to Orlando, new son-in-law to the restored Duke Senior, to Rosalind, Orlando's duchess, and to Frederick, father to Celia.

200  **victual'd**  supplied with food (victuals). If Jaques is correct, Touchstone will enjoy his 'Pleasures' for as long as he likes and then have his 'loving Voyage' yield to 'Wrangling' (line 199) and roaming. See the notes to III.iv.29–30, 34–36, 70, 82.

201  **other, then**  other than. But here 'other, then' can also function logically as a way of prophesying the dancing in Heaven that a Shakespearean contemporary, Sir John Davies, depicted as a symbol of cosmic 'Love and Harmony'; see his poem *Orchestra* (1596), and compare *Much Ado About Nothing*, V.iv.120–32. *Measures* echoes lines 186–87.

203  **Pastime**  dances and other frivolous activities.
**what you would have**  your business with me.

204  **I'll stay to know**  I'll wait to learn.
**abandon'd Cave**  The Duke's cave is abandoned now because everyone is away from it. In a brief time, however, it will be abandoned permanently, for the Duke and his companions will return from exile.

JAQUES   – Sir, by your patience: if I heard you
   rightly,
The Duke hath put on a Religious Life,
And thrown into Neglect the pompous Court.                    190
2 BROTHER   He hath.
JAQUES   To him will I: out of these Convertites
There is much Matter to be heard, and learn'd.
   – You to your former Honour I bequeath:
Your Patience, and your Virtue, well deserves it.             195
   – You to a Love, that your true Faith doth merit.
   – You to your Land, and Love, and great Allies.
   -- You to a long, and well-deserved Bed.
   – And you to Wrangling, for thy loving Voyage
Is but for two Months victuall'd. – So to your
   Pleasures,                                                 200
I am for other, then for Dancing Measures.
DUKE SENIOR   Stay, Jaques, stay.
JAQUES   To see no Pastime, I: what you would have,
I'll stay to know, at your abandon'd Cave.        *Exit.*
DUKE SENIOR   Proceed, proceed: we'll begin these
   Rights,                                                    205
As we do trust they'll end in true Delights.      *Exit.*
ROSALIND   It is not the Fashion to see the Lady
the Epilogue: but it is no more unhandsome,
then to see the Lord the Prologue. If it be

---

205   **Rights**   both (a) rites (rituals), and (b) rights (privileges). After
      the Duke speaks he may follow Jaques to the exit. Whether
      the others follow him or stay 'for Dancing Measures' (line
      224) is not clear. All we know is that either now or shortly
      hereafter Rosalind steps forward to address the audience with
      valedictory remarks.

207–   **see the Lady the Epilogue**   have a heroine present the verbal
8      postlude to a play. *Fashion* recalls III.ii.271–72.

208   **unhandsome**   inappropriate, unbecoming.

209   **then**   than. But as in line 224, 'then' can also be defended as a
      viable reading.

210    **good Wine needs no Bush**  a proverbial expression, referring to the leafy branches that vintners displayed to advertise their business. Here *Bush* means 'advertisement'. It also hints at a bushy clump of hair, such as the beard that Rosalind would wear (see I.ii.77–82) if she were still suited 'like a Man' (I.iii.120) rather than as an un-Epilogue-like 'Lady' (lines 207–8). Lines 209–18 recall III.v.72–75, IV.iii.111–19.

211    **Epilogue**  Here Rosalind probably means 'apology' (defence or justification). Compare *A Midsummer Night's Dream*, V.i.359–65, where Duke Theseus assures 'Lion' that he shouldn't trouble himself with an epilogue, 'for your Play needs no Excuse', and *The Tempest*, Epilogue, lines 15–20, where Prospero says that 'my Ending is Despair, / Unless I be reliev'd by Prayer' and 'pardon'd' by the audience's 'Indulgence'.

214    **Case**  predicament. Rosalind puns on another sense of *Case* that means 'costume', here that of a 'Lady' (line 207) whose outward 'Case' implies a pudendal 'Bush' that conceals female genitalia. See the note to III.iv.4.

215–  **insinuate . . . you**  employ the 'Smoothness' (I.iii.81) of subtle,
16     ingratiating indirection with you.

216    **in the behalf**  in support of.

217    **furnish'd**  dressed (as in III.ii.261–62). Rosalind is probably wearing a handsome wedding dress, the apparel she disclosed when she was led in by Hymen after line 115. *Beggar* echoes III.iii.84–85, where Jaques upbraids Touchstone for his willingness to be 'married under a Bush like a Beggar'.

218    **conjure you**  summon you, in the manner ('way') of a magician calling spirits into a circle with an incantation. Now the circle is no longer the forest (the 'Bush' of the play), but the round 'bare Island' (*The Tempest*, Epilogue, line 8) represented by the theatre itself. And Rosalind, as the conjurer, is functioning as the presiding genius of a space that she hopes to confirm as magical by the applause she is able to evoke from the audience. *As You Like It* was probably first performed in the Globe playhouse, almost certainly the round amphitheatre referred to as 'this Wooden O' in line 13 of the Prologue to *Henry V*. Lines 218–19 recall II.v.61–62, V.iii.10.

219    **charge**  command. Compare IV.iii.72.

220–  **to like . . . you**  Rosalind alludes to the play's title. These lines
21     echo lines 76–77 and anticipate lines 221–25.

true that good Wine needs no Bush, 'tis true            210
that a good Play needs no Epilogue. Yet to
good Wine they do use good Bushes: and good
Plays prove the better by the help of good
Epilogues. What a Case am I in then, that am
neither a good Epilogue, nor cannot insinuate        215
with you in the behalf of a good Play? I am
not furnish'd like a Beggar, therefore to beg
will not become me. My way is to conjure you,
and I'll begin with the Women. – I charge you,
O Women, for the Love you bear to Men, to like      220
as much of this Play as please you. – And I
charge you, O Men, for the Love you bear to
Women (as I perceive by your Simp'ring, none of
you hates them), that between you and the
Women the Play may please. If I were a Woman,       225

---

223  **Simp'ring**   smirking; coy, provocative smiles. Compare *King
Lear*, IV.vi.118–20, where the title character says, 'Behold
yon simp'ring Dame, whose Face between / Her Forks
presages Snow; that minces Virtue and / Does shake the Head
to hear of Pleasure's Name'.

225  **the Play may please**   Here Rosalind plays on *Play*, which refers
both to (a) the play the audience has just watched, and (b) the
sexual play that relates to 'the Love you bear to Women'
(lines 222–23).

**If I were a Woman**   Once again Rosalind has fun with the
suppositions made possible by 'if'; see the notes to lines 110,
126. As a character, of course, she remains a woman; but as a
male actor, she has never been and will never be one. See the
note to line 217.

227    **lik'd me**   gave me pleasure. Like *pleas'd me*, this phrase echoes lines 76–78; *Beards* (see the notes to lines 210, 214) echoes lines 73–74. In this line *Complexions* can means both (a) dispositions, and (b) appearances (skin and hair colourings); compare IV.iii.169–70.

228    **defied**   disliked, rejected. Here *Breaths* can refer both to (a) exhalations, and (b) expressions, words (compare II.vii.177–79). See line 230, where *sweet Breaths* can mean both (a) pleasant-smelling breaths, and (b) polite, amiable words, as in *A Midsummer Night's Dream*, IV.ii.43–44, where Bottom tells his fellow 'Actors' to 'eat no Onions, nor Garlic: for we are to utter Sweet Breath'.

230    **my kind Offer**   my hypothetical offer to kiss you. The offer is 'kind' in the sense that it is the kind of offer that is in character for the kind of speaker 'Rosalind' is. It is also a generous gesture, one that manifests an honest, open 'coming-on Disposition' (IV.i.120).

231    **bid me Farewell**   applaud me as I exit, pray that I fare (both 'go' and 'prosper') happily. As she concludes, Rosalind probably curtsies courteously.

I would kiss as many of you as had Beards that
pleas'd me, Complexions that lik'd me, and
Breaths that I defied not. And I am sure, as
many as have good Beards, or good Faces, or
sweet Breaths, will for my kind Offer, when I          230
make Curt'sy, bid me Farewell.          *Exit.*

FINIS

# PERSPECTIVES ON
## *As You Like It*

_____

*As You Like It* appears to have been little noticed by those who penned comments on Shakespeare in the seventeenth century. This may be in part because the play's early viewers and readers concurred with the sentiments of Charles Gildon, the first writer to offer extended remarks on *The Works of Mr. William Shakespear* (London, 1710) in the eighteenth century. According to Gildon, *As You Like It* 'has nothing Dramatic in it'. Nevertheless, allowed Gildon,

> The Scene betwixt Orlando and his Brother Oliver in the opening of the Play is well manag'd, discovering something, that goes before in the Quarrel between them; and Oliver's Management of the provoking Charles the Wrestler against Orlando is artful and natural.

Gildon enjoyed the 'moral Reflections' in the 'old Dukes Speech' at the beginning of Act II. He also commended the 'Pleasantry of the different Motion of Time' in II.vii and 'Rosalinda's Character of a Man in Love' in III.ii, which he described as 'very pretty'.

By mid-century critics were beginning to notice how much *As You Like It* owed to earlier publications. In the 'Notes, Critical and Explanatory' that accompanied his edition of *The Works of Shakespeare in Eight Volumes* (London, 1747), for example, a churchman named William Warburton pointed out that Touchstone's satire on 'the mode of formal dueling then so prevalent' derived from 'a very ridiculous treatise of one Vincentio Saviolo'. Warburton went on to quote and reflect upon what Saviolo says about 'the particle IF':

> *Conditional lies be such as are given conditionally thus* – IF *thou hast said so and so, then thou liest. Of these kind of lies, given in this manner, often arise much contention, whereof no sure conclusion can arise.* By which he means they cannot proceed to cut one another's throats while there is an *IF* between. Which is the reason of Shakespeare's making the Clown say, *I knew when seven justices*

could not make up a quarrel: but when the parties were met themselves, one of them thought but of an IF, as if you said so, then I said so, *and they shook hands, and swore brothers. Your IF is the only peacemaker; much virtue in IF.*

Shortly after Warburton's edition appeared in print, another theologian, Richard Hurd, who admired his friend's literary exercises, wrote Q. *Horatti Flacci Epistolae ad Pisones et Augustum* (London, 1753), an essay that compared *As You Like It* to the pastoral dramas of the Italian poet Torquato Tasso (1544–95). As Hurd noted,

The famous Tasso, by an effort of genius which hath done him more honour than even his epic talents, produced a new kind of pastoral, by engrafting it on the drama. And under this form, pastoral poetry became all the vogue. . . .

In this new form of the pastoral, what was childish before, is readily admitted and excused. A simple moral tale being the groundwork of the piece, the charms of description and all the embellishments of the scene are only subservient to the higher purpose of picturing the manners, or touching the heart.

But the good sense of Shakespeare, or perhaps the felicity of his genius, was admirable. Instead of the deep tragic air of Tasso (which has been generally followed) and his continuance of the pastoral strain, even to satiety, through five acts, he only made use of these playful images to enrich his comic scenes. . . .

In a word; if Tasso had the honour of inventing the pastoral drama, properly so called, Shakespeare has shewn us the just application of pastoral poetry; which, however amusing to the imagination, good sense will hardly endure, except in a short dialogue, or in some occasional dramatic scenes; and in these only, as it serves to the display of characters and the conduct of the poet's plot.

For Samuel Johnson, the most eminent of the eighteenth-century critics, *As You Like It* was a play whose 'fable is wild and pleasing'. In the notes to his edition of *The Plays of William Shakespeare* (London, 1765), Dr Johnson said:

I know not how the ladies will approve the facility with which both Rosalind and Celia give away their hearts. To Celia much may be forgiven for the heroism of her friendship. The character of Jaques is natural and well preserved. The comick dialogue is very sprightly, with less mixture of low buffoonery than in some other plays, and the graver part is elegant and harmonious. By hastening to the end of his work Shakespeare suppressed the dialogue between the usurper and the hermit, and lost an opportunity of exhibiting a moral lesson in which he might have found matter worthy of his highest powers.

Francis Gentleman, a contemporary of Johnson's, agreed. In *As You Like It*, he argued, 'the plot is hurried on to an imperfect catastrophe: we hear something of Oliver's being punished as an unnatural, abominable brother, but have a strong objection to crowning such a monster with fortune and love'. Writing in *The Dramatic Censor; or Critical Companion* (London, 1770), Gentleman went on to observe that

> An interview between the dukes would have afforded an opportunity for genius and judgment to exert themselves commendably; however, with all its faults, there is not a more agreeable piece on the stage; the characters are various, and all well supported; the incidents, if not striking, are certainly pleasing; the sentiments, with very few exceptions, are pregnant with useful meaning; and the language, though quaint in some places, shews in general strength and spirit worthy of Shakespeare's pen.
>
> Duke Senior is an amiable character, sustained with philosophical dignity, turning the frowns of fortune, as every man should do, into the means and motives of instruction: what he says is not of sufficient length to constitute a very conspicuous part in action, but if a performer has any declamatory merit, he may shew it to advantage here.

Five years later, Elizabeth Griffith penned *The Morality of Shakespeare's Drama Illustrated* (London, 1775). She commenced with the comment that *As You Like It*

> begins with a reflection on the first, and I may add the principal, concern in life, the education of children. Men are often more sedulous in training the brutes of their kennels, their mews and their stables, than they seem to be about the heirs of their blood, their fortunes, or their honours. In sad truth may it be said, that we seldom meet with a jockey, an huntsman, or a sportsman, who is half so well-bred as his horses, his hawks, or his hounds. . . .
>
> [In the conversation between Adam and Orlando in II.iii we hear] a pleasing description of the virtue and sobriety of the ancient Peasantry of England; and the difference of manners and morals between those times and the more modern ones, is well remarked upon.

As the eighteenth century entered its final quarter, a concern with morality began merging with an interest in the psychology of Shakespeare's dramatis personae. This tendency was exemplified by William Richardson's essay 'On the Character of the Melancholy Jaques' in *A Philosophical Analysis and Illustration of Some of Shakespeare's Remarkable Characters* (London, 1780). In Jaques, Richardson asserted, Shakespeare portrayed the effects of 'extreme sensibility'. Jaques

> discovers a heart strongly disposed to compassion, and susceptible of the most tender impressions of friendship: for he who can so feelingly deplore the absence of kindness and humanity, must be capable of relishing the delight annexed to their exercise. But sensibility is the soil where nature has planted social and sweet affections: by sensibility they are cherished, and grow mature. Social dispositions produce all those amiable and endearing connections that allieviate the sorrows of human life, adorn our nature, and render us happy. Now Jaques, avoiding society, and burying himself in the lonely forest, seems to act inconsistently with his constitution. He possesses sensibility; sensibility begets affection; and affection begets the love of society. But Jaques is unsocial. Can these inconsistent qualities be reconciled? Or has Shakespeare exhibited a character of which the parts are incongruous, and discordant? In other words, how happens it that a temper disposed to beneficence, and addicted to social enjoyment, becomes solitary and morose? . . .
>
> Though melancholy rules the mind of Jaques, he partakes of the leaven of human nature, and, moved by a sense of injury and disappointment.

> Most invectively he pierceth through
> The body of the country, city, court.

Instigated by sentiments of self-respect, if not of pride, he treats the condition of humanity, and the pursuits of mankind, as insignificant and uncertain. His invectives, therefore, are mingled with contempt, and expressed with humour. At the same time, he slows evident symptoms of a benevolent nature. He is interested in the improvement of mankind, and inveighs, not entirely to indulge resentment, but with a desire to correct their depravity. . . .

> The mixture of melancholy and misanthropy in the character of Jaques, is more agreeable to human nature than the representation of either of the extremes; for a complete misanthrope is as uncommon an object as a man who suffers injury without resentment. . . .

> Among the various desires and propensities implanted by nature in the constitution of every individual, some one passion, either by original and superior vigour, or by reiterated indulgence, gains an ascendancy in the soul. . . . The ruling passion, blended with others, augments their vehemence, and consequently enhances their plea-

sures: for the pleasure arising from the gratification of any passion, is proportioned to its force. [But if] the ruling passion [is] thwarted, it ceases to operate with success. [And] if social and beneficent affections, by gaining a superiority in the constitution, have heightened every other enjoyment, all the pleasures of sense or of ambition that formerly contributed to our felicity, though in themselves they are still the same; yet, being reft of their better part, of the spirit that enlivened them, they strike the mind so feebly, as only to awaken its attention to the loss it hath sustained; and, instead of affording comfort, they aggravate our misfortune. . . .

By the final decade of the century yet another direction in exegesis – this one based on philosopher John Locke's doctrine of 'the association of ideas' – became evident when Walter Whiter issued *A Specimen of a Commentary on Shakspere* (London, 1794). In one segment of his study Whiter focused on the 'celebrated line [in III.ii] which enumerates among the perfections of a beauty *the better part of Atalanta*'. According to Whiter:

Dr. Johnson observes, that the *better part of Atalanta* 'seems to have been her heels'; yet he is inclined to think that our Poet, though no despicable mythologist, has mistaken some other character for that of Atalanta. Dr. Farmer is of opinion, that her *better part* is her *wit*, that is, the *swiftness of her mind*, and Mr. Malone observes, that a passage in Marston's *Insatiate Countesse* might lead us to suppose that the *better part* of Atalanta was her *lips*. Mr. Tollet remarks, that 'perhaps the poet means her beauty and graceful elegance of shape, which he would prefer to her swiftness'; but he afterwards asks, whether *Atalanta's better part* may not mean 'her virtue or virgin chastity.' . . .

. . . I have always been firmly persuaded, that the *imagery*, which our Poet has selected to discriminate the more prominent perfections of *Helen*, *Cleopatra*, *Atalanta*, and *Lucretia*, was not derived from the abstract consideration of their general qualities; but was caught from those *peculiar traits* of beauty and character, which are impressed on the mind of him who contemplates their portraits [in *pictures* and in *representations in Tapestry*]. It is well known, that these celebrated heroines of romance were in the days of our Poet the favourite subjects of popular representation, and were alike visible in the coarse hangings of the poor and the magnificent arras of the rich. . . .

. . . Since the story of *Atalanta* represents that heroine as possessed of singular beauty, zealous to preserve her virginity even with the death of her lovers, and accomplishing her purposes by extraordinary swiftness in running, we may be assured that the skill of the artist would be employed in delineating the *fine proportions and elegant symmetry of her person*. . . .

The greatest of the early nineteenth-century English critics, Samuel Taylor Coleridge, jotted down some observations about *As You Like It* in notebooks that covered the years 1808–18; these reflections appeared in print (London, 1836) a couple of years after the poet's death. In one entry Coleridge quotes and comments on two passages in I.i.

> *Oli.* What, boy!
> *Orl.* Come, come, elder brother, you are too young in this.
> *Oli.* Wilt thou lay hands on me, villain?

> There is a beauty here. The word 'boy' naturally provokes and awakens in Orlando the sense of his manly powers: and with the retort, 'elder brother', he grasps him with firm hands, and makes him feel that he is no *boy*.

> *Oli.* Farewell, good Charles. . . . Now will I stir this gamester: I hope I shall see an end of him; for my soul, yet I know not why, hates nothing more than he. Yet he's gentle; never schooled, and yet learned; full of noble device; of all sorts enchantingly beloved; and indeed so much in the heart of the world, and especially of my own people, who best know him, that I am together misprized; but it shall not be so long; this wrestler shall clear all: nothing remains but that I kindle the boy thither; which I'll go about.

> . . . It is too venturous to charge a speech in Shakespeare with want of truth to nature. And yet at first sight this speech of Oliver's expresses truths which it almost seems impossible that any mind should so distinctly and so livelily have voluntarily presented to itself in connection with feelings and intentions so malignant and so contrary to those which the qualities expressed would naturally have called forth. But I dare not say that this unnaturalness is not in the nature of an abused wilfulness when united with a strong intellect.

While Coleridge was bringing new rigour to critical commentary in Shakespeare's native land, the German scholar August Wilhelm von Schlegel was delivering *A Course of Lectures on Dramatic Art and Literature* (1811) on the Continent; these influential remarks were translated by John Black and edited by Reverend A. J. W. Morrison for publication in England (London, 1846). In his essay on the 'contents' and 'narrative' of *As You Like It*, Schlegel admitted that

> nothing takes place, or rather what is done is not so essential as what is said; even what may be called the *denouement* is brought about pretty arbitrarily. Whoever can perceive nothing but what can as it were be

counted on the fingers, will hardly be disposed to allow that it has any plan at all. Banishment and flight have assembled together, in the forest of Arden, a strange band: a Duke dethroned by his brother, who, with the faithful companions of his misfortune, lives in the wilds on the produce of the chase; two disguised Princesses, who love each other with a sisterly affection; a witty court fool; lastly, the native inhabitants of the forest, ideal and natural shepherds and shepherdesses. These lightly-sketched figures form a motley and diversified train; we see always the shady dark-green landscape in the background, and breathe in imagination the fresh air of the forest. The hours are here measured by no clocks, no regulated recurrence of duty or of toil: they flow on unnumbered by voluntary occupation or fanciful idleness, to which, according to his humour or disposition, every one yields himself, and this unrestrained freedom compensates them all for the lost conveniences of life. One throws himself down in solitary meditation under a tree, and indulges in melancholy reflections on the changes of fortune, the falsehood of the world, and the self-inflicted torments of social life; others make the woods resound with social and festive songs, to the accompaniment of their hunting-horns. Selfishness, envy, and ambition, have been left behind in the city; of all the human passions, love alone has found an entrance into this wilderness, where it dictates the same language alike to the simple shepherd and the chivalrous youth, who hangs his love-ditty to a tree. A prudish shepherdess falls at first sight in love with Rosalind, disguised in men's apparel; the latter sharply reproaches her with her severity to her poor lover, and the pain of refusal, which she feels from experience in her own case, disposes her at length to compassion and requital. The fool carries his philosophical contempt of external show, and his raillery of the illusion of love, so far, that he purposely seeks out the ugliest and simplest country wench for a mistress. Throughout the whole picture, it seems to be the poet's design to show that to call forth the poetry which has its indwelling in nature and the human mind, nothing is wanted but to throw off all artificial constraint, and restore both to mind and nature their original liberty. In the very progress of the piece, the dreamy carelessness of such an existence is sensibly expressed: it is even alluded to by Shakespeare in the title.

William Hazlitt published *Characters of Shakespeare's Plays* (London, 1817) at about the same time that Samuel Taylor Coleridge was recording a few doubts about the artistry of *As You Like It*. Unlike Coleridge, Hazlitt described the comedy as 'the most perfect specimen of Shakespeare's various powers'.

Some exceptions to general excellence may be discovered in many of his productions; but this drama presents one uniform picture of surpassing beauty. Every line teems with humanity. There is the philosophy of love, of mirth, and of melancholy. . . . There is little plot to arrest attention, or to create suspense: the spell lies in the sentiments, which are clothed in language the most choice and appropriate, and in the grace and propriety of the characters. . . .

The character of Jacques bears a certain resemblance to that of Timon [in Shakespeare's *Timon of Athens*]. Jacques has fled, not from the society of men, but from their follies and their vices; he still joins in fellowship with his brothers in exile; nor has his love of solitude given him a disrelish for humour in the pointed jests of the clown. Not so with Timon – his turbulent passions are only forced into a different channel: he hates with the same violence that he once revelled – his spirit, so far from being subdued by adversity, has become more furious by being opposed – and he lives and dies a hideous example of impotent malice and disappointed ambition. Such are the shades that distinguish these two celebrated characters, which, though they bear some analogy in certain features, are, nevertheless, perfectly individualised and distinct.

The ancient clown, or fool (which characters have been strangely confounded with each other), was a domestic buffoon, whose peculiar province was to divert his lord. He had the privilege of saying that which from other lips would have been accounted treason or heresy; satirising the follies of all present, not sparing even his lord, with the utmost keenness of sarcastic wit. . . . [Touchstone] is a *material* fool, as Jacques aptly describes him. His folly, like Hamlet's madness, has both matter and method in it. His description of the knight who swore by his honour the mustard was naught – his scenes of courtship with Audrey – his dissertation upon horns, and upon the lie seven times removed, are alternate jest and apothegm. The character is worked up to the highest pitch of grotesque humour without any approach to vulgar buffoonery.

The disposition of Rosalind is gentle and confiding – sprightly as youth and innocence can make it – tinged with occasional sadness for the banishment of her father – and shaded with that most exquisite of all sensations, the melancholy of true love. Nor is the character of Celia scarcely less interesting, from her heroic friendship in following the fortunes of Rosalind; in soothing and supporting her amidst the perils of their flight; and in whimsically becoming the victim of that very passion which she rallies with such agreeable playfulness in her friend. . . .

In contemplating this romantic and beautiful drama, all opinion necessarily rises into panegyric. Every part is so perfect – the philosophy, the humour, the sentiments, and the imagery – that to rise from it without delight and improvement, would betray an obliquity of feeling wholly inconsistent with just perception and moral rectitude. We are taught by the noblest examples, that adversity is not in reality a bane to man, but to his pride and ambition. That its uses are sweet and consolatory; and while with rude hand it arrests the career of his unlicensed passions, it restores his mind to that state of healthful serenity, which, when the vain blandishments of life are past and gone, is the remaining friend and companion of virtue. The schools dedicated to morals and philosophy, the holy temples of religion, never echoed with more divine precepts than the solitudes of Arden. Mirth never sounded a merrier note, nor music a more enchanting strain, than those which glad the hearts, and sooth the cares, of these banished foresters.

A few years after Hazlitt sang the praises of *As You Like It*, Anna Brownell Jameson commended the virtues of its female characters. In *Shakespeare's Heroines* (London, 1833), she placed Rosalind on an even higher pedestal than the Beatrice of *Much Ado About Nothing*.

The portrait is one of infinitely more delicacy and variety, but of less strength and depth. It is easy to seize on the prominent features in the mind of Beatrice, but extremely difficult to catch and fix the more fanciful graces of Rosalind. . . .

. . . The first introduction of Rosalind is less striking than interesting; we see her a dependant, almost a captive, in the house of her usurping uncle; her genial spirits are subdued by her situation, and the remembrance of her banished father; her playfulness is under a temporary eclipse. . . . The sensibility and even pensiveness of her demeanour in the first instance render her archness and gaiety afterwards more graceful and more fascinating.

Though Rosalind is a princess, she is a princess of Arcady; and, notwithstanding the charming effect produced by her first scenes, we scarcely ever think of her with a reference to them, or associate her with a court and the artificial appendages of her rank. . . . She was not made to bandy wit with lords, and tread courtly measures with plumed and warlike cavaliers, like Beatrice; but to dance on the greensward, and 'murmur among living brooks a music sweeter than their own.' . . .

Celia is more quiet and retired; but she rather yields to Rosalind than is eclipsed by her. She is as full of sweetness, kindness, and intelligence, quite as susceptible, and almost as witty, though she makes less display of wit. . . . To Celia, Shakespeare has given some of the most striking and animated parts of the dialogue: and in particular, that exquisite description of the friendship between her and Rosalind. . . . We listen to her as to one who has made herself worthy of our love, and her silence expresses more than eloquence.

Phebe is quite an Arcadian coquette; she is a piece of pastoral poetry. Audrey is only rustic. A very amusing effect is produced by the contrast between the frank and free bearing of the two princesses in disguise and the scornful airs of the real shepherdess.

In *Shakespeare Commentaries* that date from 1849 or 1850, even though they were not made available in F. E. Bunnett's English translation until more than a quarter-century later (London, 1877), the German critic G. G. Gervinus offered some cogent comparisons between *As You Like It* and Thomas Lodge's *Rosalynde*, the pastoral romance that Shakespeare drew upon as his primary source for the comedy. According to Gervinus:

. . . Many of the Ovid-like reminiscences, and much of the mythological learning with which the romance abounds, still adhere to Shakespeare's play; but, on the whole, he has completely eradicated the pastoral mannerism, and, according to his wont, he simplifies the motives of the actions and ennobles the actions themselves. The rude enmity between Oliver and Orlando, which results in acts of violence in the romance, is properly moderated by our poet. He has removed the unnaturalness of Celia's banishment by her father on her protest against the banishment of Rosalind. The war, by which the exiled prince regains the throne, and the rescue of the ladies from robbers, with which in the romance Celia's love for Oliver is introduced, have been omitted by the dramatist in order that he might not disturb the peace and merry sports of his rural life by any discords. The play between Orlando and Rosalind is in the romance only a pastoral song, but Shakespeare has made it a link for the continuation of the action in the last act. In all the rest the poet adheres faithfully to the course of the story in the novel, without much addition and omission.

. . . Duke Frederick is called even by his daughter a man of harsh and envious mind; he appears to be perpetually actuated by gloomy fancies, by suspicion and mistrust, and to be urged on by covetousness. [Meanwhile Shakespeare shows us that in Oliver] there flows the same vein of avarice and envy as in the Duke. He strives to plunder his brother of his poor inheritance, he undermines his education and gentility, he first endeavours to stifle his mind, and then he lays snares for his life; all this he does from an undefined hatred of the youth, whom he is obliged to confess is 'full of noble device', but who for this very reason draws away the love of all his people from Oliver to himself; and on this account excites his envious jealousy. Both the Duke and Oliver equally forfeit the happiness which they seek, the one the heritage of his usurped dukedom, the other his lawful and unlawful possessions. And in this lies the primary impulse and the material motive for their subsequent renunciation of the world; a more moral incentive to this change of mind is given to Oliver in the preservation of his life by Orlando, and to the Duke in the warning voice of a religious man who speaks to his conscience and his fear. . . .

The misery which proceeds from these two covetous and ambitious men, who were not even contented in and with their prosperity, affects in the first place the deposed Duke. [Having] withdrawn from the dangers of the 'envious court', [he and his fellow lords] have learned to love exile beyond the painted pomp of the palace. . . .

Only the one danger does this life possess, that by its monotony it awakes, in one and another, ennui, melancholy, and ill-humour. In the hunting circle round the Duke, Jaques is in this condition. He shares with the Duke and his companions the propensity for drawing wisdom and philosophy from the smallest observation and consideration: he has to excess the gift of linking reflections to the smallest event, and in this seclusion from the world these reflections have assumed a touch of despondency. . . . Long experienced in sin, he has learned to find out the shadow side of every age of man; he has satiated himself with the world, and has not entered upon this life of retirement furnished with the patience and contentment of the others, but from a natural passion for the contrary. If his satire is directed more against things in general, and is free from bitterness towards stated individuals, this is only a result of his inactive nature, which is rather calculated for observation and reflection than for work and action, and of his isolated position in this idyllic and peaceful life, in which moreover the poet will suffer no discord to arise. This character is entirely Shakespeare's property and addition. It furnishes a fresh instance to us of the two-sidedness of the poet's mind, with which so many proofs have made us familiar. . . .

In Touchstone, Shakespeare has for the first time produced a fool of a somewhat more elevated nature. In all the earlier comedies there have been only clowns introduced, natural fools whose wit is either studied and mechanically prepared or is given out in droll unconsciousness. . . . Jaques regards him as a clown, who has 'crammed' the strange places of his dry brain with observation, which 'he vents in mangled forms'. . . . The two ladies call him by turns a natural and a fool; Celia, in his face, ascribes to him the dulness of the fool, which is the whetstone of the witty, while to the true fool the folly of others is the whetstone of his wit. And Touchstone himself assumes the appearance of being wiser than he himself knew; he shall, he says, ne'er be 'ware of his own wit, till he breaks his shins against it. On the other hand, from his expression in other passages, he regards himself as far superior to the clown and the natural philosopher, and the Duke readily perceives his design behind his interposing folly; 'he uses his folly,' he says, 'like a stalking-horse, and under the presentation of that he shoots his wit'. . . .

... It seems to me that perhaps all pastoral poetry put together scarcely contains so much real wisdom as this philosophy of the fool. He finds nothing to say against the shepherd's life, but nothing also against the contrary manner of living; and the homely simplicity of Corin himself is on his side in this, that he leaves courtly manners to the court and country ones to the country. ... In neither of the two circles does he find the condition of happiness or virtue in itself, but he sees happiness most surely dwelling, not in this or that place, but in the beings who, exiled from the world, do not feel themselves miserable, just as little so as when they are recalled to the world from their solitude. The poet knows nothing of a certain situation, condition, or age, which would be a sure source of happiness; but he knows that there are men in all classes and generations, like his Duke, his Rosalind, and his old Adam Spencer, who bear in their bosoms that equanimity and contentment which is the only fruitful soil of all true inner happiness, and who carry with them wherever they go a smiling Eden and a golden age.

A couple of decades after Gervinus's appraisal of Jaques and Touchstone, an American editor, H. N. Hudson, compared the two figures in *Shakespeare: His Life, Art, and Characters* (Boston, 1872).

Jaques is, I believe, an universal favourite, as indeed he well may be, for he is certainly one of the Poet's happiest conceptions. Without being at all unnatural, he has an amazing fund of peculiarity. Enraptured out of his senses at voice of a song; thrown into a paroxysm of laughter at sight of the motley-clad and motley-witted Fool; and shedding the twilight of his merry-sad spirit over all the darker spots of human life and character; he represents the abstract and sum-total of an utterly useless yet perfectly harmless man, seeking wisdom by abjuring its first principle. An odd choice mixture of reality and affectation, he does nothing but think, yet avowedly thinks to no purpose; or rather thinking is with him its own end. On the whole, if in Touchstone there is much of the philosopher in the Fool, in Jaques there is not less of the fool in the philosopher. ...

... Tears are a great luxury to him: he sips the cup of woe with all the gust of an epicure. Still his temper is by no means sour: fond of solitude, he is nevertheless far from being unsocial. The society of good men, provided they be in adversity, has great charms for him. He likes to be with those who, though deserving the best, still have the worst: virtue wronged, buffeted, oppressed, is his special delight; because such moral discrepancies offer the most salient points to his cherished meditations. He himself enumerates nearly all the forms of melancholy except his own, which I take to be the melancholy of self-love. ... Nevertheless his melancholy is grateful, because free from any dash of malignity. His morbid habit of mind seems to spring from an excess of generative virtue. And how racy and original is everything that comes from him! as if it bubbled up from the centre of his being; while his perennial fulness of matter makes his company always delightful.

After discussing the other characters of *As You Like It*, Hudson broadened his canvas to encompass the play as a thematic whole.

The general drift and temper, or, as some of the German critics would say, the ground-idea of this play, is aptly hinted by the title. . . . For example, touching Frederick and Oliver, our wish is that they should repent, and repair the wrong they have done, in brief, that they should become good; which is precisely what takes place; and as soon as they do this, they naturally love those who were good before. Jaques, too, is so fitted to moralize the discrepancies of human life, so happy and at home, and withal so agreeable, in that exercise, that we would not he should follow the good Duke when in his case those discrepancies are composed. . . . Indeed I dare ask any genial, considerate reader, Does not every thing turn out just *as you like it?* Moreover there is an indefinable something about the play that puts us in a receptive frame of mind; that opens the heart, soothes away all querulousness and fault-finding, and makes us easy and apt to be pleased. Thus the Poet here disposes us to like things as they come, and at the same time takes care that they shall come as we like. The whole play indeed is *as you like it.*

For Edward Dowden, an Irish poet and critic who drew upon the plays for a psychobiography of the poet, *As You Like It* was 'the sweetest and happiest' of the comedies. In *Shakspere: A Critical Study of His Mind and Art* (London, 1875), Dowden noted that in the Forest of Arden

No one suffers; no one lives an eager intense life; there is no tragic interest . . . as there is in *The Merchant of Venice*, as there is in *Much Ado about Nothing*. It is mirthful, but the mirth is sprightly, graceful, exquisite; there is nothing of the rollicking fun of a Sir Toby here; the songs are not 'coziers' catches' shouted in the night-time, 'without any mitigation or remorse of voice' [as in *Twelfth Night*], but the solos and duets of pages in the wild-wood, or the noisier chorus of foresters. The wit of Touchstone is not mere clownage, nor has it any indirect serious significance; it is a dainty kind of absurdity worthy to hold comparison with the melancholy of Jaques. And Orlando, in the beauty and strength of early manhood, and Rosalind –

A gallant curtle-axe upon her thigh,
A boar-spear in her hand,

and the bright, tender, loyal womanhood within – are figures which quicken and restore our spirits, as music does which is neither noisy nor superficial, and yet which knows little of the deep passion and sorrow of the world.

Shakspere, when he wrote this idyllic play, was himself in his Forest of Arden. He had ended one great ambition – the historical plays – and not yet commenced his tragedies. It was a resting-place. He sends his imagination into the woods to find repose. Instead of the courts and camps of England and the embattled plains of France, here was this woodland scene, where the palm-tree, the lioness, and the serpent are to be found: possessed of a flora and fauna that flourish in spite of physical geographers. There is an open-air feeling throughout the play. The dialogue, as has been observed, catches freedom and freshness from the atmosphere. . . . Shakspere was not trying to control his melancholy. When he needed to do that, Shakspere confronted his melancholy very passionately, and looked it full in the face. Here he needed refreshment, a sunlight tempered by forest-boughs, a breeze upon his forehead, a stream murmuring in his ears.

On the other side of the Atlantic, in his New Variorum edition of *As You Like It* (Philadelphia, 1890), Horace Howard Furness offered some insights into the flexible time-schemes involved in the 'Duration of the Action'. When the play opens, Furness observes,

it is necessary that the senior Duke's banishment should be recent, so recent that the usurping Duke feels his grasp of the sceptre most insecure. Time can have given to the traitor no prescriptive right. 'What is the new news at the new court?' asks Oliver. 'There's no news,' answers Charles, 'but the old news: that is, the old Duke is banished by his younger brother, the new Duke, and three or four loving lords have put themselves into voluntary exile with him.' The impression here conveyed is clear enough. The banishment is spoken of almost in the present tense. And if the news is called 'old,' it may be so called on the assumption that its limit of life is nine days. At any rate, it is not so 'old' but that the 'younger brother' is called the 'new Duke,' and the report of the banishment has not yet had time (and such news travels fast) to reach Oliver in all its details. Oliver's residence cannot be far removed from the ducal court, the wrestling match was quite in the neighborhood, and yet Oliver neither knows where the banished Duke has gone, nor whether Rosalind has accompanied her father. . . . The 'new court' cannot be many weeks old. It is so 'new' that the only news in it is the event which created it. . . .

Perhaps the first faint intimation of the lapse of time – and it is very faint but still marked enough to create an impression – is after the wrestling, when the usurping Duke says to Orlando. 'The world esteemed thy father honourable. But I did find him still mine enemy.' This must refer to old Sir Rowland's loyalty to the senior Duke and his hostility to the usurper during the recent crisis, the only time as far as we know when any proofs of enmity could have been evoked. But the first impression concerning old Sir Rowland which we receive, in the very opening of the play, is that he has been dead several years, at least long enough to account for Orlando's neglected education. This passing reference, then, to Sir Rowland's enmity during his lifetime to the usurping Duke weakens the impression that the *coup d'état* is so very recent, and for one second carries that event with it back into the past, and there is a fleeting vision of unflinching loyalty long years ago to the exiled Duke in the stress that then drove him from his throne.

This allusion, which has swiftly come and swiftly gone, is closely followed by another allusion to time long past, more marked, as it ought to be, than the former, and which can scarcely fail to leave a still more decided impression. Le Beau says to Orlando immediately after the wrestling: 'But I can tell you that *of late* this duke Hath ta'en displeasure 'gainst his gentle niece, Grounded upon no other argument But that *the people praise her for her virtues.*' Charles, the Wrestler, told us that Rosalind was 'no less beloved of her uncle than his own daughter.' To turn love thus deep into 'displeasure' time will be required. . . .

Deep as this impression is of the slow flight of time, and remote as the banishment of the Duke is beginning to grow, this impression is followed up by another still deeper. When the usurping Duke, half crazed by suspicion, wrathfully banishes Rosalind, Celia intercedes for her cousin, and recalls to her cruel father that when he 'stay'd Rosalind,' and she had not 'with her father ranged along,' he had done it out of pity and of love for his own daughter, but, pleads Celia, 'I was TOO YOUNG THAT TIME to value her; But NOW I know her,' and then she goes on to picture *the years that have passed* since that time in her unconscious childhood when the Duke was banished, and how since then she and Rosalind have grown up together, how they had learned their lessons together, played together, slept together, rose at an instant, ate together, and wherever we went 'like Juno's swans still we went coupled and inseparable.' . . .

But to one fact attention must be called, and this is, the extreme importance, dramatically, of making, just at this point, the time of the Duke's banishment recede into the past. As a present active force its power is spent. It was of vital importance to quicken the usurper's suspicion and to cause him to drive Rosalind forth. It is now equally important that it should recede into the past and . . . grow dim through a vista of years. [And why?] . . . Are not 'old custom' and 'the seasons' difference' 'the very lime-twigs' of Shakespeare's spell [at the beginning of Act II]? . . . Can it be doubted for a moment that Shakespeare did not here intend us to believe that the Duke had lived through many a season's difference, or that custom to him had not grown old?

At a time when virtually everyone else was treating Shakespeare with reverence, a modern Irish playwright went out of his way to counter the prevailing Bardolatry. In an 1896 essay that first appeared in London's *Saturday Review*, Bernard Shaw pointed out that

It was in 'As You Like It' that the sententious William first began to openly exploit the fondness of the British Public for sham moralizing and stage 'philosophy'. It contains one passage that specially exasperates me. Jaques, who spends his time, like Hamlet, in vainly emulating the wisdom of Sancho Panza, comes in laughing in a superior manner because he has met a fool in the forest [who speaks about 'how the world wags' and 'we rot and rot'].

Now, considering that this fool's platitude is precisely the 'philosophy' of Hamlet, Macbeth ('To-morrow and to-morrow,' &c), Prospero, and the rest of them, there is something unendurably aggravating in Shakespeare giving himself airs with Touchstone, as if he, the immortal, ever, even at his sublimest, had anything different or better to say himself. Later on he misses a great chance. Nothing is more significant than the statement that 'all the world's a stage.' The whole world *is* ruled by theatrical illusion. Between the Caesars, the emperors, the Christian heroes, the Grand Old Men, the kings, prophets, saints, heroes and judges, of the newspapers and the popular imagination, and the actual Juliuses, Napoleons, Gordons, Gladstones, and so on, there is the same difference as between Hamlet and Sir Henry Irving. The case is not one of fanciful similitude, but of identity. The great critics are those who penetrate and understand the illusion: the great men are those who, as dramatists planning the development of nations, or as actors carrying out the drama, are behind the scenes of the world instead of gaping and gushing in the auditorium after paying their taxes at the doors. And yet Shakespeare, with the rarest of opportunities of observing this, lets his pregnant metaphor slip, and, with his usual incapacity for pursuing any idea, wanders off into a grandmotherly Elizabethan edition of the advertisement of Cassell's 'Popular Educator.' . . .

And then Touchstone with his rare jests about the knight that swore by his honour they were good pancakes! Who would endure such humour from anyone but Shakespeare? . . . And the comfortable old Duke, symbolical of the British villa dweller, who likes to find 'sermons in stones and good in everything', and then to have a good dinner! . . . And yet so wonderful is his art, that it is not easy to disentangle what is unbearable from what is irresistible. . . .

Harking back to the kind of source study that had been developed by G. G. Gervinus, Frederick S. Boas brought the nineteenth century to a close in *Shakspere and His Predecessors* (New York, 1896) by comparing *As You Like It* with 'a novel by Thomas Lodge, called *Rosalind Euphues' Golden Legacy*'. After noting that Shakespeare 'followed the framework of Lodge's attractive though somewhat prolix tale with unusual fidelity', Boas said:

All the more remarkable therefore is it that by readjustments of the perspective, and by the addition of a series of entirely novel creations, the dramatist has given to his work a profoundly original and, in respect of his epoch, unique character. For the broad result of his treatment is to substitute for the artificial atmosphere of the Renaissance pastoral the open-air freshness, the breeze and blue of the old English ballad-poetry. . . .

. . . The novelist [Lodge] had put into the mouth of Rosalind moralizing reflections on the dangers of love, containing some pretty turns of phrase, but growing oppressive in their heavy Euphuistic brocade. For this Shakspere substituted a gushing stream of wit that carries foam and freshness into the close atmosphere of the conventional Arcadia. . . . This leisurely forest life allows ample time for weaving imaginative embroidery round not too serious themes, and thus we get Rosalind's charming little lecture on the divers paces in which time travels with divers persons, and her comparison of love to a madness, which deserves a dark house and a whip, and only escapes because the whippers share the lunacy. In a similar vein is her modernized version of the romantic stories of Troilus and Cressida, and Hero and Leander, in support of her assertion that 'men have died from time to time, and worms have eaten them, but not for love.' . . .

Amongst the couples whom Hymen unites are Silvius and Phebe, who had already made their appearance in Lodge's romance. The novelist had censured Phebe for her excessive scorn, and had emphasized the retribution in kind that falls upon her head. But his picture of the self-forgetting devotion of Silvius was, on the whole, sympathetic, and neither of the characters moved in a different plane from the remaining figures in the story. But in the drama this is exactly what they do, for, by a number of minute touches, Shakspere transposes them into the region of caricature. Unlike the other lovers, they speak uniformly in verse instead of prose, and this in itself gives a distinctly idealistic flavour to their sentiments. . . . Phebe has all the 'regulation' charms of a pastoral nymph – inky brows, black silk hair, bugle eyeballs, and cheeks of cream; but these are turned into burlesque by the addition of 'a leathern hand, a free-stone coloured hand'. . . . Silvius, who is satisfied to live upon a 'scattered smile' loosed now and then by his mistress, and who bears her letter to Ganymede in the fond belief that it has an angry tenor, is a parody of the true loyalty of heart which, as seen in Orlando, is no enemy to either cheerfulness or self-respect. . . .

To throw Silvius and Phebe into yet bolder relief Shakspere has set beside them one or two genuinely rustic figures, drawn probably from his personal observation in Warwickshire. Corin, the shepherd to a churlish master, had already appeared in Lodge's novel. With his primitive philosophy, that 'good pasture makes fat sheep, and that a great cause of the night is lack of the sun', he puts to shame the extravagances of morbid fancies, and instead of sighing and weeping after the fashion of mock swains, he finds in the honest toil of a country life an abiding content. . . . To the same genuinely rustic species, though of coarser mould, belongs Audrey, a creation completely of the dramatist. . . .

Touchstone is another figure due to Shakspere's invention, and together with [*Twelfth Night*'s] Feste he stands far above the other fools in the comedies. He entirely lacks Feste's tender lyrical vein, and the few snatches of rhyme that fall from his lips are only jingling parodies. . . . Touchstone's wit takes always and with every one a caustic turn, and though he gives practical proof of his attachment to Celia by following her to the forest, he spares her with his tongue as little as the rest. . . .

The addition of a Fool to the personages found in the original romance is in no way surprising, but far different is it with another Shaksperean creation whom we encounter within the groves of Arden. What has the melancholy Jaques to do there, and why is he drawn with such elaborate finish? In him, from yet another and more subtle point of view, the dramatist makes war against the idea that in an idyllic life every nature will find an anodyne for its peculiar malady. . . . There is one type of nature which never for a moment plants its foot on the solid rock-bed of things as they are, and which sees in existence only a constant flux of sensations after which it constantly flies. Of this type Jaques is the consummate representative, and to him Arcadia is merely a fresh field for the chase of new experiences. . . . Everywhere and always he pores morbidly upon the hollow and petty phrases of existence. The world to him is a stage, and nothing more: the men and women are merely players, with their exits and their entrances, mechanically regulated movements, in an ephemeral pageant.

One of the great scholars of the twentieth century was E. K.

Chambers, a British Education Department employee who produced such monumental, multi-volume studies as *The Medieval Stage* (1903), *The Elizabethan Stage* (1923), and *William Shakespeare: A Study of Facts and Problems* (1930). In 1905 he issued a Red Letter edition of *As You Like It*, and the introduction from that text was later incorporated in *Shakespeare: A Survey* (London, 1925). There Chambers described Rosalind as 'witty and brave, audacious and tender, with a grace that her doublet and hose cannot pervert, and a womanhood that they cannot conceal'; in his view, 'it is indeed she that gives the piece its special human charm, its note of sane and joyous vitality'.

> And yet, splendid as is Rosalind's, there is an even greater part in *As You Like It*. And that is the part of the Forest of Arden. Commentators dispute whether Arden is a duchy on the confines of France and Germany, or whether it lies north of the Avon in Warwickshire, just as they dispute whether the island of *The Tempest* is this or that little nook of land in the Mediterranean. Actually, of course, it too is the essential forest of romance, with its strange fauna and flora, its possibilities of a lioness beneath every bush, its olive-trees and its osiers, its palms and its oaks growing together. It is here that men live like the old Robin Hood of England, fleeting the time carelessly as they did in the golden world. . . . In its purlieus lie the pleasant pastoral lands which Theocritus invented, and after him Virgil and Mantuan sang of, where peaceful shepherds feed their flocks, careless of the court, and vexed only by the pains of love and the cruelty of a disdainful mistress. We are always conscious of the forest in *As You Like It*. It is something more than a mere scenic background; a spiritual force, bringing medicine to the hurt souls of men. . . . *As You Like It* does for the Elizabethan drama what the long string of pastoral poets, Spenser and Sidney, Lodge and Greene, Drayton and Browne, and the rest, had already done, or were still to do, for Elizabethan lyric. The temper of it is not strictly the temper of the actual country-dweller as that has filled our later literature for the last century. It is rather the temper of urban disillusion, the instinctive craving of the man who has been long in cities pent for green fields and quiet nights. And no doubt it yields rather a mirage of the country than a sober and realistic vision of the country as it really is. . . . The monstrous nightmare of the modern city had not yet made its appearance; but there was already reason enough, especially in days when court intrigue was merciless and none too savoury, for the finer souls to dream their dreams of Arcady or of Arden.

Using words that echoed Chambers', Sir Arthur Quiller-Couch

said, 'We know that Arden – a lovely word in itself – was endeared to Shakespeare by scores of boyish memories; Arden was his mother's maiden name.' But Quiller-Couch was unwilling to classify *As You Like It* as a romance that epitomized 'perfection'. No, he insisted in *Shakespeare's Workmanship* (London, 1917),

> I must in fairness mention a piece of sheer botchwork. I mean the introduction of Hymen in the last Act. To explain away this botch of an imposition of Shakespeare by another hand – to conjecture it as some hasty alternative to satisfy the public censor, who objected to Church rites of marriage on the stage – would be as easy as it were accordant with the nice distinctions of critical hypocrisy, were it not that Shakespeare, almost if not quite to the end of his days, was capable of similar ineptitudes. . . . Hymen in *As You Like It* is worse than Hecate in *Macbeth*.

For J. B. Priestley, as for a long line of writers before and after him, the most intriguing characters in *As You Like It* were Touchstone and Jaques. As Priestley reminded us in *The English Comic Characters* (London, 1925), Touchstone

> has no unconscious absurdities, and that is why he cannot be counted among those who wear the fine flower of the ridiculous; he is not laughable in himself, he is only droll by vocation. Although he is a Clown, a Fool, he is obviously a superior member of his order; he is no common buffoon making the most of some natural deformity and finding his fun in bladder play and monkey tricks, but the first of Shakespeare's great Fools, a professional wit and humorist, who publishes his jests and sarcasms daily at the dinner-table instead of bringing them out in octavo in the spring and autumn publishing seasons. . . . Certainly for us he is no mere butt, for we laugh with him and not at him. Even when he is gabbling nonsense, and that is not often, he is, of course, angling for a laugh and usually preparing to launch some shrewd home-truth. . . .
>
> Now, as we have seen, Jaques and Touchstone stand in somewhat similar relation to the rest of the company. They are 'the critics', detached from the main action, observing, mocking. Whatever departs from sincerity receives a flick of the whip from them: or, if you will, they supply the chorus to the piece; one, the sad-suited gentleman, this somewhat eighteenth-century figure with his exquisite sensibility and his lack of real warm human sympathy, plays the part of cynical-sentimental-moralistic chorus; the other, motleying for more than mere beef and ale, an embassy from the Spirit of Comedy, supplies the comic chorus. But while these two seem to run together most of the way, Touchstone parodying to Jaques' applause, there is a

very real and very important difference in their respective attitudes. Motley is a better critic than Melancholy. He is a better critic because, unlike Jaques, he does not completely detach himself from his fellow mortals but identifies himself with them: he does not say, in effect, 'What beasts you are!' but 'What fools are we!' and so, like a true comic genius, he is universal.

With John W. Draper, writing on 'Orlando the Younger Brother' in the journal *Philological Quarterly* (1934), discussions of *As You Like It* began focusing on some of the social and economic issues implicit in the play's structure.

The Mediaeval youngster of good family was either put out as a page to do 'hard service' in the household of his father's overlord so that he might in time become a knight; or he was forced upon some monastery to grow up into a monkish worldling like Chaucer's; or perhaps he was apprenticed to a rich merchant. In the Renaissance, however, arms became a career for professional mercenaries skilled in the mathematics of gunnery; the monasteries in England were dissolved; and trade was more and more considered 'utterly vnfit for Gentlemen'. Thus, unless his father provided the son with lands and income, he could hardly rise above the place of armed retainer, or 'servingman' in the household of his patron; and, as the tranquility of Tudor times made retainers less and less necessary, and as the rising cost of living made them more and more a burden, the servingman generally sank to a mere menial servant; and, even if he escaped being cast out upon the highway by the 'incertaintie of service,' he could look forward only to a 'contemptible' old age. . . .

Family honor and future policy required that what money there was should be spent on the eldest son; for primogeniture was an established custom consecrated in the Bible and in the laws of England. The stress of the times, therefore, left the younger brother unprovided for. . . .

This situation must have been notorious; and, in *As You Like It*, Shakespeare portrays Orlando as faced with the typical problems of the younger son. . . . His father had left Orlando a thousand crowns; but, as his elder brother refuses him even this patrimony, he is no better off than the average younger son. . . . Thus he is sinking to the rank of menial; and the dramatic value of Adam in the play is largely his vivid illustration of Orlando's future fate, unless the young man makes a break for freedom. . . . If Orlando leaves his brother's roof, however, he has no choice but the beggary that Oliver taunts him with. . . . He will not offend against the divine law of primogeniture; but rather, full of youth and spirits, he tries to do something 'notable' to win his way. His first effort is the wrestling match; and, though the wicked usurping Duke gave him no reward, yet his strength and valor 'tript vp the Wrastlers heeles' and the heart of Rosalind 'both in an instant'; and so, finally, like the impoverished Bassanio, he achieves a rich heiress [comparable to Portia in *The Merchant of Venice*]. . . .

In yet another analysis of the play in *Philosophical Quarterly* (1935), Z. S. Fink commented on the parallels between 'Jaques and the Malcontent Traveler' of the Renaissance.

. . . He has lived a licentious life abroad and has picked up the characteristic vices of all nations. He is so corrupted that he sees even nature as tainted. Either because of this fact, or because he has become a Catholic or an atheist and lost his love of his native country and his faith in life, he is also genuinely melancholy and discontented with everything. He rails at the abuses of the world when he is himself thoroughly polluted. Nor are his railings and lamentations necessarily for the benefit of others. Sometimes he avoids company and seeks a solitary spot where he quarrels with himself. . . .

. . . [True to type, Jaques] is cynical and pessimistic; . . . it is the futility of existence, not the goodness and sweetness of it, that is the burden of his complaining. As has often been pointed out, the Duke finds in the forest a relief from the corruptions of courts and cities; but to Jaques Arden is no more satisfactory in any respect than is the great world; in both he sees the same misery, cruelty and folly. . . . Finally, the action of the play and the attitudes of the other characters towards Jaques contain definite indications as to how he was intended to be taken. . . . Orlando comes in carrying Adam as a counter-blast to the 'Seven Ages' speech. Rosalind makes fun of Jaques, Orlando has no time for him. Touchstone mimics him, the Duke rebukes him and expresses it as his opinion that Jaques is one who has been 'transformed into a beast.' . . .

. . . In this connection [the malcontent's] very name is significant, for as is well known, the word *jakes* in Elizabethan times meant a privy.

For Oscar James Campbell, seeking to define 'Jaques' in *The Huntington Library Bulletin* (1935), the key to this courtier's 'state of mind' was to be found in the way Shakespeare's contemporaries related at least one 'malcontent type' to 'the theory of humors, in which melancholy played the most important part', and especially to 'the important place given to those forms of melancholy caused by the so-called adustion or burning of each one of the four humors'. Campbell begins by noting that

Natural melancholy – that produced by a considerable excess of this humor – was commonly called 'ass-like melancholy' and rendered its victim, above all, sluggish. . . . [Jaques] is clearly not suffering from any form of so-called 'Natural Melancholy.'

To understand the second, or unnatural, sort of melancholy – that produced by adustion – one must remember that, ideally, the humors were supposed not only to preserve an equilibrium among themselves, but also, as expressions of the vital moisture, to maintain, severally and collectively, a properly balanced relationship to natural physiological heat. When any humor was subjected to excessive heat, it became transformed into an unnatural humor called phlegm-, choler-, melancholy-, and blood-adust, as the case might be. Moreover, all of these states were regarded as forms of melancholy and frequently called by the general term 'choler adust,' as a short equivalent of the phrase 'melancholy formed by adustion.'. . .

Jaques' prevailing humor obviously has not been burned so deeply as to reduce it to any form of madness. But he does exhibit the emotional variability characteristic of the moderately adust temperament. He takes equal delight in weeping over the hunted deer and in laughing at Touchstone's sallies. Yet he is enough master of his mind to enlist his volatile powers of intelligence and imagination in the service of his figurative sententiousness. These are the most prominent features of his character, and of all types of the unnaturally melancholy.

The initial description of Jaques, developed with more than ordinary fulness and circumstance, suggests that Shakespeare wishes his audience to regard his eccentric as a representative of one specific form of adustion. . . . Being a cold and moist humor, phlegm was associated in everyone's mind with water. The phlegmatic were attracted to water in both their waking and dreaming hours. . . .

A character who was introduced to an Elizabethan audience poring over a brook and there weeping and meditating, would write himself down at once as a phlegmatic person who had been rendered melancholy.

In *The Fool: His Social and Literary History* (London, 1935), a pioneering investigation of the role of folly in medieval and Renaissance culture, Enid Welsford pointed out that

In *As You Like It* the fool's name indicates his dramatic rôle: he serves as a touchstone or test of the quality of men and manners, and so helps to poise an otherwise somewhat kaleidoscopic play. For here, as elsewhere, Shakespeare expresses a complex point of view, making the most of the comic as well as the romantic possibilities of his theme, and even at times burlesquing the pastoral convention in which his play is written. In such a play as this, where so much depends on a skilful use of allusion, contrast, and a variety produced by constant shift of focus, the rôle of the court-jester can be turned to very useful account. As privileged truth-teller, he can both serve as a mouthpiece for his author's criticism of prevailing literary fashions, and also by an occasional tartness preserve the play from the insipidity which so often mars pastoral literature. As an onlooker by profession he can supply us with that *punctum indifferens*, or point of rest, which, as Coventry Patmore has well remarked, is particularly necessary for the enjoyment of a complicated work of art.

The plan of *As You Like It* is indeed unexpectedly subtle. Touchstone is, as it were, the authorized commentator, but he has a rival in the person of that self-constituted critic of society, the melancholy Jaques. It is as though, the curtain which veils Arcadia having been drawn aside, two of the inhabitants separate themselves from the rest, and step forward to the front of the stage offering themselves as guides to the spectators in the auditorium. Both of them are equally ready to act as showmen, but in every respect they are sharply contrasted: the one a sophisticated traveller, professedly intellectual, melancholy and dressed in black, the other a natural court-jester, professionally mad, merry and dressed in motley. This contrast of colour is not unimportant in a play which derives much of its charm from its picturesque qualities, and has many affinities with masque and ballet. But the contrast of outward appearances corresponds to a contrast of critical attitudes, which is still more significant. In spite of his varied experiences, Jaques is a superficial critic of life, because his apparent curiosity as to the doings of other people is really only an intense interest in his own relations. He is essentially a poseur. Touchstone, on the other hand, exposes affectation; but he is capable of sympathy as well as of criticism, and his judgments are really impartial because his mental peculiarities and his degraded social position prevent him from having any private axe to grind. So, although Jaques and Touchstone stand side by side as showmen, their points of view are not equally valid; and it is the fool, not the cynic, who is the touchstone of the play.

Mark Van Doren could always be counted upon to say something pithy, and in his eloquent *Shakespeare* (New York, 1939) he argued that

The airiness of 'As You Like It' is as much the work of thought as the reward of feeling. The comedy seems to balance like a bubble on a point of thin space; yet space in its neighborhood has not worn thin, and the bubble is as tough as eternity, it does not break. . . . We see an idea anatomized until there is nothing left of it save its original mystery. We watch an attitude as it is taken completely apart and put completely together again. And all of this is done without visible effort. . . .

'As You Like It' is a criticism of the pastoral sentiment, an examination of certain familiar ideas concerning the simple life and the golden age. It is not satire; its examination is conducted without prejudice. For once in the world a proposition is approached from all of its sides, and from top to bottom. . . . When Rosalind has made her last curtsy and the comedy is done, the pastoral sentiment is without a leg to stand on, yet it stands; and not only stands but dances. The idea of the simple life has been smiled off the earth and yet here it still is, smiling back at us from every bough of Arden. The Forest of Arden has been demonstrated not to exist, yet none of its trees has fallen; rather the entire plantation waves forever, and the sun upon it will not cease. The doctrine of the golden age has been as much created as destroyed. We know there is nothing in it, and we know that everything is in it. We perceive how silly it is and why we shall never be able to do without it. . . . There is only one thing sillier than being in love, and that is thinking it is silly to be in love. Rosalind skips through both errors to wisdom.

She, not Jaques, is the philosopher of the play. Hers is the only mind that never rests; his bogs down in the mire of melancholy, in the slough of self-love. He is too fond of believing he is wise to be as wise as he sounds, either in the set speech he makes about man's seven ages (II, vii) or in the insults he considers himself privileged at all times to deliver. His distrust of manners turns out to be the disaffection of a boor. His melancholy, like his wit, is an end in itself, a dyspeptic indulgence, an exercise of vanity that serves none of wisdom's purposes. . . . Jaques has seen much and can say anything, but he has nothing. Experience has made him sad. The more experience Rosalind has the merrier she grows. She too is a traveler, but she has not sold her own lands. She has taken her integrity with her to Arden, tucked under her three-cornered cap. It is proper that the limitations of Jaques should be stated by her, for if in him we have the pastoral sentiment criticized we have in her the only intelligence capable of judging the criticism.

C. L. Barber shared Van Doren's sense of the paradox implicit in Shakespeare's wit, and he analysed it perceptively in a *Philological Quarterly* article (1942) on 'The Use of Comedy in *As You Like It*'. 'In reality', Barber noted,

the finest comedy is not a diversion from serious themes but an alternative mode of developing them: not only the placing of the humor but also its content is determined by its function in the whole play. . . .

. . . A good way to begin is to ask the simple but much-begged question 'What is the comedy in *As You Like It* about? What does

Shakespeare ridicule?' At times one gets the impression that it doesn't matter very much what the characters make fun of so long as they make fun. The wit seems directed almost at random, not criticism by laughter, but a buoyant sort of game, high spirits overflowing in high jinks with language. . . .

This practice of making fun of something which is presented seriously a moment before or a moment after is standard throughout the play. It raises the question whether the play is divided against itself. But the humor is not really critical of the ideals on which the serious action is founded: its contribution is of a different kind. Touchstone's remarks make fun of the ideal of marriage, not as a bad ideal, but as an ideal which life does not live up to. His humor thus expresses the difference between the ideal existence represented in the play and life as a whole, which so frequently is not ideal. . . .

This comic method is precisely the reverse of satire. The satirist presents life as it is and ridicules it because it is not ideal, as we would like it to be and as it should be. Shakespeare goes the other way about: he represents or evokes ideal life, and then makes fun of it because it does not square with life as it ordinarily is. . . .

. . . In *As You Like It* the court fool for the first time takes over the work of comic commentary and burlesque from the clown of the earlier plays; in Jaques's praise of Touchstone and the corrective virtues of fooling, Shakespeare can be heard crowing with delight at his discovery. The figure of the jester, with his recognized social rôle and rich traditional meaning, enabled the dramatist to embody in a character and his relations with other characters the relation of his comic to his serious action, to make explicit the comedy's purpose of maintaining objectivity. . . .

Romantic participation in love and humorous detachment from its follies, the two polar attitudes which are balanced against each other in the action as a whole, meet and are reconciled in Rosalind's personality. Because she remains always aware of love's illusions while she herself is swept along delightfully by its deepest currents, she possesses as an attribute of character the power of combining whole-hearted feeling and undistorted judgment which gives the play its value. Shakespeare exploits her situation in disguise to permit her to furnish the humorous commentary on her own ardent love affair, thus keeping comic and serious actions going at the same time. In her pretended rôle of saucy shepherd youth, she can mock at romance and burlesque its gestures while playing the game of putting Orlando through his paces as a suitor, to 'cure' him of love. But for the audience, her disguise is transparent, and through it they see the very ardor which she mocks. . . .

Without this technical resource, Rosalind could never have been created; for her peculiar charm lies less in what she does as a lover than in her attitude towards being in love. The full realization of this attitude in the great scene of disguised wooing marks the climax of the play's romantic movement. It is achieved when Rosalind is able, in the midst of her golden moment, to look beyond it and mock its illusions, including the master illusion that love is an ultimate and final experience, a matter of life and death. . . . Love has been made independent of illusions without becoming any the less intense; it is therefore safe against life's unromantic contradictions. To emphasize by humor the limitations of the experience has become a way of asserting its reality. . . .

In an essay on 'As You Like It' (Shakespeare Survey, 1955) that has been cited in every study that has appeared in its wake, Harold Jenkins observes that the play draws its basic frame from

the world of fairytale or folklore. This is a world which supplied the plots of a number of Shakespeare's plays, including the greatest, notably King Lear. And fairytales have many advantages for the dramatist, among which is their total disregard of practical probabilities. In fairytales, for example, evil is always absolute, clearly recognized, and finally overthrown; all of which may have something to do with the Aristotelian theory that while history records what has happened, poetry shows what should happen. . . .

Shakespeare . . . builds up his ideal world and lets his idealists scorn the real one. But into their midst he introduces people who mock their ideals and others who mock them. One must not say that Shakespeare never judges, but one judgement is always being modified by another. Opposite views may contradict one another, but of course they do not cancel out. Instead they add up to an all-embracing view far larger and more satisfying than any one of them in itself. . . .

. . . There are of course many other lovers in the play, but the story of Silvius and Phebe is of the pure pastoral world, the familiar literary norm against which all the others may be measured. First against Silvius and Phebe are set Rosalind and Orlando, and the immediate result of this is that Rosalind and Orlando, though they clearly belong to the pastoral world, seem much closer to the ordinary one. Indeed, since Silvius and Phebe relieve them of the necessity of displaying the lovers' more extravagant postures, Rosalind and Orlando are freer to act like human beings. Rosalind need only play at taunting her adorer while allowing her real woman's heart to be in love with him in earnest. . . .

Shakespeare, then, presents the conventional pastoral, and duly burlesques it. But with a surer knowledge of life than many poets have had, he seems to suspect that the burlesque as well as the convention may also miss the truth. . . .

In Corin Shakespeare provides us with a touchstone with which to test the pastoral. Corin's dialogue with the Touchstone of the court, dropped into the middle of the play, adds to the conventional antithesis, between courtier and countryman, a glimpse of the real thing. Our picture of the court as a place of tyranny, ambition and corruption is no doubt true enough. But its colours are modified somewhat when Touchstone gives us the court's plain routine. For him, as he lets us know on another occasion, the court is the place where he has trod a measure, flattered a lady, been smooth with his enemy and undone three tailors. Though Touchstone seeks to entangle Corin in the fantastications of his wit, his arguments to show that the court is better than the sheepfarm have a way of recoiling on himself. What emerges from the encounter of these two realists is that ewe and ram, like men and women, are put together and that though the courtier perfumes his body it sweats like any other creature's. In city or country, *all* ways of life are at bottom the same, and we recognize a conclusion that Jaques, by a different route, has helped us to reach before. . . .

. . . Dominating the centre of the play, playing both the man's and woman's parts, counsellor in love and yet its victim, Rosalind gathers up into herself many of its roles and many of its meanings. . . . Heroine of numerous masquerades, she is none the less always constant and never more true than when insisting that she is counterfeiting. For she is an expert in those dark riddles which mean exactly what they say. Though things are rarely what they seem, they may sometimes be so in a deeper sense. What is wisdom and what is folly is of course never decided – you may have it 'as you like it'. Or, as Touchstone rejoined to Rosalind, after her gibe about the medlar, 'You have said; but whether wisely or no, let the forest judge'.

Shortly after Harold Jenkins set down his thoughts about the play, Helen Gardner delivered an influential lecture on '*As You Like It*'; her reflections were later collected by editor John Garrett in *More Talking of Shakespeare* (London, 1959). After noting that, 'As its title declares, this is a play to please all tastes', Dame Helen remarked that

*As You Like It* is the most refined and exquisite of the comedies, the one which is most consistently played over by a delighted intelligence. It is Shakespeare's most Mozartian comedy. . . .
Shakespeare added virtually nothing to the plot of Lodge's novel. There is no comedy in which, in one sense, he invents so little. He made the two Dukes into brothers. As in *King Lear* he put together two stories of good and unkind children, so here he gives us two examples of a brother's unkindness. This adds to the fairy-tale flavour

of the plot, because it turns the usurping Duke into a wicked uncle. . . .

The Forest of Arden ranks with the wood near Athens and Prospero's island [in *A Midsummer Night's Dream* and *The Tempest*, respectively] as a place set apart, even though, unlike them, it is not ruled by magic. . . . Arden is not a place where the laws of nature are abrogated and roses are without their thorns. If, in the world, Duke Frederick has usurped on Duke Senior, Duke Senior is aware that he has in his turn usurped upon the deer, the native burghers of the forest. . . . At times Arden seems a place where the same bitter lessons can be learnt as Lear has to learn in his place of exile, the blasted heath. Corin's natural philosophy, which includes the knowledge that 'the property of rain is to wet', is something which Lear has painfully to acquire:

> When the rain came to wet me once and the wind to make me chatter, when the thunder would not peace at my bidding, there I found 'em, there I smelt 'em out. Go to, they are not men o' their words: they told me I was everything; 'tis a lie, I am not ague-proof.

[Here Lear] is echoing Duke Senior, who smiles at the 'icy fang and churlish chiding of the winter's wind', saying

> This is no flattery: these are counsellors
> That feelingly persuade me what I am.

Amiens's lovely melancholy song:

> Blow, blow, thou winter wind,
> Thou art not so unkind
> As man's ingratitude . . .
> Freeze, freeze, thou bitter sky,
> That dost not bite so nigh
> As benefits forgot . . . ,

is terribly echoed in Lear's outburst:

> Blow, winds, and crack your cheeks! rage! blow! . . .
> Rumble thy bellyful! Spit, fire! spout, rain!
> Nor rain, wind, thunder, fire, are my daughters:
> I tax not you, you elements, with unkindness;
> I never gave you kingdom, call'd you children. . . .

And Jaques's reflection that 'All the world's a stage' becomes in Lear's mouth a cry of anguish:

> When we are born, we cry that we are come
> To this great stage of fools.

. . . Like other comic places, Arden is a place of discovery where the truth becomes clear and where each man finds himself and his true way. This discovery of truth in comedy is made through errors and mistakings. The trial and error by which we come to knowledge of ourselves and of our world is symbolized by the diguisings which are a recurrent element in all comedy, but are particularly common in Shakespeare's. Things have, as it were, to become worse before they become better, more confused and farther from the proper pattern. By misunderstandings men come to understand, and by lies and feignings they discover truth. . . . This discovery of truth by feigning, and of what is wisdom and what folly by debate, is the centre of *As You Like It*. . . .

In an article entitled ' "No Clock in the Forest": Time in *As You Like It*' (*Studies in English Literature*, 1962), Jay L. Halio reinforced Helen Gardner's observation about the function of Arden.

. . . The forest may be enchanted – the appearance of a god is only the least subtle indication that it is – but the enchantment is of an unusual kind; the forest still admits of other, qualifying realities. For the right apprehension of a natural, humane order of life, which emerges as Shakespeare's standard, takes account of both the ideal (what should or could be) and the actual (what is). . . . If Duke Senior finally returns along with the others to his dukedom (despite his earlier assertion that he would not change his 'life exempt from public haunt'), he returns not only because his dukedom is ready to receive him, but also (we must infer) because he is prepared to resume his proper role. Tempered by adversity, his virtue matures. To provide this temper, or balance, is the true function of the forest, its real 'magic'. Neither the Duke nor anyone else who comes to Arden emerges the same. . . .
. . . To the forest, the repository of natural life devoid of artificial time barriers, the champions of regeneration repair in order to derive new energy for the task before them. There they find refuge, gain strength, learn – and return.

Writing on *As You Like It* in a British Council publication, *William Shakespeare, the Later Comedies* (London, 1962), G. K. Hunter emphasized the role of 'meaningful *play*' in the comedy.

. . . This *play* is a uniquely powerful way of presenting the richness and complexity of a relationship [such as that between Rosalind/Ganymede and Orlando]; but it requires a suspension of place, time and intrigue, and this becalming of the play makes it difficult to steer it to a satisfactory conclusion. Shakespeare has to rescue his characters from their 'dream' or 'holiday' at the end of the play, and to tie up the various strands of interest and intention, and do so in such a way that we can believe that the knots will last.

He solves the problem in an unexpected way. He achieves the fulfillment of a character as real as Rosalind by keeping his *play* motif open, and deliberately exploiting its theatrical naivety. The couples are paired off with comic efficiency. . . . Rosalind acts as impresario, not only for their wedding but also for her own, seeing as well as enjoying the naivety that underlies the proper ceremonial of a great social occasion. . . .

The formal arrangements of the lovers and the final appearance of Hymen, to bless and organize, only reflect the formality which life, no less than art, thinks appropriate to the presentation of marriage. Hymen admits that these are 'strange events'. . . . But this *wonder* is not a new or unprepared element in the play; it has sustained Rosalind throughout the action. . . . We may see the formality of Hymen as only the emergence of a subdued current which has run throughout the play.

What is more, the Masque of Hymen serves to bring to the surface an idea which has had recurrent emphasis throughout the play, the idea of life itself as a 'play', which only the most poised can master, and in which the others are tied to stage-struck or incoherent roles.

In his provocative book *Shakespeare Our Contemporary*, translated by Boselaw Taborski (New York, 1964), Polish critic Jan Kort spoke even more insistently on what he referred to as 'the borderlines between illusion and reality' in *As You Like It*.

The theatre represents in itself all human relationships, but not because it is their more or less successful imitation. The theatre is the image of all human relationships because it is based on falseness – original falseness, rather like original sin. The actor plays a character he is not. He is who he is not. He is not who he is. To be oneself means only to play one's own reflection in the eyes of strangers. . . .

In the closing scenes of *As You Like It* one can discern this double significance of disguise: the spiritual and the physical; the intellectual and the sensual. Everything has been mixed up: the bodies of boys and girls; desire and love. Silvius loves Phebe, the shepherdess; Phebe loves Ganymede; Ganymede loves Orlando; Orlando loves Rosalind, Ganymede is Rosalind, but it is Rosalind who is Ganymede, because Rosalind is a boy, just as Phebe is a boy. Love is an absolute value, and at the same time most absolutely a matter of chance. Eroticism goes through bodies like electric current and makes them tremble. Every Rosalind is Ganymede, and every Ganymede is Rosalind. . . .

In a Shakespearean forest the lovers [in *A Midsummer Night's Dream*] in the course of a summer night went through the dark sphere of animal eroticism. They came to know the urgency of desire and possession. They exchanged partners. In another of Shakespeare's forests, four characters of *As You Like It* will pass through tempest and hurricane [in *King Lear*]: the prince who has renounced his crown; the exiled minister; the exiled brother; and the clown. They will be reduced to bare existence, which must suffice for itself and in itself find reasons for being, as there can be no appeal from it, whether to empty heavens, to bloody history, or to nonrational nature. In the last of the Shakespearean forests [in *The Tempest*], on Prospero's island, the history of the world will be performed in quick motion, in three hours.

First, the Forest of Arden means escape; escape from the cruel kingdom where, as always in Shakespeare, two themes obsessively repeat themselves: exile of the lawful prince depriving the younger brother of his inheritance. For Shakespeare this is rudimentary social history in a nutshell. . . . A tyrant has ascended the throne, a brother persecutes a brother, love and friendship have been destroyed by ambition, the world is ruled by sheer force and money. From the Duke's feast wrestlers are being carried away with broken ribs. The opening of *As You Like It* has the atmosphere of the Histories; the air is stuffy and everyone is afraid. The new prince is distrustful, suspicious, jealous of everything and everybody, unsure of his position, seeing the enemy in everyone. As in the Histories, the only hope of salvation is in escape: escape at any price and as fast as one can. . . .

The Forest of Arden is a return to the golden age, the only place in the feudal world where alienation has ceased to operate. And in this Forest of Arden, it is Jaques who feels his alienation most fully and is, to use our terminology, most thoroughly frustrated. . . .

The Forest of Arden makes mockery of Arcadia and constitutes a new Arcadia. Love is escape from cruel history to an invented forest. Shakespeare is like a Bible; he creates his own myths. The Forest of Arden is a place in which all dreams meet; it is a dream and the awakening from a dream.

As if in response to Jan Kott's stress on the grim realism of *As You Like It*, Sylvan Barnet came forward a few years later with a *Shakespeare Studies* article (1968) on ' "Strange Events": Improbability in *As You Like It*'.

It is probably true that most of us cannot quite escape from a view of literature that in one respect may be called Aristotelian: we expect to see in literature (as distinct from history) deeds growing out of motives, and motives growing out of the conjunction of personality and circumstances. . . . This paper will argue that Shakespeare goes out of his way to heighten the improbabilities in *As You Like It*, presumably for a purpose, and that it is therefore an error to dismiss them or to suggest that they are to be accepted unthinkingly as conventions. . . .

. . . In *As You Like It*, Hymen himself is part of the wonder that concludes the play; he is never explained in the play, and those productions that make him recognizably one of the Duke's men, or a Corin whose Falstaffian girth reveals his identity beneath his sheet, do an injustice to this element in the play.

In keeping with the strangeness of this world, Shakespeare in several places *lessens* the motivation he found in Lodge's *Rosalynde*. . . . Shakespeare might have followed Lodge [for example] in having the eldest son envious of his young brother's ample possessions, but instead Shakespeare makes Oliver's conspiracy against Orlando *less* intelligible by giving Orlando only a 'poor thousand crowns,' a 'poor allottery' that does not seem to interest Oliver. Near the end of the first scene, after we have witnessed the quarrel between the brothers but have been given no explanation for Oliver's treatment of Orlando, Oliver confesses he can offer no explanation. . . .

The reasons for Frederick's banishment of Rosalind are similarly less detailed and less plausible than those for Torismond's banishment of Rosalynde. . . . Rosalind's very excellence is Celia's enemy because it diminishes Celia's excellence. This indeed is a reason, but it is a bad one, and we can only echo Le Beau's earlier conclusion: 'The Duke is humorous.' . . .

But of course in *As You Like It* the most unpredictable happenings (from the point of view of psychology, not of literary conventions) are the instantaneous love affairs and the conversions of the villains. . . . [Unlike Lodge,] Shakespeare . . . goes out of his way to insist upon the suddenness and the improbability of the love between Celia and Oliver. . . .

[The play's] insistence on the suddenness and improbability of the experience suggests not that Shakespeare is winding things up quickly because (in Johnson's words) he is 'in view of his reward,' or that (in Paul V. Kreider's words) Shakespeare is mocking his 'patently inadequate plot,' but that suddenness and improbability are part of the meaning of the play. . . . Oliver speaks of his 'conversion,' [a change] which utterly transforms one's personality, as, for example, on the road to Damascus Paul's personality was transformed. . . .

. . . Like Oliver's conversion, Frederick's is apparently triggered by a sudden experience, and it has 'an element of marvel,' to use words that William James in Lecture IX of *The Varieties of Religious Experience* used of conversion. . . . Jaques' discords, like Frederick's discordant actions, betoken a personality that has not become integrated, and at the conclusion of the play, after the report of Frederick's conversion, Jaques' intention to visit Frederick reminds us of this sort of anxious personality and it reminds us also of its great potentiality for change. In Jaques' statement that he hopes to learn 'much matter' from the convertite, we hear, very faintly, a voice like that of the jailer who asked Paul and Silas, 'What must I do to be saved?' Zera Fink says Jaques 'has lost any real faith in life,' but the implication of the play is, I think, that his dissatisfaction with things as they are prepares him for the possibility of conversion. . . .

. . . In comedy we find things absurd to reason. As the etymology indicates, the preposterous is that in which the natural order is broken, the first coming last, and the conversions we have been speaking of involve the unnatural, the implausible. . . .

Early in the play Jaques describes as a 'strange eventful history' man's unhappy progress through seven rather uneventual ages; in the last act, when conflicts have been wondrously reconciled through patently unreasonable (but not therefore perfunctory or meaningless) transformations, Hymen justly speaks of 'strange events.' Had Shakespeare wished to write a more plausible play, he needed only to have followed his source more closely. But he apparently took pains to make his play implausible, and we ought not to let our awareness of conventions, or our tolerance for occasional perfunctoriness, mislead us into thinking that the plot of *As You Like It* is negligible, or that the play is about anything less than 'strange events.'

Shortly after Sylvan Barnet published his analysis of the play, D. J. Palmer drew attention to the relationships between 'Art and Nature in *As You Like It*' (*Philological Quarterly*, 1970).

When Rosalind steps forward to speak the Epilogue to *As You Like It*, she does so both as the heroine of the play just concluded, and as the boy actor of that part. Such an ambiguous coupling of art with reality is appropriate to any epilogue, which effects the transition from make-believe to truth, but it is especially fitting to a play with the self-conscious artifice of *As You Like It*. The Epilogue links the play to its spectators in the real world, by appealing to the men and women, for the love they bear to each other, to applaud this comedy of lovers. Rosalind's charge to the men, 'that between you and women the play may please,' contains a bawdy pun on 'play' which expresses in a word the correspondence between the lovers on the stage and those who have been watching them. The stage holds up a mirror to life, and the men and women whose favor is now solicited, as they like it, are reminded that they have seen their own image in the business of the play. . . .

As a pastoral world, the forest itself possesses this mirrorlike quality, and upon our first entry there the banished Duke describes its peculiar virtue for us. . . . The Duke's discovery of books in the running brooks, and sermons in stones, shows that there is an Art in Nature itself. Arden is a meeting-place of Art and Nature, a world whose inhabitants may recognize themselves more truly in the reflections that are cast back upon them. . . .

Rosalind's counterfeiting with Orlando is the most elaborate and artificial pageant of the play. It is a mock-courtship where each finds a reflection of his true love, and where reality and its counterfeit image are eventually revealed as one and the same. . . .

. . . The Forest of Arden represents Nature as Art, not only when we accept it as an unreal pastoral world, but equally in its properties as a teacher and as a restorer of Nature's equilibrium. For those who enter there, and encounter each other under its auspices, are cast by reflection into their natural roles. Such confrontations are analogues of the play in the theatre, as Art holding up the mirror to Nature, because 'all the world's a stage, and all the men and women merely players.'

Many of Palmer's points were amplified, with variations, a year later when Albert R. Cirillo printed As You Like It: Pastoralism Gone Awry' in the 1971 volume of ELH (English Literary History).

The shifting perspective between actual and ideal that is so integral a part of the pastoral world in Renaissance literature is infused with urbanity, wit, and mild but revealing cynicism in As You Like It. . . .

The amorous situation itself in the perspective provided by the Forest of Arden becomes a trial which leads to harmony. Rosalind is the instrument who effects this order and therein lies a great deal of the ironic humor of the play. For the name Rosalind had become, by the time Shakespeare wrote the play, almost a stock symbol for the loved-one in romantic situations; she was, almost in virtue of her name, the lovely lass for whom poetic shepherds pined, and her name evoked all of the sweet melancholy associated with literary lovers. By making the object of Orlando's youthful ardor a figure with inherent associations of romantic pastoral – a Rosalind who, somewhat paradoxically, acts as a cynical iconoclast towards the standard romantic convention – Shakespeare makes his play and its setting a self-reflective commentary on the unreality of the pastoral convention.

This is not to say that the play rejects the significance of the pastoral as a symbol; what it rejects is the naive belief in the pastoral fiction as an attainable ideal in life. . . .

The image of the circle, which is a standard one in magic or occult rites, becomes integral to the final resolution of the play and, in retrospect, casts light on all that has preceded. . . . Rosalind will later become a Prospero (the general resemblance between this play and *The Tempest*, which represents a more mature vision, are worth recognition); and she is here just as much a surrogate for Shakespeare, the artist, as that later magician is. Within the magic circle of the forest Rosalind/Ganymede can, like a true Renaissance *magus*, proceed to set everything according to nature; as the image of the circle suggests, she will bring everything to a harmonious conclusion. . . .

But if the Forest has been a magic circle for the characters in the play, so has the play been for the audience. Again, it is Rosalind who makes this clear in her Epilogue. By stepping out of the play, as if out of the fiction, she exercises the genuine force of her magic on us by bringing us *into* the fictional. The play is our Arden. What Rosalind does in directly begging the audience for applause is to *invoke* us, to bring us into the circle of her magic. . . .

In *The Heart's Forest: A Study of Shakespeare's Pastoral Plays* (New Haven, 1972), David Young developed many of the same themes that had been touched on by D. J. Palmer, Albert Cirillo, and previous commentators. According to Young,

The tendency of *As You Like It* to keep before us the artificial basis of the pastoral design is closely linked to its stress on the relativity and subjectivity of the experience of sojourn. The forest is constant in its imaginary character and changeable in each contact with a separate imagination. The essential subjectivity of pastoral thus emerges with considerable force; and since each character's encounter with Arden differs, the play offers a growing awareness of the fundamental relativity of human experience.

The forest of Arden, like the theater or any art, can be likened to a special sort of mirror that reflects the subject under the guise of objects. It is not surprising that its viewers so seldom realize that they are seeing themselves when they look at it. . . .

It is not only in nature that the characters find themselves reflected, but in each other as well. Rosalind and her party have no sooner arrived than they have an opportunity to hear Silvius on the subject of his love for Phebe. Rosalind is immediately referred to her own passion for Orlando. . . .

[But] it is Touchstone, parodist supreme, who proves the deftest reflector of others in the play, partly because it is his professional role. . . . He is as much a chameleon as the forest, although this fact seems to have escaped the commentators who have disapproved of him as a show-off, cynic, and lecher. Touchstone is either a grotesque reflection of those he encounters, as with Jaques, Silvius, and Orlando, or a reflection of what they think a courtier must be like, as with Corin, William, and Audrey. He exists to score off other characters and conventional attitudes, and as such he is a source of pure, and at times extremely subtle, enjoyment. . . .

Jaques does not fare very well in the holding up of mirrors. . . . He is usually taken in. When Touchstone gives him some exaggerated euphuism, he takes it straight. And when he meets Orlando [in III.ii], and for a moment their two kinds of melancholy mirror each other, it is Orlando who points out their difference and scores off Jaques with a stale joke [about looking in the brook and finding his 'own figure']. . . .

No character is more contradictory than Jaques, a fact which has led to frequent misunderstandings. His melancholy must not be taken too literally because it is in fact an enthusiasm. No one has more zest for life than this declared solitary. He can 'suck melancholy out of a song as a weasel sucks eggs' [as we hear in III.v], an appropriate image, surely, in its suggestion of furtive pleasure. His encounter with Touchstone arouses him to a frenzy of happy excitement [in II.vii], and leads him on to a spirited defense of satire and his Seven Ages speech. He admits to Rosalind of his melancholy that 'I do love it better than laughing.' It is his own artful compound, in which he takes great pride and pleasure, and it would be wrong to find anything but complacent satisfaction in his account of the way his 'often rumination' wraps him 'in a most humorous sadness.' . . .

There is scarcely an element in *As You Like It* unaffected by a sense of relativity. Sex, rank, fortune, the ages of man, the forest itself, are all seen as variables rather than constants. And so is Time, not only in the play as a whole, but quite particularly in Rosalind's opening gambit [in III.ii] when she encounters Orlando in the forest. 'Time,' she tells him, 'travels in divers paces with divers persons,' and ambles, trots, gallops, and stands still. . . . It is, in effect, Orlando's first lesson, and it is a good one, a lesson that the play takes to heart. We may suppose that the title is related to it, as a kind of warning against categorical judgments. Pastoral is not always true or always false or always anything; it is as you like it. And it is not just to pastoral that this applies, but to Time, to Nature, to Art, and to life itself.

Alexander Leggatt focused on the 'freedom' afforded by *As You Like It* when he discussed the play in *Shakespeare's Comedy of Love* (London, 1974). Commencing with an analysis of the 'mingling of conventions' in Shakespeare's treatment of artistic genres, he went on to note a similar diversity in his portrayal of the 'native population of Arden':

for one kind of wedding, the forest can produce an Elizabethan hedge-priest, Sir Oliver Martext, whose very name suggests the real problems the church has always faced in country parishes; for another kind of wedding, it can produce Hymen himself. There is one shepherd, Corin, whose language, pungent and concrete, is rooted in his occupation, and who experiences the hard facts of economic reality. . . . There is another shepherd, Silvius, who 'little cares for buying anything,' and whose language has no particular roots in rural experience (pleading with Phebe, he uses a very urban image, drawn from public executions). . . . The female population is equally mixed: there is Phebe, a shepherdess who can quote Marlowe in a gracefully allusive manner. . . . And there is Audrey, a country wench (a very distinct breed from the shepherdess) who finds the very word 'poetical' hard to understand. These figures represent not simply different types of character, but different types of dramatic idiom. Yet they mingle freely – Corin and Silvius are first seen together – and no one coming to Arden remarks on the incongruity. . . .

. . . No fixed attitude to court or country emerges from [the play's debates], unless it be the idea that everything is relative. But to state this idea so clearly [as Touchstone and Corin do in III.ii] is to bring it out into the open, and that makes it vulnerable. A Shakespearian comedy is a very dangerous place for an abstract idea to be wandering loose. And the idea that all experience is relative, that everything depends on your point of view, is no safer than any other. . . .

Much of the comic effect of *As You Like It* comes, as we have seen, from a swift interplay of perspectives. But this is not the play's final effect. In the forest scene we seem for a while to be suspended beyond time, enjoying an endless afternoon. The only movement is a back-and-forth shuttling as the various characters wander in, confront each other and wander out again. But just as there is a controlling attitude behind the interplay of perspectives, so in the play as a whole there is a steady forward motion behind the apparent casualness. . . .

. . . If this play is peculiarly successful in showing the reality behind convention, this may be because it sees convention as strongest where it embodies recognizable, predictable experiences: in love in particular, all the clichés come true. . . . [Here Shakespeare] concentrates on a conviction – the Noah's Ark ending – which allows us in the audience to feel that we are not merely spectators but participants. We are entitled to poke fun at it if we wish. The liberty of Arden will admit almost any point of view. But if we do laugh, we must also recognize that, like Rosalind when she played Ganymede, we are laughing at ourselves.

Harking back to studies as early as Walter Whiter's 1794 essay on the pictorial motifs behind such phrases as 'the better part of Atalanta', Harry Morris related *As You Like It* to the *et in Arcadia ego* motto (echoed in II.iv in Touchstone's 'Now I am in Arden')

speech) that figured in early seventeenth-century paintings by Guercino and Poussin. Writing in the 1975 volume of *Shakespeare Quarterly*, Morris suggested that, like those two artists, the author of *As You Like It* went out of his way to include '*memento-mori* elements' (reminders of the inevitability of death) in 'a pastoral setting of great loveliness, peopled by youths of great beauty'.

> Glosses [on Jaques's Seven Ages speech in II.vii] have always indicated that the final line is a description of advanced decrepitude, the lack of teeth and taste to be regarded as literal, but the lack of eyes and everything to be regarded as metaphorical. But if we read the line as modifying 'mere oblivion' rather than 'second childishness,' the description may be regarded as literal throughout. Lack of teeth, of taste, of eyes, of everything then presents the charnel-house skull. . . .
>
> For Shakespeare, then, to add a dead shepherd to the skull strongly suggests some link between *As You Like It* and the *et-in-Arcadia-ego* tradition, for both the skull and the shepherd are parts of the Guercino-Poussin pictorial iconography. And in choice of his dead shepherd, Shakespeare is perfect: 'Dead shepherd, now I find thy saw of might, / Who ever lov'd that lov'd not at first sight?' (III.v.80–81). By quoting from *Hero and Leander*, Shakespeare glances at Christopher Marlowe. This is a brilliant device, for Marlowe as pastoral poet lived in Arcadia, but Marlowe as murdered poet died in the real world. . . . As Marlowe, Shakespeare's 'dead Shepherd' reminds us that shepherds, poets, and playwrights 'all must, / As chimney-sweepers, come to dust' [to recall the eulogy that adorns IV.ii of *Cymbeline*]. As pastoral poet he reminds us that all golden lads and girls, all famous lovers. . . . will have only the briefest span of life.

A year after Morris's article, in an examination of 'Jaques' Distortion of the Seven-Ages Paradigm' (*Shakespeare Quarterly*, 1976), Alan Taylor Bradford showed that 'the common rationale for all seven-ages schemes [in Renaissance iconography] is astrological and that in such schemes the ages correspond in number, sequence, and characteristics to the planetary spheres.' Bradford then argued that by his alterations of the 'sequence of the ages . . . Jaques has tendentiously distorted that paradigm'.

> Jaques' first three ages – in fact, schoolboy, and lover (moon–Mercury–Venus) – conform to the paradigm. His distortions begin with the fourth age, which is traditionally allotted to the sun: symbol of young manhood, the prime of life. In Jaques' speech Mars the soldier has displaced the sun – an anticlimactic substitution. Jupiter

follows in the person of the justice, advanced from the sixth to the fifth position in the sequence to fill the vacuum caused by Mars's promotion. Next is the grotesque portrait of 'the lean and slippered pantaloon,' followed by the 'last scene of all,' Jaques' stunning image of total decrepitude. But the last two ages, as envisioned by Jaques, are in fact one: both represent degrees of senility and are under domination of Saturn. If we superimpose Jaques' sequence of ages on the paradigm as Shakespeare received it, two striking discrepancies emerge: (1) Jaques' cosmos is sunless; (2) the baleful planet Saturn has extended its dominion over the final *two* phases of human life. These aberrations, moreover, are directly related to each other. The significance of Jaques' omission of the solar age cannot be overemphasized; for in terms of the astrological paradigm, that age was the climax of human life – what Sir Walter Ralegh called 'the strong, flourishing, and beautiful age of man's life.' . . . That Shakespeare could have omitted the climax of man's life through oversight or through ignorance is inconceivable. He knew perfectly well why the sun occupied the fourth of the seven planetary spheres. . . . With the abdication of 'the glorious planet Sol' [a phrase from I.iii of *Troilus and Cressida*] . . . the uncorrected influence of the evil planet Saturn has penetrated the sphere of Jupiter (or the sixth age) and threatens to run amok through the heavens. To look at the situation another way, a 'Saturnine' perspective distorts Jaques' view of life. . . .

The distorted paradigm thus operates as a kind of subtextual metaphor. As such, it would seem to reinforce the point of Jaques' speech: that human life is without meaning, purpose, or value. . . . [As a consequence] it declines into protracted senility (the double age of Saturn) and ends fittingly in 'mere oblivion . . . sans everything.' Such, at any rate, appears to be *Jaques'* intention in rearranging the scheme of things to fit his own nihilistic philosophy. *Shakespeare's* intentions, on the other hand, were no doubt far different; he must have felt that such irresponsible tampering with absolutes would automatically invalidate itself in the minds of right-thinking people. From Jaques' point of view, the seven-act play being performed on the stage of the world obviously belongs to the Theatre of the Absurd – a school of dramaturgy with which Shakespeare, in spite of certain current directorial trends, has very little in common.

In an investigation of 'The Reform of a Malcontent' (*Shakespeare Studies*, 1976), Robert B. Bennett revisited the implications of Jaques's 'refusal to join the marriage celebration and his intention to return with the company to court' at the end of *As You Like It*.

. . . Harold Jenkins, Jay Halio, and Helen Gardner deny any change in

Jaques and maintain that his cynicism is confirmed by his departure at the end. . . . John Russell Brown [in *Shakespeare and his Comedies* (London, 1957)] states that a change has taken place:

> Jaques cannot join the dance which celebrates the new order of the lovers; unappeased, he must seek more matter for his contemplation. But having seen them all endure 'shrewd days and nights' (V.iv.179), he accepts this as testimony of their inward virtues, and, for the first time in the play, sees promise of order, not of disorder.

I agree with Brown's argument, but it still leaves unanswered the question, why is Jaques 'unappeased'? The general confusion over Jaques' position in the final scene rests, I believe, on the failure to keep in mind the distinction between practiced fashionable melancholy and genuine intellectual melancholy. The conversion that one must expect, or hope, for Jaques is not one from cynical philosopher to reveler but one from fashionable intellectual to true intellectual – and it takes place. As cynicism lies at the core of the fashion, its absence in the final scene is a crucial indication of Jaques' change. . . .
. . . He has come to see the natures of the Arden inhabitants, including his own, and has replaced rancor with measure. . . . Were he like Malvolio [in the concluding scene of *Twelfth Night*], he would merely have left the scene with a few harsh words for the Duke, Rosalind, and Orlando, who purged his humor with rather harsh physic [in an earlier encounter]. . . . [But Jaques] no longer plays the malcontent by such actions as calling for music and then saying that he dislikes it. He does not disdain the dancing and pastime. He only sees that in choosing the sober intellectual and religious life, he is choosing not to participate in the pleasures allied to court and marriage. His departure is not absurd, as his former poses of unsociability had seemed, but is fitting and calls for reluctant acceptance, not censure, from those who like his company but respect his choice.

Meanwhile, in her study of another passage from the final scene of *As You Like It* (*Shakespeare Quarterly*, 1977), Maura Slattery Kuhn found broad significance in Touchstone's observation that there is 'Much Virtue in If'.

> *If* is a springboard that propels the quester from the premise to a conclusion beyond. The forest of Arden embodies an unreal condition for the exiles. By accepting its premises they are rewarded with conclusions transcending their expectations. Oliver's case is revealing: he surrenders so completely as to give up his inheritance for the love of a poor shepherdess – a shepherdess who will turn out to be the daughter of a Duke.

The unreal condition of the forest is contained within the larger unreal condition of the play itself. The many *If*'s of the forest are amplified by the large *If* of the play. By virtue of *If*, a contract is drawn up between the players and the audience. If you will suspend your disbelief, you will be delighted by our play. . . . In a sexual encounter [such as the one implied in Rosalind's Epilogue], there must be a mutual yielding for the love-play to please. At a stageplay the audience must yield its disbelief to be pleased. The players, for their part, yield truth of one kind to show truths of a higher kind – to show things as they should be, to use Sidney's language. The audience feigns an *If*. If you say so, then I say so.

*As You Like It* begins in one kind of seriousness, passes through a magic circle of Huizingian play, and ends in an advanced kind of seriousness. The circle of play has been constantly characterized by the conditional. *If* saves the game, for it defines the condition and shapes the consequence. In saving the game it makes the play. To employ a musical metaphor, *As You Like It* is a series of inspired improvisations in the key of *If*.

In yet another approach to 'the end of *As You Like It*', Margaret Boerner Beckman connected 'The Figure of Rosalind' (*Shakespeare Quarterly*, 1978) to the wonders she claims to be able to perform in V.ii.

I would like to suggest that Rosalind ends the play as a magician because throughout the play she has made extraordinary, seemingly impossible – and thus 'magical' – conjunctions between contrary things. Her own person is a seemingly impossible reconciliation of opposites. The magic she performs brings contrarieties together and harmonizes them. The 'strange things' she does, then, are not incidental to the play, but rather a logical development from what she has been doing all along. . . .

For if the plot of this plotless play is about anything, it is about man and wife, about 'getting married and living happily ever after.' . . . To make 'earthly things . . . even' [as Hymen promises to do in V.iv] is not to make them the same or to make one subordinate to another; it is to reconcile them and make them one ('atone') in a creative relationship. The name for this kind of relationship is 'harmony,' and its central representative in *As You Like It* is Rosalind. She *is* harmony, a coincidence of opposites, promising to 'make all this matter even' and to 'make the doubts all even' (V.iv.18, 25). Her 'way is to conjure you,' she says in the play's Epilogue, because *concordia discors* ['the harmonious combination of true opposites'] defies logic and seems impossible.

Since marriage is a *concordia discors*, Rosalind's image is a complex one. She starts out simply enough as a woman who [falls in love]. She therefore first stands for 'idealism.' But when she later comes to 'speak to [Orlando] like a saucy lackey and under that habit play the knave with him' (III.ii.312–13), she stands for the 'realism' that is opposed to Orlando's idealism. . . .

Maintaining these two alternative perspectives, she already represents a *concordia discors*. But Shakespeare heightens the paradox of her figure through a number of other devices. The most important one is that she is a *woman* presenting the voice of critical realism about love. . . .

. . . When Shakespeare presents Rosalind as a woman disguised as a man pretending to be a woman, then, he does more than merely 'permit her to furnish the humorous commentary on her own ardent love affair' [as C. L. Barber noted]. He offers us a symbolic image of 'earthly things made even.'

Rosalind's disguise is in fact even more complex, for on the stage she is actually a boy playing the part of a woman disguised as a man pretending to be a woman: the boy actor playing Rosalind disguised as Ganymede pretending to be Rosalind. . . .

. . . Shakespeare had a strong interest in the androgynous, but not epicene, sexual figure. But it is important to note that his androgynous figure does more than set forth paradox for its own sake. Such a figure symbolizes the natural union of those opposites that are made for each other. Male and female are thus images for all reconcilable contraries. . . . It is not that *As You Like It* allegorizes the coincidence of Mars and Venus. It is rather that such coincidences as those involving Mars and Venus or Rosalind and Ganymede can be used to symbolize the natural harmony of opposed forces that constitutes man's 'possible perfection.' And in comedy, man's perfection is epitomized in marriage.

When the figure of Rosalind is seen as in itself a *concordia discors*, her word-play reveals itself to be the rhetorical expression of her symbolic function. . . . Like male compassion, female wit is part of a fully realized human character. Thus, although Shakespeare establishes clear differences between the 'masculine' and the 'feminine' in his plays, he often implies that characters who are totally one or the other are sterile. . . .

. . . Rosalind's word-play serves as a necessary verbal imitation of 'earthly things made even,' bringing together in union things that are at odds. And her word-play in turn reinforces her magical power to bring about the unions at the end of the play. . . .

To know Rosalind is to know that opposites can be reconciled.

Recent commentary on *As You Like It* has focused increasingly on the social, political, and gender issues the play reflects. Illustrating these concerns, Louis Adrian Montrose has written an important article on ' "The Place of a Brother": Social Process in *As You Like It*' (*Shakespeare Quarterly*, 1981). As Montrose observes:

As the play begins, Orlando and Adam are discussing the terms of a paternal will; the first scene quickly explodes into fraternal resentment and envy, hatred and violence. By the end of the second scene, the impoverished youngest son of Sir Rowland de Boys finds himself victimized by 'a tyrant Duke' and 'a tyrant brother' (I.iii.278). . . .
[But contrary to the view of Harold Jenkins and other critics, what] happens to Orlando at home is not Shakespeare's contrivance to get him into the forest; what happens to Orlando in the forest is Shakespeare's contrivance to remedy what has happened to him at home. . . .
The tense situation which [commences] *As You Like It* was a familiar and controversial fact of Elizabethan social life. . . . In the sixteenth and seventeenth centuries, primogeniture was more widely and rigorously practiced in England – by the gentry and lesser landowners, as well as by the aristocracy – than anywhere else in Europe. . . .
It is precisely in the details of inheritance that Shakespeare makes one of the most significant departures from his source. Sir John of Bordeaux is on his deathbed at the beginning of Lodge's *Rosalynde*; he divides his land and chattels among his three sons. . . . Saladyne, the eldest born, inherits his father's authority. Rosader [the youngest] receives more land and love – he is his father's joy, although his last and least [like Cordelia in *King Lear*]. Saladyne, who becomes Rosader's guardian, is deeply resentful and decides not to honor their father's will. . . .
Lodge's text . . . reminds us that primogeniture was not a binding law but rather a flexible social custom in which the propertied sought to perpetuate themselves by preserving their estates intact through successive generations. Shakespeare alters the terms of the paternal will in Lodge's story so as to alienate Orlando from the status of a landed gentleman. The effect is to intensify the differences between the eldest son and his siblings, and to identify the sibling conflict with the major division in the Elizabethan social fabric. . . .
The reunion of the de Boys brothers is narrated retrospectively [in IV.iii] by a reborn Oliver, in the alien style of an allegorical dream romance. . . .
Agnes Latham suggests [in the introduction to her Arden edition of *As You Like It* (London, 1975)] that the snake and the lioness which menace Oliver are metaphors for his own animosities: as the snake 'slides away, Oliver's envy melts, and his wrath goes with the lion.' The text suggests that it is Orlando who undergoes such an allegorical

purgation. . . . In killing the lioness which threatens to kill Oliver, Orlando kills the impediment to atonement within himself. Oliver's narrative implies a causal relationship between Orlando's act of self-mastery and purgation and Oliver's own 'awakening.'

. . . The spiritual principle of 'brotherly love' is reconciled to the jural principle of primogeniture; 'real brothers' are made 'blood brothers' – as the napkin borne by Oliver so graphically testifies.

. . . Orlando sheds his own blood for his elder brother, which becomes the sign of Oliver's conversion rather than the mark of his [Cain-like] fratricidal guilt.

. . . Oliver is not defeated, eliminated, supplanted; he is converted, reintegrated, confirmed. In the subplot of *King Lear*, the unbrotherly struggle for mastery and possession is resolved by fratricide [as Edgar slays Edmund in a duel at the end of the play]; the comic resolution of *As You Like It* depends instead upon an expansion of opportunities for mastery and possession. . . .

With his patrimony restored and his marriage effected, Oliver legitimately assumes the place of a patriarch and emerges into full social adulthood; he is now worthy to be the son and heir of Sir Rowland de Boys. Orlando, on the other hand, has proved himself worthy to become son and heir to the Duke. . . . The de Boys brothers atone together when the eldest replaces a father and the youngest recovers a father. . . .

. . . It is by the conjurer's art that Shakespeare manages to reconcile the social imperatives of hierarchy and difference with the festive urges toward leveling and atonement. The intense and ambivalent personal bonds upon which the play is focused – bonds between brothers and between lovers – affect each other reciprocally and become the means of each other's resolution. And as the actions within the play are dialectically related to each other, so the world of Shakespeare's characters is dialectically related to the world of his audience. *As You Like It* is both a theatrical *reflection* of social conflict and a theatrical *source* of social conciliation.

In another recent example of 'new historicist' approaches to Renaissance theatre, *Patriarchal Structures in Shakespeare's Drama* (Berkeley, 1985), Peter Erickson explores the 'Sexual Politics' of *As You Like It*. Commenting on the roles she plays in the comedy, Erickson argues that, though Rosalind has 'access to both male and female attributes',

the impression she conveys of androgynous wholeness is misleading. Neither Rosalind nor the play question the conventional categories of masculine and feminine. She does not reconcile gender definitions in the sense of integrating or synthesizing them. Her own insistence on the metaphor of exterior (male) and interior (female) keeps the categories distinct and separable. The liberation that Rosalind experiences in the forest has built into it the conservative counter-movement by which, as the play returns to the normal world, she will be reduced to the traditional woman who is subservient to men. . . .

Though she teases Orlando with the wife's power to make him a cuckold and then to conceal her duplicity with her 'wayward wit' [in IV.i], this is good fun, and it is only that. It is clear to the audience, if not yet to Orlando, that Rosalind's flaunting of her role as disloyal wife is a put-on rather than a genuine threat. She may playfully delay the final moment when she becomes a wife, but we are reassured that, once married, she will in fact be faithful.

. . . We may wish to give Rosalind credit for her cleverness in forestalling male rivalry between her father and her fiancé. Unlike Cordelia [who has not been so wise in *King Lear*], she is smart enough to see that in order to be gratified, each man needs to feel that he is the recipient of all her love, not half of it. Yet Rosalind is not really in charge here because the potential hostility between the younger and older man has already been negotiated in the forest in act 2, scene 7, a negotiation that results in the formation of an idealized male alliance. Rosalind submits not only to two individual men but also to the patriarchal society that they embody. . . .

The convention of males playing female roles gives men the opportunity to imagine sex-role fluidity and flexibility. Built into the conditions of performance is the potential for male acknowledgment of a 'feminine self' and thus for male transcendence of a narrow masculinity. . . . In the boy-actor motif, woman is a metaphor for the male discovery of the feminine within himself, of those qualities suppressed by a masculinity strictly defined as aggressiveness. Once the tenor of the metaphor has been attained, the vehicle can be discarded – just as Rosalind is discarded. The sense of the patriarchal ending in *As You Like It* is that male androgyny is affirmed whereas female 'liberty' in the person of Rosalind is curtailed. . . .

. . . The Epilogue is, in effect, a second ending that provides further security against women by preserving on stage the image of male ties in their pure form with women absent. Not only are women to be subordinate; they can, if necessary, be imagined as nonexistent. Rosalind's art does not, as is sometimes suggested, coincide with Shakespeare's: Shakespeare uses his art to take away Rosalind's female identity and thereby upstages her claim to magic power. . . .

We have too easily accepted the formulation that says that Shakespeare in the mature history plays concentrates on masculine development whereas in the mature festive comedies he gives women their due by allowing them to play the central role. *As You Like It* is primarily a defensive action against female power rather than a celebration of it. . . . These two elements − female vitality kept manageable and male power kept loving − provided a resolution that at this particular moment was 'As Shakespeare Liked It.'

# SUGGESTIONS FOR FURTHER READING

Many of the works quoted in the preceding survey, or excerpts from those works, can be found in modern collections of criticism. Of particular interest or convenience are the following anthologies:

Bloom, Harold (ed.), *Rosalind* (Major Literary Characters), New York: Chelsea House, 1992.

—— *William Shakespeare's 'As You Like It?'*, New York: Chelsea House, 1988.

Halio, Jay L. (ed.), *Twentieth Century Interpretations of 'As You Like It'*, Englewood Cliffs, NJ: Prentice-Hall, 1968.

Scott, Mark W. (ed.), *Shakespearean Criticism*, vol. 5, Detroit: Gale, 1987.

Other studies (including modern editions) that include pertinent discussions of *As You Like It*:

Allen, Michael J. B., 'Jaques against the Seven Ages of the Proclan Man', *Modern Language Quarterly*, 42 (1981), 331–46.

Aston, Elaine, and George Savona, *Theatre as Sign-System: A Semiotics of Text and Performance*, London: Routledge, 1991.

Babb, Lawrence, *The Elizabethan Malady: A Study of Melancholia in English Literature from 1580 to 1642*, East Lansing: Michigan State College Press, 1951.

Baker, Susan, 'Shakespeare and Ritual: The Example of *As You Like It*', *Upstart Crow*, 9 (1989), 9–23.

Barber, C. L., *Shakespeare's Festive Comedy*, Princeton: Princeton University Press, 1959.

Barnet, Sylvan, '*As You Like It* on the Stage', in his Signet Classics volume on *As You Like It*, ed. Albert Gilman, New York: Penguin Books USA, 1986.

Berry, Ralph, 'No Exit from Arden', *Modern Language Review*, 66 (1971), 11–20.

—— *Shakespeare's Comedies: Explorations in Form*, Princeton: Princeton University Press, 1972.

Bethell, S. L., *Shakespeare and the Popular Tradition*, London: P. S. King and Staples, 1944.

Bono, Barbara J., 'Mixed Gender, Mixed Genre in Shakespeare's *As You Like It*', in *Renaissance Genres: Essays on Theory, History, and Interpretation*, ed. Barbara Kiefer Lewalski, Cambridge, Mass: Harvard University Press, 1986.

Bowe, John, 'Orlando in *As You Like It*', in *Players of Shakespeare*, ed. Philip Brockbank, Cambridge: Cambridge University Press, 1985.

Brissenden, Alan (ed.), *As You Like It*, Oxford: Clarendon Press, 1993.

Brown, John Russell, *Shakespeare and His Comedies*, London: Methuen, 1975.

Carlson, Susan, *Women and Comedy: Rewriting the British Theatrical Tradition*, Ann Arbor: University of Michigan Press, 1991.

Carroll, William C., *The Metamorphoses of Shakespearean Comedy*, Princeton: Princeton University Press.

Charlton, H. B., *Shakespearian Comedy*, London: Methuen, 1938.

Chaudhuri, Sakunta, *Renaissance Pastoral and its English Developments*, Oxford: Clarendon Press, 1989.

Coghill, Nevill, 'The Basis of Shakespearian Comedy', in *Shakespeare Criticism*, ed. Anne Ridler, London: Oxford University Press, 1963.

Colie, Rosalie, *Shakespeare's Living Art*, Princeton: Princeton University Press, 1974.

Daley, A. Stuart, 'The Dispraise of the Country in *As You Like It*', *Shakespeare Quarterly*, 36 (1985), 300–14.

—— 'The Idea of Hunting in *As You Like It*', *Shakespeare Studies*, 21 (1993), 72–95.

—— 'Where are the Woods in *As You Like It*?', *Shakespeare Quarterly*, 34 (1983), 172–80.

Doebler, John, 'Orlando: Athlete of Virtue', *Shakespeare Survey*, 26 (1973), 111–17.

Evans, Bertrand, *Shakespeare's Comedies*, Oxford: Clarendon Press, 1960.

Evans, Malcolm, 'Deconstructing Shakespeare's Comedies', in *Alternative Shakespeares*, ed. John Drakakis, London: Methuen, 1985.

Fortin, René E., ' "Tongues in Trees": Symbolic Patterns in *As You Like It*', in *Shakespeare's Christian Dimension: An Anthology of Commentary*, ed. Roy Battenhouse, Bloomington: Indiana University Press, 1994.

Fowler, Alastair, *Pastoral Instruction in 'As You Like It'* (John Coffin Memorial Lecture), London: University of London, 1984.

Fraser, Russell, 'Shakespeare's Book of Genesis', *Comparative Drama*, 25 (1991), 121–28.

Frey, Charles, 'The Sweetest Rose: *As You Like it* as Comedy of Reconciliation', in *Comedy: New Perspectives*, ed. Maurice Charney, New York: New York Literary Forum, 1978.

Frye, Northrop, 'The Argument of Comedy', in *English Institute Essays 1948*, New York: Columbia University Press, 1949.

—— *A Natural Perspective*, New York: Columbia University Press, 1965.

Garber, Marjorie, 'The Education of Orlando', in *Comedy from Shakespeare to Sheridan*, ed. A. R. Braunmuller and James C. Bulman, Newark: University of Delaware Press, 1986.

—— 'The Transvestite's Progress: Rosalind the Yeshiva Boy', in *The Appropriation of Shakespeare: Post-Renaissance Reconstructions of the Works and the Myth*, ed. Jean I. Marsden, New York: St Martin's Press, 1991.

Goldsmith, Robert H., *Wise Fools in Shakespeare*, East Lansing: Michigan State University Press, 1955.

Greenblatt, Stephen, 'Culture', in *Critical Terms for Literary Study*, ed. Frank Lentricchia and Thomas McLaughlin, Chicago: University of Chicago Press, 1990.

Halio, Jay L., and Barbara C. Millard, '*As You Like It*': An Annotated Bibliography, 1940–1980, New York: Garland, 1985.

Hassel, R. Chris, Jr, *Faith and Folly in Shakespeare's Romantic Comedies*, Athens, Ga: University of Georgia Press, 1980.

Hawkins, Sherman, 'The Two Worlds of Shakespearean Comedy', *Shakespeare Studies*, 3 (1968), 62–80.

Hayles, Nancy K., 'Sexual Disguise in *As You Like It* and *Twelfth Night*', *Shakespeare Survey*, 32 (1979), 63–72.

Hodges, Devon L., *Renaissance Fictions of Anatomy*, Amherst: University of Massachusetts Press, 1985.

Howard, Jean E., 'Crossdressing, the Theatre, and Gender Struggle in Early Modern England', *Shakespeare Quarterly*, 39 (1988), 418–40.

Hunt, Maurice, '*Kairos* and the Ripeness of Time in *As You Like It*', *Modern Language Quarterly*, 52 (1991), 113–35.

Iser, Wolfgang, 'The Dramatization of Double Meaning in Shakespeare's *As You Like It*', *Theatre Journal*, 35 (1983), 307–32 (see also Iser's *Prospecting: From Reader Response to Literary Anthropology*, Baltimore: Johns Hopkins University Press, 1989).

Jensen, Ejner, *Shakespeare and the Ends of Comedy*, Bloomington: Indiana University Press, 1991.

Kimbrough, Robert, 'Androgyny Seen Through Shakespeare's Disguise', *Shakespeare Quarterly*, 33 (1982), 17–33.

Knowles, Richard (ed.), *'As You Like It': A New Variorum Edition of Shakespeare*, New York: Modern Language Association of America, 1977.

Kott, Jan, 'The Gender of Rosalind', *New Theatre Quarterly*, 7 (1991), 113–25 (reprinted in Kott's *The Gender of Rosalind: Shakespeare, Büchner, Gautier*, Evanston: Northwestern University Press, 1992).

Latham, Agnes (ed.), *As You Like It* (The Arden Shakespeare), London: Methuen, 1975.

Lifson, Martha Ronk, 'Learning by Talking: Conversation in *As You Like It*', *Shakespeare Survey*, 40 (1988), 91–106.

McCombie, Frank, 'Medium and Message in *As You Like It* and *King Lear*', *Shakespeare Survey*, 33 (1980), 67–80.

McFarland, Thomas, *Shakespeare's Pastoral Comedy*, Chapel Hill: University of North Carolina Press, 1972.

Marshall, Cynthia, 'Wrestling as Play and Game in *As You Like It*', *Studies in English Literature*, 33 (1993), 265–87.

Nevo, Ruth, *Comic Transformations in Shakespeare*, London: Methuen, 1980.

Nicholl, Charles, *The Reckoning: The Murder of Christopher Marlowe*, London: Jonathan Cape, 1992, New York: Harcourt Brace, 1992 (includes a chapter on allusions to Marlowe in *As You Like It*).

Paglia, Camille, *Sexual Personae: Art and Decadence from Nefertiti to Emily Dickinson*, New Haven: Yale University Press, 1990 (includes a discussion of Rosalind). (Reprinted Penguin, 1991).

Palmer, D. J., '*As You Like It* and the Idea of Play', *Critical Quarterly*, 13 (1971), 234–45.

Park, Clara Claiborne, 'As We Like It: How a Girl Can Be Smart and Still Popular', in *The Woman's Part: Feminist Criticism of Shakespeare*, ed. Carolyn Ruth Swift Lenz, Gayle Greene, and Caarol Thomas Neely, Urbana: University of Illinois Press, 1980.

Parrott, Thomas Marc, *Shakespearean Comedy*, London: Oxford University Press, 1949.

Phialas, Peter G., *Shakespeare's Romantic Comedies*, Chapel Hill: University of North Carolina Press, 1966.

Reynolds, Peter, *'As You Like It': A Dramatic Commentary*, London: Penguin, 1988.

Riemer, A. P., *Antic Fables: Patterns of Evasion in Shakespeare's Comedies*, New York: St Martin's Press, 1980.

Salingar, Leo, *Shakespeare and the Traditions of Comedy*, Cambridge: Cambridge University Press, 1974.

Scoufos, Alice-Lyle, 'The *Paradiso Terrestre* and the Testing of Love in *As You Like It*', *Shakespeare Studies*, 14 (1981), 215–28.

Shaw, Fiona, and Juliet Stevenson, 'Celia and Rosalind in *As You Like It*', in *Players of Shakespeare 2*, ed. Russell Jackson and Robert Smallwood, Cambridge: Cambridge University Press, 1988.

Smith, James, '*As You Like It*', *Scrutiny*, 9 (1940), 9–32.

Soule, Lesley Anne, 'Subverting Rosalind: Cocky Ros in the Forest of Arden', *New Theatre Quarterly*, 7 (1991), 126–36.

Stanton, Kay, 'Remembering Patriarchy in *As You Like It*', in *Shakespeare: Text, Subtext, and Context*, ed. Ronald Dotterer, London: Associated University Presses, 1989.

Stevenson, David L., *The Love-Game Comedy*, London: Oxford University Press, 1946.

Suzman, Janet, '*As You Like It*', in *Shakespeare in Perspective*, vol. 1, ed. Roger Sales, London: Ariel Books (British Broadcasting Corporation), 1982.

Swinden, Patrick, *An Introduction to Shakespeare's Comedies*, London: Macmillan, 1979.

Thompson, Sophie, 'Rosalind (and Celia) in *As You Like It*', in *Players of Shakespeare 3*, ed. Russell Jackson and Robert Smallwood, Cambridge: Cambridge University Press, 1993.

Traub, Valerie, 'Desire and the Difference it Makes', in *The Matter of Difference: Materialist Feminist Criticism of Shakespeare*, ed. Valerie Wayne, Ithaca: Cornell University Press, 1991.

Van Den Berg, Kent Talbot, 'Theatrical Fiction and the Reality of Love in *As You Like It*', *PMLA: Publications of the Modern Language Association of America*, 90 (1975), 885–93.

Waddington, Raymond B., 'Moralizing the Spectacle: Dramatic Emblems in *As You Like It*'. *Shakespeare Quarterly*, 33 (1982), 155–63.

Ward, John Powell, *As You Like It*, New York: Twayne, 1992.

Wilson, John Dover, *Shakespeare's Happy Comedies*, London: Faber & Faber, 1969.

Wilson, Richard, ' "Like the old Robin Hood": *As You Like It* and the Enclosure Riots', *Shakespeare Quarterly*, 43 (1992), 1–19.

Background and general critical studies, and useful reference works:

Abbot, E. A., *A Shakespearian Grammar*, New York: Haskell House, 1972.

Allen, Michael J. B., and Kenneth Muir (eds), *Shakespeare's Plays in Quarto: A Facsimile Edition*, Berkeley: University of California Press, 1981.

Andrews, John F. (ed.), *William Shakespeare: His World, His Work, His Influence*, 3 vols, New York: Scribners, 1985 (articles on 60 topics).

Barroll, Leeds, *Politics, Plague, and Shakespeare's Theater*, Ithaca: Cornell University Press, 1992.

Bentley, G. E., *The Profession of Player in Shakespeare's Time, 1590–1642*, Princeton: Princeton University Press, 1984.

Berry, Ralph, *Shakespeare and Social Class*, Atlantic Highlands, NJ: Humanities Press, 1988.

Blake, Norman, *Shakespeare's Language: An Introduction*, New York: St Martin's Press, 1983.

Bullough, Geoffrey (ed.), *Narrative and Dramatic Sources of Shakespeare*, 8 vols, New York: Columbia University Press, 1957–75 (printed sources, with helpful summaries and comments by the editor).

Calderwood, James L., *Shakespearean Metadrama*, Minneapolis: University of Minnesota Press, 1971.

Campbell, O. J., and Edward G. Quinn (eds), *The Reader's Encyclopedia of Shakespeare*, New York: Crowell, 1966.

Cook, Ann Jennalie, *Making a Match: Courtship in Shakespeare and His Society*, Princeton: Princeton University Press, 1991.

—— *The Privileged Playgoers of Shakespeare's London*: Princeton: Princeton University Press, 1981 (an argument that theatre audiences at the Globe and other public playhouses were relatively well-to-do).

De Grazia, Margreta, *Shakespeare Verbatim: The Reproduction of Authenticity and the Apparatus of 1790*, Oxford: Clarendon Press, 1991 (interesting material on eighteenth-century editorial practices).

Eastman, Arthur M., *A Short History of Shakespearean Criticism*, New York: Random House, 1968.

Gurt, Andrew, *Playgoing in Shakespeare's London*, Cambridge: Cambridge University Press, 1987 (an argument for changing tastes, and for a more diverse group of audiences than Cook suggests).

—— *The Shakespearean Stage, 1574–1642*, 2nd edn, Cambridge: Cambridge University Press, 1981 (theatres, companies, audiences, and repertories).

Hinman, Charlton (ed.), *The Norton Facsimile: The First Folio of Shakespeare's Plays*, New York: Norton, 1968.

Muir, Kenneth, *The Sources of Shakespeare's Plays*, New Haven: Yale University Press, 1978 (a concise account of how Shakespeare used his sources).

Onions, C. T., *A Shakespeare Glossary*, 2nd edn, London: Oxford University Press, 1953.

Partridge, Eric, *Shakespeare's Bawdy*, London: Routledge & Kegan Paul, 1955 (indispensable guide to Shakespeare's direct and indirect ways of referring to 'indecent' subjects).

Rabkin, Norman, *Shakespeare and the Common Understanding*, New York: Free Press, 1967.

Righter, Anne, *Shakespeare and the Idea of the Play*, London: Chatto & Windus, 1962.

Schoenbaum, S., *Shakespeare: The Globe and the World*, New York: Oxford University Press, 1979 (lively illustrated book on Shakespeare's world).

—— *Shakespeare's Lives*, 2nd edn, Oxford: Oxford University Press, 1992 (readable informative survey of the many biographers of Shakespeare, including those believing that someone else wrote the works).

—— *William Shakespeare: A Compact Documentary Life*, New York: Oxford University Press, 1977 (presentation of all the biographical documents, with assessments of what they tell us about the playwright).

Spevack, Marvin, *The Harvard Concordance to Shakespeare*, Cambridge, Mass: Harvard University Press, 1973.

Vickers, Brian (ed.), *Shakespeare: The Critical Heritage, 1623–1801*, 6 vols, London: Routledge & Kegan Paul, 1974–81.

Wells, Stanley (ed.), *The Cambridge Companion to Shakespeare Studies*, Cambridge: Cambridge University Press, 1986.

Whitaker, Virgil K., *Shakespeare's Use of Learning*, San Marino, Cal.: Huntington Library, 1963.

Wright, George T., *Shakespeare's Metrical Art*, Berkeley: University of California Press, 1988.

# PLOT SUMMARY

I.1    In the orchard of the late Sir Rowland de Boys, Orlando, one of his sons, talks to Adam, an old servant. Orlando believes that Oliver, his eldest brother, is not giving him the upbringing that befits a gentleman. He confronts his brother with this accusation when he arrives, and they fight briefly. When Orlando and Adam have left, Oliver calls for Charles, the Duke's wrestler. He persuades him to try to maim or kill Orlando at the next day's wrestling-match.

I.2    In the grounds of Duke Frederick's palace, Rosalind talks with Celia, her cousin. Celia, who is Duke Frederick's daughter, promises to give Rosalind back the throne that her father has usurped from his brother (and Rosalind's father), Duke Senior. The court Fool, Touchstone, enters to call Celia to her father. Le Beau, one of Frederick's courtiers, arrives with news of the wrestling, in which Charles has already severely injured three contestants.

    The Duke and his company arrive, and after Rosalind and Celia have wished the unknown Orlando well, the bout begins. Orlando wins, but in declaring who he is offends the Duke, as Sir Rowland was the Duke's enemy. The two cousins, and Rosalind in particular, compliment him as recompense; he finds he cannot speak in Rosalind's presence. Le Beau warns him to leave before the Duke's displeasure is displayed more obviously.

I.3    Rosalind discusses her love for Orlando with Celia. The Duke enters and banishes Rosalind from the court. The cousins resolve to disguise themselves and set out together to find Duke Senior.

II.1    At his camp in the Forest of Arden, Duke Senior discusses the merits of his new life with his lords. They tell him how their hunting of deer upsets Jaques. The company leave to find this melancholy lord.

II.2    The next morning, Celia, Rosalind and Touchstone are discovered missing. The cousins' admiration for Orlando was noted, and so the Duke sends for him.

II.3    Adam meets Orlando before his brother's house, and warns him that Oliver plans to kill him. Adam persuades Orlando to set off elsewhere.

II.4    Rosalind and Celia, now disguised respectively as the servant Ganymede and his mistress Aliena, reach the Forest. Touchstone has come with them. Here they meet Corin and Silvius, an old and a young shepherd. Silvius explains the extent of his love for a shepherdess, Phebe. When he leaves, the travellers ask Corin for food. He tells them of his poverty, and they decide to alleviate this by buying the cottage, pasture and flock from his absent and miserly master.

II.5–7  Elsewhere in the forest, Amiens, another lord, sings 'Under the greenwood tree' to Jaques. Nearby, Adam protests to Orlando that he is about to die from hunger. Duke Senior and the lords arrive where Jaques was last seen, and lay a table with food. Jaques returns, and describes his recent meeting with Touchstone. Suddenly Orlando enters and demands food. When this is offered to him willingly, he goes to fetch Adam. Jaques reflects on the seven ages of man. While they eat, 'Blow, blow, thou Winter Wind' is sung.

III.1   In his palace, Duke Frederick orders Oliver to bring his brother to him, and confiscates Oliver's lands and possessions until he has done so.

III.2   In the forest, Orlando is putting love-poems on to trees. Touchstone discusses the merits of rural, as opposed to courtly, life with Corin. Rosalind enters as Ganymede, reading out a love-poem that she has found; Touchstone parodies it. Celia enters as Aliena, reading another. When the Fool and Shepherd have left, Celia tells Rosalind that Orlando is the author. He enters with Jaques, and while the cousins look on, the two men quarrel wittily. Jaques having departed, Rosalind, as Ganymede, questions Orlando concerning the sincerity of love. He agrees to come to her cottage every day to woo her as if she were Rosalind.

III.3   Elsewhere, with Jaques looking on, Touchstone talks to Audrey, a goat-herd whom he has decided to marry. The vicar, Sir Oliver Mar-text, arrives. Jaques persuades Touchstone to be married in a more respectable manner.

III.4–5 Rosalind is upset at Orlando's failure to turn up. Corin arrives and takes her and Celia to see a scene of True Love meeting Proud Disdain. This is the meeting of Silvius and Phebe. Rosalind rebukes Phebe for her pride, and Phebe promptly falls in love with Rosalind as Ganymede, at which Rosalind and her companions leave. Phebe employs Silvius as her messenger to Ganymede.

IV.1–2  Nearby, Rosalind and Celia meet Jaques. Rosalind and he match wits until Orlando arrives, at which Jaques leaves. Rosalind as Ganymede forces Orlando to apologize, and

Orlando proceeds to woo Ganymede as Rosalind. Orlando leaves to have lunch with the Duke, vowing to return at two o'clock. Elsewhere, Jaques and other lords have killed a deer, and now sing a song.

IV.3    While Rosalind and Celia are waiting for Orlando's return, Silvius arrives with Phebe's love-letter for Ganymede. Rosalind sends Silvius back to say that Ganymede wishes Phebe to love Silvius.

Oliver arrives, bearing a handkerchief red with Orlando's blood. Orlando had found Oliver sleeping in the forest, watched over by a lioness. Instead of leaving his brother to his fate, Orlando killed the beast, an act of kindness that has made his brother recognize the error of his ways. However, in the fight Orlando was injured in the arm: he sent Oliver with the handkerchief as an apology for missing his appointment. Rosalind faints.

V.1    Touchstone, with Audrey's approval, sends away William, one of her country sweethearts. Corin tells Touchstone that he is wanted by his master and mistress.

V.2    Oliver declares to Orlando that he has fallen in love with Aliena and that they are to marry on the next day. Rosalind arrives and discusses this news with Orlando. Mentioning a magician, she promises Orlando that he will marry Rosalind when his brother marries Aliena. Phebe enters, with Silvius behind, and she declares her love for Ganymede. Rosalind as Ganymede promises to bring everyone's loves to a happy conclusion if they will meet him tomorrow.

V.3    Touchstone and Audrey are also to be married on the next day. One of the Duke's pages sings 'It was a lover and his lass'.

V.4    The next day, the company are gathered. Rosalind as Ganymede extracts promises: Orlando promises to marry Rosalind; the Duke promises to give Rosalind, his daughter, away to Orlando; Phebe promises that if she refuses to marry Ganymede she will marry Silvius; Silvius promises to marry Phebe. Rosalind exits with Celia.

Touchstone arrives with Audrey, and Jaques draws him out into some foolery. Rosalind and Celia, now dressed as themselves, enter in the company of Hymen. Hymen unites the four couples and sings 'Wedding is great Juno's Crown'.

Orlando's and Oliver's other brother arrives with news of Duke Frederick. The Duke had been coming to capture and kill Duke Senior, but then met a religious man on the outskirts of the forest. There Frederick realized the injustice of his past actions, and resigned the throne to its rightful possessor, Duke Senior.

Duke Senior commands the wedding celebrations to begin. Before they do, however, Jaques leaves to find Duke Frederick. Rosalind steps forward and addresses the final lines to the audience.

# ACKNOWLEDGEMENTS

The editor and publishers would like to thank the following for permission to reproduce copyright material:

Peter Erickson for material from *Patriarchal Structures in Shakespeare's Drama*, University of California Press, 1995;

Doubleday, a division of Bantam Doubleday Dell Publishing, for material from Jan Kott, *Shakespeare Our Contemporary*, trs. Boselaw Taborski, Anchor Books, 1961;

Faber and Faber Ltd for material from Enid Welsford, *The Fool: His Social and Literary History*, 1935;

Huntington Library Press for material from Oscar James Campbell, 'Jaques', *Huntington Library Bulletin*, 8, 1935, pp. 81–4.

The Johns Hopkins University Press for material from Albert R. Cirillo, '*As You Like It*: Pastoralism Gone Awry', *English Literary History*, 1971. Copyright © 1971 by The Johns Hopkins University Press;

Philological Quarterly for material from John W. Draper, 'Orlando the Younger Brother', *Philological Quarterly*, 1934, Z. S. Fink, 'Jaques and the Malcontent Traveler', *Philological Quarterly*, 1935; C. L. Barber, 'The Use of Comedy in *As You Like It*', *Philological Quarterly*, 1942; and D. J. Palmer, 'Art and Nature in *As You Like It*', *Philological Quarterly*, 1970;

Routledge for material from Alexander Leggatt, *Shakespeare's Comedy of Love*, 1974, Methuen & Co;

The Society of Authors on behalf of the Bernard Shaw Estate for material from Bernard Shaw, '*As You Like It*', *Saturday Review*, 1896;

SEL Studies in English Literature 1500–1900 for material from Jay Halio, 'No Clock in the Forest; Time in *As You Like It*', *SEL*, 2, 2 Spring 1962;

Charles Van Doren for material from Mark Van Doren, *Shakespeare*, 1939;

Yale University Press for material from David Young, *The Heart's Forest: A Study of Shakespeare's Pastoral Plays*, 1972.

Every effort has been made to trace all the copyright holders, but if any have been inadvertently overlooked the publishers will be pleased to make the necessary arrangement at the first opportunity.

# SHAKESPEARE
## IN EVERYMAN

*Edited by John Andrews, the Everyman Shakespeare is the
most comprehensive, up-to-date paperback edition of
the plays and poems, featuring:*

**face-to-face** text and notes

**chronology** of Shakespeare's life and times

a rich selection of **critical and theatrical responses**
to the play over the centuries

**foreword by an actor or director** describing
the play in performance

**up-to-date commentary** on the play

**Antony and Cleopatra**  £3.99

**Hamlet**  £2.99

**Julius Caesar**  £3.99

**King Lear**  £2.99

**Macbeth**  £2.99

**Measure for Measure**  £3.99

**The Merchant of Venice**  £2.99

**A Midsummer Night's Dream**
£1.99

**Othello**  £3.99

**Romeo and Juliet**  £2.99

**The Tempest**  £2.99

**Twelfth Night**  £3.99

**The Winter's Tale**  £3.99

All books are available from your local bookshop or direct from:
Littlehampton Book Services Cash Sales, 14 Eldon Way, Lineside Estate,
Littlehampton, West Sussex BN17 7HE (*prices are subject to change*)

To order any of the books, please enclose a cheque (in sterling) made payable to
*Littlehampton Book Services*, or phone your order through with credit card details (Access,
Visa or Mastercard) on 01903 721596 (24 hour answering service) stating card number
and expiry date. (*Please add £1.25 for package and postage to the total of your order.*)

In the USA, for further information and a complete catalogue call 1-800-526-2778

# DRAMA
## IN EVERYMAN

**The Oresteia**
AESCHYLUS
*New translation of one of the
greatest Greek dramatic trilogies
which analyses the plays in
performance*
£5.99

**Everyman and Medieval
Miracle Plays**
edited by A. C. Cawley
*A selection of the most popular
medieval plays*
£4.99

**Complete Plays and Poems**
CHRISTOPHER MARLOWE
*The complete works of this great
Elizabethan in one volume*
£5.99

**Restoration Plays**
edited by Robert Lawrence
*Five comedies and two tragedies
representing the best of the
Restoration stage*
£7.99

**Female Playwrights of the
Restoration: Five Comedies**
edited by Paddy Lyons
*Rediscovered literary treasures in
a unique selection*
£5.99

**Plays, Prose Writings
and Poems**
OSCAR WILDE
*The full force of Wilde's wit
in one volume*
£4.99

**A Dolls House/The Lady from
the Sea/The Wild Duck**
HENRIK IBSEN
*introduced by* Fay Weldon
*A popular selection of Ibsen's
major plays*
£4.99

**The Beggar's Opera and
Other Eighteenth-Century Plays**
JOHN GAY et. al.
*Including Goldsmith's* She Stoops
To Conquer *and Sheridan's* The
School for Scandal, *this is a volume
which reflects the full scope of the
period's theatre*
£6.99

**Female Playwrights of the
Nineteenth Century**
edited by Adrienne Scullion
*The full range of female nineteenth-
century dramatic development*
£6.99

---

All books are available from your local bookshop or direct from:
Littlehampton Book Services Cash Sales, 14 Eldon Way, Lineside Estate,
Littlehampton, West Sussex BN17 7HE *(prices are subject to change)*

To order any of the books, please enclose a cheque (in sterling) made payable to
*Littlehampton Book Services*, or phone your order through with credit card details (Access,
Visa or Mastercard) on 01903 721596 (24 hour answering service) stating card number
and expiry date. *(Please add £1.25 for package and postage to the total of your order.)*

In the USA, for further information and a complete catalogue call 1-800-526-2778